HOLY WAR
IN THE BIBLE

Christian Morality and
an Old Testament Problem

EDITED BY
HEATH THOMAS,
JEREMY EVANS AND
PAUL COPAN

IVP Academic

An imprint of InterVarsity Press
Downers Grove, Illinois

InterVarsity Press
P.O. Box 1400, Downers Grove, IL 60515-1426
World Wide Web: www.ivpress.com
E-mail: email@ivpress.com

©2013 by Heath Thomas, Jeremy Evans and Paul Copan

*InterVarsity Press® is the book-publishing division of InterVarsity Christian Fellowship/USA®, a movement of students
and faculty active on campus at hundreds of universities, colleges and schools of nursing in the United States of America,
and a member movement of the International Fellowship of Evangelical Students. For information about local and
regional activities, write Public Relations Dept., InterVarsity Christian Fellowship/USA, 6400 Schroeder Rd., P.O. Box
7895, Madison, WI 53707-7895, or visit the IVCF website at <www.intervarsity.org>.*

Cover design: Cindy Kiple
Interior design: Beth Hagenberg
Images: Sword (metal), English School at Royal Armouries, Leeds, UK / Bridgeman Art Library

ISBN 978-0-8308-3995-7

Printed in the United States of America ∞

 *InterVarsity Press is committed to protecting the environment and to the responsible use of natural
resources. As a member of Green Press Initiative we use recycled paper whenever possible. To learn more
about the Green Press Initiative, visit <www.greenpressinitiative.org>.*

Library of Congress Cataloging-in-Publication Data

A catalog record for this book is available from the Library of Congress.

P	22	21	20	19	18	17	16	15	14	13	12	11	10	9	8	7	6	5	4	3	2	1
Y	32	31	30	29	28	27	26	25	24	23	22	21	20	19	18	17	16	15	14	13		

Contents

PART ONE

*The Challenge of "Holy War"
for Christian Morality*

1

ORIENTATION AMIDST
THE DIVERSITY

An Introduction to the Volume

Geth Allison and Reid Powell

———————————— ✚ ————————————

THE "HOLY WARS" OF THE OLD TESTAMENT stand in many ways as a theological crux in the goal of a right interpretation of Holy Scripture. The challenge of a seemingly genocidal God who commands ruthless warfare has bewildered biblical readers for generations. Much more confusion than clarity continues to surround such texts and themes of the Bible as the blight of religious violence rages now more than ever. Far from ignoring or suppressing the presence of "holy war" in the biblical witness, careful attention and thorough interpretation is due the controversial yet theologically vital theme of divine warfare.

The present volume began with the concern of two seminary students over the challenge of prevalent Old Testament divine war imagery in light of Christ's call to peace. Subsequently, a colloquium was organized in order to wrestle with the concern and work toward a proper understanding of Scripture. The colloquium, composed of professors from Southeastern Baptist Theological Seminary and Duke University Divinity School, was held at Wake Forest Baptist Church on April 20, 2009. From that first conversation the list of contributors eventually grew to include the authors of the present work, with the overarching hope of providing clarity and guidance through the persistent challenge of coming to terms with "holy war" in Christian Scripture.

Ultimately, the problem of "holy war" in the Old Testament is one that spans the entire spectrum of biblical studies, theology and ethics, thereby demanding an interdisciplinary approach. The difficulties raised by particularly violent Old Testament texts are not a monochromatic problem for one niche of scholarship but intersect with a wide spectrum of scholarly concern. The phrase "Old Testament 'holy war'" itself clearly focuses the challenge on the biblical text, with the tradition of "holy war" (or better, "Yahweh war" or "divine war," as will be demonstrated in the volume) as a long-standing issue in biblical studies. Further, the embrace of the Old Testament as Christian Scripture introduces a farther-reaching concern. Christian morality takes as its foundation the testimony of Jesus Christ and his moral imperatives for the world. For many the violence of "holy war" seems at odds with his call to "turn the other cheek" (Mt 5:39). Thus, this volume seeks to approach the challenge of Old Testament "holy war" from the unique but equally vital perspectives that make it a Christian problem. As such, this volume will address six primary areas of concern relating to the problem of "holy war" and Christian morality.

The opening part of this volume emphasizes the importance of an accurate understanding of the historical use and influence of the "holy war" texts themselves. Far from being benign records of ancient Israelite lore, these texts have a long history of *mis*interpretation and *mis*appropriation, which leads to prolonged stereotypes and misunderstandings of the "holy war" theme in history.

In chapter two Douglas Earl challenges the widespread and largely accepted notion that the texts of Joshua, the primary locus of "holy war" texts, bear a direct relationship to the Christian Crusades, being used as biblical grounding, if not justification, for these infamous acts of violent aggression. The problem with this widespread assumption is that little evidence supports a direct link of Joshua to the propaganda and historical writings surrounding the Crusades. Through a careful study of primary sources surrounding the Crusades, Earl argues that, in fact, Joshua was not generally used as justification for these religious conquests and thus the popular assumption that the "holy war" themes in Joshua justified the violence of the Crusades are unwarranted. Accordingly, "That this is surprising might indicate that something has gone wrong with our interpretation of the Crusades and with our reading of Joshua." Addressing the challenge of "holy war" and divine violence requires an accurate appreciation of how texts were actually used in troublesome scenarios in the past. Earl works to refocus modern interpretation of the biblical texts to avoid attribution of violent legacies to texts unjustly.

The Old Testament canon itself, the focus of part two, is the original record of the "holy war" accounts and thereby requires particularly careful interpretation. Upon examining the corpus of the entire Old Testament, it is clear that the "holy war" theme is not one sequestered away in the ancient historical narratives of Joshua. From the accounts of divine violence in the Torah, the wars of Canaan rage on in Joshua and Judges and remain a theme of the Prophets and Writings. The function of a sustained "Yahweh war" theme across the Old Testament canon is significant for properly interpreting it as a theological motif, not simply a historical phenomenon.

Stephen Chapman, in chapter three, quickly dispels the misnomer of Old Testament "holy war." Nowhere in the Bible is war called holy. Instead, "holy war" was a descriptive phrase coined by early twentieth-century scholarship. Thus, while popular scholarship labels the texts of divinely sanctioned warfare as "holy war," the Old Testament itself does no such thing. This explains the use of quotation marks around "holy war" throughout this volume. Chapman suggests "Yahweh war" or "divine war" as much more appropriate phrases. They are particularly fitting because the relevant texts depict God himself as the primary actor in his sanctioned warfare. In this light, the "ban" that was to be carried out under God's command was meant to destroy the affront and threat of idolatry. "The wholesale slaughter of human beings for this reason is not any less horrible, but it should still be taken into account that such slaughter is not being authorized out of vengeance, rage or ethnic hatred, but self-protection."

But Chapman continues by showing that Israel's martial memory, its recounting of relating with God in history, moves progressively toward peace. "And apparently—this is the hard part—God was not able, given the violence of the world, to preserve Israel purely nonviolently, although even so Israel's history witnesses to and moves toward nonviolence as it moves toward Christ." Chapman suggests that Yahweh's condescension as warrior is significant for the future incarnation of Christ and builds an incarnational model for interpreting the divinely sanctioned violence of the Old Testament. Far from being random acts of vengeance or oppression, the divine wars were God's personal intervention in and preservation of the life of Israel. Subsequent to the survival of Israel is the incarnation of Christ, the ultimate harbinger of peace. "With Christ's work accomplished, furthermore, there now does exist a faithful and efficacious nonviolent response to the threat of violence, a response that is available to and enjoined upon those who follow Jesus."

In chapter four, Heath Thomas examines the human response to the presence of "holy war" through the lens of the Writings. This oft-neglected portion of Christian Scripture provides an essential insight into the canonical witness to divine war, whether it be celebrating God's fighting on behalf of his people in the Psalms or the mourning of God's warfare against his own people in Lamentations. Thomas draws out the direct allusions to the divine warrior theme in Israel's lament of the wrath of God particularly in Lamentations 2. From within the Old Testament itself, the reality of divine war is challenged through the petition of God's own people. Israel's lament models the appropriate response to apparent injustice and terrible violence from within the realm of faith. "For those who doubt the justice of God's warring activity, Lamentations offers a response that engages the divine warrior directly and then awaits God's response."

A surprisingly neglected aspect to the problem of "holy war" is the New Testament, the subject of part three. When the reader of the Old Testament turns to Matthew, he or she quickly comes to the Sermon on the Mount in Matthew 5, where Jesus says, "You have heard that it was said to the people long ago, 'You shall not murder, and anyone who murders will be subject to judgment.' But I tell you that anyone who is angry with a brother or sister will be subject to judgment'" (Mt 5:21-22 NIV). This proclamation of peace signifies a dramatic event in the drama of biblical redemption.[1] However, beyond Jesus' calls for peace are warnings of a coming warrior who will judge the earth in wrath. John foresaw a final war carried out by the Lamb:

---

[1]As Richard Hays writes, "The delivery of the Sermon from a mountain probably echoes the Exodus story of Moses and suggests that Jesus' teaching is a new Torah, a definitive charter for the life of the new covenant community" in *The Moral Vision of the New Testament* (San Francisco: Harper, 1996), p. 321.

"They called to the mountains and the rocks, 'Fall on us and hide us from the face of him who sits on the throne and from the wrath of the Lamb! For the great day of their wrath has come, and who can withstand it?'" (Rev 6:16-17 NIV). Thus, the New Testament does not abrogate the notion of divine war as presented in the Old Testament but carries it forward in light of Christ.

In chapter five, Timothy Gombis addresses the prevalence of divine warfare imagery in Ephesians and argues that far from promoting "Christian" violence, Paul envisions self-sacrificial Christians who promote peace. The enemies of the church are not physical entities but are the spiritual powers that oppose God and the goodness of his creation. The model of the divine warrior in Ephesians proves to be cruciform, one that calls for self-sacrificial love and service to the world in the pattern of Jesus Christ. As Christians follow the image of the divine warrior, they are ultimately following one who is fighting to redeem the world through love and justice. Ultimately Gombis establishes that the divine war tradition in the New Testament is not used to encourage violence or warfare but to promote the peace of Christ. "God defeats the powers through the death and resurrection of Jesus Christ, which is a radically subversive way of doing things. The cross turns everything on its head—God wins by losing; the powers lose by winning." New covenant "holy war" is war against the spiritual powers opposed to Christ's church, instead of physical warfare against God's opponents.

The book of Revelation is perhaps the biblical book most associated with violence. In chapter five, Alan S. Bandy shows through sociohistorical evaluation of the apocalypse that John intentionally used warfare imagery to inform the theological goals of his writing. "Theodicy represents a major theological thrust of the Apocalypse, providing the reader with a clear sense of God's justice." The hope of the victimized and suffering Christians of the first-century Roman Empire was realized in the God who would ultimately bring retribution and establish justice. The temporary injustices of the Roman Empire and the voices of the martyrs will ultimately be answered by the coming retribution of Jesus Christ as divine warrior.

A careful study of the unique setting of the divine war theme within the Old and New Testaments allows for a proper assessment of the canonical perspective of biblical theology, which is the aim of part four. With so much confusion surrounding individual passages associated with death and destruction, an approach to the entire message of both the Old and New Testaments is necessary in order to assess the holistic biblical message of divine war. Through the lens of biblical theology, the overarching biblical narrative of divine redemption unfolds and shows the place of divine war in the salvific movement of God.

David Lamb seeks to understand the motivations and purposes for divine warfare in chapter seven. In doing so, he argues for an intrinsic link between divine wrath and compassion and the actions of Yahweh as recorded in the Old Testament. A clear pattern in Exodus develops wherein God responds with violent judgment when his anger and compassion are roused by injustice. Lamb shows that anger and compassion are the principle motivators of divine warfare as recorded throughout the Old Testament following the model of Exodus. In arguing this point, Lamb surveys a wide spectrum of biblical texts, from Exodus to Acts, in order to show the consistent interplay of these themes in God's wrath. In doing so, Lamb holds that God violently intervenes in order to uphold his will for the world, while not acting out of capricious rage or frivolous wrath.

Douglas Earl focuses, in chapter eight, on perhaps the most challenging term of all related to the Yahweh war tradition, "the ban" (ḥērem). He develops a biblical theology of "the ban" itself in order to articulate its meaning in Christian Scripture. From his analysis, "the ban" should not be interpreted as a literal, historical idea but as a symbol employing rhetorical, imaginative meaning. Instead of interpreting the history of Joshua as strictly literal, Earl suggests Origen's reading of Joshua through a symbolic hermeneutic. In fact, Earl argues, it would be going against the intent of the original authors themselves to assume a literal meaning for "the ban." The poetic genre of the relevant Old Testament texts establishes a symbolic use of this term. "This is not to detract from their value and nature as inspired revelatory texts, but rather to rethink the way in which they are revelatory— to rethink their genre, and thus how and what we can learn from them." Ultimately, Earl provides a promising model for a biblical theology of "the ban," one in which this theological symbol is appropriated by Christian theology and expressed in the reality of Christ.

In part five, each author provides their perspective on a particular aspect of the ethical and philosophical problems that arise from attempts to harmonize the concept of Old Testament "holy war" with Christian morality. Daniel Heimbach's chapter, "Crusade in the Old Testament and Today" assesses whether or not an Old Testament "crusade ethic" could justifiably be employed today. Heimbach begins by clarifying the distinction between the concepts of "holy war," or what he terms *crusade*, and just war, listing twelve features of the former that distinguish it as unique. He goes on to compare Israel's practice of crusade with the practice of warfare conducted by its ancient Near Eastern contemporaries, noting that while Israel's crusade ethic was not unique in form, it nevertheless was unique in moral authority. Heimbach identifies the particular difficulty faced by those who accept the accounts of crusade in the Old Testament in which God is credited with the commands to kill, burn and destroy entire populations. He concludes his assessment with criteria by which crusade may legitimately be waged, arguing that such conditions could never allow for crusade to be a human decision. As such, strict rules for the identification of divinely sanctioned war obtain. Heimbach's essay addresses the timely question that many have asked, particularly in light of violent acts done in the name of God: can the texts of the Bible that describe divinely sanctioned war be used to justify violence today?

In their chapter, "The Ethics of 'Holy War' for Christian Morality and Theology," Paul Copan and Matthew Flannagan address the moral problem of Old Testament "holy war" for Christian theism in light of Raymond Bradley's "inconsistent tetrad." Against Bradley, Copan and Flannagan contend that the Christian theist can argue both that (1) if certain special conditions obtain, it may be morally permissible for moral agents to kill other persons who are innocent of any serious wrongdoing, and (2) the Bible does not tell us that God commands us, or commanded others in the past, to kill persons who are innocent of any serious wrongdoing. In support of the first point, Copan and Flannagan respond to two objections, one from Bradley regarding nihilism, the second from Robert Adams concerning the conceptual coherence of God's goodness. To support their second point, Copan and Flannagan argue extensively for a hyperbolic interpretation of many texts associated with Old Testament holy war, drawing upon arguments originally put forth by Alvin Plantinga and Nicholas Wolterstorff. They conclude that more defensible, modified versions of Bradley's tetrad still fail to show that Christian theism is inconsistent with holy war as it is described in the Old Testament. If Copan and Flannagan are correct, the Christian theist need not deny the authority of the texts of the Old Testament that describe these events, nor be committed to a concept of God that is inconsistent.

Glen Stassen takes a different approach in "The Prophets' Call for Peacemaking Practices," in which he evaluates which particular practices either *cause* or *prevent* unholy war, with much of the chapter focusing upon Norman Gottwald's *All the Kingdoms of the Earth*. Stassen opens by claiming that two opposite philosophies, Platonic idealism and American pragmatic consequentialism, have corrupted our thought, making us blind to the critical social and religious roles embodied by the prophets of the Old Testament, as well as Jesus himself. Stassen notes that often war is a sign of judgment and, as such, is an effect of unjust practices, particularly in the case of the nation of Israel in the Old Testament. Furthermore, Stassen argues that warfare often displays an idolatrous trust in weaponry, which itself becomes the cause of "foolish warmaking," and that in the Hebrew prophets there is a strong beginning of "a genuine religious universalism which forms the matrix of international law." He concludes that much of the paradigm of the contemporary ethic of "just peacemaking" can be found in the ancient writings of the prophets of Israel. Because this ethic is presently helping to prevent many wars and deaths, Stassen urges churches to become "followers of Jesus' call to peacemaking."

Robert Stewart's chapter, "'Holy War,' Divine Action and the New Atheism," considers both the logical and existential problems of Old Testament "holy war." Although Stewart can find no formal argument in the writings of the New Atheists, he does respond to an argument based upon Old Testament "holy war" against biblical inerrancy from fellow Christian Randal Rauser. He considers four possible, traditional responses and explores a relevant philosophical entailment that speech-act theory has for our understanding of God's commands to kill the Canaanites. Yet even if all of the logical problems can be solved, the existential worries still present a challenge to both believer and non-believer alike. In response to the rhetoric of the New Atheism, Stewart argues that their message is often an incomplete and misrepresentative theological caricature of God. Although "holy war" texts present deep existential worries, the Christian theist is not without countervailing texts of God's trustworthiness, justice, love and kindness. For Christians who have concerns about trusting such a person as this God, the entirety of the Bible reassures them that he is a trustworthy and loving father, savior, comforter and giver of life, both temporal and eternal.

The proceeding chapters take up the challenge of divine violence and "holy war" from the perspective of dogmatic theology. Murray Rae begins part six by arguing for Christian pacifism in his essay, "The Unholy Notion of 'Holy War': A Christian Critique," Rae surveys the Christian just war and pacifist traditions from the church fathers to the twentieth century, with an emphasis on the writings of Reinhold Niebuhr, Karl Barth and Oliver O'Donovan. He notes that in its early history the church took a strong position in favor of pacifism and that it was not until the rise of the Holy Roman Empire that its stance was reversed. After surveying the just war theories of all three twentieth-century theologians above, Rae offers a critique of each of their views and concludes that all fall short of capturing the full implication of that which is entailed by the concept of Christian ethics: Jesus' resurrection from the dead brings with it a new order that has as its first priority "God's intention that the creature should have life triumphs over death and over our death-dealing ways." Modeling Jesus' example, Christians should seek to combat evil with sacrificial love devoid of violence. Although Rae acknowledges the importance of understanding the Old Testament "holy war" texts, there can be no justification for any kind of armed conflict for Christians.

In this section's second essay, "'Holy War' and the New Atheism," Stephen N. Williams discusses the claims made by New Atheist authors and some possible apologetic responses open to their Christian interlocutors. Williams notes that although New Atheist authors frequently lack rational support for their arguments, Christians must nevertheless respond to some of their criticisms in light of their rhetorical force and cultural impact. He identifies New Atheism's principal point of contention with the belief that "dogmatic religious conviction, irrationally maintained, breeds violence." Williams, however, argues that Christianity has a rich intellectual history and system of beliefs that preclude action based upon irrational thoughts and desires. In light of these considerations, it is clear that the New Atheists misunderstand Christianity, a fact evidenced particularly in any worry that past violence done in God's name can be used to justify present or future violence in the same manner. Rather than analyzing the concept of "holy war," it is better to consider the character of the God who commanded it. God's character is ultimately displayed by Jesus on the cross and provides some contrast to some of the violence in the Old Testament. Perhaps it is the case, says Williams, that the wrath of God is a reaction to sin and not something that is immanently in his nature. Williams concludes with thoughts on Francis Bacon's commentary on "holy war" and how it might actually have been the instrument of opponents of Christianity, as well as the source of anti-religious sentiment that continues today.

It is hoped that the present volume will provide a sense of orientation amidst the diversity of biblical texts that speak to the issue of Old Testament "holy war," as well as the voices that engage the text through a variety of angles of vision. This volume is designed to be a kind of "reader," a resource that will enable discussion and deliberation from a number of different perspectives: biblical, ethical, philosophical and theological. It is certainly in order to say that not all has been addressed and there is more to be said. However, it is hoped that the present volume will provide *an* entry point into the discussion. The variety of responses and approaches that emerge in the volume are warranted. Such a difficult and delicate topic cannot be cleanly "answered," as if theological questions such as these can be resolved in a simplistic manner. Biblical, moral, philosophical and theological threads inevitably weave together in arguments laid before the issue of divine war. These threads need to be identified and addressed in order to deal with "holy war" robustly. Indeed, it was just such an entry point that we searched out in preparing the colloquium on the subject that sparked the interest in this project.

2

JOSHUA AND THE CRUSADES

Douglas S. Earl

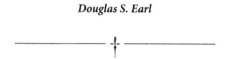

IF ONE READS THE BOOK OF JOSHUA or studies the history of the church in a twenty-first century Western context, one is often encouraged to engage in the moral critique of the Bible or of the history of the church through ethical, "colonial," "postcolonial" or similar kinds of ideological methods of criticism. In such a setting it might be natural to assume that Joshua is a narrative that would have played a significant role in the preaching of the Crusades. Indeed, in many contemporary frames of reference it seems almost inevitable that Joshua, and probably the Crusades, will be interpreted using categories of divinely-legitimated xenophobia, oppression and conquest—the Bible and its violent legacy.

So, for example, in Roland Bainton's *Christian Attitudes Toward War and Peace*, he titles a chapter "The Origins of the Crusading Idea in the Old Testament" and cites and discusses texts from Deuteronomy and Joshua, as well as other accounts of what he terms "crusading" in the Old Testament.[1] As the title of the chapter suggests, he links the narrative of Joshua to the idea of "crusade," repeatedly using the category of "crusade" in relation to Joshua and other Old Testament narratives. Moreover, he concludes this chapter by stating, "The architects of the Christian crusade, therefore, drew their warrant from the books of the conquest and of the Maccabean revolt."[2]

---

[1]Roland H. Bainton, *Christian Attitudes Toward War and Peace: A Historical Survey and Critical Re-evaluation* (Nashville: Abingdon, 1960), pp. 44-52.
[2]Ibid., p. 52. Also see p. 111.

But, rather surprisingly, he makes this claim without referring to any primary source materials that cite or allude to Deuteronomy or Joshua in relation to *the* Crusades, or indeed in relation to any other "crusading" activity. The implication is that for Bainton there is an inherent association or family resemblance between *the* Crusades and the book of Joshua via the category of "crusading," and that the crusaders found warrant for such activity in the book of Joshua. But neither does Bainton supply any documentary evidence for such a link, nor does he seek to justify the use of the category "crusading" in relation to Joshua. Rather, he adopts his own category of "crusading," construed as something like "religiously backed militarism or conquest" and imports it to interpret both Joshua and the Crusades, thus interpreting each in the light of each other as essentially manifestations of the same phenomenon.

Bainton's work has been influential in relation to establishing a moral critique of the Bible and its violent legacy of use. His work has helped to create a context for further analysis of the Bible's use in relation to certain forms of "religiously backed militarism" through the history of the church. Whilst others have been less explicit than Bainton in specifically linking Joshua with the Crusades, in contexts where his work is used approvingly this association seems implicitly accepted. Or at least the effect on the reader is that such a link is implied.[3] For example, his analysis is followed by D. H. Green,[4] and Susan Niditch who, in her influential work *War in the Hebrew Bible*, remarks that "European Christians were encouraged to join in the crusading wars against the Saracens by religious leaders quoting Hebrew Scriptures (Bainton: 112-33). . . . It comes as no surprise that modern students of war trace a trajectory of justified crusade back to the Hebrew Scriptures."[5] Moreover, while Bainton wrote before the rise of colonial and postcolonial studies, his work has been used in the development of this field.

---

[3]Bainton's work has been widely used, but I am not aware that anyone has questioned his association of Joshua with the Crusades.

[4]D. H. Green, *The Millstätter Exodus: A Crusading Epic* (Cambridge: Cambridge University Press, 1966), pp. 207-8.

[5]Susan Niditch, *War in the Hebrew Bible: A Study in the Ethics of Violence* (New York: Oxford University Press, 1993), p. 4. However, Niditch appears to nuance the interpretation of the nature of the portrayal of warfare in the Hebrew Bible as a whole, going on to remark, "within the Hebrew Bible the sort of war of extirpation waged against the Canaanites in Joshua is one among many war ideas as Bainton himself implies (46)" (p. 5).

In Michael Prior's *The Bible and Colonialism*, in which Prior argues for a moral critique of the Bible and its use in colonialism, while not discussing the Crusades at length, he juxtaposes a discussion of Joshua with a discussion of the Crusades, suggesting that the "Crusades provide a striking example of the link between religious and political power, and exemplify how the Bible has been employed as an agent of oppression."[6] Here he refers to Bainton's work, suggesting that "Roland Bainton provides numerous examples from the period of the Crusades (1960: 112-33) up to such eighteenth-century preachers as Herbert Gibbs who thanked the mercies of God for extirpating the enemies of Israel in Canaan (i.e. Native Americans) (1960: 168)."[7] Thus Prior completes the trajectory implicit in Bainton's work that draws a straight line from Joshua through the Crusades to examples of religiously backed militarism in the modern era. But in the section of Bainton's work that Prior refers to, Bainton in fact cites rather few examples of the kind that Prior suggests, especially with reference to the Crusades, and supplies only two references to biblical texts being used in relation to the Crusades: Jeremiah 48:10, "Cursed be he that keepeth back his hand from blood," and Psalm 118:24, "The Lord made this day, and we rejoiced and exulted in it."[8] Thus Bainton's material cited by Prior fails to provide sufficient warrant for Prior's claim and the implications that he wishes to draw, quite apart from the question of whether or not Bainton's analysis is well-founded in its own right.

Most recently, however, in a detailed study of the significance of Joshua for King Louis IX of France's crusading activities, M. C. Gaposchkin claims that

> Old Testament typology also played an important role in crusading ideology and rhetoric from its inception, since the story of the Israelites' battles to secure the Promised Land seemed elegantly to echo the crusaders' own goals.
> . . . Louis IX *may* not *have articulated his relationship to Joshua explicitly* as that of type and antitype, but the story of Joshua *must have been read* at the court with the crusades . . . in mind.[9]

---

[6]Michael Prior, *The Bible and Colonialism: A Moral Critique* (Sheffield, UK: Sheffield Academic Press, 1997), p. 35; see pp. 29-36.

[7]Ibid., p. 263.

[8]Translations as they appear in Bainton, *Christian Attitudes Toward War and Peace*, pp. 112-13.

[9]M. C. Gaposchkin, "Louis IX, Crusade and the Promise of Joshua in the Holy Land," *Journal of Medieval History* 34 (2008): pp. 246, 273 (emphasis added); see pp. 245-74. She suggests

Again, we see how pervasive and powerful is the assumption that Joshua *must have been read* with the Crusades in mind without needing an explicit articulation of the claim. One might say that this sort of approach to Joshua has become a worldview.[10]

Thus there is a clear tendency to conflate Joshua, the Crusades and perhaps some forms of more recent religiously backed militarism and colonialism, often through an ill-defined category such as "Holy War" or "crusading," where certain kinds of interpretation of each are read into the interpretation of the others so as to mutually reinforce "the problem." This *creates* the need for a certain kind of moral critique out of a phenomenon that is possibly the construct of modern scholars. An analysis such as Bainton's seems plausible and might sit well today, rather ironically, in both colonialist and postcolonialist ideologies. For those with "colonial" sympathies it provides a possible mandate for colonialism in Scripture. For the postcolonialist Bainton's analysis, read through Prior, unmasks oppressive crusading ideologies found in the Bible and its purportedly violent legacy, thus suggesting the need for a forceful critique of Scripture and of much Western history.[11] It seems plausible to think that Joshua is a text glorying in divinely mandated genocide and conquest, and that it would play a part in legitimizing the Crusades, and that each are best interpreted now in terms of categories derived from colonial (or postcolonial) theory.

But is this correct? I have already argued at length elsewhere that Joshua has been misread as a text of conquest and genocide. This is not what the text reflected as discourse in ancient Israel, and it was not read in this way in the early church.[12] Here I wish to reconsider Joshua's history of reception in the Crusades to consider whether or not Bainton's thesis is correct, or at least a helpful framework for understanding the use of certain Old Tes-

---

that the Ste.-Chapelle glass cycle is the "strongest evidence" for establishing Joshua as a type for the crusade leader, reflecting a "tradition of looking to the Israelite conquest of the Holy Land as a model for crusading, and specifically of recalling Joshua as a type for the crusading price" (p. 247).

[10]Gaposchkin does, however, cite a number of crusade texts that refer to Joshua in a detailed and careful study. See below for discussion of the significance of these texts.

[11]For discussion on the use of the category "postcolonial" see Ania Loomba, *Colonialism/Postcolonialism*, 2nd ed., The New Critical Idiom (London: Routledge, 2005), esp. pp. 7-22.

[12]See Douglas S. Earl, *Reading Joshua as Christian Scripture*, JTISup 2 (Winona Lake, IN: Eisenbrauns, 2010).

tament texts such as the book of Joshua. A study of every extant text relating to the Crusades is not feasible here; so first I shall consider how the Bible was interpreted in the context of the Crusades using one of the *Bible Moralisées*. Second, I shall consider how Joshua was used through various representative compilations of primary texts relating to the Crusades in general, including the major works *De praedicacione crucis*, a treaty on crusade preaching, and *Opus tripartium*, a crusade apologetic work, as well as through recent compilations of sermons that preached the Crusades. Finally, I shall consider the use of Joshua more broadly in the Middle Ages and specifically in texts relating to "just war" in particular, such as Gratian's *Decretum*. My thesis will be that the book of Joshua was *not* central to the justification and preaching of the Crusades.

JOSHUA AND THE *BIBLE MORALISÉE*

Before considering primary materials explicitly concerned with the Crusades, I would like to consider a medieval work, the *Bible Moralisée* (Codex 2554), to set the use of the Bible in this era in context, given that it is a systematic presentation of biblical interpretation *and application* in a historical context that reflects the pinnacle of crusading ideology. The *Bible Moralisée* ÖNB codex 2554 is a beautifully illustrated pictorial Bible with accompanying texts that explain the illustrations. Each folio has eight "medallions" in two rows each with an explanatory text. Each biblical medallion illustrates a biblical text and "is related to the medallion immediately below, which offers a moralizing interpretation of that biblical passage."[13] According to Christoph Maier, codex 2554 is an early *Bible Moralisée*, produced between 1215 and 1230 for a member of the French Royal Family:

> Considering this date and provenance, it should come as no surprise that the theme of crusading features in ÖNB codex 2554. The period between 1215 and 1230, like the first half of the thirteenth century in general, was a time of great crusading activity both in France against the Albigensian heretics and elsewhere, and the members of the French royal family—past, present and future—were fervent supporters and active participants of the crusade

---

[13]C. T. Maier, "The bible moralisée and the Crusades," in *The Experience of Crusading*, vol. 1, *Western Approaches*, ed. Marcus Bull and Norman Housley (Cambridge: Cambridge University Press, 2003), p. 212; see pp. 209-22.

movement. . . . Daniel Weiss . . . hinted at the fact that crusade ideology had a strong impact on the pictorial programme and biblical exegesis of lavishly illustrated bibles originating, as the *bible moralisées* did, in the second quarter of the thirteenth century under the influence of the French royal family.[14]

Thus if Joshua was an important resource in relation to the Crusades in the context of the production of codex 2554—to the French royal family of the thirteenth century—one would expect to find the interpretation of Joshua in relation to the Crusades developed in the *Bible Moralisée*. So what does *Bible Moralisée* do with Joshua? The text relating to Joshua is reproduced here in full:

[Illustration:] Here Joshua comes and finds at the issue of the river .XII. precious stones and he takes them and keeps them with him and leaves behind him other bad ones. (*Joshua 4:8-9*)
[Interpretation:] That Joshua took the .XII. precious stones and kept them and left the other bad ones signifies Jesus Christ who took the .XII. Apostles from the world and drew them to Himself, and left behind the Jews and all the miscreants and trampled them beneath Him.

[Illustration:] Here Joshua comes and has his trumpets sound and has the ark carried to the city of Jericho and the walls fall and are completely destroyed. (*Joshua 6:15-16, 20*)
[Interpretation:] That the sons of Israel sounded their trumpets and carried the ark and the walls fell signify the Apostles who spread their preaching through the world and carried the Holy Church, and the Jews and the miscreants and their idols fell and came to nothing.

[Illustration:] Here the sons of Israel come and enter into the city and kill and cut up all those whom they find and the woman signals herself apart, and she is saved and protected from death, and her family, and her things. (*Joshua 6:20-25*)
[Interpretation:] That the sons of Israel entered the city and cut up the wicked people signifies the Apostles who came to the world and pulled down *Synagoga* and all miscreance [*sic*]. The woman signifies the Holy Church who was saved by the martyrdom of Jesus Christ.

[Illustration:] Here Joshua comes and commands his people to make of-

---

[14]Ibid., p. 211.

ferings of gold and of silver and warns them not to keep anything, and they make offerings and God receives them. (*Joshua 6:18-19, 24*)

[Interpretation:]That Joshua commanded them to make offerings of that which they had won in the city and not keep anything signifies Jesus Christ who commands kings and counts and all princes to make offerings of their conquest in gratitude, and they do so, and God receives their offering.[15]

This treatment of Joshua and its thirteenth century application is striking. Apart from the vague treatment of conquest in the interpretation of Joshua 6:18-19, 24, there is nothing on the Crusades. The interpretation presented here, although saturated with anti-Jewish polemic, is close to traditional Christian interpretation of Joshua, exemplified in Origen's homilies on Joshua and reflected in the Middle Ages in the *Glossa Ordinaria*, a reference work that collates traditional interpretations of biblical texts.[16] So it seems likely that Joshua was read more in terms of the typology of the church than as a manifesto for conquest or crusade.[17]

But is codex 2554 simply silent on the Crusades? It is not, with the first reference to the Crusades being found in what we might consider an unusual location: the call of Abraham in Genesis 12 (fol. 4r). Maier's analysis of

[15]Gerald B. Guest, trans., *Bible Moralisée Codex Vindobonensis 2554, Vienna, Österreichische Nationalbibliothek* (Manuscripts in Miniature 2; London: Harvey Miller, 1995), fol. 34r, pp. 94-95. Guest suggests that there are probably two leaves missing from Joshua, probably illustrating Joshua 1.

[16]M. Gibson, "The Twelfth-Century Glossed Bible," in *Studia Patristica 23: Papers Presented to the Tenth International Conference on Patristic Studies, Oxford 1987*, ed. E. A. Livingston (Leuven, Belgium: Peeters Press, 1989), pp. 243-44; see 232-44. See Barbara Bruce, trans., *Origen: Homilies on Joshua* (FC 105; Washington, DC: Catholic University of America Press, 2002).

[17]Gaposchkin notes that codex 2554 was one of four moralized Bibles produced for the Capetain court between ca. 1215 and ca. 1240, the others being Oxford-Paris-London, the Toledo Bible, and Vienna ÖNB 1179 ("Louis IX," p. 260). While she discusses these in a section entitled "Joshua in the rhetoric of the crusades," she does not indicate how any of these works might actually refer to the Crusades. However, the so-called Morgan Picture Bible (ca. 1244–1254), whose patron was probably Louis IX, does use imagery from the Crusades to depict scenes from the book of Joshua (Daniel Weiss, "Portraying the Past, Illuminating the Present: The Art of the Morgan Library Picture Bible," in *The Book of Kings: Art, War and the Morgan Library's Medieval Picture Bible*, ed. William Noel and Daniel Weiss [London: Third Millenium, 2002], pp. 10-35). But little space is devoted to Joshua in this work, covering only fols. 10r-11v, whereas Judges covers 12r-17r, and 1 and 2 Samuel covers fols. 19r-46v. Thus the tendency to interpret the Crusades using Joshua (and vice versa) in these works is slight and may not be significant.

the treatment of Genesis 12 in the *Bible Moralisée* is revealing and introduces a number of important themes in the Crusades. The medallions
portray the difficulties for the crusader in leaving family and home in a
situation of economic uncertainty on a difficult journey of uncertain
outcome, an outcome which might include death. But the crusaders are
depicted as confidently leaving their families, indicating their love of God
and renunciation of worldly affairs, taking up their crosses and accepting
the sacrifices involved in going on a spiritual, penitential journey. In the
accompanying text Genesis 12:1 is typologically associated with Luke 9:23
("Then [Jesus] said to them all, 'If any want to become my followers, let
them deny themselves and take up their cross daily and follow me'" [NRSV]),
a text that is of considerable importance in the preaching of the Crusades.[18]

So the *Bible Moralisée* codex 2554 presents the motivation and practice
of the Crusades rather differently than is often implied today within certain
contemporary frames of reference. Interpreted in their own era and on their
own terms, rather than being about conquest, the Crusades reflect sacrifice
and a spiritual journey, probably to martyrdom. These themes are developed here in the *Bible Moralisée* in a careful canonical hermeneutic.[19]

JOSHUA IN PRIMARY TEXTS RELATING TO THE CRUSADES

In the contemporary context fostered by Bainton's work, as evidenced in
works such as Prior's, the *Bible Moralisée* may seem anomalous. But if one
takes as a starting point Louise and Jonathan Riley-Smith's compilation of
primary texts relating to the Crusades, a collection designed for classroom
use to provide a general overview of the crusading movement and the theology behind it, then it is surprising how few references one finds to Joshua.
There are far fewer references or allusions to Joshua (and/or Deuteronomy)
in this compilation of primary texts than there are in Bainton's short chapter,
"The Origins of the Crusading Idea in the Old Testament."[20] While there are

---

[18]Maier, "The bible moralisée," pp. 212-16.

[19]Two other explicit references to the Crusades in codex 2554 are found in fol. 38r, depicting 1
Kings 17:1-9, and fol. 40v, depicting 1 Sam 25:12-13. It is interesting that in fol. 38r Goliath
and his army are explicitly interpreted as being Saracens, (Guest, *Bible Moralisée*, p. 112)
whereas in Joshua the Canaanites, such as the inhabitants of Jericho, are not.

[20]L. and J. Riley-Smith, *The Crusades: Idea and Reality 1095–1274*, Documents of Medieval
History 4 (London: Edward Arnold, 1981), hereafter *Crusades*. Moreover, in J. A. Brundag-
es's earlier compilation, *The Crusades: A Documentary Survey* (Milwaukee: Marquette Uni-

many references to the Old Testament in the justification of the Crusades, it would seem from the Riley-Smiths' collection that it is primarily to the books of Maccabees that appeal is made, presumably because the books of Maccabees narrate a piously-motivated response (that includes martyrdom) to liberate and re-establish what had been aggressively captured, thus providing a narrative that is appropriate for analogical use in the context of the Crusades, or the earlier Crusades at least.[21] However, and perhaps rather surprisingly, in this compilation it appears that it is often to the Gospels that appeal is made in the preaching and justification of the Crusades. If we assume that the compilation is reasonably representative of Crusade literature, then this is surprising, for it is possible to provide a competent overview of the Crusades and their theology from primary texts almost without reference to Joshua. Hence it would seem difficult to sustain the claim that the book of Joshua provided inspiration, motivation or legitimation for the Crusades. There does not appear to be any inherent "family resemblence" between Joshua and the Crusades. That this is surprising might indicate that something has gone wrong with *our* interpretation of the Crusades and with *our* reading of Joshua.

I would like to look at a variety of foundational crusading texts and Crusade sermons in some detail so as to consider how Joshua is (or is not) used here and what theological themes are important in the Crusades. Two statements by Pope Urban II have been taken as programmatic for the encouragement to participate in the Crusades: "No one must doubt that if he dies on this expedition for the love of God and his brothers his sins will surely be forgiven and he will gain a share of eternal life through the most compassionate mercy of our God."[22] And, "Whoever for devotion alone, not to gain honour or money, goes to Jerusalem to liberate the Church of God can substitute this journey for all penance."[23] Thus whatever rhetoric may or may not

---

versity Press, 1962), as well as in S. J. Allen and E. Amt's more recent compilation, *The Crusades: A Reader*, Readings in Medieval Civilizations and Cultures VIII (Peterborough, Ontario: Broadview Press, 2003), there are *no* references or allusions to Joshua.

[21] For a discussion of the use of the books of Maccabees in crusade preaching see P. J. Cole, *The Preaching of the Crusades to the Holy Land, 1095–1270* (Cambridge, MA: The Medieval Academy of America, 1991), pp. 27-32.

[22] Urban to the counts of Besalú, Empurias, Roussillon and Cerdana and their knights (ca. January 1096–29 July 1099), in Riley-Smith, *Crusades*, p. 40.

[23] Indulgence from the Council of Clermont, 18–27 November 1095, in Riley-Smith, *Crusades*, p. 37.

lie behind Urban's words, the motivation encouraged in participants in crusading is love of God and brothers and devotion and not a desire for gain or
conquest *per se*. Moreover, in her study of the preaching of the Crusades
Penny Cole notes that in his crusading preaching Urban II refers to the Holy
Land using Exodus 3:8, the land "which flows with milk and honey,"[24] but
there is no reference to Joshua in his sermons represented here. Exodus 3:8 is
explicitly referred to by Robert of Rheims at a similar date, although its use is
not developed. Here we do find some of the most xenophobic material that
relates to the Crusades, including the one example cited by Prior to illustrate
his thesis about the nature of the Crusades.[25] Robert writes, "Race of the
French . . . race chosen and beloved by God. . . . Take the road to the Holy
Sepulchre, rescue that land from a dreadful race and rule over it yourselves,
for that land *that*, as scripture says, *floweth with milk and honey* was given by
God as a possession to the children of Israel." Significantly however, Robert
does not refer to Joshua explicitly. Indeed, he turns to the Gospels—"He that
loveth father or mother more than me is not worthy of me"—a citation he
uses to argue for the need to *go* crusading, without possessions or family
holding one back. Robert concludes with another Gospel citation: "Whosoever doth not carry his cross and come after me is not worthy of me."[26]
These themes, developing the Gospel citations, are common throughout the
crusading material, suggesting that it is the ideals of love and sacrifice and not
gain and conquest that are the dominating ideals of much crusading activity.
This might account for the lack of appeal to Joshua.

Indeed, in this same era, Guibert of Nogent in *Historia quae dicitur Gesta
Dei per Francos* (before 1108) develops these themes and shows an acute
awareness of the problem of motive in war, contrasting unjust war with the
Crusade. "Until now you have fought unjust wars: you have often savagely
brandished your spears at each other in mutual carnage only out of greed
and pride, for which you deserve eternal destruction and the certain ruin of
damnation! Now we are proposing that you should fight wars which contain
the glorious reward of martyrdom."

---

[24]Cole, *Preaching*, p. 15.
[25]Prior, *Bible*, p. 35.
[26]Robert of Rheims, *Historia Iherosolimitana* (before 1107), in Riley-Smith, *Crusades*, pp. 42-
45.

Most significant for Guibert are the Maccabees; "If the Maccabees in days of old were renowned for their piety because they fought for the sacred rituals and the Temple, then you too, Christian soldiers, may justly defend the freedom of the fatherland by the exercise of arms."[27] The Maccabees are here the main exemplars for the crusaders from the biblical materials, owing to their piety and willingness to accept martyrdom to re-establish what had been aggressively taken.

While the paucity of allusions to or citations of Joshua is striking in these examples, it is not entirely absent, even if its use is rare. Guibert does allude to Joshua and to the procession around Jericho in *Historia*,[28] and Baldric of Bourgueil, in *Historia Jerosolimitana* (ca.1108) alludes to Joshua, although it is in the context of martyrdom:

> O Stephen, first of all the martyrs, how blessed are the stones which won you a martyr's crown! O John the Baptist, how blissful are the streams of the River Jordan which you used to baptize the Saviour! The children of Israel, who were led out of Egypt and prefigured you after crossing the Red Sea, appropriated by force, with [Joshua] as their leader, this land for themselves; they ejected the Jebusites and other communities and they lived in the earthly Jerusalem, the type of the heavenly Jerusalem.[29]

While alluding to Joshua, there is no development of Joshua here. Instead he develops Exodus 17:8-13, the story of Moses and Amalek: "Yours [duty] must be to fight against the Amalekites. We will hold out tireless hands like Moses, praying to heaven; you must draw and brandish your swords, you fearless warriors against Amalek." Moreover, he compares the Turks to the Jebusites: "you . . . wage war for your own rights over Jerusalem and attack and throw out the Turks, more unholy than the Jebusites, who are there." But Baldric is deeply concerned with the motive for crusading: "Gird yourselves, I say, and act like mighty sons, because it is better for you

---

[27] Guibert of Nogent, *Historia quae dicitur Gesta Dei per Francos*, in Riley-Smith, *Crusades*, pp. 45-46.

[28] Although not in the excerpt in Riley-Smith, *Crusades*. For the text see *The Deeds of God Through the Franks: A Translation of Guibert de Nogent's Gesta Dei per Francos*, ed. R. Levine (Woodbridge, UK: Boydell Press, 1997), pp. 107, 129. A similar allusion to Jericho occurs in Peter Tudebode, *Historia de Hierosolymitano itinere* (1099) (Riley-Smith, *Crusades*, pp. 164-65).

[29] Baldric of Bourgueil, *Historia Jerosolimitana*, in Riley-Smith, *Crusades*, p. 51.

to die in battle than to tolerate the abuse of your race and your Holy Places. Do not let the seductive lures of your women and possessions persuade you not to go." Baldric concludes with the usual Gospel citation of taking up the cross—anyone who does not take up their cross is not worthy to be Jesus' disciple.[30]

In a slightly later period, in the Second Crusade, we see the same kind of emphases and use of biblical texts. Pope Eugenius III, writing to King Louis VII of France (1146) and proclaiming the Second Crusade, is concerned with defending the Eastern Church and turns to the book of Maccabees. "Let the good Mattathias be an example to you," he wrote. "He did not hesitate for a moment to expose himself with his sons and relatives to death and to leave all he had in the world to preserve his ancestral laws; and at length with the help of divine aid and with much labour he and his offspring triumphed powerfully over their enemies."

Eugenius continues, expressing a concern with motivation for crusading:

Since . . . those who fight for the Lord ought not to care for precious clothes or elegant appearance or dogs or hawks or other things that are signs of lasciviousness, we, in the Lord, impress upon your understanding that those who decide to begin so holy a work ought to pay no attention to multi-coloured clothes or minivers or gilded or silvered arms.[31]

Again it is striking that there is no reference to Joshua here, especially in this citation, as it might be natural to appeal to Achan's story in Joshua 7, where Achan takes a valuable robe, gold and silver from Jericho (Josh 7:21) and is stoned to death for so doing.

Later in the twelfth century (1187) it is again the Maccabees that are exemplars for Gregory VIII: "the Maccabees, on fire with zeal for the divine law, exposed themselves to every danger to liberate their brothers, and taught that not only riches but also persons ought to be laid down for the salvation of their brethren." Gregory also speaks of those "who with contrite hearts and humbled spirits undertake the labour of this journey and die in penitence for their sins and with right faith we promise full indulgence of their faults and eternal life."[32] Again, there is no appeal to Joshua, and the

---

[30]Ibid., pp. 51-53.
[31]Pope Eugenius III writing to King Louis VII of France, in Riley-Smith, *Crusades*, pp. 58-59.
[32]Gregory VIII, *Historia de expeditione Friderici imperatoris*, in Riley-Smith, *Crusades*, pp. 65-67.

same interpretative themes emerge: contrition, a sacrificial journey and love for brethren. The books of Maccabees are quite appropriately taken as a paradigm for the Crusades while Joshua is not.

Turning to the early-mid thirteenth century, while Riley-Smith describes Pope Innocent III's proclamation of the Fifth Crusade (1213) as the "apogee of papal crusading propaganda," there are no references or allusions to Joshua in the material that Riley-Smith cites, despite various citations from the Gospels and Revelation. However, the theme of martyrdom and the concern of motive are still prevalent. "How many men, converted to penance, have delivered themselves up to the service of the Crucified One in order to liberate the Holy Land and have won a crown of glory as if they had suffered the agony of martyrdom, men who perhaps might have died in their wicked ways, ensnared in carnal pleasures and worldly enticements!"[33] Moreover, in a sermon of John of Abbeville (1217–1218) on Lamentations 5:1, in which he uses the language of Deuteronomy 23:1-3 to denounce the captors of the land as Moabites and Ammonites, he refers to Judges 19, but not to Joshua.[34]

However, in Christoph Maier's compilation of Crusade sermons, in a sermon by James of Vitry in this era reference is made to Rahab's story (Josh 2), being imaginatively interpreted through Psalm 77:54 in the Vulgate:[35]

About the scarlet string and the line of distribution:

Therefore, pray to the Lord that today the sinners may be led out of their caves by the string of the cross of Christ. This is the scarlet string by which Rahab was freed while the others perished; thus today, while the hardened and obstinate perish, the others, amongst whom *the Lord divided the promised land by the line of distribution* [Ps 77:54], are drawn to Christ by the string of the cross.[36]

---

[33]Ibid., p. 120; see pp. 118-24.

[34]Cole, *Preaching*; sermon Paris, Bibliothèque Nationale, MS nouv. acq. Lat. 999, folios 169va-179ra, in Cole, *Preaching*, pp. 222-26 as "The Sermon of John of Abbeville," cf. pp. 150-56 for discussion.

[35]Psalm 77:54 in the Vulgate reads: *et induxit eos in montem sanctificationis suae montem quem adquisivit dextera eius et eiecit a facie eorum gentes et sorte divisit eis terram in funiculo distributionis.* This reading seems to derive from the LXX Ps 77:55 which reads ἐκληροδότησεν αὐτοὺς ἐν σχοινίῳ κληροδοσίας for the MT (Ps 78:55) ויפילם לבהב נהלה, taking הבל as cord or line rather than territory.

[36]Sermon II.5 in Christoph T. Maier, *Crusade Propaganda and Ideology: Model Sermons for Preaching the Cross* (New York: Cambridge University Press, 2000), p. 103.

But in James of Vitry's other Crusade sermons in Maier's compilation there are no references to Joshua. Indeed, in another sermon of his that takes Ezekiel 9:4-6 as the point of departure, Christians are reminded of their moral duty to take up the cross. This sermon turns to Kings, Haggai, Maccabees and Judges, but not Joshua.[37]

James of Vitry's use of Joshua 2 and Psalm 77:54 (Vulgate) is very similar to Gilbert of Tournai's in this same era, who develops this sort of reading further:

> The cross of Christ is the *scarlet string*, by which the sinners are led from their caves, meaning the hideouts of their sins, and by which Rahab was freed, while the others perished. So while the hardened and the obstinate are killed, the faithful crusaders are drawn to Christ by this string and the promised land is given to them *by the line of distribution*, because true crusaders, who are truely [sic] contrite, have confessed their sins and prepare for the service of God and then die, are considered true martyrs, freed from mortal and venial sins and absolved from all penance enjoined on them, the punishment for their sins in this world and the punishment of purgatory in the next, they are safe from the tortures of hell and will be invested by this sign with eternal glory.[38]

Here the traditional "spiritual" reading of Joshua, in this case of Rahab's story, is reinterpreted and developed in the context of crusading. Yet Joshua himself is not presented as an exemplar for a crusader, and the book of Joshua does not provide a paradigm for crusading as such, although we come much closer to seeing the use of Joshua for legitimating the Crusades than anything that we have seen yet. It seems that the point here is that of fostering a penitential attitude in the crusader rather than an attitude of violence in crusading.

However we do in fact find, in a sermon of Eudes of Châteauroux (1268/69) written for Charles of Anjou following a crusade against Muslims in Lucheria, the kind of use of Joshua as a type for the crusade leader that has been commonly claimed. In a sermon based upon Joshua 7 Eudes preaches, "Hec ystoria parabola est instantis temporis: Dominus dedit

---

[37]Riley-Smith, *Crusades*, pp. 133-35.
[38]Sermon I.20 in Maier, *Crusade Propaganda*, p. 189.

terram Apulie nostre Iosue, id est domino Karolo."[39] ("This history is a parable for the present time: The Lord gave the land of Apulie to our Joshua, i.e., to lord Charles.") Eudes also refers to Joshua in other sermons. For example, in a sermon of 1240 he makes a passing allusion to the Israelites crossing the Jordan in Joshua 3, although this is not developed.[40] It would seem, then, that Eudes's use of Joshua in relation to the Crusades is innovative—it is unusual and atypical.

In the latter thirteenth century there are two major works by Humbert of Romans that demand particular consideration. Humbert was an experienced crusade preacher who was Master General of the Dominican Order. He wrote *De praedicacione crucis*, a treaty on crusade preaching, and *Opus tripartium*, an important text in which he replies to objections to crusading, written at the request of Gregory X before the Second Council of Lyons in 1274.[41] In *Opus tripartium* he offers an apologetic response to a series of "condemnations." In reply to the "first kind of condemnation" he argues that crusading is a defence of what is established. He appeals to the story of the Maccabees fighting on the Sabbath against enemies who attacked them, even though "this might seem to have been against the law" in order to deal with questions of justice and law. A biblical precedent is set by the Maccabees. There is no appeal to Joshua here. Likewise in his reply to the "second kind of condemnation," he does not refer to Joshua but repeatedly appeals to Judges and, again, in his reply to the "third kind of condemnation" there is no appeal to Joshua, although he does appeal to the stories of David, Elisha, Judas Maccabaeus and Deuteronomy 32:30, in the context of leadership and of fighting for justice. In the reply to the "fourth kind of condemnation" Humbert asks, "How, therefore, can Christians be without fault if they are at peace with the Saracens and do not resist their deeds, which are so evil, especially since the Lord commanded the children of Israel never to make a treaty with the gentiles who lived among them?" Here there appears

---

[39]Christoph T. Maier, "Crusade and rhetoric against the Muslim colony of Lucera: Eudes of Châteauroux's *Sermones de Rebellione Sarracenorum Lucherie in Apulia*" in *Journal of Medieval History* 21 (1995): 379; see pp. 343-85. Eudes was a papal legate and crusade preacher and accompanied Louis IX to the Holy Land. See also Gaposchkin, "Louix IX," p. 258 for further discussion.

[40]Sermon II.20, in Maier, *Crusade Propaganda*, p. 151.

[41]Riley-Smith, *Crusades*, p. 103.

to be an allusion to Deuteronomy 7:2, a text related to Joshua that finds
virtually no use in Crusade materials. Again, there is no reference to Joshua
here. Humbert goes on to use the story of Sodom and Gomorrah as an example in his next response, together with citations from Luke 19, Matthew
and Hebrews 6. But interestingly, in his reply to the "sixth kind of condemnation" he notes that some are saying that "when we gain their [Saracen]
lands we do not occupy them like colonists . . . and so there seem to be no
spiritual, corporeal or temporal fruits from this sort of attack," a criticism
that implies that the Crusades were not "colonial," and indeed were being
criticized for not being sufficiently "colonial"—a criticism that Humbert *rejects*! Here Humbert appeals to Judith but, again, not to Joshua.[42] In the
reply to the "seventh kind of condemnation" he cites Psalms, Ecclesiastes,
Habakkuk, Judges, Samuel, Judith and Maccabees, and it is only in the final
paragraph of the work that there is any reference or allusion to Joshua in
the whole of *Opus tripartium*, and its context is revealing:

> [W]e should correct evildoers, as was done to Achan: the children of Israel
> stoned him when they discovered that he was the man in the army of the
> Lord who had stolen something under the ban against the Lord's command
> and that because of his crime they had been defeated. And . . . we should
> grieve over the abasement of the name of the Lord, as Joshua grieved when
> the people he had sent against Ai were defeated.[43]

Joshua is used here in the context of correcting crusaders who are thieves
and in the context of defeat, not of conquest. Joshua is used as the basis for
self-critique. In summary, the almost total absence of Joshua in *Opus tripartium* is significant and striking.

Humbert's other major crusade work, *De predicacione crucis*, survives
in numerous manuscripts,[44] being written for crusade preachers. But Cole
notes that *De predicacione crucis* was not just a preaching aid but "more
like an omnibus, a reference collection of ideas and information about
crusading up to his own day."[45] For Humbert "the model of the religious

---

[42]Humbert of Romans, *Opus tripartium*, in Riley-Smith, *Crusades*, pp. 105-13.

[43]Ibid., pp. 115-17.

[44]Cole suggests that Vat. lat. 3847, folios 1ra-25vb is possibly the earliest, dating from the
fourteenth-century (Cole, *Preaching*, p. 202).

[45]P. J. Cole, "Humbert of Romans and the crusade," in *The Experience of Crusading*, p. 164; see
pp. 157-74.

warrior which he would have all crusaders follow is that of the Maccabees, who fought for justice right up to death (fol. 4b)." Humbert uses the examples of Mattathias and Phinehas "who fought to defend their laws and resisted infidel oppressors," as well as other examples of men "who acted out of brotherly love to save others (fol. 7va)," such as the apostles, Judas Maccabeus and Abraham. Following 1 John 4:21, people are admonished to love God and brother. Humbert promotes crusading as a devotional act, a pilgrimage.[46] *De predicacione crucis* exists in short and long versions. In the long version, represented in a fifteenth-century manuscript in Madrid,[47] there is a section that addresses the benefits obtained by those who undertake the warfare of God. Humbert emphasizes that the "army of God enjoys the 'society of angels,'" something that he develops using 2 Kings 6:8-17 and Joshua 5:13-15. "From those two histories," Humbert explains, "we realize that in those ancient armies of the faithful, the angels joined against the infidels as companions, as leaders, as helpers and as teachers in the wars. If that is true about those armies then how much more should we believe this about the Christian army fighting for Christ crucified."[48] Again, we find that Joshua is of little significance for the Crusades. Moreover, the usage that we do find—only present in one of the manuscript families—does not legitimize the crusade as conquest of the land in any way analogous to Joshua, but simply illustrates a point about divine assistance.

However, *De predicacione crucis* is written in two parts. The second part consists of 142 biblical *themata* for use in crusade preaching—biblical texts that could be used in sermons.[49] Here, in the Vatican MS (fols. 15rb-18ra), Humbert provides a comprehensive list of preaching texts for crusade sermons, drawing on twenty-seven Old Testament books and eighteen New Testament books, which "provide a panorama of the religious wars of sacred history . . . although none of the texts is amplified and some consist of only one line."[50] Here there are 103 Old Testament texts and thirty-nine New Testament texts cited in canonical order. Most of the Old Testament books

---

[46]Cole, *Preaching*, pp. 206-7.
[47]Biblioteca Nacional 19423, ff.87r-126v (Cole, "Humbert," pp. 160-1).
[48]Quoted in Cole, "Humbert," p. 161, cf. MS Biblioteca Nacional 19423, fol. 88v.
[49]Cole, "Humbert," pp. 160-61.
[50]Cole, *Preaching*, p. 212.

are represented, but "a disproportionate weight of seventeen *themata* is given to the books of Maccabees.... The New Testament texts tend to stress Christian discipleship, and especially the duty to suffer for Christ and follow him to the cross. The texts from the Apocalypse underline the glorious reward that awaits these faithful followers."[51] But it is striking that of these themata *only two* are taken from Joshua—Joshua 10:7-8 and Joshua 18:3—and the biblical texts are simply quoted without amplification.[52] Thus once again it is Maccabees rather than Joshua that is central for the crusaders, with the use of Joshua being almost nonexistent. Cole concludes that for Humbert it is devotion to the cross and the emulation of the martyrs that is central to crusading.[53]

The paucity of references to Joshua in these major works on crusading by Humbert, works that may said to exemplify the legitimation, theology and preaching of the Crusades, is surely significant.

However, as with Eudes's sermon of 1268/69, it is again in the late thirteenth or early fourteenth century that we discover another sermon that uses Joshua more in the sense of the legitimizing of crusading, even though the reading of Joshua is still "spiritualized." It is a sermon of Bertrand de la Tour's based upon Joshua 8. It is unlike many previous materials considered above (apart from Eudes's sermon on Joshua 7), which have generally made only passing reference to Joshua. His sermon commences:

> Raise the shield against Ai, Joshua 8. Ai, a city hostile to the Lord, a nuisance to God's people, burned down by fire, represents a faithless people armed against the Lord, standing ready against God's troops, destined for disgrace, against whom the Lord orders the shield to be raised. Thus it says: Raise the shield etc., where using a metaphor he addresses Joshua, the prince or standard-bearer of the army, with these words, which taken in the spiritual sense contain the encouragement of the leader, the exaltation of the cross and the threat to the enemy.[54]

---

[51]Cole, "Humbert," p. 165. Moreover, again there is a variation between manuscripts, and the so-called "O" version (Österreichische Nationalbibliothek [Palatinus] 4329, ff. 169-87, dated 1433) omits the themata (Cole, "Humbert," p. 162).

[52]I am indebted to Dr. Christoph Maier for these references, taken from chapter 27 (*Sequuntur themata ex tota biblia ad predicandum crucem*) of the 1495 printed edition of the work.

[53]Cole, *Preaching*, pp. 215-16.

[54]Sermon III.1, in Maier, *Crusade Propaganda*, pp. 243-45.

Perhaps this sermon might typify the shift in the aims and goals of the later crusading movement,[55] coupled with shifting trends in biblical interpretation in the Middle Ages. Indeed, Riley-Smith suggests that the motivation behind the crusade movement changed over time, noting that there had been a widening of the goal of crusading in 1105, and that in a papal encyclical of 1198 Innocent III extended crusades to heretics and political opponents. Revenge becomes a theme in twelfth-century crusade poetry, a theme absent in the First Crusade in which crusading was motivated by piety and not the gain of land, entailing much suffering and hardship.[56] So it is noteworthy that in Gaposchkin's analysis of Joshua's use in crusading rhetoric there are, I believe, only two references dating from the twelfth century but seventeen references from the thirteenth century.[57] This would correspond to the shift in interpretative practice of the Old Testament that she claims occurred in the thirteenth century and would be consistent with the analysis above, even if such an approach to Joshua was probably still a minority approach. It is not reflected in Humbert's major works, for example, or much in later works as we shall see below.

Moving to the fourteenth century and beyond, it is noteworthy that in Norman Housley's collection of primary materials relating to the Crusades between 1274 and 1580,[58] there is only a single reference to Joshua (Josh 7) in this era in Erasmus' *Consultatio de bello Turcis inferendo* (1530). It is striking, however, that the text is used as the basis of the self-critique of crusaders rather than as justifying crusading:

> [I]f theft by a single man, Achan, brought ill-fortune to the whole people of Israel in its combat with the enemy, what hope is there for us, laden with sins, and fighting through sinful soldiers, who in a spirit of venality think of nothing but evil-doing, who pillage as they set off to war and pillage as they come back, are sometimes crueller to their own people than to the enemy, cart harlots around with them, and when in camp get drunk, play at dice, swear, quarrel and brawl? For these men war consti-

---

[55]See P. Lock, *The Routledge Companion to the Crusades* (London: Routledge, 2006) for a recent account of the development of the Crusades.

[56]Riley-Smith, *Crusades*, pp. 11–29.

[57]Gaposchkin, "Louis IX."

[58]N. Housley, *Documents on the Later Crusades, 1274–1580* (New York: St. Martin's Press, 1996).

tutes an open season for sinning and a chance for plunder.

If we want God to fight on our side, and if we cannot be like those soldiers whom St. Bernard describes, whom he doesn't know whether to call monks or knights, so great was their moral probity and their warrior courage, then at least the spirit should be free of guilt, and we should refrain from provoking the Lord by our sins while marching under His banners.[59]

Thus even as there is development in the crusading movement and ideals, Joshua remains a minor influence on the movement and cannot be said to provide a warrant for the activities of the crusaders.

JOSHUA AND THE "JUST WAR" IN THE MIDDLE AGES

The idea of the "just war" saw much of its development in Augustine and was further developed in the medieval period. But, in general, little use is made of Joshua in the context of "just war" theory, apart perhaps from Joshua 8, which forms the locus for debates on the legitimacy of ambush in warfare.[60]

J. W. Baldwin suggests that Gratian assembled the main elements of the just war theory in the twelfth century in the *Decretum* (*Concordia discordantium canonum*), a work which became a textbook that was the basis for reflection by theologians contemporary with the Crusades.[61] Gratian deals with warfare in C.23 q.1-5, and in particular how to appropriate narratives

---

[59]*Consultatio de bello Turcis inferendo*, in Housley, *Documents*, p. 180.

[60]For discussion of the development of the "just war" theory in this period see F. H. Russell, *The Just War in the Middle Ages* (Cambridge: Cambridge University Press, 1975), or more recently Henrik Syse and Gregory M. Reichberg, eds., *Ethics, Nationalism, and Just War: Medieval and Contemporary Perspectives* (Washington, DC: Catholic University of America Press, 2007). There are no references to Joshua in *Ethics and Nationalism* in relation to the medieval era. Russell's work contains few references to Joshua and the majority, and all those that refer to actual uses of the text, are to Joshua 8 (pp. 20, 23, 90, 235 and 271). His other reference to Joshua in a discussion of Robert of Courson prematurely conflates Joshua with the war against the Amorites in Num 21:21-24, a text which appears to be the locus for much of the discussion of the legitimacy of warfare as derived from Old Testament texts (Russell, *Just War*, pp. 252-3). See also T. R. Elssner, *Josua und seine Kriege in jüdischer und christlicher Rezeptionsgeschichte* (Theologie und Frieden 37; Stuttgart: W. Kohlhammer, 2008), pp. 255-89. He does not discuss the use (or lack of use) of Joshua in the Crusade materials and confines his discussion to Joshua's reception in major figures such as Aquinas and Gratian, with the use of Joshua 8 highlighted.

[61]J. W. Baldwin, *Masters, Princes and Merchants: The Social Views of Peter the Chanter and His Circle* (Princeton: Princeton University Press, 1970), 1.206.

of warfare in the Old Testament in a Christian context.[62] He cites a homily of Origen on Joshua (which he incorrectly ascribes to Gregory),[63] which implied that since the wars "were only figures of spiritual conflicts for instructing Christians, they lent no sanctions to actual hostilities."[64] Gratian proceeds to develop an account of warfare, using Old Testament texts in the process, initially through appeal to Augustine. But he avoids appealing to Joshua,[65] presumably because Origen's interpretation of Joshua was so well established.[66]

Robert of Courson, part of the circle of Peter the Chanter, devotes some attention to legitimizing crusades in his *Summa*, taking the *Decretum* as a point of departure.[67] Here the focus is primarily the use of the story of the Amorites in Numbers 21:21-24 rather than Joshua. So Baldwin notes that for Robert, "A crusade to the holy land for liberating the eastern Christian provinces was legitimate because it regained the church's rightful inheritance. Just as God's promise justified the Hebrew conquest of the Amorites, so the present "land of promise" could be rightfully taken by Christians."[68]

Thus there is remarkably little use of Joshua in just war discourse in the Middle Ages,[69] with Joshua's use essentially limited to addressing the legit-

---

[62]Cf. Russell, *Just War*, pp. 68-76. See also G. M. Reichberg et al., eds., "Gratian and the Decretists (Twelfth Century): War and Coercion in the *Decretum*," in *The Ethics of War: Classic and Contemporary Readings* (Oxford: Blackwell, 2006), pp. 104-24, esp. pp. 104-8.

[63]*Decretum* C.23 q.1, cf. Origen, *Joshua* 15.1, *PG* 12:897 and Baldwin, *Masters*, 2.145n10.

[64]Baldwin, *Masters*, 1.207 (cf. *Decretum*, C.23, q.1, c.1). Tertullian also considered Joshua to be inapplicable to the question of warfare in a Christian context (*De idolataria* 19.3), unlike Augustine (e.g. *Questions on Joshua* 10-11 [*PL* 34:780-81]) and Ambrose (*De officiis ministorum* [1.40.195]).

[65]Apart from discussion of the legitimacy of ambush in Joshua 8 which Gratian takes from Augustine (C.23, q.2. c.3; cf. Elssner, *Josua*, pp. 271-2). Indeed, the locus of Joshua's significance for just war theory is very limited, essentially limited to the question of the legitimacy of ambush in warfare (Joshua 8, cf. Augustine, *Questions on Joshua* 10–11 and Thomas Aquinas, *ST* 2a2ae, 40.1). See further B. Smalley, *The Study of the Bible in the Middle Ages*, 3rd ed. (Oxford: Basil Blackwell, 1983), pp. 212-13.

[66]Texts such as Num 21:21-24 form Gratian's point of departure, read through Augustine (C.23 q.2; cf. Augustine's treatment of Num 21:21-24 in *Questions on Numbers* 4.44 [*PL* 34:739]). Augustine judged the conquest of the Amorites to be a just war (cf. Baldwin, *Masters, Princes and Merchants* 1.207 and *Decretum*, C.23, q.2, c.3).

[67]Cole, *Preaching*, p. 127.

[68]Baldwin, *Masters, Princes and Merchants* 1.208-209 (cf. Robert of Courson, *Summa*, xxvi, 10: fol. 92rb, va; xv, 2,3: fols. 63vb-64ra).

[69]To take another study, there are no references to Joshua's use in this era in J. E. Damon's *Soldier Saints and Holy Warriors: Warfare and Sanctity in the Literature of Early England* (Aldershot, UK: Ashgate, 2003).

imacy of ambush. Numbers 21:21-24 is the more significant text for relating
Old Testament narratives to the just war and to the Crusades considered in
this perspective.

JOSHUA IN THE MIDDLE AGES

Joshua's use recedes generally in the Middle Ages[70] in contrast to its earlier
popularity as exemplified in Origen's *Homilies on Joshua*. So in an edition of
Mirour of Mans Saluacioune (ca. 1475), a translation of *Speculum Humanae
Salvationis* (ca. 1310–1324) written, according to the prologue, as a guide to
instruct laity and clergy, a work for which the number of extant copies witnesses to its popularity,[71] there are few instances of the use of Joshua, and
each reflects the traditional use of Joshua's typology with reference to the
crossing of the Jordan, Rahab and Achan.[72] Moreover, in a major collation
of extant Middle English sermons, there are only eight references to Joshua,
five of which concern Achan.[73] But in a woodcut version (ca. 1460) of the
Biblia Pauperum (a title that is rather misleading and not original), a very
early printed work that was probably a devotional aid depicting various Old
Testament scenes together with their typological fulfilment,[74] there is no
use of the book of Joshua at all. So Joshua seems to fall out of use generally
in the later Middle Ages.

Finally, however, an imaginative interweaving of traditional Christian

---

[70]Smalley's work makes little reference to Joshua, it being Joshua 8 that receives attention in
relation to ambush in warfare (Smalley, *The Study of the Bible*, pp. 212-13).

[71]A. Henry, *The Mirour of Mans Saluacioune: A Middle English Translation of Speculum Humanae Salvationis: A Critical Edition of the Fifteenth-Century Manuscript Illustrated from
Der Spiegel der menschen Behältnis, Speyer: Drach, c.1475* (Philadelphia: University of Pennsylvania Press, 1987), pp. 10-11.

[72]The references are to Joshua 3–4 (lines 1469-1504 in ibid., p. 89); to Rahab (line 1697, p. 97)
and to Achan (lines 3935 and 4084, p. 187 and 193).

[73]V. O'Mara and S. Paul, eds., *A Repertorium of Middle English Prose Sermons*, SERMO (Turn-
hout, Belgium: Brepols, 2007). Other books in the Old Testament receive significantly more
treatment. Significantly, there is only a single reference to Deut 7, the text that seemingly
commands the Canaanite genocide that finds its fulfilment in Joshua. The reference is to
Deut 7:1 in a fifteenth-century parchment which develops the idea that to reach the promised
land the Israelites had to defeat the seven nations which signified the seven deadly sins.
(Cam/StJo/G.22/007 in ibid., 1.111) This reflects the "stable" Christian reading of Deut 7 in
the *Glossa ordinaria* where Deut 7:1 is developed, with the "seven nations" being the seven
main vices which the 'spiritual warrior' overcomes by God's grace (*PL* 113, col. 459).

[74]A. Henry, *Biblia Pauperum: A Facsimile and Edition* (Ithaca, NY: Cornell University Press,
1987), pp. 3-18.

typological reading of Joshua with the concerns of crusading is found in Dante (ca. 1265–1321), in Division III, Canto IX, lines 109-42 of the *Paradiso*.[75] W. W. Vernon comments

> Folco now names Rahab, and draws a contrast between the zeal of her, who favoured the cause of God entrusted to Joshua in the Holy Land, and the perfect indifference of Pope Boniface VIII, who takes no pains to recover it from the Infidels. He inculpates the accursed Lily stamped upon the form of Florence as the cause of the Pope's thoughts being turned to Avarice and Simony instead of to the Holy Sepulchre, and assigns to the same cause the neglect and disuse of the Holy Scriptures and the Gospels, whose place is usurped by the Decretals, the collection of the constitutions and traditions of the Papal See.[76]

This is an interesting and unusual use of Joshua demonstrating an imaginative development of traditional typological reading in a new context, a use having some resonance with James of Vitry's and Gilbert of Tournai's use of Rahab's story.

CONCLUSION

The analysis above paints a picture of the theological themes and biblical texts that were important in the Crusades, providing in particular a representative (if not exhaustive) portrait of Joshua's use in the crusading literature. While Joshua was quoted or alluded to in the crusading literature, its use was rare and generally undeveloped, especially when compared with the usage of other books such as Maccabees and the Gospels. The book of Joshua and its interpretation in the Middle Ages was not inherent to the theology of the Crusades, and there appears to be no "family resemblance" that associates Joshua with the Crusades.[77] The books of Maccabees provide the primary Old Testament exemplars for the Crusades, while Numbers 21:21-24 forms the focus for the development of just war theory in relation to the Old Testament in the Middle Ages. To give an idea of the frequency of Joshua's use, in Maier's compilation of Crusade sermons there are 512

---

[75]See W. W. Vernon, *Readings on the Paradiso of Dante*, vol. 1 (London: Macmillan, 1900), pp. 318-27. Dante also refers to Joshua in *Parad.* XVIII.38 and *Purg.* XX.109-111.

[76]Vernon, *Readings*, p. 318.

[77]Likewise there is little appeal to Deut 7 in the crusade literature.

biblical references, of which only thirteen are to Joshua (with forty-nine to the Gospels),[78] and in Cole's shorter compilation, there are 137 biblical references, of which there are *none* to Joshua (and thirty-one to the Gospels).[79]

The absence of Joshua in such accounts may reflect two factors primarily: first, the normativity of Origen's "spiritual reading" of Joshua in which Joshua was not read in terms of military activity; and second, a recognition that the situation of the books of Maccabees spoke more directly to the situation of the Crusades than Joshua, since they reflect the pious and costly liberation of that which was aggressively taken, through martyrdom. The focus on martyrdom, "taking up the cross," and love of brother or sister is also developed in the crusading literature through the use of New Testament texts and, in particular, the Gospels. Indeed, it is interesting to observe that the use of the Gospels in preaching the Crusades is far more widespread than that of Joshua. This resonates with Riley-Smith's suggestion that crusading was in fact an act of love:

> [A]s manifestations of Christian love, the crusades were as much the products
> of the renewed spirituality of the central Middle Ages, with its concern for
> living the *vita apostolica* and expressing Christian ideals in active works of
> charity, as were the new hospitals, the pastoral work of the Augustinians and
> Premonstratensians and the service of the friars. The charity of St. Francis
> may now appeal to us more than that of the crusaders, but both sprang from
> the same roots.[80]

Thus some contemporary interpretative frames of reference have led to poor interpretation of Joshua, its history of reception and the Crusades. By attempting to identify a family resemblance or trajectory connecting Joshua, the Crusades and more recent forms of "religiously legitimated militarism," reading one phenomenon through and in terms of the others, the understanding of each has been distorted. A moral problem has been created as a scholarly construct, perhaps using a category such as "Holy War." This has fueled projects to morally critique the Bible and its purported "violent legacy," leading to the sidelining of Scripture, and the premature characterization (a characterization that

---

[78]Maier, *Crusade Propaganda.*
[79]Cole, *Preaching.*
[80]J. Riley-Smith, "Crusading as an Act of Love," *History* 65 (1980): 192; see pp. 177-92.

lacks nuance) of the history of the church as violent.[81]

While it is clear that there *are* morally difficult texts in the Bible that we may wish to critique, such as Genesis 34,[82] and that there *are* instances of atrocities committed in which appeal has been made to biblical texts,[83] it is important to locate and to clarify the actual difficulties that we face. For it would appear that certain post-Enlightenment categories and frames of reference may distort our interpretation not only of events such as the Crusades, but also of our understanding of the reception of Joshua and the book of Joshua itself. There is no straight line that one can draw from Joshua, through the Crusades, to more recent examples of colonialism and religiously legitimated militarism.

---

[81]I have argued elsewhere that the message and significance of Joshua is not in fact one of genocide or conquest. See Earl, *Reading Joshua*.

[82]See Douglas S. Earl, "Toward a Christian Hermeneutic of Old Testament Narrative: Why Genesis 34 Fails to Find Christian Significance," *CBQ* 73.1 (2011): 30-49.

[83]See R. A. Warrior, "Canaanites, Cowboys and Indians: Deliverance, Conquest, and Liberation Theology Today" in *The Postmodern Bible Reader*, ed. D. Jobling et al. (Oxford: Blackwell, 2001), pp. 188-94.

PART TWO

Old Testament Perspectives

3

MARTIAL MEMORY, PEACEABLE VISION

Divine War in the Old Testament

Stephen B. Chapman

———————— ✝ ————————

ALTHOUGH IT HAS BECOME CUSTOMARY to refer to "holy war" in the Old Testament, the expression is a misnomer. The Old Testament never once calls war "holy." The phrase "holy war" nowhere appears; neither is the adjective "holy" ever used attributively or substantively in reference to warfare or any battle. This linguistic phenomenon is much more than an accident or a curiosity. It instead points distinctly both to the Old Testament's true witness concerning war and to the way in which that witness has often been tragically misunderstood.

The expression "holy war" did not always have an accepted place within Old Testament scholarship. It was Friederich Schwally's 1901 volume, *Der heiligen Krieg im alten Israel*, that introduced the term into research in the field, and it was the term's continued use by various scholars, especially by Gerhard von Rad in his influential monograph *Holy War in Ancient Israel*, that won its broad acceptance.[1]

---

[1] These two points are made by Ben C. Ollenburger in "Gerhard von Rad's Theology of Holy War," his introduction to Gerhard von Rad, *Holy War in Ancient Israel*, trans. Marva J. Dawn (Grand Rapids: Eerdmans, 1991), pp. 4-6. They now receive more detailed discussion and further confirmation in Friedrich Wilhelm Graf, "Sakralisierung von Kriegen: Begriffs- und problemgeschichtliche Erwägungen," in *Heilige Kriege: Religiöse Begründungen militärischer Gewaltanwendung: Judentum, Christentum und Islam im Vergleich*, ed. Klaus Schreiner and Elisabeth Müller-Luckner, Schriften des Historischen Kollegs 78 (Munich: Oldenbourg, 2008), pp. 24-25.

Schwally had set out to write a comparative study of ancient warfare in which Israel's attitudes and practices would be viewed in relation to those of other Semitic cultures.[2] In keeping with the comparative nature of his study, Schwally borrowed the term "holy war" from treatments of *jihād* in Islam. This Qur'ānic word literally means "struggling" or "striving," although there is an established convention of translating it by the phrase "holy war."[3] Traditionally in Islam there were twin goals to *jihād*: the conversion of non-Muslim individuals, often by force, and the compulsory imposition of taxes on non-Muslim peoples.

However, especially in view of a modern brand of Islamic terrorism in which *jihād* is seen as a religious duty to engage in military battle against infidels, it is all the more necessary to observe that classical Islam emphasized the spiritual and non-military dimensions of *jihād*, even as it sought to limit the applicability of military *jihād* to defensive, rather than aggressive, warfare. So, as many are pointing out with renewed emphasis in the present, conventional use of the term "holy war" already involves an inappropriate conceptual reduction with respect to Islam.[4] Actually the term "holy war" is not of Islamic origin either but emerges first in the West among the ancient Greeks.[5] This originating context suggests that the association between warfare and holiness is at home within ancient Greek culture rather than Jewish tradition or Islamic teaching.[6]

Yet Schwally borrowed the term "holy war" not only out of convenience. For him, the term usefully illuminated the distinctive organization and

---

[2]Friedrich Schwally, *Der heilige Krieg im alten Israel* (Leipzig, Germany: Deiterich, 1901).

[3]For this definition and the following differentiation of *jihād* see Peter C. Craigie, *The Problem of War in the Old Testament* (Grand Rapids: Eerdmans, 1978), pp. 22-26. According to Graf, it is not yet possible to trace the origin of the European-language translation "holy war" for *jihād* ("Sakralisierung," pp. 26-27).

[4]For the view that *jihād* has been illegitimately hijacked by terrorists, see John L. Esposito, *Unholy War: Terrorism in the Name of Islam* (New York: Oxford University Press, 2003). For criticism of this view, see Christopher J. van der Krogt, "*Jihād* Without Apologetics," *Islam and Christian-Muslim Relations* 21 (2010): 127-42. Helpful comparisons are found in Reuven Firestone, "Conceptions of Holy War in Biblical and Qur'ānic Tradition," *Journal of Religious Ethics* 24 (1996): 99-123 and Schreiner, *Heilige Kriege*.

[5]Ollenburger ("Theology," p. 6) cites Thucydides, *Peloponnesian Wars*, i.112 and Aristophanes, *The Birds*, v. 556. For other Greek parallels, see Philip D. Stern, *The Biblical ḥērem: A Window on Israel's Religious Experience* (Brown Judaic Studies 211, Atlanta: Scholars Press, 1991), pp. 58-60.

[6]Graf, "Sakralisierung," p. 24.

worldview of early Israelite society. Prior to the establishment of the monarchy, he maintained, Israel had existed as a tribal confederation in which God was venerated as a divine warrior and worshiped through joint sacrificial rites.[7] War was prosecuted not only as a means of preserving the confederation but also as a form of religious belief. For this reason, Schwally held, war was approached in Israel with a religious mentality and accompanied with various other religious practices; war was in fact an *extension* of cultic sacrifice and therefore a holy act. It was this idea of war as holy sacrifice, war as an elemental expression of Israelite faith, which persuaded Gerhard von Rad to retain Schwally's term "holy war," even as he attempted to refine it through more detailed analysis.

For his part, von Rad submitted the martial traditions of the Old Testament to exacting critical investigation in an effort to delineate the precise sociohistorical contours of Israelite warfare as a sacral institution. Ordinary warfare was secular, he argued, but a distinctive subset of warfare practice proceeded along the lines that Schwally had sketched. Von Rad focused on this subset of "holy war" and assembled its characteristic practices from the biblical narratives detailing its prosecution. Fundamental to von Rad's reconstruction was also the full participation of the Israelite tribal confederation in such warfare, as well as the fact that it was strictly defensive in nature.[8] Von Rad agreed with Schwally that war in Israel had been religious, but he did not think the Israelites fought "for" a religion.[9]

Von Rad's observations regarding the biblical text were characteristically perceptive and can still be read with great profit, but relatively little of his historical reconstruction has been sustained in recent scholarship. Where von Rad imagined a stable and distinctive set of early Israelite religious practices relating to "holy war"—"holy war" as a "cultic institution," he termed it[10]—the response of other scholars has increasingly been to view the same literary materials as more diverse than uniform, more typical of

---

[7]On this point, and for further discussion, see Ollenburger, "Theology," pp. 4-5. Ollenburger, p. 3, also helpfully demonstrates how Schwally's conception of early Israel as a military confederation is dependent upon the previous scholarship of Julius Wellhausen.

[8]Von Rad, *Holy War*, p. 65.

[9]Ibid., p. 72.

[10]E.g., von Rad, *Holy War*, p. 52.

the ancient Near East than unique, and mostly too late historically to shed much light on the military aspects of Israel's early existence.[11]

This scholarly response has also included a rejection of von Rad's use of the term "holy war" in favor of the expressions "Yahweh war" and "divine war."[12] Rudolf Smend in particular is to be credited with the term "Yahweh war," by which he intends specifically to signal the noncultic character of early Israelite warfare. According to Smend, individual Israelite tribes engaged in battles, but there was not a special type of sacred battle involving the confederation as a whole. So-called holy war in the Old Testament expressed the theological conviction that Yahweh was fighting for Israel rather than Israel fighting for Yahweh.[13] It should be noted again that while von Rad understood the nature of the Israelite tribal confederation differently, he had agreed with Smend's judgment about just who fought for whom: "in the holy wars Israel did not arise to protect faith in Yahweh, but Yahweh came on the scene to defend Israel."[14] In this way it can be said that von Rad's use of the term "holy war" stood in some tension with his own presentation. If "holy war" is taken to mean an offensive military initiative with the twin purpose of conversion and territorial expansion, undertaken on behalf of a deity or religious ideal, then such warfare is decidedly *not* to be found in the pages of the Old Testament.[15] However, such warfare is not what von Rad had in mind either, although the phrase "holy war" carries

---

[11]See especially Sa-Moon Kang, *Divine War in the Old Testament and in the Ancient Near East*, BZAW 177 (Berlin: de Gruyter, 1989); Alexander Rofé, "The Laws of Warfare in the Book of Deuteronomy," *Journal for the Study of the Old Testament* 32 (1985): 23-44; Rudolf Smend, *Yahweh War and Tribal Confederation: Reflections upon Israel's Earliest History* (Nashville: Abingdon, 1970; German orig. 1963); Fritz Stolz, *Jahwes und Israels Krieg: Kriegstheorien und Kriegserfahrungen im Glauben des alten Israel*, ATANT 60 (Zurich: Theologischer Verlag, 1972); Moshe Weinfeld, "Divine Intervention in War in Ancient Israel and in the Ancient Near East," in *History, Historiography and Interpretation*, ed. Hayim Tadmor and Moshe Weinfeld (Jerusalem: Magnes, 1983), pp. 121-47; Manfred Weippert, "'Heiliger Krieg' in Israel und Assyrien: kritische Anmerkungen zu Gerhard von Rads Konzept des 'Heiligen Krieges im alten Israel,'" *Zeitschrift für die alttestamentliche Wissenchaft* 84 (1972): 460-93.

[12]In addition to Kang, *Divine War*; Smend, *Yahweh War*; and Stolz, *Jahwes und Israels Krieg*; see also Craigie, *The Problem of War*, pp. 48-49. A proposal to retain the language of "holy war" in reference to Israel's ideology of war rather than its actual practice (which then would be denoted by the term "Yahweh war") has been made by G. H. Jones, "'Holy War' or 'Yahweh War'?" *Vetus Testamentum* 25 (1975): 642-58, but has not been widely influential.

[13]Smend, *Yahweh War*, pp. 4-6. Cf. Roland de Vaux, *Ancient Israel: Its Life and Institutions* (New York: McGraw-Hill, 1961), p. 262.

[14]Von Rad, *Holy War*, p. 72.

[15]De Vaux, *Israel*, p. 262.

exactly those kinds of connotations today. This is why the term should now be avoided with reference to the Old Testament.

Divine War and the Old Testament

The expressions "Yahweh war" and "divine war" not only elude the web of common assumptions relating to "holy war," they also have the benefit of remaining closer to the idiom of the Old Testament itself. The Old Testament speaks in the plural of "the wars of Yahweh" (Num 21:14; 1 Sam 18:17; 25:28), in the singular of specific wars or individual battles as authorized or "belonging to" Yahweh (Ex 17:16; 1 Sam 17:47) and of Yahweh as a "man of war" or "warrior" (Ex 15:3; Is 42:13; Zeph 3:17) "mighty in battle" (Ps 24:8). Similarly the "angel of the Lord" is a warrior figure stand-in, who directs warfare in Yahweh's stead (e.g., Ex 14:19-20; 23:23-24; Josh 5:13-15; 2 Kings 19:35).

It is true that the Hebrew root for "holy/holiness" (*qdš*) does appear in two restricted contexts relating to war. First, persons and objects affiliated with warfare can be called "holy." Israelite soldiers could apparently be conceived as functioning within a heightened state of purity; accordingly they can be described as "consecrated" (*qdš*, Josh 3:5) to their mission.[16] Captured booty can also be termed "consecrated" or "holy" (*qdš*, Josh 6:19; cf. Is 23:18). These usages indicate how a conception of holiness could exist in relation to the activity of warfare, but they do not characterize warfare itself as holy. Secondly, the prophetic corpus several times uses the peculiar linguistic idiom "to consecrate a war" (*qdš* Piel, Jer 6:4; Joel 4:9[3:9]; Mic 3:5; cf. "consecrate destroyers" in Jer 22:7; "consecrate nations" in Jer 51:27-28) in the sense of declaring or inaugurating military hostilities. But this usage seems conventional and formulaic; it also refers properly to the way in which a war is begun rather than to the actual fighting.[17] Especially in light of how readily many interpreters continue to refer to "holy war" in the Old Testament, the really striking thing is how little semantic overlap exists between the discourse of holiness and phenomenon of war.[18]

---

[16]Von Rad, *Holy War*, p. 42.

[17]Preparation for war might be thought of as a holy matter because a sacrifice would be made, or an oracle sought, or because soldiers would undergo ritual purification, or some combination of any (or all) of these possibilities.

[18]Cf. the conclusion of Georg Fohrer, *History of Israelite Religion*, trans. David E. Green (London: SPCK, 1972), p. 118: "Like everything in life, the conduct of war was surrounded by re-

Even though considerable historical uncertainties persist with respect to the dating of various Old Testament texts, it is possible to trace the distinctive shape of "divine war" in Israel's martial memory.[19] Clearly there is a process of idealization at work in these texts; the basic historical question is how early to locate the characteristically theocentric aspect of this tradition, particularly its disregard for common sense calculations of fighting strength and force capability. Texts that seem naively "spiritual" have routinely been dated late within Old Testament scholarship; historical-critical appraisals of Israel's early military outlook often assume that it must have been much more "realistic." But the danger of anachronism is significant in such judgments, which may only be inscribing modern prejudices within reconstructions of Israel's history under the guise of exegetical correctness. Yet even without attempting to resolve such historical questions, it is nevertheless possible to characterize the overall effect of the various biblical witnesses.[20]

Straightaway it has to be said that many battle accounts in the Old Testament feature some form of divine involvement.[21] Some wars, especially those in the context of Israel's entry into the land, are portrayed in biblical narrative as divinely authorized (e.g., Ex 17:8-16; Deut 7:1-5; Josh 6:1-5). As the so-called conquest narratives depict,[22] such wars are primarily but not

---

ligious conceptions and accompanied by religious rites. But these do not make it a 'holy' war and a sacral institution any more than the religious conceptions, rites, and formulas that surround birth, weaning, marriage, death, and sheep-shearing make them holy."

[19]Ultimately I prefer the term "divine war" out of consideration for those who find printing or speaking the word "Yahweh" to be disrespectful. For a concise presentation of the features of such warfare, see my entry "Holy War" in the *Dictionary of Scripture and Ethics*, ed. Joel B. Green (Grand Rapids: Baker Academic, 2012), pp. 369-70. See also von Rad, *Holy War*, pp. 41-51.

[20]In this attempt at characterization I am less interested in what war was actually like for ancient Israel and more interested in what was considered the ideal. This ideal is nevertheless rooted in history, at least in Israel's memory of its history. For a somewhat kindred approach, one also stressing the nature of biblical warfare as memory, see Robert L. Hubbard, "Only a Distant Memory: Old Testament Allusions to Joshua's Days," *Ex Auditu* 16 (2000): 131-48. However, I would stress even more than Hubbard the historical distance already obtaining between the book of Joshua and the memories it relates. My further goal here is to sketch how Israel's memory of war grew into a distinctive vision of peace.

[21]The following list of features is based on von Rad, *Holy War*, p. 42, but further elaborated.

[22]As recent scholarship has come to acknowledge, "conquest" is also a misnomer in reference to Israel's entry into the land. For a sense of the lively historical debate, see Mark G. Brett, "Israel's Indigenous Origins: Cultural Hybridity and the Formation of Israel's Ethnicity," *Biblical Interpretation* 11 (2003): 400-12; William G. Dever, "Archaeology and the Emergence of Early Israel," in *Realia dei: Archaeology and Biblical Interpretation: Essays in Honor of Edward F. Campbell, Jr. at His Retirement*, ed. Prescott H. Williams Jr. and Theodore

exclusively defensive actions.[23] Weapons can be anointed to their task with oil (2 Sam 1:21),[24] and soldiers consecrated through purification rituals (Josh 3:5) and by refraining from sexual intercourse (1 Sam 21:6[5]; 2 Sam 11:11). Military camps should be ritually clean (e.g., Deut 23:9-14). Religious vows appear in connection with battle (e.g., Num 21:2; Judg 11:36; 1 Sam 14:24). Sacrifices (1 Sam 7:7-11; 13:8-12) are frequently made prior to battle in order to seek the divine will and secure divine aid. Military threats and defeats could elicit rites of mourning and repentance (e.g., Judg 20:19-26; 1 Sam 11:1-4; 30:1-4). Moreover, Yahweh is to be consulted prior to battle (Judg 20:18-28; 1 Sam 7:9; 14:36-37; 23:1-5, 9-12; 28:5-6; 30:7-8; 2 Sam 5:17-24; 1 Kings 22:5).

Divine warrior, divine king

For his part Yahweh can be celebrated as a divine "warrior,"[25] who personally wields a sword and commits bloodshed (Deut 32:39-42; Is 34:5-6; 63:1-6; Jer 25:30-38). He commands heavenly troops or "hosts" (e.g., 1 Sam 17:45; Is 13:4)

Hiebert, Scholars Press Homage Series 23 (Atlanta: Scholars Press, 1999), pp. 20-50; Israel Finkelstein, "The Rise of Early Israel: Archaeology and Long-Term History," in *The Origin of Early Israel—Current Debate: Biblical, Historical and Archaeological Perspectives,* ed. Shmuel Ahituv et al. (Beer-Sheva, Israel: Ben-Gurion University of the Negev Press, 1998), pp. 7-39; Niels Peter Lemche, "Early Israel Revisited," *Currents in Research* 4 (1996): 9-34; Lawrence E. Stager, "Forging an Identity: The Emergence of Israel," in *The Oxford History of the Biblical World,* ed. Michael D. Coogan (New York: Oxford University Press, 1998), pp. 122-75; K. Lawson Younger Jr., "Early Israel in Recent Biblical Scholarship," in *The Face of Old Testament Studies: A Survey of Contemporary Approaches,* ed. D. W. Baker and B. T. Arnold (Grand Rapids: Baker, 1999), pp. 176-206.

[23]As already noted, von Rad, *Holy War,* p. 65, thought that holy war proper was "exclusively defensive." But he also reads Joshua 1–9 as a later violation of that principle. For the view that Joshua 1–9 moves literarily and redactionally in the direction of circumscribing war, in part by elevating its defensive aspect, see Lawson G. Stone, "Ethical and Apologetic Tendencies in the Redaction of the Book of Joshua," *Catholic Biblical Quarterly* 53 (1991): 25-35; Daniel L. Hawk, "Conquest Reconfigured: Recasting Warfare in the Redaction of Joshua," in *Writing and Reading War: Rhetoric, Gender, and Ethics,* ed. Brad E. Kelle and Frank Ritchel Ames (Atlanta: SBL, 2008), pp. 145-60.

[24]However, T. R. Hobbs, *A Time for War: A Study of Warfare in the Old Testament,* Old Testament Studies 3 (Wilmington, DE: Michael Glazier, 1989), pp. 134-35, thinks that shields, which ordinarily consisted of animal hide over wood, would have been rubbed with oil in order to preserve them rather than to anoint them for battle.

[25]For tradition-historical background and ancient Near Eastern parallels, see particularly Henning Frederiksson, *Jahwe als Krieger: Studien zum alttestamentlichen Gottesbild* (Lund, Germany: Gleerup, 1945); Patrick D. Miller Jr., *The Divine Warrior in Early Israel,* Harvard Semitic Monographs 5 (Cambridge, MA: Harvard University Press, 1973). For theological reflection, see Richard Nysse, "Yahweh Is a Warrior," *Word and World* 7 (1987): 192-201.

and celestial chariots (2 Kings 7:6; Ps 68:18[17]; Hab 3:8),[26] which prophets—
rather than kings or generals—perceive and direct (2 Kings 2:11-12; 6:17;
13:14). In battle accounts it is Yahweh himself who is said to be fighting
against these enemies (Josh 10:10; 1 Sam 7:10), although anthropomorphic
representations of Yahweh actually doing battle are rare (e.g., Gen 19:24-25;
Josh 10:11). The "enemies" at issue are *his* (Judg 5:31; 1 Sam 30:26).[27] Israel's
own military participation is viewed as either practically unnecessary or as
merely providing support (phrased as "coming to help Yahweh," as in Judg
5:23[28]) rather than ensuring victory in and of itself. The biblical pattern of
discourse consistently attributes decisive military activity to Yahweh alone
(Ex 14:4, 14, 18; Deut 1:30; Josh 10:14, 42; 11:6; 23:10; Judg 20:35; 1 Sam 14:23).[29]
The conception that emerges from these various components is thus a theocentric one in which Israel's security is based in God's sovereignty rather
than human war craft.

Indeed, as Israel's true king (Ex 15:18; Judg 8:23; Ps 44:5[4]; 47:1-9; 146:6-10;
Is 6:5; Jer 7:6-10) God reigns supreme over life and death (Deut 32:39-42)
and is ultimately responsible for Israel's security and defense (Ps 44:2-9[1-8];
48; Is 31:4-5). Precisely for this reason, faith in weapons (Josh 24:12; Ps 76:3),
horses and chariots (Ps 20:8[7]; 33:17; Is 31:1-3; Hos 14:4[3]; Mic 1:13)[30] and/
or international treaties (Is 30:1-5; Hos 12:2[1]) is viewed as illusory and
deceptive. Although the exploits of heroes can be recounted with pride and
enjoyment (e.g., Judg 3:15-30; 14:1–15:20), the ideal form of warfare deci-
sively subverts the importance of bigger (e.g., 1 Sam 17), stronger (e.g., Ps
33:16) or more numerous warriors (e.g, Judg 7:2-8; 1 Sam 14:1-15; Hos 10:13).

The paradigmatic expression of this outlook occurs in Deuteronomy 20,

---

[26]This divine fighting force can include Israel (Ex 12:41). In 1 Sam 17:45 the phrase "Yahweh
of hosts" is paralleled with "God of the ranks/armies of Israel," further demonstrating its
military connotation (cf. Joel 2:11). The phrase "Yahweh of hosts" can also take a longer
form, "Yahweh, God of hosts" (e.g., 2 Sam 5:10; 1 Kings 19:10, 14; Ps 89:9[8]). For further
evidence of a military meaning to this term and scholarly discussion of the matter, see C. L.
Seow, "Hosts, Lord of," in *Anchor Bible Dictionary*, ed. David Noel Freedman (New York:
Doubleday, 1992), 3:204-7.

[27]Von Rad, *Holy War*, p. 44.

[28]Ibid., p. 49.

[29]Ibid., pp. 44-45.

[30]On the theological significance of horse and chariot throughout the Old Testament, see further Walter Brueggemann, *Divine Presence and Violence: Contextualizing the Book of Joshua*
(Eugene, OR: Cascade Books, 2009), esp. pp. 55-60.

where explicit instructions for warfare are recounted.[31] After a speech by a priest in which the troops are reminded that it is God "who goes with you to fight for you against your enemies" (Deut 20:4), military officers question the soldiers about their personal situations and state of mind:

> Has anyone built a new house but not dedicated it? Let him go back to his home, lest he die in battle and another dedicate it. Has anyone planted a vineyard but never harvested it? Let him go back to his home, lest he die in battle and another harvest it. Has anyone gotten engaged but not yet married? Let him go back to his home, lest he die in battle and another marry her. . . . Is anyone afraid and disheartened? Let him go back to his home, lest he cause the heart of his comrades to melt like his. (Deut 20:5-8, my translation)

By any ordinary measure of military procedure, this line of questioning is of course ridiculous and self-defeating. Indeed, the purpose of the deuteronomic instructions might initially appear to be that of limiting the size of the fighting force as much as possible, on the understanding that a wholly committed few will be more effective than a larger deployment of distracted and conflicted soldiers. But even this pragmatic formulation misses the central aim of the text, which is concerned to proceed with wholly committed fighting men not as an alternative technique or strategy, but because such men will not confuse the military action of God with their own efforts.

This aim is made even more explicit in Judges 7 when God tells Gideon, "You have too many troops with you for me to deliver the Midianites into their hands; Israel might claim for itself the glory due to me, saying 'Our own hand has brought us victory.' Therefore, announce to the men, 'Let whoever is fearful and trembling turn back'" (Judg 7:2-3, my translation). But the subsequent departure of most of Gideon's men still proves an insufficient remedy to God, who has a seemingly arbitrary method of whittling down their number even further (Judg 7:4-8).[32] The same point of view, clearly at home in deuteronomic tradition whatever its ultimate origins, can be identified in the account of Jonathan's attack on a Philistine

---

[31]For a fuller exegetical treatment of Deut 20, see Rüdiger Schmitt, *Der "Heilige Krieg" im Pentateuch und im deuteronomistischen Geschichtswerk: Studien zur Forschungs-, Rezeptions- und Religionsgeschichte von Krieg und Bann im Alten Testament*, AOAT 381 (Münster: Ugarit-Verlag, 2011), pp. 52-65.

[32]For further discussion of Judg 7, see Schmitt, *Krieg*, pp. 116-18.

garrison in 1 Samuel 14. Accompanied only by his armor-bearer, Jonathan does not hesitate to engage the enemy: "Come, let us cross over to the garrison of these uncircumcised ones. Perhaps the Lord will act on our behalf, for nothing hinders the Lord from victory by many or by few" (1 Sam 14:6). Human estimations of military strength are turned upside down by Israel's conviction that God will reliably protect the faithful and wring deliverance out of threat.

Even counting the size of an army seems to have been viewed as a sign of a lack of faith (Ex 30:12; 2 Sam 24:1-10), most likely because it signaled a misplaced trust in human ability at the expense of total reliance upon God. It also placed control of the army into the hands of the nation-state, a move that stood at variance from the charismatic dimension of the biblical warfare tradition.[33] The fundamental theological paradigm for this tradition is thus Israel's Exodus from Egypt,[34] a pre-state liberation brought about by the direct action of God and involving a corresponding passivity on the part of Israel: "Do not fear, stand firm, and see the deliverance that the Lord will work for you today . . . the Lord will fight for you; you keep still" (Ex 14:13-14). The expression "do not fear" frequently appears in battle contexts within the Old Testament (e.g., Deut 20:3; Josh 8:1; 10:8, 25; 11:6).[35] As these instances of the formula illustrate, ascription of warfare to God actually serves to limit rather than promote militarism on Israel's part. Even though Israel remembered war as something properly left to God, and even though Israel's memory assigned martial features to God's own character, Israel's tradition also preserved these ideas predominantly as warrants for nonimitation instead of imitation. In other words, by assigning war to God Israel distanced itself from the pursuit of war. Israel's ideal war is characterized by trust and not fear, because fear is the anxiety that arises from

---

[33]John Howard Yoder, *The Original Revolution: Essays on Christian Pacifism* (Scottdale, PA: Herald Press, 1977), p. 105.

[34]See Millard C. Lind, *Yahweh Is a Warrior: The Theology of Warfare in Ancient Israel* (Scottdale, PA: Herald, 1980), esp. pp. 46-64. Lind attempts to make this case historically by dating the Exodus tradition early and treating all other Israelite warfare accounts as later outgrowths of this decisive early witness. Whether or not his historical model succeeds is open to doubt, but to my mind his case for the centrality of the Exodus tradition still stands as a judgment about the canonical presentation of war within the Old Testament.

[35]Von Rad, *Holy War*, p. 45. See further Edgar W. Conrad, *Fear Not Warrior: A Study of ʾal tîrāʾ Pericopes in the Hebrew Scriptures*, Brown Judaic Studies 75 (Chico, CA: Scholars Press, 1985).

expediency, and expediency is in reality an "atheistic" pragmatism (e.g., Num 14:1-12; 2 Chron 20:13-17).

Ḥērem *regulations.* Even the *ḥērem* or "ban" (e.g., Deut 7:1-5; 20:16-18; Joshua 6-7)—the permanent committal of booty and captives to God, sometimes through their destruction (Lev 27:28-29) and sometimes by delivering them to temple priests (Lev 27:21; Num 18:14; Ezek 44:28-30) or a temple treasury (Josh 6:18-24; Ezra 10:8)—can be viewed as a prohibition of personal gain through battle (contrast Deut 20:10-15 with 20:16-18), and thus another reminder that only God grants the victory.[36] Booty was a major incentive for soldiers in the ancient world and was normally shared (Judg 5:30; 2 Kings 3:23; Is 9:2[3]; Ps 119:162).[37] The ban was conceived as the state or condition of Yahweh's exclusive ownership, and it therefore mandated the withdrawal of something from ordinary human use.[38] So only some invocations of the ban occur within a military context.

The explicit reason given for the ban is the prevention of idolatry (Ex 22:19[20]; 23:24, 32-33; Deut 7:4-5; 20:18). It was feared that not destroying idols and other holy objects, or incorporating foreign worshipers into the Israelite community, would occasion idolatry or religious syncretism on the part of the Israelites. The wholesale slaughter of human beings for this reason is not any less horrible, but it should still be taken into account that such slaughter is not being authorized out of vengeance, rage or ethnic hatred but self-protection.

Contrary to what previous scholarship has often concluded, it is now

---

[36]Yoder, *Revolution*, pp. 105-6. Yoder also makes the cogent point that this is precisely how later biblical writings, illustrated by the books of Chronicles, understand the divine war tradition. This understanding in fact worked *"against* the development of a military caste, military alliances, and political designs based on the availability of military power" (p. 106, his emphasis).

[37]See further De Vaux, *Israel*, p. 255.

[38]See my entry "Ban, The," in Green, *Dictionary of Scripture and Ethics*, p. 89. For more detailed reflections, see G. Braulik, "Die Völkervernichtung und die Rückkehr Israels ins Verheissungsland: hermeneutische Bemerkung zum Buch Deuteronomium," in *Deuteronomy and Deuteronomic Literature*, ed. M. Vervenne and J. Lust, BETL 133 (Leuven, Belgium: Leuven University Press, 1997), pp. 3-38; J. P. U. Lilley, "Understanding the Ḥērem," *Tyndale Bulletin* 44 (1993): 169-77; R. D. Nelson, "Ḥērem and the Deuteronomic Social Conscience," in Vervenne and Lust, *Deuteronomy*, pp. 39-54; C. Sch2äfer-Lichtenberger, "Bedeutung und Funktion von Herem in biblisch-hebräischen Texten," *Biblische Zeitschrift* 38 (1994): 270-75. As stressed by Nelson, Lilley and Schäfer-Lichtenberger, "destruction" is a secondary implication of *ḥērem* and not its primary meaning.

becoming increasingly clear that the military use of the ban predates Israel and is solidly attested in other ancient Near East cultures: e.g., the inscriptions of the Old Babylonian ruler Iddi(n)-Sin of Simurrum[39] and King Mesha of Moab,[40] as well as the Hittite proclamation of Anitta of Kuššar.[41] The ban is remembered in the Old Testament primarily as an expression of

---

[39]For the text, see William W. Hallo, ed., *The Context of Scripture*, 3 vols. (Leiden: Brill, 1997-2002), 2:106:255. For further discussion, see Stern, *The Biblical Ḥērem*, pp. 39-40. This inscription tells of a consecration of a city to the gods by its destruction.

[40]For the text, see Hallo, *Context*, 2:223:137-38. For discussion, see Stern, *The Biblical Ḥērem*, pp. 19-56. The inscription is dated ca. 835 B.C.E. and describes the killing of the entire population of Nebo as *ḥrm*. This apparent technical term also appears in two other extra-biblical sources, the late bronze Ugaritic text KTU 1.13 and the seventh-century B.C. (?) South Arabian Sabaean text RES 3945. For a convenient English-language presentation of KTU 1.13, a hymn to Anat, see N. Wyatt, *Religious Texts from Ugarit*, The Biblical Seminar 53 (Sheffield, UK: Sheffield Academic Press, 1998), pp. 169-73. On the Sebaean text, see Lauren A. S. Monroe, "Israelite, Moabite and Sabaean War- *ḥērem* Traditions and the Forging of National Identity: Reconsidering the Sabaean Text RES 3945 in Light of Biblical and Moabite Evidence," *Vetus Testamentum* 57 (2007): 318-41. The parallel between Israel's *ḥērem* tradition and the Mesha inscription is acknowledged almost universally by scholars. For an example of one who disputes the claim, but for unclear reasons, see Aarnoud van der Deijl, *Protest or Propaganda: War in the Old Testament Book of Kings and Contemporaneous Ancient Near Eastern Texts*, SSN 51 (Leiden: Brill, 2008), p. 339.

[41]For the text, see Hallo, *Context*, 1:72:182-84. For discussion, see Stern, *The Biblical Ḥērem*, pp. 78-79. This text refers to captives as *ḥappar* or a "devoted thing." Although there are differences in vocabulary among these various inscriptions, the practices described seem highly similar. They effectively counter the claim that the only parallel to Israelite *ḥērem* is the Moabite Stone, and that Israel is therefore distinctive or unique with regard to the ban, as in Kang, *Divine War*, p. 81. They also cast doubt on the claim that Joshua 1–11 is pure fiction and that *ḥērem* was never actually practiced in ancient Israel, as in Reinhard Müller, "Jahwekrieg und Heilsgeschichte," *Zeitschrift für Theologie und Kirche* 106 (2009): 277. The criteria for determining what will count as *ḥērem* are, of course, very much at issue. For additional possible textual parallels at Mari, in Uruk, in Egypt and among the Hittites, see Stern, *The Biblical Ḥērem*, pp. 67-87. On the possibility of archaeological evidence for the practice of total war among the Canaanites, see William G. Dever and S. M. Paul, *Biblical Archaeology*, Library of Jewish Knowledge (Jerusalem: Keter, 1973), pp. 202-3. They describe a find reminiscent of the divine war tradition, a find that was discovered by Flinders Petrie west of Tell al-ʿAjjūl. Petrie dated it to the beginning of the second millennium B.C. A brief discussion can be found in Stern, *The Biblical Ḥērem*, pp. 65-66. Stern concludes with respect to the Iddi-Sin inscription in particular that it "gives every ground for belief in the oft repeated conclusion that the origins of the חרם [are] to be found in the pre-Israelite world and world-view" (*The Biblical Ḥērem*, p. 79). For broad ancient Near Eastern parallels to the conception of a warrior deity fighting on behalf of his/her people, see K. Lawson Younger Jr., *Ancient Conquest Accounts: A Study in Ancient Near Eastern and Biblical History Writing*, JSOTSup 98 (Sheffield, UK: Sheffield Academic Press, 1990); Weinfeld, "Divine Intervention"; Weippert, "Heiliger Krieg." For an analysis of new research on this topic, see K. Lawson Younger, "Some Recent Discussion on the Ḥērem," in *Far from Minimal: Celebrating the Work and Influence of Philip R. Davies*, ed. Duncan Burns and J. W. Rogerson, LHBOTS 484 (London: T&T Clark, 2012), pp. 505-22.

God's sovereignty, and its appearances in the biblical narrative cluster around Israel's entry into the land.[42]

The book of Deuteronomy invokes the ban against the indigenous residents of Canaan, none of whom are to be spared (Deut 7:1; 20:17; cf. Ex 23:23),[43] but in this way the book also restricts the ban from wider application.[44] Only with respect to these nations and only within the specific context of gaining and protecting the land is the military ban to be employed by Israel. Outside of Canaan, in fact, terms of peace are to be offered first, and only if peace is rejected are captured males to be killed. Women, children, livestock and booty may be kept by the Israelites in this case (Deut 20:10-15). Although some of the details vary, several biblical narratives turn on the centrality of the ban within Israel's martial memory (Josh 2; 6-7; 10-11; 1 Sam 15). In these narratives its absolute nature is treated as a test of full obedience to God, but the accompanying bloodshed, while accepted as normative, is literarily downplayed in the actual telling of the stories. The focus is on the obedience of the characters, not the gore.[45]

It bears mentioning in this connection that the divine command to "blot out" or "erase" (*mḥh*) the Amalekites (Ex 17:14-16; Deut 25:17-19) is not technically an example of the ban but a supplementary injunction whose rationale is obscure.[46] In Exodus 17, God is proclaimed to inaugurate eternal war with Amalek, but the nature of this warfare is highly metaphorical: God will "utterly erase *the remembrance* of Amalek from under heaven" (Ex 17:14;

---

[42]C. L. Crouch, *War and Ethics in the Ancient Near East: Military Violence in Light of Cosmology and History*, BZAW 407 (Berlin: de Gruyter, 2009), p. 177. While there are exceptions, and thus not complete unanimity among the biblical witnesses, most of the war narratives center on Israel's receipt and defense of the land. The typological use of the Exodus tradition also emphasizes its paradigmatic nature (Josh 3:7-17). Theoretical statements ground Israel's warrant for war in the particular time and circumstance of its entry into the land (e.g., Ex 23:30; Deut 7:1; Ps 44:2-4[1-3]). It is also sometimes overlooked that everything in the book of Deuteronomy is situated in the time prior to Israel's entry into the land by virtue of its literary presentation as a series of addresses by Moses.

[43]There is a strong argument to be made that hyperbole was an accepted feature of such accounts, not only in Israel but throughout the ancient Near East; see Paul Copan, *Is God a Moral Monster? Making Sense of the Old Testament* (Grand Rapids: Baker Books, 2011), pp. 170-77; John Goldingay, *Old Testament Theology: Volume Three, Israel's Life* (Downers Grove, IL: IVP Academic, 2009), pp. 570-72.

[44]Yair Hoffmann, "The Deuteronomistic Concept of the Ḥērem," *Zeitschrift für die alttestamentliche Wissenschaft* 111 (1999): 196-210; Stern, *The Biblical Ḥērem*, pp. 102-3.

[45]Schäfer-Lichtenberger, "Bedeutung," p. 275.

[46]Amalek is not one of the nations listed in Ex 23:23; Deut 7:1; 20:17.

my emphasis). And he will do so himself; the Israelites are not explicitly commanded to take up this duty as their own. In Deuteronomy 25 the Israelites do receive an injunction to "erase the remembrance of Amalek from under heaven" when they come into the land (Deut 25:19), but the text does not specify what is meant. Even if this tradition has actual killing in mind,[47] once again it may have been understood as limiting a tendency toward indiscriminate slaughter by the designation of a single prototypical enemy. However, the metaphorical language also suggests that Amalek is being treated more symbolically than realistically, which is how much of later Jewish and Christian interpretation has viewed these texts.[48]

Martial memory and exile. Even more significantly, Israel's memory held divine promise together with divine threat, Exodus with Exile. In other words, not only did Israel remember how God had fought on its behalf, Israel also remembered that God could fight against it (Num 14:42-43; Is 63:10; Jer 21:3-7; Lam 2:5). This aspect of the tradition moves God's military leadership past nationalism to a transnational standard of justice (Amos 1–2). If the Israelites themselves are disobedient and sinful, God will also war against *them* (2 Kings 23:27; Amos 2:4–3:2; Jer 21:5; Ezek 21:6-22[1-17]), even using other nations to do it (Is 5:25-30; 9:8–10:11; 13:3; Jer 34:21-22). Thus the ban can also be invoked against apostate Israelite cities (Deut 13:6-8), and the Exile is described by the prophets, frighteningly, in terms of a divine ban against Israel as an entire people (Is 43:28; Jer 25:9).[49]

The divine warrior against the nations. In the end, perhaps the most

---

[47]Use of the root *mḥh* in the Flood narrative might suggest actual killing (Gen 6:7; 7:4, 23), although it appears there without reference to "remembrance." Is "erasing a memory" a euphemism in this tradition for killing people, or does it mean to "forget" them? 1 Samuel 15 is regularly introduced as a parallel text illustrating that the Amalekites are in fact to be massacred, but it is not clear that the two traditions really are parallel (even granting the appeal to past history in 1 Sam 15:2). 1 Samuel 15 is ultimately constructed on the basis of the divine war tradition and not the Amalekite tradition per se.

[48]Stephen B. Chapman, "Perpetual War: The Case of Amalek," in *The Bible and Spirituality: Exploratory Essays in Reading Scripture Spiritually*, ed. J. Gordon McConville, Andrew T. Lincoln and Lloyd K. Pieterson (Eugene, OR: Cascade Books, forthcoming); Avi Sagi, "The Punishment of Amalek in Jewish Tradition: Coping with the Moral Problem," *Harvard Theological Review* 87 (1994): 323-46; Hans Andreas Tanner, *Amalek, der Feind Israels und der Feind Jahwes: eine Studie zu den Amalektexten im Alten Testament*, TVZ Dissertationen (Zurich: Theologischer Verlag, 2005).

[49]See further J. A. Soggin, "Der prophetische Gedanke über den heiligen Krieg als Gericht gegen Israel," *Vetus Testamentum* 10 (1960): 79-83.

challenging Old Testament texts are those that do seem to encourage Israel to imitate the military activity of Yahweh (Num 31:1-3; Ps 18:34), especially outside the context of Israel's entry into the land (e.g., in the royal wars described in 2 Sam 8–11). In this connection special mention should be made of the material at the end of the book of Jeremiah because of the violence that it directs toward other nations, most of all Babylon (Jer 50–51). Jeremiah 48:10 is particularly infamous for its use as a biblical warrant during the medieval Crusades:[50] "Whoever keeps back the sword from bloodshed is cursed" (cf. Ezek 21:33-34[28-29]). But there are genre considerations here: all of this material appears within a series of oracles against the nations.

While fundamental obscurities remain regarding the social and historical role of this genre of oracle, it seems likely that its purpose was highly rhetorical and directed more to Israel than to other nations.[51] In other words, these oracles may have been delivered in order to instruct Israel by using other nations as rhetorical object lessons. Still, the perspective found within this material does cut against the nonimitative ascription of warfare to God, which clearly predominates in Israel's tradition. The oracles against the nations reinforce the obvious point that Israel is never banned from making war within the biblical tradition, even if the notions of God as a warrior and of retribution as properly belonging to him alone (Deut 32:39-43) move steadily in the direction of military inaction, indeed, of quietism or nonviolence.

THE PEACEABLE KINGDOM AND CHRISTIAN PRAXIS

Moreover, the consistent goal of God's activity in the world is not violence but peace (Ps 46:10[9]; 11:1-7; Zech 9:9-10).[52] "Nation shall not lift up sword

---

[50]Craigie, *The Problem of War*, p. 28.

[51]See H. G. L. Peels, "'You Shall Certainly Drink!': The Place and Significance of the Oracles Against the Nations in the Book of Jeremiah," *European Journal of Theology* 16 (2007): 81-91; Paul R. Raabe, "Why Prophetic Oracles against the Nations?" in *Fortunate the Eyes that See: Essays in Honor of David Noel Freedman in Celebration of His Seventieth Birthday*, ed. Astrid Beck (Grand Rapids: Eerdmans, 1995), pp. 236-57. The origin of this oracle tradition is disputed, but warfare is one likely source (Num 22–24). The possibility that Israelite prophets may have traveled to another land in order to deliver oracles cannot be discounted (2 Kings 8:7-15), although it seems somewhat unlikely to have been a regular event. Another possibility is that such oracles were delivered to foreign envoys visiting Jerusalem (Jer 27:7). Interestingly, Schwally also pioneered the academic study of the oracles against the nations; for further details, see Peels, "You Shall Certainly Drink," p. 83.

[52]See further Paul D. Hanson, "War and Peace in the Hebrew Bible," *Interpretation* 38 (1984): 341-62; Rolf P. Knierim, "On the Subject of War in Old Testament and Biblical Theology,"

against nation, neither shall they learn war any more" (Is 2:4; Mic 4:3). Israel's prophetic heritage includes a prediction of the *end* of the ban at the
day of the Lord (Zech 14:11; cf. Mal 3:24 [4:6]). In this way, all war in Israel's
memory—whether divinely authorized or not—carries the quality of a
temporary reality, a concession to current circumstances that make it necessary for the time being but not permanent. The heavy use of cosmological
language in Old Testament battle accounts (e.g., Ex 14:26-29; Josh 10:11-13;
Judg 5:20-21; Ps 18:12-15; 77:16-20)[53] indicates a similar perspective: warfare
is an unnatural disruption within the created order and not a feature of "the
way things are supposed to be."[54] Battle accounts in the Old Testament
therefore imply that war represents the suspension of God's normal main-
tenance of creation (Ps 104:30) and a return of chaos.[55] In this sense, then,
warfare is ultimately remembered in Israel as the withdrawal of God's compassionate oversight rather than as God's positive will for humankind (Ps
81:12-13 [11-12]; Is 50:11; 64:6[7]; cf. Rom 1:18-32).[56] In the biblical perspective,
the state of war results from a removal of divine protection and an ensuing
subjection to elemental, demonic forces (Ezek 38; Dan 8; cf. Rev 6:3-4).

Thus in Israel's distinctive use of various ancient Near Eastern traditions
regarding warfare, and in Israel's consistent effort to limit justifiable warfare
primarily to the context of its entry into the land,[57] and in Israel's location
of its true security in God's faithfulness rather than in human might, the

---

Horizons in Biblical Theology 16 (1994): 1-19; Elmer A. Martens, "Toward Shalom: Absorbing
the Violence," in *War in the Bible and Terrorism in the Twenty-First Century*, ed. Richard S.
Hess and Elmer A. Martens, Bulletin for Biblical Research Supplements (Winona Lake, IN:
Eisenbrauns, 2008), pp. 33-57.

[53]On cosmological motifs in biblical and ancient Near Eastern battle accounts, see especially
Crouch, *War*; Stern, *ḥērem*.

[54]On this point, see further H. Eberhard von Waldow, "The Concept of War in the Old Testament," *Horizons in Biblical Theology* 6 (1984): 27-48.

[55]The most penetrating analysis of this perspective is found in Hans Heinrich Schmid, *Altori-
entalische Welt in der alttestamentlichen Theologie* (Zurich: Theologischer Verlag, 1974), pp.
91-120. The link between war and chaos is also emphasized by Müller, "Jahwekrieg," and
Stern, *Ḥērem*. Cf. Tryggve N. D. Mettinger, "Fighting the Powers of Chaos and Hell: Towards
the Biblical Portrait of God," *Studia Theologica* 39 (1985): 21-38. Mettinger offers helpful
tradition-historical details but ultimately moves in a dualistic direction that is, in my view,
insufficiently supported by the biblical text.

[56]Raymund Schwager, *Must There Be Scapegoats? Violence and Redemption in the Bible* (San
Francisco: Harper & Row, 1987), pp. 63-71, 214-20. Note the use of the divine war term *mwg*
in the unamended Hebrew text of Is 64:6[7].

[57]De Vaux, *Israel*, p. 262.

canonical Old Testament presents war as a time-conditioned, concessive practice at odds with God's ultimate will for humankind.[58] To be sure, such warfare is presented as religious in nature, but there was no such thing as "secular" warfare in the ancient Near East.[59] The Old Testament does not intend to glorify vengeful slaughter through its inclusion of war traditions but to confess God as the sole source of Israel's deliverance. That is again why it is so important to avoid the term "holy war" with respect to the Old Testament, to come full circle, because the Old Testament contains no legitimate textual warrant at all for believers to shoulder arms and do physical battle with unbelievers in order to convert them or to conquer their territory.[60] To the contrary, the Old Testament tradition of "Yahweh war" means exactly what it says: war belongs to God to prosecute, not humankind (Deut 32:35).[61] If the price of this tradition is to involve God in killing and death, it nonetheless upholds the involvement of God in every aspect of life.[62] From this perspective, Christians can view God's willingness to enter even into the morally contested and compromised arena of Israelite warfare as pointing ahead to the incarnation of Christ.[63]

Warfare in the Old Testament, as indeed all killing in the Old Testament,

---

[58]Yoder, *Revolution*, pp. 95-98, discusses the possibility of viewing Old Testament warfare as a divine concession but rejects the idea. He describes two kinds of concession: one a "concession to disobedience"; the other a "pedagogical concession." He does find a parallel for the first in the way that Mt 19:8 characterizes the divorce law of Deut 24. However, he then rejects this possibility for warfare because he says it is not explicitly described in concessive terms in the biblical text. By contrast, he argues, divorce was "never commanded in the Old Testament . . . only grudgingly permitted" in the first place (p. 96). Yoder does not consider whether, as I argue below, all violence is characterized within the Old Testament as a divine concession. As for a pedagogical concession, I agree with Yoder that it too easily collapses into the kind of "evolutionist liberal theological perspective" that views "the ancient Israelites with a sense of moral superiority which is difficult to justify on objective grounds" (p. 97).

[59]Richard S. Hess, "War in the Hebrew Bible: An Overview," in Hess and Martens, *War*, p. 25.

[60]De Vaux, *Israel*, pp. 258 and 262. Copan, *God*, p. 179, also notes how in Deuteronomy's presentation of the Exodus Israel is specifically prohibited from military engagement with the nations surrounding Canaan (Deut 2).

[61]For a comprehensive statement of this view, see Lind, *Yahweh*.

[62]Patrick D. Miller, "God the Warrior: A Problem in Biblical Interpretation and Apologetics," *Interpretation* 19 (1965): 39-46.

[63]Craigie, *The Problem of War*, pp. 99-100. For efforts to deal with biblical warfare theologically within Jewish tradition, see Shalom Carmy, "The Origin of Nations and the Shadow of Violence: Theological Perspectives on Canaan and Amalek," *Tradition* 39 (2006): 57-88; Reuven Firestone, "Holy War in Modern Judaism? 'Mitzvah War' and the Problem of the 'Three Vows,'" *Journal of the American Academy of Religion* 74 (2006): 954-82; Sagi, "Punishment."

needs to be recognized within Christian theology as a strictly circum-
scribed divine concession to the brutal reality of human sin (Gen 9:3-6).[64]
However, someone still might ask, "Couldn't God design a world in which
war wasn't necessary?" The appropriate theological response is that God in
fact did so (Gen 1-2), but human sinfulness spoiled it precisely by gener-
ating violence (Gen 6:11-13). Someone might push further and say, "Even
with the advent of human violence, couldn't God have devised a strictly
nonviolent method for dealing with it?" Here again the theological response
is that God did just that in Jesus Christ, but in order for Christ to appear in
the fullness of time (Gal 4:4) it was necessary for God to elect and preserve
the people of Israel.[65] And apparently—this is the hard part—God was not
able, given the violence of the world, to preserve Israel purely nonviolently
although, even so, Israel's history witnesses to and moves toward nonviolence as it moves toward Christ.[66]

---

[64]The same concessive quality governs the killing of animals as well as humans and, therefore,
predation, sacrifice and meat eating (cf. Gen 1:29-30). It is important to note how each of
these activities is carefully subordinated, controlled and restricted within the biblical tradition (e.g., Gen 9:4-6; Lev 7:22-27; Deut 12:20-27) and, more than in Christianity, within Judaism. The goal of God's creative acts in history is a world without predation (Is 11:6-7),
sacrifice (Ps 40:7[6]; 50:13; Is 1:11-15; Jer 7:21-26; Hos 6:6) and any animal killing (Is 11:8-
9)—in other words, the restoration of paradise.

[65]James Barr, *Biblical Faith and Natural Theology* (Oxford: Clarendon, 1993), p. 218, rejects
this kind of logic and asks, "If God's people needed a land of their own to live in and work
out their role in the world's salvation, why could the inhabitants of Jericho and other cities
not have been offered the choice of emigration, which they might well have grasped as an
alternative to total extermination?" There is honestly no answer to this kind of question,
which is not addressed in the biblical text. However, there are many reasons why this kind of
option might not have been practicable at the time. What if the inhabitants really did not
want to move? And what if their presence constituted a critical threat to Israel's very survival?

[66]John Allister, "The Amalekite Genocide," *Churchman* 124 (2010): 217-26, makes a similar
point, arguing that God had determined to protect Israel and that such protection entailed the
possibility of violence. However, "protection" is less convincing as a justification for offensive
military action and for the killing of noncombatants, as the ban dictates. With my own formulation I am attempting to adopt an incarnational stance, one that does not presume Israel always acted in accordance with God's will, but also one that views God as entering fully into the
world of the ancient Near East in order to work on behalf of its transformation. I am also attempting to avoid making a distinction between the supposedly illegitimate ancient Near Eastern features of Israel's heritage and Israel's true theological witness, as in Müller, "Jahwekrieg,"
p. 281: "Diese Vorstellung zählt nicht zu den Propria des Alten Testaments." In contrast I take
the view that everything in the Old Testament partakes of the ancient Near East, all the way
down, and that the effort to draw such a distinction, while well intentioned, is conceptually
muddled and theologically misguided. For more on this way of viewing the issue, see Peter
Enns, *Inspiration and Incarnation* (Grand Rapids: Baker Academic, 2005), pp. 23-70.

As Emil Fackenheim once observed, God could not free the Israelites without also killing Egyptians.[67] The further conclusion to draw is not that God's involvement in war renders it holy, but rather that God, who alone is holy, is willing to participate in what is profane and wicked in order to bring about what is good. War is always evil, but God can work redemptively with it, even with war, because God works redemptively with *everything*.[68] For some, such a perspective provides a biblical basis for "just war." But the biblical concession to a sin-soaked realism is also finally time-bound and thus temporary. Within the Old Testament, as already noted, warfare traditions are primarily located and restricted to the event of Israel's entry into the land. With Christ's work accomplished, furthermore, there now does exist a faithful and efficacious nonviolent response to the threat of violence, a response that is available to and enjoined upon those who follow Jesus.

The view just sketched does not fully extricate God from violence and will therefore be unacceptable to some.[69] However, those who reject the idea that God could be involved in violence in any fashion must take care not to imagine that a state of "pure" non-involvement in violence truly exists today. Any citizen of a modern nation-state is implicated in violence. Not recognizing God's presence on the battlefield does not mean that God

---

[67]Emil L. Fackenheim, *God's Presence in History* (New York: New York University Press, 1970), p. 25.

[68]Cf. Craigie, *The Problem of War*, p. 42 (his italics): "divine activity takes as its stage the world *as it is*, namely the world of sinful men and activities, and this understanding is the primary condition for understanding war: *war is always evil*. The participation of God in evil human activity has a positive end in view; that is to say, the judgment of God, in the larger perspective, is the other face of the coin which is the mercy of God."

[69]The only real alternative, it seems to me, is to question the truth of the biblical ascription of war to God. This is the line taken by Paul N. Anderson, "Genocide or Jesus: A God of Conquest or Pacificism?" in *The Destructive Power of Religion: Violence in Judaism, Christianity, and Islam*, ed. J. Harold Ellens (Westport, CT: Praeger, 2004), pp. 31-52, who writes of the need to "recognize the anthropomorphic projections involved in the narrative traditions" of the Bible (p. 51). Eric A. Siebert, *Disturbing Divine Behavior: Troubling Old Testament Images of God* (Minneapolis: Fortress, 2009), pp. 169-81, goes even further and argues for a thoroughgoing theological distinction between "the textual God" and "the actual God." Thom Stark, *The Human Faces of God* (Eugene, OR: Wipf & Stock, 2011), p. 150, most fully articulates the contours of this view: "[M]y contention is that God never did command the Israelites to slaughter entire peoples wholesale. These accounts reflect a standard imperialistic ideology that Israel shared with many of its ancient neighbors, and I read them as products of ancient culture, not as products of pure divine revelation." As Anderson rightly notes, "In the end, the way one looks at these things and the manner in which one interprets these matters depends completely on one's theology of sacred scripture" (p. 51).

is not there or does not want to be there, even in all the confusion and brutality of war. Modernity is arguably no less brutal than the ancient world for conducting a secularized, technologized, indiscriminate form of war that excludes God from the kill zone on principle, thereby seducing the strong into believing that they are masters of their own destiny.[70] Indeed, the biblical witness unblinkingly confronts modernity most sharply right at this point: "Assyria will not save us; we will not ride upon horses; we will say no more, 'Our God,' to the work of our hands" (Hos 14:4[3]; cf. Deut 32:27; Judg 7:2).

Despite what is often thought, the New Testament does not simply reject what the Old Testament has to say about war but lays claim to the mainstream of Old Testament tradition in which God is sovereign over life and death, God rules over the affairs of nations as well as over individual hearts, and retribution is left to God alone (compare Rom 12:19 with Deut 32:35). The New Testament continues to use martial imagery to describe God's ongoing war against the demonic powers of the world (1 Cor 15:24-28), Jesus' distinctive role in that divine campaign (2 Thess 1:6-10; Rev 19:11-16) and the character of the Christian life as a spiritual battle (Mt 10:34; 2 Cor 10:3-5; Eph 6:10-17; 1 Tim 1:18-19a).[71] The holy warrior is transformed into the holy martyr.[72] The nonviolent impulse already present in Israel's memory of war is strengthened and deepened through reflection on a messiah who did not slaughter but was slaughtered (Rev 5:6-14)[73] and on the conviction that the long-promised day of the Lord has finally arrived. Enemies are now to be loved (Mt 5:43-48) rather than fought. Taking up the sword is unproductive and self-defeating (Mt 26:52). The role of the Christian is to live out the eschatological peaceableness of Christ's kingdom within the present world as a sign and a foretaste that the day of the Lord is indeed at hand.[74]

---

[70]For further reflections along this line, see Jeph Holloway, "The Ethical Dilemma of Holy War," *Southwestern Journal of Theology* 41 (1998): 44-69.

[71]For further examples, see Tremper Longman III and Daniel G. Reid, *God Is a Warrior*, Studies in Old Testament Biblical Theology (Grand Rapids: Zondervan, 1995).

[72]See further W. H. Brownlee, "From Holy War to Holy Martyrdom," in *The Quest for the Kingdom of God: Studies in Honor of George E. Mendenhall*, ed. Huffmon et al. (Winona Lake, IN: Eisenbrauns, 1983), pp. 281-92.

[73]See especially Tremper Longman, "The Divine Warrior: The New Testament Use of an Old Testament Motif," *Westminster Theological Journal* 44 (1982): 304.

[74]See the discussion in Richard B. Hays, *The Moral Vision of the New Testament: Community, Cross, New Creation* (San Francisco: Harper, 1996), pp. 317-46.

The ethical decision confronting modern Christians is thus whether there remains, after the resurrection, any satisfactory theological reason to sanction violence as a concession to human sin and whether such violence can truly be conducted in a manner that does not contradict the peaceable intentions of both biblical testaments—or whether Christ's peace is in fact worth martyrdom. In today's world concrete cases make for hard choices. But those choices need to be made in constant awareness and full confidence that the shared vision of the Old and New Testaments is one of peace.

4

A NEGLECTED WITNESS TO
"HOLY WAR" IN THE WRITINGS

Heath A. Thomas

————————— ✝ —————————

THIS ESSAY BRIEFLY EXPLORES RESPONSE to the divine warrior
from the context of the Writings, that is, the third section of the Hebrew
Bible. The rationale behind this is fairly straightforward: the Writings
provide a *human response* to the issue of divine war (YHWH war) not particularly advocated or explored in the rest of the canon, and this perhaps
may provide a shape to Christian response in regards to the theme of Old
Testament "holy war" and Christian morality. But to get to this point, some
ground must be cleared.

In the first place, when dealing with the issue most commonly called
"holy war" this term remains a misnomer, as Chapman argues in his essay in
this volume. Why is this? Building upon Chapman's argument, one further
notes a cultural and worldview disconnect between the ancient and modern
conceptions of reality. The language of "holy war" can bring a number of
things to our modern minds: crusade, "fighting *in the name of God* for the
benefit of the deity" (or rather for *human benefit* for those a bit more skep-
tical of those who speak or act for god), or the like. But in the Old Testament, in accordance with her ancient Near Eastern neighbors, Israel
viewed warfare, as Roland de Vaux understood years ago, at the very least
associated with the sacred sphere of life.[1] More to the point, war was, like

---

[1] Roland de Vaux, *Ancient Israel: Its Life and Institutions* (London: Darton, Longman & Todd,
1988 [1961]), pp. 258-67.

the rest of the fabric of existence in ANE worldviews, an act naturally implicated by a people's relationship with the sacred. As such, in the ancient world it is challenging to designate some wars "holy" and other wars "normal." Most ANE nation-states related war (in some way) to the activity of the divine, and so war as a concept could not be dissected from the rest of life in terms of "sacred" and "secular," as do many modern western people.

Modern sensibilities of identifying as *secular* aspects of life such as economy, family, work, state and warfare on the one hand, and then labeling as *sacred* aspects of life such as church or spirituality is an anachronism. In the ancient world, *all of life*—whether a people's economic policy, international policy, family institutions, or even the conduct of warfare—was interwoven with the sphere of the sacred, culminating in a relationship between a people, their God and their land.[2] These triangulated entities were not as conceptually divorceable as they may be today, and this holds true when we use the language "holy war" to describe what we find in the Old Testament. In fact, the portrait there is better described as an integrated picture in which the sacred infuses the fabric of existence.[3]

Moreover, when we think of "holy war" in the Old Testament—or as I shall identify it throughout this paper "Divine War" or "Yнwн War" in accord with the other essays in this volume[4]—the rhetoric of these texts actually leads us to conclude that there is, in fact, a divine focus to this kind of warfare. Emphasis lay not upon human beings with swords and spears but rather upon God himself, who fights for his people, who receives the spoils of war (as opposed to random looting or personal benefit from the

---

[2]See Christopher J. H. Wright, *God's People in God's Land* (Grand Rapids: Eerdmans, 1990). This holds true even for the wisdom tradition in Israel, which has often been thought to be a line of thinking that is more concerned with quotidian life apart from sacred concerns. A recent work effectively speaks against this suggestion and constructively argues that all of life was lived under the auspices of God, even wisdom thinking: Craig G. Bartholomew and Ryan P. O'Dowd, *Old Testament Wisdom Literature: A Theological Introduction* (Downers Grove, IL: IVP Academic, 2011), esp. pp. 35-46. Note as well the now dated but immensely important edited volume: Henri Frankfort, H. A. Groenewegen-Frankfort, John Albert Wilson, Thorkild Jacobsen and William A. Irwin, eds., *The Intellectual Adventure of Ancient Man: An Essay on Speculative Thought in the Ancient Near East* (Chicago: The University of Chicago Press, 1946).

[3]This holds true even if one adheres to Niditch's claim that different ideologies of war permeate the biblical material. In each of the ideologies that she identifies, the integration of the divine into the human realm remains. See Susan Niditch, *War in the Hebrew Bible: A Study in the Ethics of Violence* (Oxford: Oxford University Press, 1994).

[4]See Chapman's article in this volume for further discussion on the title "Divine War."

warriors) and (oddly, to our minds) even receives *worship* through the process of warfare.[5] Thus many scholars rightly understand that the concept in the Old Testament is not to be described as "holy war" at all, but as *divine war*.[6]

Much more could be said here, but however one *names* this warfare, it still carries all sorts of challenges for interpretation. In the first place, in terms of Jewish or Christian morality, how can one view this God as just and good? A modern Jewish impulse recognizes the inherent unpredictability of God's justice and goodness as reflected in the Hebrew Bible. Sometimes this God is good and just, sometimes not. So Blumenthal can argue that when God is good it is appropriate to praise him. Otherwise, when he is violent and unjust (as may be the case in sanctioned divine warfare), the faithful response is to face the abusing God and confront his dark side in protest.[7] Blumenthal develops a faithful Jewish theology of praise and protest.

In Christian tradition, one temptation is to move in the direction of Marcion, who viewed the Old Testament and its characterization of a violent and wrathful God as profoundly opposed to the loving and gracious portrait of Jesus. As such, it is possible to expunge the faith of the Old Testament God in favor of a more palatable New Testament vision.[8] The God of the Old Testament and his warring ways does not comport with the peace, justice and grace of Jesus. In terms of Christian faith and practice, Patrick Miller long ago conceded the wars of the Lord constitute an "apologetic problem . . . the incompatibility of these wars with basic aspects and characteristics of the Christian faith."[9]

The contributions in this volume provide response from a variety of angles of vision, although (no doubt) further attention is warranted. To my

---

[5]See Niditch, *War in the Hebrew Bible*, pp. 28-89.

[6]For example: G. W. Jones, "'Holy War' or 'Yahweh War'?" *Vetus Testamentum* 25 (1975): 642-58; J. P. U. Lilley, "Understanding the *Herem*," *Tyndale Bulletin* 44 (1993): 169-77, esp. pp. 171-3; Eugene H. Merrill, "The Case for Moderate Discontinuity," in *Show Them No Mercy: 4 Views on God and Canaanite Genocide*, ed. Stanley N. Gundry, Counterpoints (Grand Rapids: Zondervan, 2003), pp. 65-94.

[7]David R. Blumenthal, *Facing the Abusing God: A Theology of Protest* (Louisville: Westminster John Knox, 1993).

[8]Heikki Räisänen, *Challenges to Biblical Interpretation: Collected Essays 1991–2000*, BIS 59 (Leiden: Brill, 2001), pp. 191-208, esp. pp. 193-95.

[9]Patrick Miller, "God the Warrior: A Problem in Biblical Interpretation and Apologetics," *Interpretation* 19 (1965): 41.

mind, Patrick Miller rightly argues that the concept of the wars of the Lord must in fact be integrated into a full Christian theology—at least in some manner. Movements down the road to Marcion's place will not do for Christian reflection on Old Testament "holy war" and Christian morality.[10]

Further, Christians must refuse to relegate YHWH war to a "primitive" or less enlightened past, over which we today stand as inheritors of a more reasonable reality. After all, the wars that go on in the ancient world and their supposed primitive thought processes are not so far removed from analogues and (mis)applications in the modern world. The activity of Puritan Christians driving Native Americans from their land with the echoes of Canaanite conquest on their lips did not occur in the too far distant past of American history. Other historical analogues might be brought to bear as evidence as well, as John C. Collins highlights.[11] The issue of divine war, both in terms of its presence in the biblical text as well as its application in various ways, must be understood as part and parcel of Christian Scripture and tradition.

But how does the Christian proceed? On the one hand, one may focus upon the questions that arise as a result of a holy and good God commanding the obliteration of the Amalekites or the Canaanites in the book of Deuteronomy. This may lead one to view with Dawkins that God is genocidal and maniacal and breeds an "us versus them" mentality. But then again, YHWH war is not isolated to foreign nations or ethnicities. In the Old Testament, God is no respecter of persons, nations or ethnicities when it comes to divine war. In the prophets (Isaiah and Jeremiah especially) it becomes clear that the Lord enacts divine war against his own people—and for their injustice which is, within the Old Testament portraiture, ultimately creation-destroying. Thus by neglecting action on the issue of his people's injustice, God would effectively abandon his creation. And this is something that God doesn't seem anxious to do. So an us-versus-them viewpoint

---

[10]So the view advocated here goes in a different way than Eric Siebert, *Disturbing Divine Behavior: Troubling Old Testament Images of God* (Minneapolis: Fortress, 2009). For a helpful review, see David T. Lamb, "Review of Eric Siebert, *Disturbing Divine Behavior*," *STR* 2, no. 1 (2010): 71.

[11]John C. Collins, "The Zeal of Phinehas: The Bible and the Legitimation of Violence," *JBL* 122 (2003): 3-21, esp. pp. 13-14. See also Conrad Cherry, ed., *God's New Israel: Religious Interpretations of American Destiny* (Englewood Cliffs, NJ: Prentice Hall, 1971). Though see Earl, "Joshua and the Crusades," in this volume.

on divine war for the Old Testament does not comport with the biblical evidence, contrary to the kind of argument made by Dawkins on this issue.[12] As far as God being maniacal or genocidal, that is another issue altogether and cannot be tackled here though other contributions do so in the present volume.[13] I would just say at the outset that in the Old Testament God acts in ways that are *not* maniacal though sometimes difficult for readers to appropriate and understand rationally or emotionally.

Once one recognizes that God indeed enacts divine war against foreign nations and his own people as well, how then should one respond? One response is to observe specific internal testimony within the Old Testament to the divine warrior. A helpful outcome of Niditch's masterful analysis of war in the Hebrew Bible lay in her recognition of various responses to, or "ideologies" of, this topic of "holy war" in the biblical corpus. But Niditch overlooks a neglected witness in the Writings that holds promise for modern appropriation.

DIVINE WAR IN THE WRITINGS: POSITIVE PORTRAYAL

In the Writings one discovers human response to the divine warrior. At points one finds positive response—praise—to God for his enactment of divine war. In the Psalter especially, a number of praise hymns extol God for his majestic defeat of enemies. These may be explored in Longman and Reid's fine analysis and Klingbeil's exceptional monograph.[14] However, it is in place to mention two examples to show how the Psalter affirms the divine warfare: Psalms 18 and 21.

Psalm 18 praises God for his defeat of an individual enemy. The psalmist describes God as a warrior, with lightning for arrows and thunder as a kind of bludgeon. This theophanic and anthropomorphic language declares that

---

[12]See also the comments by Niditch elucidating a similar point in *War in the Hebrew Bible*, pp. 151-55.

[13]Also note recent works that address the issue in their own ways: Paul Copan, *Is God a Moral Monster? Making Sense of the Old Testament* (Grand Rapids: Baker Books, 2011); David Lamb, *God Behaving Badly: Is the God of the Old Testament Angry, Sexist and Racist?* (Downers Grove, IL: InterVarsity Press, 2011). See also their contributions in this volume.

[14]Tremper Longman III and Daniel G. Reid, *God Is a Warrior*, SOTBT (Grand Rapids: Zondervan, 1995). A more detailed analysis can be found in the exceptional work of Martin Klingbeil, *Yahweh Fighting from Heaven: God as Warrior and as God of Heaven in the Hebrew Psalter and Ancient Near Eastern Iconography*, OBO 169 (Göttingen: Vandenhoeck and Ruprecht, 1999).

God "thundered in the heavens" and "sent forth his arrows,"[15] scattering the enemies (Ps 18:13, 14). With these accoutrements of war, God fights against those that would oppose him. Accompanying God's victory, God defeats the chaos waters that threaten to encompass not just the psalmist's life, but even creation itself (vv. 14-15).

This theme of God defeating the chaos waters that threaten his creation comes up over and again in the Psalter as a whole and should be understood as a permutation of the theme of divine war.[16] This imagery recurs in a number of psalms that highlight the sovereignty of God in defeating the enemies of his elect people, whether an individual or community, as the divine warrior from heaven. In essence, God defeats enemy nations as well as the cosmic foe of chaos/water in his descent from heaven to earth.

This is also true in Psalm 21, a hymn that celebrates Yнwн's defeat of the rivals of the divinely appointed king. Armed for battle, the God of heaven fights and wins victory for his king. So on the earthly plane, Psalm 21:8-11 ushers forth God's praise:

> Your hand found all your enemies,
>   Your right hand discovered those who hate You.
> You placed them in a fiery furnace at the time of Your presence,
>   O Yнwн.
>   In his anger he swallowed them and fire consumed them.
> Their offspring You terminated from the land,
>   Their seed from the descendants of humanity.[17]

Note that the rivals of the king are the enemies of God. Verse 13 [v. 12] states that God took aim against their faces with his bowstring (note the similarity to the archer imagery in Psalm 18). His/the king's enemies are wiped out and consumed, and their seed/children are terminated from the face of the earth. This sounds horrific, but the justification comes by way of these enemies' actions, discovered in Psalm 21:12 [v. 11]: these foes extended evil (רעה) against God/the king, planning wicked plans (מזמה) against him. This reveals a theological rationale for God's warring. His holy, just and righteous personhood demands warring action against all those who would

---

[15]All translations in this chapter are mine unless otherwise noted.
[16]Longman and Reid, *God Is a Warrior*, pp. 72-82; Klingbeil, *Yahweh Fighting*, pp. 57-74.
[17]I have translated from the Hebrew; the English verses of the same are Ps 29:8-10.

contend against both him and his righteous rule through its divinely appointed king. This action, at least in the mind of the biblical writer, remains essentially action against creation-threatening evil.[18]

Other psalms praise the divine warrior for his activity as well (Ps 46:7-12; 65:10-14; 68:15-22; 83:14-18; 144:5-8). In each of these, the divine warrior is praised for his action against enemies and chaos/waters. In some of these texts, the divine victory over chaos is part of a deliberate vision and theology of God's kingship in Zion (e.g., Ps 46:7-12; 65:10-14). But in others, God is celebrated as a divine victor over the enemies either of Israel (e.g., Ps 68:15-22; 83:14-18) or of God's divinely appointed king (e.g., Ps 21:8-11; 144:5-8). In each of these, however, the divine warrior fights on behalf of his people. Because of this, God is pictured on the side of his people *against* the forces of evil. In this way, the portrayal of Yhwh war in the Psalter can be related to Yhwh war in the destruction of the Amalekites and in the rhetoric of Joshua.

Divine War in the Writings: Negative Portrayal

But indeed this is not the only rejoinder to Yhwh war in the Psalter and not the one I particularly want to focus upon. Alternatively one sees a protest against the activity of the divine warrior in some psalms and particularly in the book of Lamentations. These texts question the divine warrior about his activity—his inherent justice, fairness and goodness. I will briefly attend to the Psalter but concentrate on Lamentations.

A prominent psalm that questions the action of the divine warrior is Psalm 89:38-45. Interestingly, in the early verses of the psalm, God is praised because he fights for his people/king and defeats the chaos waters (Ps 89:8-10, 22-25), using language similar to that of the positive portrayals of the divine warrior outlined above. But as the psalm progresses, it becomes apparent that God has turned against his own people and king, rejecting them in wrath (v. 38). Yhwh then lays siege to his people and king (v. 39) enabling their enemies to rejoice at their defeat. In short, Yhwh becomes a warrior against his own people, leading the psalmist to cry out, "How long,

---

[18]Of course ideological and postcolonial criticism will have something to say against this theological construction. See George Aichele et al., *The Postmodern Bible: The Bible and the Culture Collective* (New Haven, CT: Yale University Press, 1996), pp. 272-308.

O Lord? Will you hide yourself forever? How long will your wrath burn like fire?" (v. 46). The aim of the prayer is to draw the divine warrior back on the side of the afflicted and against the enemies of Israel and the king (vv. 49-51). Other texts that draw a similar line are Psalms 74 and 80. Lamentations takes up its protest against the divine warrior as well.

The following section explores perhaps the most strident response to God against his warring activity: Lamentations 2. Here the poetry poses fundamental questions to YHWH about the war enacted against his own people. This is accomplished, first, by highlighting the extensive range of God's destruction and, second, by bringing that portraiture of trauma to God in prayer, raising fundamental questions about its justice. The thesis argued here is that Lamentations 2 reveals an alternative response to divine war within the biblical canon, which is grounded in faith and spirituality but nonetheless enables questioning the deity. That is to say, Lamentations 2 responds to YHWH war by rooting itself in *spirituality* and *prayer* that moves beyond relationally disembodied *explanations* or *justifications* of YHWH war.

In order to make this case, it must be shown that Lamentations 2 actually speaks to the issue of YHWH war and the divine warrior. Lamentations 2:1-9 vividly displays divine judgment in a manner unparalleled in the Old Testament. Thirty active verbs concentrate upon the day of wrath.[19] The alphabetic acrostic draws the reader steadily through graphic depictions of judgment and reinforces its divine authority in which the deity is presented

---

[19]Lam 2:2a: He beclouded (יעיב); Lam 2:1b: He cast from heaven to earth the beauty of Israel (משמיך ארץ תפארת ישראל); Lam 2:1c: He forgot his footstool (ולא־זכר הדם־רגליו); Lam 2:2a: He swallowed (בלע); Lam 2:2a: He did not pity (לא חמל); Lam 2:2b: He tore down (הרס); Lam 2:2c: He hurled to earth her kingdom and officials (הגיע לארץ ... ממלכה ושריה); Lam 2:2c: He profaned her kingdom and officials (חלל ממלכה ושריה); Lam 2:3a: He cut off every horn of Israel (נדע ... כל קרן ישראל); Lam 2:3b: He withdrew his right hand (השיב אחור ימינו); Lam 2:3c: He burned in Jacob (ויבער ביעקב); Lam 2:3c: He consumed everything (אכלה סביב); Lam 2:4a: He strung his bow (דרך קשתו); Lam 2:4b: He slaughtered (ויהרג); Lam 2:4c: He poured out wrath like fire (שפך כאש); Lam 2:5a: He swallowed (בלע); Lam 2:5b: He swallowed (בלע); Lam 2:5b: He annihilated (שחת); Lam 2:5c: He increased mourning and lamentation (וירב ... תאניה ואניה); Lam 2:6a: He treated violently (ויחמס); Lam 2:6a: He annihilated (שחת); Lam 2:6b: He abolished (שכח); Lam 2:6c: He spurned (וינאץ); Lam 2:7a: He spurned (זנח); Lam 2:7a: He repudiated (נאר); Lam 2:7b: He delivers the walls of Jerusalem's citadels into the hand of an enemy (הסגיר ביד־אויב חומת ארמנותיה); Lam 2:8a: He planned to annihilate the walls of dear Zion (חשב יהוה להשחית חומת בת־ציון); Lam 2:8b: He stretched out a line and did not turn back his hand from swallowing (נטה קו לא־השיב ידו מבלע); Lam 2:8c: He put in mourning rampart and wall (ויאבל־חל וחומה); Lam 2:9a: He destroyed and shattered her bars (אבד ושבר בריאיה).

as a warrior through imagery of the cloud, fire and the bow. Drawing from Old Testament texts and Canaanite mythological tradition, YHWH is depicted as an adversarial warrior who pours out his anger against his city, people and temple.

Note the language used to describe God's activity. In Lamentations 2:1-9, fire and wrath belong to divine warrior imagery,[20] prevalent in Old Testament and Canaanite literature. Miller explains in the Old Testament, "The image of the 'devouring fire' seems to be predominantly expressive of the divine warrior's wrath and destruction," drawn from Canaanite theological traditions.[21] YHWH pours out wrath like fire against pastureland,[22] cities and temple; the observer can rightly say the fire of the Lord consumed everything.

Along with the weapon of fire, YHWH is an enemy warrior with a bow. The divine warrior with a bow appears in iconography with the deity holding the bow from the heavens;[23] the Old Testament often pictures YHWH as an archer with bow or arrows, possibly understood as thunderbolts and lightning (Deut 32:23-24; Job 6:4; 34:6; Ps 18:14; 21:12; 38:2; 64:7; 77:17; 120:4; 144:6; Is 41:2, Hab 3:9; Zech 9:13). In Lamentations 2:4a the deity has strung his bow and has it tensed ready to fire in his hand. The tensed bow seems to be the force of "strong (in) his right hand."[24]

Allusions in Lamentations 2:3-4 reverse previous depictions of YHWH in Exodus tradition to portray the deity as a warrior against his own people. Boecker sees allusions to Exodus in the Song of the Sea in Lamentations 2:3b-4a. In Exodus 15:6, YHWH's right hand wins glory for himself and his right hand shatters his enemy. Where the Lord has formerly fought enemies with the strength of his right hand, Lamentations 2:3b-4a reverses this tradition and presents YHWH as an enemy warrior fighting against his people

---

[20]Antje Labahn, "Fire From Above: Metaphors and Images of God's Actions in Lamentations 2.1-9," *JSOT* 31 (2006): 239-56.

[21]Patrick D. Miller, "Fire in the Mythology of Canaan and Israel," *CBQ* 27 (1965): 256-61, esp. p. 259.

[22]נאות means "grazing place" or "pastureland" as in Jer 9:9: "Over the mountains I raise weeping and lamentation; and over the pastureland of the wilderness, a dirge," על־ההרים אשא בכי ונהי ועל־נאות מדבר קינה.

[23]Klingbeil, *Yahweh Fighting*, fig. 88.

[24]BHS suggests emending נצב ימינו to "an arrow in his right hand" (חץ בימינו). Yet the Niphal participle from נצב suggests the bow is raised and tensed, ready to fire at its target. Thus Boecker translates נצב ימינו: "erhoben seine Rechte," "raised in his right hand." Hans Jochen Boecker, *Klagelieder* (ZBAT 21; Zürich: Theologischer Verlag Zürich, 1985), p. 38.

with a bow in his right hand. Moreover, he withdraws his right hand from the face of the enemy.[25] Reversal of Exodus 15:6 in Lamentations 2:3b-4a presents a dark divine victory song: YHWH remains victorious, but his enemy is his *own people* rather than *Egypt*.

Lamentations 2 includes further imagery of divine war. Cloud imagery in Lamentations 2:1 draws upon specifically theological conceptions of divine war both from Old Testament traditions and from Canaanite mythology. The only instance of "cloud" as a verb in the Old Testament occurs in Lamentations 2:1a: "he has beclouded." Re'emi and Lee recognize cloud imagery is often associated with theophany and divine protection in the Old Testament.[26] The cloud was usually a sign of God's favor on his people, as in the Sinai revelation of Exodus 19:9 where, after defeating Egypt and the miracle of the sea, YHWH says to Moses, "Behold! I am coming to you in a cloud," and Exodus 34:5-6, where God descends in a cloud and promises his presence: "YHWH, YHWH! A God compassionate and merciful; slow to anger, and full of lovingkindness and faithfulness."

Cross believes the Sinai theophany and divine battle theophany (as in Ex 15) are variant aspects of similar conceptions of the divine warrior. He demonstrates that the Old Testament draws from Canaanite imagery, usually ascribed to Ba'al, and transforms it polemically to refer to YHWH's power.[27] Contrasted against the imagery of divine war against a foreign people (like Egypt), YHWH is figured as a storm god who has gone to war against Jerusalem and her people with his cloud of wrath in Lamentations 2:1a.[28] This theophanic "storm god," YHWH, comes from the clouds and has arrows of lightning (Lam 2:4a) to ravage his own land in a storm.[29]

Further, the poetry employs the verb construction "not pity," which is the same verbal construction used in God's command to Saul in his YHWH war against Amalek in 1 Samuel 15:3: "Now go and attack Amalek, and utterly

[25]Boecker, *Klagelieder*, pp. 38-39.

[26]R. Martin-Achard and S. Paul Re'emi, *God's People in Crisis: Amos and Lamentations*, ITC (Grand Rapids: Eerdmans, 1984), p. 92; N. C. Lee, *The Singers of Lamentations: Cities Under Siege, From Ur to Jerusalem to Sarajevo*, BIS 60 (Leiden: Brill, 2002), p. 133.

[27]F. M. Cross, *Canaanite Myth and Hebrew Epic: Essays in the History of the Religion of Israel* (Cambridge, MA: Harvard University Press, 1973), pp. 156-77.

[28]F. W. Dobbs-Allsopp, *Weep, O Daughter of Zion: A Study of the City-Lament Genre in the Hebrew Bible*, BibOr 44 (Rome: Pontifical Biblical Institute, 1993), p. 62.

[29]Cross, *Canaanite Myth and Hebrew Epic*, pp. 161-63.

destroy all that they have; *do not pity them*, but kill both man and woman, child and infant, ox and sheep, camel and donkey." Lamentations 2:2 reads, "The Lord swallowed, *he did not pity*, all the habitations of Jacob. He tore down in his rage the fortified cities of dear Judah. He hurled to earth, he profaned her kingdom and her officials." The Lord is even described as "like an enemy" and "like a foe" in Lamentations 2:4-5. He is pictured as an enemy warrior brandishing a bow and firing upon his people. So the connection between YHWH war and Lamentations 2 is sustainable.

The scope of the divine warrior's battle plan is impressive as well. In Lamentations, God either directly destroys or uses his instrument of war (the Babylonian army) to destroy physical, political, religious and social structures. The divine warrior literally slaughters (הרג) the precious things of Jerusalem's eye in Lamentations 2:4b. He fights like an "enemy" and a "foe" (v. 4) against city, people and temple. The leaders of the city, the inhabitants of the city and even the physical environs cannot escape the wrath of God. Repetition of the term "precious thing" in 2:4b exploits its polyvalence and suggests another depiction of victims of destruction. "Precious things" of Jerusalem's "eye" refers to the city's children when read with the information gained from Lamentations 1:7b, 11b. But the "precious things" in Lamentations 2:4b takes on a different meaning, namely, her leaders. The similar syntactical constructions in Lamentations 2:3a-4b conjoin "leaders" with "precious things." The syntactic repetition creates another meaning to "precious things." Not only the city's children but also her leaders are precious, but YHWH slaughtered them both like a foe.

Lamentations 2:4c-9 explicitly depicts God's rejection of his temple, cult and city, as well as the leadership of Jerusalem, though this has already been intimated in Lamentations 2:1. In Lamentations 2:4c he pours out his wrath like fire into the tent of Zion. The "tent of the daughter of Zion" likely indicates the temple itself, as it recalls the description of the tabernacle or "Tent of Meeting" in Exodus 27–40.[30] Moses is unable to enter into the Tent of Meeting because YHWH settles upon it in a cloud and fills it with his glory (Ex 40:35). As in Lamentations 2:1—where the Lord's "beclouding" his people inverts the cloud imagery in Exodus 19:9 and 34:5-6—his pouring

---

[30]Ex 27:21; 28:43; 29:4, 10, 11, 30, 32, 42, 44; 30:16, 18, 20, 26, 36; 31:7; 35:21; 38:8, 30; 39:32, 40; 40:2, 6, 7, 12, 22, 24, 26, 29, 32, 34, 35; see also Lev 1:1.

out fire on the tent of the daughter of Zion in Lamentations 2:4c exposes a reversal: YHWH is no longer present in the Tent of Meeting through the cloud and glorified (Ex 40:35). He now pours out his fire upon the Tent of the daughter of Zion in wrath (Lam 2:4c). God has utterly rejected all prior systems in Jerusalem. He abolishes festival and Sabbath (2:6), destroys pastureland, habitations and fortified cities (2:1) and rejects his altar, sanctuary (2:7) and temple (2:4). The divine warrior spurns king and priest (2:6), he exiles Jerusalem's king and princes (2:9), he denies Torah (2:9), and he enacts the failure of prophecy (2:9). Elders sit on the ground (2:10a) and maidens grieve (2:10c). Children and infants are exposed and vulnerable (2:11-12). The devastation of every structure of order in society here is presented as a result of divine wrath—the people are victims of judgment against them.

In light of these indicators, it is apparent that Lamentations exploits divine warrior and "divine war" motifs. God is presented as enacting "holy war" against his own people. As a result, nothing in society remains unaffected. All is left devastated at the hand of the warrior.

ENGAGING THE DIVINE WARRIOR

Once one recognizes the connection between Lamentations and "holy war"/divine war, it is in place to query how or if the poetry responds to this presentation of God and his actions in war. At this point, one may simply walk away from the theology of the poetry as being unjust and immoral in a desire to remove it from cultural discourse.[31] But such a move must be resisted because the poetry does not stop at a mere description of the fact of divine warfare. Rather, the poetry enables response and engagement to the divine warrior through prayer. The speaker, Zion personified, engages the Lord in Lamentations 2:20-22, opening her address with the language of prayer:

> Look, O YHWH, and consider with whom you have dealt with in this way! Should mothers eat their own fruit, little children raised to health? Should priest and prophet be slaughtered in the sanctuary of the Lord? Young and old lie down on the ground of open places; maidens and young men fell by

---

[31]E.g., Deryn Guest, "Hiding Behind the Naked Women in Lamentations: A Recriminative Response," *BI* 7 (1999): 413-48.

the sword. You slaughtered in the day of your wrath, you butchered, you did not pity. You called as on a festal day terrors on every side. There was not—in the day of the wrath of the Lord—fugitive or survivor. Who I brought forth and reared, the enemy destroyed.

Much of what Zion personified says here actually picks up the language of the poem (Lam 2:1-19), showing a "response" to the description of divine activity and suffering on display in the preceding verses.

While confirming God's sovereignty in the warfare, this prayer has the effect of redressing the issue of justice, at least from the perspective of the sufferers. The aim is to draw the Lord's attention to the issue of pain and suffering—which God has caused as a result of "not pitying" and "slaughtering" his people—and persuade him to move to act out of his mercy to the one who prays. Note the petition that is made here: not forgiveness for sin, not for God to counteract the work of enemies, not the issue of shame or disgrace to be removed.[32] No, it is *the Lord's* activity that motivates the appeal: consider what he has done! The interrogatives that follow in Lamentations 2:20 highlight the effects of divine activity—cannibalism and slaughter—and protest against them. The appeal may be designed to persuade YHWH to act on Zion's behalf. Liturgically, the complaint/lament function provides the community a means to engage the divine warrior in the way they have experienced him: as an enemy. This is not a theodicy—either an explanation of why this disaster occurred or a justification of the activity of God—but rather lament prayer.

It is important to address this passage for a couple of reasons. First, it shows how challenging the very concept of divine war and the divine warrior is at this point in the biblical testimony. The poetry of Lamentations 2 forecloses upon a *facile* understanding of divine war in the Bible that flattens this prayer speech. And yet it remains crucial to note that the very logic of this prayer remains grounded in a tacit view of God's goodness and faithfulness. Lament prayer presupposes the Lord's goodness and depends

---

[32]For a discussion on the variety of formulaic address to the deity in Lamentations, including Lam 2:20-22, see H. A. Thomas, "The Liturgical Function of the Book of Lamentations," in *Thinking Towards New Horizons. Collected Communications to the XIXth Congress of the International Organization for the Study of the Old Testament, Ljubljana 2007*, ed M. Augustin and H. M. Niemann; BEATAJ 55 (Frankfurt am Main: Lang Verlag, 2008), pp. 137-47.

upon divine fidelity in order to ground its prayer.[33] Without both God's fidelity and his goodness, lament prayer remains impotent. The primary issue that stands between praise and lament lay in their temporal relationship: lament *anticipates* God's goodness in order to extol him while praise *participates* in God's goodness and rejoices in him. The language of Lamentations 2:20-22, then, is certainly not praise speech. Rather it is rhetorical and persuasive speech designed to move God to act on behalf of the petitioner. This prayer is grounded firmly with a view to God but set within the horizons of the human perspective. So Dawkins and others, who would attempt to caricature the biblical witness to the issue of divine war as *unquestioned* approval of slaughter, are in fact incorrect. The biblical testimony does have internal points that question the concept of divine war, particularly from Lamentations 2.

Once we recognize that there is biblical testimony that enables questions about divine war enacted against God's own people (particularly in the context of the sixth century B.C.), we must press further to query *how* in fact the questioning is done. The *mode* by which Lamentations 2 questions God's activity and divine war is from within the realm of faith. That is to say, it does not attempt to stand outside of relationship with God and judge divine activity to *then* make an assessment of its justice. No, what is witnessed in Lamentations 2 is a response to divine war that is marked by spirituality and relationship, even communion, with God. One way to approach the issue of divine war is to sit, or at least to suppose to sit, *outside* of God's activity and judge its inherent rightness or injustice. After one arrives at his or her conclusion, then one may either accept or reject this deity as unjust or irrational. This is not what one finds in the biblical picture, at least in Lamentations. Rather, the petitioners of Lamentations 2 face the problem of divine war head-on, in all its gruesome detail, but do so *coram deo*.[34] Therefore communion with God and anticipated divine response (*actual* response) provides the framework by which to tackle the complexities and

---

[33]Patrick D. Miller, *They Cried to the Lord: The Form and Theology of Biblical Prayer* (Minneapolis: Fortress, 1994), pp. 55-134; C. C. Broyles, *The Conflict of Faith and Experience in the Psalms: A Form-Critical and Theological Study*, JSOTSup 52 (Sheffield, UK: JSOT Press, 1989), pp. 36-37.

[34]This is a characteristic of lament prayer in general. See the discussion of Miller, *They Cried to the Lord*, pp. 55-134.

atrocities of violence, war and even (what seems to be) sanctioned death. This is a radically different response to the issue of Yhwh war as one finds, say, in Deuteronomy or Joshua. But it is a response that must be heard.

Conclusion

In conclusion, it is in place to address *why* this engagement of the divine warrior in Lamentations 2 remains fruitful and necessary for Christian morality. In the first place, it shows the challenge of the very issue itself. The Bible does not give a sugarcoated picture of divine war. Though it certainly presents a view of God as powerful in war, it also provides a view in which this power may be questioned, at least in Lamentations 2. This shows us that divine war remains a difficult issue that must be taken seriously in all of its explicit violence and the challenges that presents.

Second, it appropriately sets a context for questioning God. Too often, in honest attempts to deal with the issue, some may tend to move outside of life before God and address challenging issues, like divine war, as if God would not actually respond to the prayers and tears of humanity. Lamentations 2 provides a context for engaging difficult issues like Yhwh war within Christian spirituality. It was Christ on the cross, for instance, who actually prayed to God using the same speech form in his time of distress: "My God, my God, why have you forsaken me?" (Mk 15:34).

Did Jesus really not know? Could he really not explain his situation? Could he not justify why God had done what he had done? On the logic of the apostle Mark and other gospel writers, it certainly appears that Jesus could rationally and logically explain why he was dying on the cross, but that in no way diminishes the force of his lament to God. Jesus cried out to God because he was, at that instant, God-forsaken—and this moment comprises a crucial bridge that links the humanity and deity of Jesus as recorded in the gospels.[35]

In an analogous way, Lamentations *knows* and can *explain* the nature of and reasons for divine war that its petitioners experience. But cognition and explanation of the reality of divine war is not the primary point of the

---

[35]See the discussion of R. Bauckham, *Jesus and the God of Israel: God Crucified and Others Studies on the New Testament's Christology of Divine Identity* (Grand Rapids: Eerdmans, 2008), pp. 254-68.

poetry. Lamentations establishes and displays the sense of communion and spirituality between the petitioner and God (as Christ did on the cross in his cry of dereliction). Ultimately, the Father did respond to the Son. And Lamentations' petitioners may surmise that God will provide response to their prayers as well (which, on the response from the larger Old Testament, God does).[36] This hope, however, is not a certainty, at least not in the book of Lamentations. If we identify the logic of hope on display in Christian prayer as an analogue to the kind of prayer we find in Lamentations 2, then we see that Lamentations provides a context for a spirituality that takes difficult issues to God and awaits his response. For those who doubt the justice of God's warring activity, Lamentations offers a response that engages the divine warrior directly and then awaits God's response. In such spirituality of faith, life from the broken shards of experience may emerge.

---

[36]Isaiah 40–66; Zechariah 1–2, for example. See N. K. Gottwald, *Studies in the Book of Lamentations*, SBT 14 (London: SCM Press, 1962), pp. 44-46; C. Seitz, *Word Without End: The Old Testament as Abiding Theological Witness* (Grand Rapids: Eerdmans, 1998), pp. 130-49.

PART THREE

New Testament Perspectives

5

THE RHETORIC OF
DIVINE WARFARE IN EPHESIANS

Timothy G. Gombis

———————— ✝ ————————

THE LANGUAGE OF DIVINE WARFARE in the New Testament is often misused to endorse militant Christian social action and aggressive engagement in the culture wars. The use of such aggressive rhetoric by Christians seems at odds with other fundamental Christian behavioral norms and invites the charge of hypocrisy. What's more, the presence of this language in the New Testament raises the question of whether or not Christianity is inherently violent.

I will argue in this essay that the language and ideology of divine warfare in Ephesians cannot be utilized to endorse political postures or social strategies of aggressive power-grabbing. That is, it does violence against the text of Ephesians to equate Christian "spiritual warfare" with loyalty to the agenda of one political party against another; with efforts to advance a "Christian" agenda through party power-politics on the national, state or local level; with any effort to gain social or political power over other people or groups; and certainly with any endorsement of violence. I hope to make clear that Ephesians presents a powerfully subversive vision of divine warfare, one that resonates with the notion that the reality of Jesus Christ and the existence of the church is good news for the world. Paul utilizes Scriptural divine warfare language in Ephesians in order to persuade the people of God to adopt redemptive and inviting postures of self-sacrifice and embodied love. What is more, Paul actually calls upon his readers to *reject* power-grabbing strategies that seek to gain leverage over others. They are, rather, to adopt postures and patterns of life that *surrender* social and political power in imitation of both Jesus and Paul.

OLD TESTAMENT BACKGROUND

The background for the imagery Paul utilizes in Ephesians 6 is found in Isaiah 59, a text that already contains some surprising elements. In order to understand this properly, we must consider the covenantal relationship between the God of Israel and the nation of Israel. The God of Israel had made himself known internationally by choosing the enslaved and weak people being held by imperial Egypt. Yahweh thoroughly trounced Pharaoh and the gods of Egypt at the exodus and had intended to bring Israel into the land of Canaan in order to bless them as his own special possession. Not only did Yahweh act as the "divine warrior" in this great battle, but he promised to continue to fight on Israel's behalf so long as the nation remained faithful to him (Deut 1:30).

Israel was chosen by God in order to be a "holy nation," a people set apart by the Creator God as agents in his mission to reclaim and restore the nations to his blessing. As a holy nation, Israel was to seek the good of the nations, and they were to look after the poor, the orphan and the widow within their borders. They were to be a nation of justice, where the rich used their resources to care for the poor and to make sure that no one was socially marginalized. Everyone was to participate in the holistic flourishing of the nation (*shalom*). So long as Israel cultivated this sort of national pattern of life, they could trust that Yahweh would fight on their behalf just as he did at the exodus.

As it happened, however, Israel did not remain faithful to Yahweh. They did not seek the life and blessing of the nations but longed for their destruction. They took a perverted view of their election by Yahweh, forgetting that they were chosen *for* this special mission of extending God's gracious reign to the nations. Rather, they considered that they were chosen *instead of* the nations, so they took a condescending and judgmental posture toward them. The prophet Jonah is the chief example of this attitude. He refused to preach to Nineveh for fear that they might repent and be spared judgment.

Further, rather than being a holy nation—a people radically unlike the nations—Israel became a nation just like the nations. The rich exploited the poor, and the orphan and the widow were neglected and abused. Israel became a nation of injustice rather than one of justice. Because of this, Isaiah announced that Yahweh was going to do something extremely subversive. Rather than fighting *on behalf of* Israel against its enemies, Yahweh would take up arms *against* Israel:

> The LORD saw it, and it displeased him
>   that there was no justice.
> He saw that there was no one,
>   and was appalled that there was no one to intervene;
> so his own arm brought him victory,
>   and his righteousness upheld him.
> He put on righteousness like a breastplate,
>   and a helmet of salvation on his head;
> he put on garments of vengeance for clothing,
>   and wrapped himself in fury as in a mantle.
> According to their deeds, so will he repay;
>   wrath to his adversaries, requital to his enemies;
>   to the coastlands he will render requital.
> So those in the west shall fear the name of the Lord,
>   and those in the east, his glory;
> for he will come like a pent-up stream
>   that the wind of the Lord drives on. (Is 59:15-19)[1]

Isaiah's use of the divine warrior tradition is quite subversive in that it turns expectations on their heads and reverses all assumptions about how the God of Israel acts. Yahweh had declared, of course, that he would do this, but Israel had grown complacent and presumptuous. They figured that because they were God's special possession they could rely on their insider status with God to avoid any consequences for their failure to love one another and serve the nations on God's behalf. Yahweh took up arms, therefore, against his own people because they had proved disloyal to him and his cause of restoring the nations. They had become a people who did not re-

---

[1] All Scripture references are from the New Revised Standard Version (NRSV) unless otherwise noted.

flect properly his character in their national life. Because of this, Yahweh went to war against his own people.[2]

Those who assume the righteousness of their cause and rally people to their efforts using biblical military imagery ought to keep in mind two things about the divine warrior tradition from the Old Testament. First, it is presumptuous for anyone to assume that they do their fighting or politicking in God's name. One of the leaders of Israel—God's chosen people!—learned this lesson in a divine warfare passage:

> Once when Joshua was by Jericho, he looked up and saw a man standing before him with a drawn sword in his hand. Joshua went to him and said to him, "Are you one of us, or one of our adversaries?" He replied, "Neither; but as commander of the army of the LORD I have now come." And Joshua fell on his face to the earth and worshiped, and he said to him, "What do you command your servant, my lord?" The commander of the army of the LORD said to Joshua, "Remove the sandals from your feet, for the place where you stand is holy." And Joshua did so. (Josh 5:13-15)

Humanity, including the people of God, must take pains to search out and adjust to God's agenda and strategies. The assumption that God endorses our agenda brings disastrous consequences.

Second, the appearance of Yahweh waging war against unjust Israel in Isaiah 59 highlights God's impartiality and commitment to judge injustice among all peoples (Rom 2:11; 1 Pet 1:17). Israel confessed daily their identity as the people of Yahweh and celebrated the feasts and rituals that attended this identity. But when their daily behavior failed to live up to that identity because of selfishness and exploitation of others, they experienced the judgment of "Yahweh of armies." Sadly, it is far too common in our day for political figures who posture provocatively in the public square to utilize religious language of "spiritual warfare" only later to be exposed as morally compromised in various ways.

Isaiah 59, the text to which Paul refers in Ephesians 6, is already a subversive text. Non-Christians are right to flinch at aggressive Christian utilization of divine warfare language to endorse supposedly Christian

---

[2]On the use of Isaiah 59 in Ephesians 6 and other texts, see Thomas R. Yoder Neufeld, *"Put on the Armour of God": The Divine Warrior from Isaiah to Ephesians*, JSNTSS 140 (Sheffield, UK: Sheffield Academic Press, 1997).

political efforts to influence public policy. The use of such language *against the people of God*, however, ought to serve as a warning to Christian people against careless presumption of the righteousness of a chosen cause. As I hope to demonstrate in the remainder of this chapter, this notion is only intensified by Paul's call to the church to engage in divine warfare.

DIVINE WARFARE IN EPHESIANS

Paul's appropriation of divine warfare ideology, language and themes is just as subversive and surprising when we consider our current political climate. The most obvious place to start is the rhetorically powerful conclusion to Ephesians. Paul sums up his letter with the following:

> Finally, be strong in the Lord and in the strength of his power. Put on the whole armor of God, so that you may be able to stand against the wiles of the devil. For our struggle is not against enemies of blood and flesh, but against the rulers, against the authorities, against the cosmic powers of this present darkness, against the spiritual forces of evil in the heavenly places. Therefore take up the whole armor of God, so that you may be able to withstand on that evil day, and having done everything, to stand firm. Stand therefore, and fasten the belt of truth around your waist, and put on the breastplate of righteousness. As shoes for your feet put on whatever will make you ready to proclaim the gospel of peace. With all of these, take the shield of faith, with which you will be able to quench all the flaming arrows of the evil one. Take the helmet of salvation, and the sword of the Spirit, which is the word of God. (Eph 6:10-17)

This conclusion, citing and expanding upon Isaiah 59, draws together Paul's use of divine warfare themes throughout Ephesians. In the remainder of this chapter I will demonstrate how this is so and how his use of this language and imagery resists being put to use to endorse violence and triumphalism.

God's triumph and Christ's exaltation. The first instance of divine warfare ideology in Ephesians occurs just after the letter opening and Paul's first prayer report. In Ephesians 1:20–2:22, Paul utilizes what scholars call "the pattern of divine warfare" in order to articulate the exaltation of Christ to his position of cosmic lordship and the attendant victories that give him the right to hold that position.[3] The pattern of divine warfare appears throughout the Old Testament as a common narrative structure that allowed for Israel to rehearse and confess the supremacy of Yahweh over all other gods. Where this pattern appears, the God of Israel is proclaimed as supreme king over all others. The victories of God are then listed, the triumphs that demonstrate God's supremacy and exalted status. The people then gather at the temple of Yahweh, the "royal seat" from which God reigns, and there they celebrate their triumphant and sovereign God. The basic pattern of divine warfare runs like this: kingship, conflict-victory, celebration, temple building.

Ephesians 1:20–2:22 follows this structure. Paul asserts the cosmic lordship of Christ in Ephesians 1:20-23, noting that Christ has defeated the powers and authorities and now sits as Lord over them, exalted far above them in the heavenly realm. This assertion of cosmic supremacy needs a defense. That is, anyone claiming ultimate cosmic supremacy needs a list of triumphs to validate such a contention. Paul does this in two cycles of the pattern of divine warfare. In the first cycle, in Ephesians 2:1-10, Paul portrays a desperate situation in which Satan, conspiring with his angelic and demonic lieutenants, enslaves humanity in death by corrupting creation so that people will walk in transgressions and sins. God has triumphed in Christ by freeing God's people from death through the death and resurrection of Jesus. He gives his people life, transforming them so that they now walk in good deeds, doing the will of God.

In the second cycle of the pattern, in Ephesians 2:11-18, Paul portrays another desperate situation in which the powers that rule the present evil age had divided humanity against itself, fostering racial and ethnic hostility. As we see every day in the news, humanity no longer seeks the flourishing of the other according to God's design. We now seek the other's destruction and death, relishing the prospect of dominating the other. Cultures proclaim their superiority over others and nations turn against one another. In a dramatic transformation of this horrible condition, God has united hu-

---

[3]On the pattern of divine warfare throughout the Bible, see Tremper Longman III and Daniel G. Reid, *God Is a Warrior* (Grand Rapids: Zondervan, 1995). For a fuller development of the structure of Ephesians 1:20–2:22, see Timothy G. Gombis, *The Drama of Ephesians: Participating in the Triumph of God* (Downers Grove, IL: IVP Academic, 2010), pp. 85-106.

manity in Christ, killing the enmity by the cross. God has created a radically new people—*a new humanity*—one in which racial, ethnic and gender differences are no longer sources of division and destruction. They are now opportunities for doing good, celebrating the wonderful variety of humanity in God's good world and rejoicing in one another.

These two cycles defend Paul's claim that Christ is cosmic champion, triumphant and exalted far above the powers and authorities. The two remaining elements of the pattern of divine warfare, temple building and celebration, appear in the final portion of Ephesians 2. In verses 19-22, Paul depicts the church as the new temple of God, and the church gathers no longer *at* the temple but now *as* the temple, in order to celebrate and do "temple service" as the restored humanity. The church is now the dwelling place of God in Christ by the Spirit.

It is crucial to note *the manner* in which God achieves his victory over the powers, since the way God triumphs determines how the church participates in his triumph. God defeats the powers through the death and resurrection of Jesus Christ, which is a radically subversive way of doing things. The cross turns everything on its head—God wins by losing; the powers lose by winning. The powers' triumph over Christ on the cross was their own defeat, and Christ's defeat won him victory.

This is radically subversive of the normal way of doing things. According to the corrupted social logic of "how things work" in the world, we get things done by winning or by dominating others. We typically manipulate situations to bring about certain ends and goals. We win by winning. We triumph by triumphing. If that means that there are losers or that we have to step on people as we advanced our cause, so be it. We "win" in personal encounters through power moves and intimidation. We must dominate others, grab for power and exploit the weak.

But this is not God's way. God does not act according to the conventions of perverted human imagining. God comes in weakness and his logic is upside-down, if we look at it in human terms. Jesus speaks from this logic when he says that the one who seeks to save his life will lose it, and the one who loses his life will save it (Mk 8:35). Elsewhere, Paul draws out this subversive way that God works when he says that God's way of working is totally foreign to the power hungry cosmic rulers. In 1 Corinthians 2:8, he says that if the rulers of this age had understood God's upside-down logic, God's wisdom of working his power through weakness, they would not have crucified the Lord of glory. The way of the cross is so subversive that even Christians often overlook it in their rush to grab for power or for some leverage in the contemporary culture wars. Such pursuits are idolatrous and constitute losses in spiritual warfare. God triumphs through self-giving unto death, and cruciformity—conformity to the cross of Christ—is the mode of life to which Paul calls the people of God.

This upside-down way of working and the self-expending character of God must shape how we conceive of "spiritual warfare" language in Ephesians. Further, the enemies over whom God triumphs throughout Ephesians 2 are also the enemies against whom the church battles in Ephesians 6. That is, "spiritual warfare" is not waged against other people but against God's cosmic enemies, those who seek to ruin creation in various ways, especially by holding humanity enslaved to destructive patterns of life. Who are these cosmic enemies and what do they do?

The powers and authorities appear prominently in Ephesians and at key points in the letter's argument (Eph 1:20-21; 3:10; 6:10-13). They originally fulfilled a God-given role in creation, having been created to be mediators of God's rule over the world. According to Jewish thought, the nation of Israel was deemed to be the special inheritance of the God of Israel, but he appointed cosmic ruler figures to rule over the nations (Deut 32:8-9; Sir 17:17).[4] They were given a stewardship to rule the nations and to order their corporate lives in such a way that the nations would glorify the Most High God. However, these figures have rebelled so that their rule is characterized by a perversion of their original commission. They have corrupted their cultures and have ordered their nations in such a way that those in positions of authority now exploit the weak and powerless, grasping after power and seeking to take any advantage they can in order to satisfy their own lusts for more power, prestige, possessions and sensual gratification. They hold creation enslaved and sow within creation perverse ideologies and destructive modes of life.

In Paul's thought, reflected throughout Ephesians, God has defeated

---

[4]For a fuller description of these figures, see Gombis, *The Drama of Ephesians*, pp. 35-58.

them in the death and resurrection of Christ. He has broken their hold over creation and is freeing his world and humanity from their enslaving grip. He will complete his victory at the day of Christ in the future at which point he will also destroy the powers that rule the present evil age forever. They still exercise influence over the world and humanity as they go down to eventual destruction, though this is counteracted by God's Spirit acting in his people, the church.

Summing up, the church is the monument to God's triumph in Christ. The existence of the church signifies to the rebellious powers that God has triumphed in the death and resurrection of Christ. As we will see, God's glory in the cosmic realm is magnified when the church imitates the self-giving and cruciform life of Christ on earth.

God's triumph in Paul's humiliation. In Ephesians 3, Paul digresses from his prayer report and gives his readers an insight into his apostolic ministry. As this passage begins, Paul reports to his readers how he prays for them. Just as he begins to do this, however, he breaks off and embarks on an extended description of his ministry. The NRSV translates Ephesians 3:1 so that it appears that Paul is explaining why he is a prisoner: "This is the reason that I Paul am a prisoner for Christ Jesus." A better translation, however, would find that the opening of verse 1 reads the same as Ephesians 3:14: "For this reason I, Paul, a prisoner of Christ Jesus." By "this reason," Paul is referring to his rehearsal of the great drama of God's redemption in Ephesians 2. His initial aim here is to report how he is praying for them now that God has made them participants in the gospel drama.

But Paul interrupts his prayer report as soon as he begins it. Here's my translation: "For this reason, I, Paul, a prisoner of Christ Jesus for the sake of you gentiles—surely you have heard of the administration of the grace of God that was given to me." Paul then goes on to write about his ministry and the mystery of what God is currently up to, after which he continues the report of his prayer in Ephesians 3:14. He actually repeats his wording from verse 1: "For this reason I bow my knees before the Father." Why does Paul break off his prayer, embark on a long digression about his ministry and then jump back into his report about his prayers for his readers?

Paul adopts this strategy because he is keenly aware that it sounds jarringly inconsistent to rehearse the victories of God in Christ over the fallen powers and then to identify himself as someone who is occupying a position of defeat. According to the first-century logic, if Paul is in a Roman prison, then the gods of Rome are stronger than the God whom Paul serves. It certainly seems that the powers that rule the present evil age have Paul right where they want him.

Paul's ironic reference to himself as "the prisoner of Christ" would have resonated with those who were fully aware of the nature of his ministry. But Ephesians most likely is a circular letter, written not only to the church in Ephesus but to many others in Asia Minor who were unfamiliar with Paul. He needs to make explicit the paradox of his situation so that they might rightly understand his imprisonment. We can see that this is his intention because the discussion is framed by his imprisonment in Ephesians 3:1 and his sufferings in Ephesians 3:13. And just before he returns to his prayer in Ephesians 3:14, he tells his readers that he doesn't want them to be shaken up because of his sufferings.

Paul, therefore, gives his readers an insight into the nature of his apostleship, demonstrating that it takes the same shape as the upside-down and subversive victory of God in Christ. Just as God's triumph comes through the "defeat" of Christ on the cross, so Paul's ministry is carried out through humility, suffering and weakness. Paul situates his present circumstances squarely within the biblical tradition of God's power being demonstrated in human weakness. He does this by emphasizing the paradox of his life and ministry—at the same time that he occupies this terribly shameful and utterly weak situation as a prisoner, he fulfills a cosmically crucial commission as the administrator of the grace of God. In so doing, Paul wonderfully embodies the same paradox of God's victory in Christ. Jesus Christ conquered the powers and authorities through his shameful and humiliating death on a Roman cross. Because of God's upside-down logic, human embodiments of God's triumph will inevitably involve displays of God's power through human weakness, loss, shame and humiliation.

The key to this passage comes in Ephesians 3:8-10. Paul says that his apostolic commission involves two activities, and these are indicated by two infinitives in Greek (Eph 3:8-9). I translate Ephesians 3:8-9 here, since this passage involves just a bit of tangled grammar: "To me, the very least of all the saints, this grace was given, *to preach* to the gentiles the unfathomable riches of God, and *to enlighten* everyone what is the administration of the mystery which had been hidden from past ages in God who created all things."

Paul's two tasks are to "preach to the gentiles" and "to enlighten everyone" about the administration of the mystery. These two tasks are not merely restatements of the same thing. Rather, the second builds upon the first so that the following dynamic is at work. The enlightening is built upon the preaching so that it is the *result* of the preaching. Paul's logic comes into focus when we realize that there are different audiences for each of these tasks. The audience for Paul's preaching is the gentiles and when they hear the proclamation, the church is called into existence. The audience for the enlightenment is the powers. When the church comes into being through the preaching of *Paul the prisoner*, the powers are enlightened about the mystery. And this enlightenment is not through education or information but demonstration.

It makes no sense, according to the powers' perverted logic, that a prisoner under their domination would have any ability at all to accomplish God's purposes in the world. Surely they are in control—Paul is in prison! But when this shamed and dominated figure preaches and gets the message out and God's power is unleashed, the powers are enlightened as to how God is accomplishing his mysterious and wonderful work in the world. He's not doing it through power-grabbing but through self-giving love, suffering and weakness. In the face of the powers and authorities who are powerless to create and whose rule over this present evil age is characterized by destruction, division, exploitation and oppression, God demonstrates his power by his ability to create his one new people and to make them flourish in the midst of enemy territory, thus confounding the evil powers. As Paul the prisoner preaches the riches of Christ, God creates the church, and this coming-into-being is a powerful lesson for the powers about God's power.

The "enlightenment" in Ephesians 3:9, then, does not refer to Paul's ministry of proclamation directly, as if his explanation of the content of the mystery helps people to understand it more clearly. Rather, the church's very coming-into-existence is in view, so that the entire cosmos is enlightened as to the administration of the mystery through the object lesson of the church's coming-into-being.

Not only is Paul's preaching the means by which God calls the church into being, but the church's coming-into-existence in this manner serves as a visible display of the "rich variety of God's wisdom" to the rebellious powers. The enlightenment in Ephesians 3:9 has a distinct purpose, which Paul indicates by "so that" in Ephesians 3:10. The logic runs like this: God creates the church through the prisoner Paul's preaching, enlightening the stunned powers regarding God's working out of the mystery of a united humanity, "*so that* through the church the wisdom of God in its rich variety might now be made known to the rulers and authorities in the heavenly places" (Eph 3:10).

The triumph of God in Christ takes place in two ways in this passage. First, the powers are notified about the wisdom of God "through the church." This is not the church's proclamation to the powers, as some suggest. Paul, rather, claims that the manner in which God has made known his richly varied wisdom to the powers is by confounding them in his creation of the church. The powers have ordered the present evil age in such a way as to exacerbate the divisions within humanity (Eph 2:11-12). God confounds them by creating in Christ one unified, multiracial body consisting of formerly divided groups of people. And it is the existence of the church as such a body set within the hostile environment of the present evil age that proclaims to them the wisdom of God.

What is more, Paul stresses *the manner* in which the church comes into being. It further confounds the powers and overturns expectations that God creates the church through "Paul the prisoner," the one who is less than the least of all the saints. In his imprisonment, Paul is in a position of utter defeat, completely under the thumb of the powers. Seen in terms of the present age, he could not be in a weaker, more shameful or more vulnerable position. Yet, astonishingly, it is by his preaching of the gospel that God unleashes his creative power and calls the church into existence.

Paul's paradoxical existence—being in a shameful position by virtue of the powers' perversion of the present evil age and carrying out a cosmically significant commission as apostle of the exalted and triumphant Lord Jesus—gives him a perfect opportunity to demonstrate for his readers how the victory of God in spiritual warfare is embodied by God's people. The church does not participate in God's triumph through power-grabbing, ag-

gressive social movements to influence social policy or to assert social influence over others. We follow the pattern set by Jesus Christ, who triumphed through defeat. This passage again emphasizes that our mode of
life ought to be characterized by weakness and self-giving love. And our
enemies are not fellow humans but God's cosmic enemies from whom God
is reclaiming creation.

Waging warfare as the divine warrior. Thus far we have seen that God
triumphs through self-giving love and that his authorized agents participate in that triumph through cruciform love—through adopting postures
and modes of life that are not characterized by coercion or aggressive strategies to dominate others but by self-sacrificial love. With all of this in view,
we may now consider the place of Ephesians 6:10-18 in the letter. This
passage is a rhetorical conclusion to the entire letter, in which Paul depicts
the church as intimately identified with the exalted Lord Jesus. In Ephesians
1:23, Paul says that the church is "his body, the fullness of him who fills all in
all." The presence of Jesus Christ fills the church by God's Spirit so that it
literally is "the body of Jesus" on earth. Just as Jesus, during his time on earth,
was the very presence of God in a human person, so the church is now the
presence of Jesus in the world. For Paul, there is an intense unity between
Jesus Christ and the church.

In Ephesians 6:10-18, then, Paul is addressing the entire gathered church.
They are the presence of God in Christ on earth, a reality brought about by
the Spirit of God. It is the Spirit who draws the community up into the
presence of God and radiates the presence of God among the community.
The church, then, is the place where the world encounters Jesus Christ and
the agency through which Jesus Christ blesses the world with his love and
grace. And just as Jesus was subject to the assaults of the powers during his
time here on earth, the church now battles against the powers and authorities arrayed against God's purposes in the world.

If the church is the divine warrior, called by God to engage the spiritual
conflict, then how does the church carry this out? There are certainly many
good people who are alarmed by Christians talking about becoming *even
more militant.* The Christian church has a shameful historical record of crusading injustice and oppression, treating people in ways that are directly
contrary to the character of Jesus Christ. Further, in the hotly contested

political climate of North America, evangelical Christians are seen as militant crusaders bent on taking away the freedoms of others. Christians are seen as those who are already skilled at angry denunciation driven by triumphalist rhetoric. Do we really need any more Christians who feel that they are doing God's will by advancing a supposedly Christian agenda on the rest of us?

As we have said, this is not at all what Paul is getting at. The church's warfare is not against the world, nor people in the world, but against the rebellious powers and authorities—the rulers of this present evil age. And, as we'll see, the strategy is not at all *militant*. In fact, Paul's instructions for engaging the spiritual conflict are quite subversive, upending notions of militancy.

If Paul's rhetorical summary appears in Ephesians 6:10-18, then his instructions for engaging in divine warfare are contained in the "ethical" section of the letter—Ephesians 4:17–6:9. Here we will see that the church engages in warfare against the powers in ways that defy and overturn our expectations. Our warfare involves resisting the corrupting influences of the powers. The same pressures that produce practices of exploitation, injustice and oppression in the world are at work on church communities. The church's warfare involves resisting such influences, transforming corrupted practices and replacing them with life-giving patterns of conduct that draw upon and radiate the resurrection power of God. *The church's warfare, then, involves purposefully growing into communities that become more faithful corporate embodiments of Jesus on earth.* Far from being a frightening prospect, this is good news for the world.

Communities of resistance. Paul calls the church to a strategy of *resistance*. It is not the church's task to defeat the powers. God has already defeated them in the death and resurrection of Jesus. God has broken their enslaving grip over creation, signaling that their eventual day of complete destruction is on its way. The church is called to inhabit the victory that God has already accomplished. The powers are not completely destroyed. They continue to exercise a perverting and corrupting influence within creation as they go down to eventual complete destruction. We are to resist these influences, standing "against the wiles of the devil" (Eph 6:11), resisting "on that evil day" (Eph 6:13).

But what are the "wiles of the devil"? From a study of the role of the powers throughout Scripture and early Jewish texts, and from the reflections of this tradition in Ephesians, it is most likely that one of their strategies is to tempt the church to compromise its holiness. The church is called to be a "holy people," appointed by God to conduct its life in radically different and redemptive ways. We are to operate according to God's resurrection logic, not the logic of the world. The powers, however, pressure the church to conform to the patterns of corrupted creation. It is a struggle, then, for the church to be a redemptive force in the world, radiating the life of God to the world.

One way that the church compromises its holiness is by participating in the culture wars. We fail to perform our roles faithfully as God's holy people when we ally ourselves with any one "side" in the culture war or with any one political party over another. The culture wars have become so tragically intense over the closing several decades of the last century. It's tempting for Christian churches to "get involved" and become drawn into supporting the cause we feel stands for righteousness. Unfortunately, however, this often involves vigorously and unquestioningly supporting one political party and its leaders while also demonizing another side and its leaders. It doesn't take too long before Christian people are loudly denouncing public figures, speaking foolishly in anger. Such behaviors have become a commonplace in American culture so that the term "evangelical Christian" is virtually synonymous with "angry, judgmental bigot."

When this happens, *the church aids the destructive cause of the powers.* We become partners in the powers' project of corrupting God's good world. Their aim is to set groups of humanity over against each other, so when we participate in the destructive culture wars, we fail to be faithful to our identity as God's holy people.

Waging warfare does not mean that the church militantly opposes the world. When the church performs the role of the divine warrior, it has the same social effect as that of Jesus. When he came to earth, he encountered a culture with its own corruptions, and he reached out to the poor and marginalized. He refused to conduct himself in culture according to the corruptions by the powers. In doing so he provided the perfect example for the church's own performance.

Communities of transformation. According to Ephesians 4:17-31, the church embodies the divine warrior faithfully by cultivating a dynamic of constant transformation. The church is to be the always-transforming and the always-being-transformed people of God. God's people must constantly be involved in becoming more and more the presence of God on earth, more and more faithful at performing the role of Jesus himself in the world. A major component of what this means is the constant transformation in which the church is to participate.

Paul speaks of two distinct realms in Ephesians 4:22-24: the Old Humanity and the New Humanity. Some versions translate these two as the "old self" and "the new self," or, "the old man" and "the new man," perhaps pointing to the old internal self and the new internal self of an individual. But Paul isn't talking about the inner tendencies toward both good and evil within each individual. He is speaking of cosmic realms, two different holistic modes of existence. The Old Humanity is a synonym for the present evil age, that cosmic realm over which the powers of darkness rule and have influence. It points to the corrupted practices and habits of life on both individual and corporate levels. The Old Humanity is undergoing decay and dissolution—it is coming undone. In his death and resurrection, Jesus Christ signaled the eventual demise of the present evil age. It is slowly listing toward destruction like a massive sinking Titanic until it is finally destroyed. Paul says that this realm is "being corrupted in accordance with the lusts of deceit" (Eph 4:22 NASB). Those who share its form of life will share its eventual destruction.

The New Humanity, on the other hand, is that new reality brought into being with the resurrection of Jesus from the dead. It is the realm of new life and new creation that is constantly being renewed by God. Christ himself is the source of life for the New Humanity and also provides for its growth. It is the sphere of existence within creation that God has created and in which he is at work with his renewing power. At the end of Ephesians 4:24, Paul says that this realm has been "created according to God in righteousness and holiness of the truth" (my translation). The New Humanity is an inaugurated form of the fully renewed creation—it's what the entire world will be like when God comes to finally make it fully new.

Because salvation is "already" but "not yet," God has brought us into the

New Humanity by his Spirit. We have been raised up with Christ, brought to life and freed from slavery to sin and death. But in some sense we are still in this world, and our salvation has not yet been completed. We still inhabit the present evil age, even though that age is going down to eventual destruction. Even though we have been raised up into the New Humanity, joined to Christ by the Spirit of God, we also participate in the Old Humanity.

Paul recognizes that we live in this "already" but "not yet" tension. In Ephesians 4:17-24, he exhorts churches to develop dynamics of transformation within their communities. The pattern of transformation is found in Ephesians 4:22-24, and it constitutes what the church has been taught regarding "the truth as it is in Jesus": "That you put off—according to your former way of life—the Old Humanity which is being corrupted according to the lusts of deceit; that you be renewed in the spirit of your mind; and put on the New Humanity, which according to God has been created in righteousness and holiness of the truth" (my translation).

This dynamic of transformation involves three elements. First, churches are to identify practices, habits and patterns of life that are characteristic of the Old Humanity and take steps to rid them from their lives and their communities. Second, they are to renew their imaginations. God's people must find new ways of conceiving of themselves and of one another, reminding themselves of the drama they inhabit and the characters they've become. A renewed imagination is powerful, since it shapes how we view ourselves, our place in this world and our relations with others. We must seek to have our community imaginations shaped and reoriented constantly by Scripture and our Christian identity. This is crucial so that we can fulfill the third step. We must imagine, create and then cultivate practices, habits of mind and patterns of thought, speech and action that are characteristic of the New Humanity. This dynamic of transformation is a key component of the church's performance of the role of divine warrior. According to Paul, a community's cultivation of this, and their constant practice of it, faithfully performs the role of Jesus on earth (Eph 4:21).

Paul's instruction is quite revolutionary here. The church rightly acts as the divine warrior when it focuses on its own need to be transformed and take on with increasing faithfulness the character of Jesus Christ. There is no room here for denouncing others or for taking a condescending posture toward the world, naming its failings and demanding that it be transformed. Such behavior, according to Paul, is a surrender of Christian identity. It is to fail at performing the divine warrior. We are faithful when we confess that we are the ones who are sick and in need of the Physician. We are those who are in need of transformation.

Communities of justice. The final section of Ephesians before the rhetorical finish in 6:10-18 is the extended instruction on Christian families in 5:22–6:9. Why does Paul talk about families in closing this letter, and what does family life have to do with spiritual warfare? Paul's point here is that the church, in filling the role of divine warrior on earth, is to be a community that embodies God's justice.

This passage appears in a distinct literary form called a "household code," which is a form of ethical instruction that appears throughout the writings of ancient political philosophers. Whenever political thinkers wanted to talk about the ideal model for community life, they would talk about the smallest political unit: the family. That is, if the household runs well, and it's the smallest political unit, then the whole society would flourish. Political thinkers, therefore, focused on life within households, which included these fundamental relationships: husband and wife, father and children, master and slaves.[5]

When he uses this form, then, Paul is not necessarily giving instruction to families in our modern conception of that social unit. *He is laying out a broader political vision.* This is something more like a manifesto for how the church is to flourish as a political entity—as God's new community among whom God dwells. This will, obviously, have huge implications for how families enjoy God's rule. But Paul considers these family relationships a concrete example of how the church should enjoy its life together as a community. Several aspects of New Humanity political life become clear when we read this household code against contemporary political expressions.

First, the New Humanity is a community of God's justice for everyone. Paul's political vision is radical in that all members of God's new people enjoy dignity and honor as humans and fully participate in the flourishing

---

[5]For a fuller treatment of this passage in light of household codes from the ancient world, see Timothy G. Gombis, "A Radically New Humanity: The Function of the *Haustafel* in Ephesians," *JETS* 48 (2005): 317-30.

of the community. This is quite different from contemporary political visions. In other household codes, the same sets of relationships appear (husband-wife, father-children, master-slaves), but the point of the instruction is for the ultimate comfort of the husband/patriarch. That is, the counsel is directed toward the well-ordered household with a view to how the patriarch would maintain control over every other member of the community. Paul's instruction, therefore, is radically subversive. Where there are hierarchical relationships, Paul addresses the subordinate member first, giving them dignity. They are full participants in the people of God. In contemporary visions of society, these members are not addressed at all. They only appear as objects of control by the patriarch. In God's new people, there is no place for control, domination, manipulation of others or exploitation.

For most ancient political thinkers, the patriarch is seen as the only one who is truly human. Others are denigrated or not regarded as worthy of full dignity. According to Aristotle, because women lack the rational capacity of men, wives must be ruled by their husbands, but Paul rejects this notion, recognizing the full dignity of everyone in the people of God.

Second, the church as God's New Humanity is ordered under the lordship of Jesus Christ. This is in radical contrast to alternative political visions in which communities have Caesar at their head. According to a Roman political system, a person's social rank determined his worth. If one is closer to Caesar, he has greater value. Such a vision fostered all sorts of mistreatment and injustice. Under the lordship of Jesus Christ, no one has any greater value than anyone else. Paul reminds slave owners that they share the same Master as their slaves and are accountable for how they treat them (Eph 6:9). The treatment of slaves in the Roman Empire—and throughout history—is horrifying to consider. They had no recourse to justice.

Third, the New Humanity conducts relationships of love and honor. Again this is radically different from relationships in alternative political arrangements. Many ancient philosophers recognized that people were fallen, or at least badly motivated. Because of this, relationships needed to function from standpoints of power and manipulation. Those in positions of social or cultural weakness would need to gain a foothold of power through manipulation. If they complied with those in authority, it was only a calculated response to avoid punishment. And those in authority would rule through domination, exploitation and oppression.

But such relational strategies have no place in the church. We are to adopt cruciform postures toward one another. God's new people are to love and honor others, give themselves for the sake of others and operate through weakness and cruciformity. Even those in authority must care for those for whom they are responsible. If there are relationships of power, then those with a superior position must use their power *on behalf of* others, not *against* them. Love and justice, not manipulation and exploitation, are to flow along relational networks. When a community conducts itself with justice—with God's justice—then that community faithfully embodies the divine warrior on earth, giving glory to God in the cosmic realm.

We can't leave this section without noting that many modern ethicists have trouble with Paul's vision of human relationships in the household code. Most obviously, Paul does not call for the overthrow of slavery, and he maintains the cultural hierarchy in marriage. Can we really say that Paul's political vision is radically redemptive when he maintains relationships of inequality? We need to note carefully what Paul does here. His ethical vision does not transform first-century corruptions with post–Enlightenment solutions. To judge Paul based on a cultural and ethical situation two millennia removed from his situation is quite unfair. Paul addresses his contemporary context and transforms the structures as he encounters them. While he doesn't call for the overthrow of societal structures, he does demand that structures operate with justice so that people in every social station are treated with dignity. The gospel of Jesus Christ enters the first-century situation and transforms it. We read Ephesians faithfully when we read it to gain wisdom for how the gospel seeks to enter our situation to transform it.

CONCLUSION

Paul's adoption of divine warfare rhetoric in Ephesians fully resonates with God's mission to redeem the world, driven by his overpowering love. It also reflects the counter—cultural character of the people of God throughout Scripture. God's people have always been called to embody his love for the world by adopting postures of self-giving love toward outsiders and cultivating relationships of cruciform love toward one another. Those outside the Christian faith who react with alarm at the strident rhetoric and militant aggression displayed by professing Christians are right to call such rhetoric into question. As I have shown, such uses of language and imagery borrowed from Scripture are highly inappropriate. Further, misusing Scripture in this way puts those who do so in the precarious position of those against whom the "Lord of armies" executes his judgment.

6

VENGEANCE, WRATH AND WARFARE AS IMAGES OF DIVINE JUSTICE IN JOHN'S APOCALYPSE

Alan S. Bandy

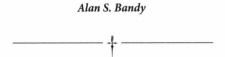

JOHN'S APOCALYPSE IS EASILY THE MOST VIOLENT BOOK of the New Testament. No other book in the New Testament is filled with imagery depicting scenes of carnage, destruction and death on an epic scale. What is more, it vividly attributes the most severe scenes of immolation to the vengeance of God displayed in an outpouring of divine warfare and wrath. As the blood readily flows throughout the pages of this vision, it provokes the senses, engages the mind and forces us to ask probing questions about the nature and purpose of such violence. It is little wonder that historically the book of Revelation has been notoriously difficult to interpret and often resulted with some aberrant radical group convinced that they will usher the Apocalypse. Other readers have shunned the violence as contrary to the ethics of Jesus and either rejected the Apocalypse or opted for nonviolent interpretations. This essay will examine the language and imagery of vengeance, wrath and divine warfare as essential to the theology, ethics and purpose of the book. It will be argued that John is writing in response to the brutality and injustice of the Roman Empire as perceived by marginalized Christians who need assurance that God's justice will ultimately prevail through retribution and recompense. As such, divine wrath and warfare is not arbitrary but central to the question of divine justice.

CRYING VENGEANCE AND DIVINE JUSTICE (REVELATION 6:9-11)

While the local religious and political climate of each city varied, John, as one who experienced unjust exile, wrote to believers feeling some sense of injustice (Rev 1:9). Believers might succumb to despair over the triumph of a corrupt justice system that condemns the innocent in some way stemming from their faith and practice. John's vision, however, assuages these fears by depicting the eventual reversal of this miscarriage of justice. This concern for justice and vindication is voiced by the cry of the martyred souls under the altar (Rev 6:9-11; 16:7).

When Jesus breaks open the fifth seal, John sees a group of souls under the altar (Rev 6:9). The altar resides in heaven and reappears throughout the Apocalypse in connection with the execution of divine justice through judgment (Rev 6:9; 8:3, 5; 9:13; 14:18; 16:7). It most likely represents the altar of incense due to its location before the throne and its connection with the prayers of the saints (Rev 8:3, cf. Rev 8:6).[1] These souls were murdered. The term indicating their death, ἐσφαγμένων, was used to describe Jesus as the slain Lamb (ἐσφαγμένον) in Revelation 5:6. This term also occurs in Revelation to indicate any form of brutal murder that humans inflict on one another (Rev 6:4; 13:3, 8; 18:24). Here it forms an associative link between the murder of these souls and the crucifixion of Jesus.[2] The reason they were executed was because of (διά) the word of God and because of (διά) the testimony they had maintained.[3]

Variations of the phrase, "the word of God and the testimony of Jesus,"

---

[1]J. P. Heil, "The Fifth Seal (Rev 6, 9–11) as a Key to the Book of Revelation," *Bib* 74 (1993): 224. That the souls are under the altar is reminiscent of Lev 4:7. See Pierre Prigent, *Commentary on the Apocalypse of St. John*, trans. Wendy Pradel (Tübingen: Mohr Siebeck, 2004), p. 273; George B. Caird, *The Revelation of Saint John*, BNTC (Peabody, MA: Hendrickson, 1966/1999), p. 84; Craig S. Keener, *Revelation*, NIVAC (Grand Rapids: Zondervan, 2000), p. 218. However, one may detect a stronger thematic parallel with Lev 17:11 (LXX) based on the shared lexical occurrences of the ψυχὴ, θυσιαστήριον, αἷμα. See Stephen Pattemore, *The People of God in the Apocalypse: Discourse, Structure, and Exegesis*, SNTS 128 (Cambridge: Cambridge University Press, 2004), p. 77.

[2]Prigent, *Commentary on the Apocalypse*, p. 273.

[3]Grant R. Osborne, *Revelation*, BECNT (Grand Rapids: Baker, 2002), p. 285. Compare Isbon T. Beckwith, *The Apocalypse of John: Studies in Introduction with A Critical and Exegetical Commentary* (London: Macmillan, 1919; repr., Grand Rapids: Baker, 1967), p. 526; R. H. Charles, *The Revelation of St. John*, vol. 1, ICC (New York: Charles Scribner's Sons, 1920), p. 174; Robert H. Mounce, *The Book of Revelation*, NICNT (Grand Rapids: Eerdmans, 1977), p. 147; David E. Aune, *Revelation 6–16*, WBC 52B (Nashville: Thomas Nelson, 1998), p. 406.

occur four times throughout the Apocalypse. Every instance pertains to the persecution of Christians with varying degrees of intensity (Rev 1:2, 9; 6:9; 12:17; 20:4; cf. 14:12). Undoubtedly this group would include Antipas (Rev 2:13), victims of the Neronic persecution, as well as any other Christians killed because of their faith in Christ, but it may also include all of God's people who died as a result of their faith.[4] These souls, then, represent witnesses in a lawsuit against the nations, because instead of taking matters into their own hands they present their case to the ultimate judge. They represent the plaintiffs in a wrongful death lawsuit pleading their case in the divine court, demanding that justice be served on their behalf through his retributive vengeance (Rev 6:10).

These martyrs cry out in a loud voice inquiring as to how long until he renders a verdict in their behalf and thereby avenges them (κρίνεις καὶ ἐκδικεῖς). Although it is possible to see their plea as a vindictive cry for vengeance[5] or a question of theodicy,[6] contextually it is best to take it as an appeal for justice through judgment.[7] The imagery of Christians demanding vengeance has caused some scholars to reject these passages as antithetical to the Christian ethic of love and forgiveness.[8] The theology here is about the question of ultimate justice and not personal retaliation. These souls demand justice because their blood was unjustly shed (cf. Ps 78:2; Zech 1:12 LXX).

The verb κρίνω ("I judge") occurs in various forms in Revelation 6:10;

---

[4]Heinz Giessen, *Die Offenbarung des Johannes*, RNT (Regensburg: Friedrich Pustet, 1997), p. 183.

[5]Charles, *Revelation*, 1:175; Martin Kiddle, *The Revelation of St. John*, MNTC (London: Hodder and Stoughton, 1940), p. 119; J. Massyngberde Ford, *Revelation*, AB (New York: Doubleday, 1977), p. 4; William Klassen, "Vengeance in the Apocalypse of John, *CBQ* 28 (1966): 300-311; A. Y. Collins, "Persecution and Vengeance in the Book of Revelation," in *Apocalypticism in the Mediterranean World*, ed. David Hellholm (Tübingen: J. C. B. Mohr [Paul Siebeck], 1983), pp. 729-50.

[6]Mounce, *Revelation*, p. 158; Elisabeth Schüssler Fiorenza, *The Book of Revelation: Justice and Judgment*, 2nd ed. (Minneapolis: Fortress, 1998), p. 64; Jürgen Roloff, *The Revelation of John: A Continental Commentary*, trans. John E. Alsup (Minneapolis: Fortress, 1993), p. 90.

[7]Aune, *Revelation 6–16*, pp. 407-10; Greg K. Beale, *The Book of Revelation*, NIGTC (Grand Rapids: Eerdmans, 1999), p. 392; Prigent, *Commentary on the Apocalypse*, p. 275; Osborne, *Revelation*, p. 287; Caird, *The Revelation of St. John*, pp. 84-85; Keener, *Revelation*, p. 218; Richard Bauckham, *The Climax of Prophecy: Studies on the Book of Revelation* (London: T&T Clark, 1993), pp. 48-56; Pattemore, *People of God in the Apocalypse*, p. 84.

[8]Charles, *Revelation*, 1:175; Kiddle, *The Revelation of St. John*, p. 119; Ford, *Revelation*, p. 4; Klassen, "Vengeance in the Apocalypse of John," pp. 300-311; Collins, "Persecution and Vengeance in the Book of Revelation," pp. 729-50.

11:18; 16:5; 18:8, 20; 19:2, 11; 20:12, 13. The first occurrence, in Revelation 6:10, plays a determinative role for all the subsequent uses.[9] Osborne states, "This verb functions as a prelude to the rest of the book as God pours out his judgment on 'those who dwell on the earth.'"[10] The additional occurrences of κρίνω in Revelation 16:5-7, 18:20 and 19:2 all directly refer back to the plea of the souls in Revelation 6:9-10 to indicate God's answer to their prayers for justice and vindication.[11]

John's use of ἐκδικέω ("I avenge" or "I vindicate") stems from the concept of justice prevalent throughout the Old Testament.[12] Several Old Testament passages provide background examples of God avenging the blood of his people (Ps 79:10; Hos 1:4; Is 26:21; Deut 32:43). Numerous Old Testament passages provide conceptual backgrounds for Revelation 6:10: (1) oppressed saints often ask God how long will it be until he acts in their behalf (Ps 6:3; 13:1-2; 35:17; 74:10; 94:3; 119:84; Hab 1:2-3); (2) the idea of blood crying out for justice (Gen 4:10; Job 16:18; Ps 9:12; cf. Mt 23:35; Lk 11:51); (3) prayers for divine vengeance (2 Sam 3:28-39; 2 Kings 1:10, 12; Neh 4:4-5; Jer 11:20; 15:15; 17:18; 18:21-23; 20:12; Amos 7:17); and (4) the general tenor of imprecatory prayers whereby an innocent one appeals to God for retribution against his enemies (Psalms 7; 35; 55; 58; 59; 69; 79; 83; 109; 138; 139).

In Revelation 6:10, however, John specifically alludes to Psalm 79[78]:10 and Deuteronomy 32:43, but it appears that Psalm 79:10 echoes Deuteronomy 32:43.[13] In Deuteronomy 32:43, the Song of Moses promises that God will exact vengeance on those who have harmed his people. One may easily observe a clear allusion between οὐ κρίνεις καὶ ἐκδικεῖς τὸ αἷμα ἡμῶν ("will you not judge and avenge our blood") (Rev 6:10) and ὅτι τὸ αἷμα τῶν

---

[9]Heil, "The Fifth Seal," pp. 220-22. His article utilizes "verbal repetitions and conceptual correlations to demonstrate the interrelationship between Rev 6, 9–11 and the rest of the book. The extensive connections will illustrate how the opening of the fifth seal functions as a key part within a unified whole." Cf. André Feuillet, "Les martyrs de l'humanité et l'Agneau égorgé. Une interprétation nouvelle de la prière des égorgés en Ap 6, 9-11," *NRT* 99 (1977): pp. 189-207; Pattemore, *People of God in the Apocalypse*, pp. 68-116.

[10]Osborne, *Revelation*, p. 287. See also Pattemore, *People of God in the Apocalypse*, p. 85. He argues that κρίνω is frequently used of action of God or Christ (Cf. Rev 11:18; 16:15; 18:8, 20; 19:2; 20:12, 13; 19:11).

[11]Cf. Caird, *Revelation of St. John*, pp. 228-30; Keener, *Revelation*, pp. 431-34.

[12]Used to translate the Hebrew terms נקם, פקד, and שפט. See Joel Nobel Musvosvi, *Vengeance in the Apocalypse*, AUSDDS 17 (Berrien Springs, MI: Andrews University Press, 1993), pp. 37-148.

[13]Beale, *Book of Revelation*, p. 393; Pattemore, *The People of God in the Apocalypse*, p. 84n78.

υἱῶν αὐτοῦ ἐκδικᾶται καὶ ἐκδικήσει ("he will avenge the blood of his sons and he will take vengeance") (Deut 32:43 LXX). In addition, both passages pertain to God vindicating his people who were wrongfully persecuted. The mention of the martyrs' blood (τὸ αἷμα ἡμῶν) makes their request for justice in accordance with the divine law of *lex talionis* (Deut 19:21). This is also echoed in Jewish apocalyptic writings which frequently depict similar scenes of appeals to God for justice.[14] The Song of Moses promises that God will vindicate his saints and exact wrathful vengeance against the wicked in due time. John N. Day contends that Deuteronomy 32 constitutes the theological foundation for the theme of divine justice through vengeance, which had direct implications for the book of Revelation:

> Moreover, the Song of Moses has an ongoing prophetic function. It is a witness to the ongoing covenant of God with his people—the application of which carries through the end of the canon. Through the canon, the cry for divine vengeance for the blood of saints is raised until [*sic*] Revelation 6:9-10, and in 19:1-2, those gathered around the throne rejoice in its accomplishment. This prophetic nature illustrates both the primary and secondary purpose of the Song. It is primarily a witness against Israel for their rebellions. . . . Secondarily it is a testimony to the faithfulness of God in the face of his people's faithlessness, including his faithfulness in taking vengeance against oppressors (cf. Deut 32:4, 31-43).[15]

The language of vengeance in Deuteronomy 32:43 is the backbone of the imprecatory prayers.[16] These prayers represent the way in which suffering saints expressed their trust in the justice of God who will avenge them. John's Apocalypse continues this theme of divine justice through retributive vengeance in accordance to the *lex talionis* because God will render judgments based on what people deserve (Rev 18:6; 20:12).

Joel N. Musvosvi's dissertation on the concept of vengeance in the Apocalypse aims to present a thematic study of the vengeance motif in Revelation in light of the Old Testament and Ancient Near East literature.[17] The problem

---

[14]See also Charles, *The Revelation of St. John*, 1:176; Aune, *Revelation 6–16*, pp. 408-9; Keener, *Revelation*, p. 218.

[15]John N. Day, *Crying for Justice: What the Psalms Teach Us About Mercy and Vengeance in an Age of Terrorism* (Grand Rapids: Kregel, 2005), p. 56.

[16]Ibid., p. 107.

[17]Musvosvi, *Vengeance in the Apocalypse*, p. 1.

he attempts to address relates to how the attitude of vengeance corresponds to the New Testament ethic of love and mercy toward one's enemies. His analysis of the Hebrew and Greek words for vengeance offers a covenantal view for interpreting the concept of vengeance. The term נקם and its cognates occur in at least seventy-eight passages in the Old Testament.[18] Musvosvi examines each instance and demonstrates its connection to the covenant and covenantal lawsuit.[19] His survey reveals that the dominant use of vengeance describes God as the avenger against those who attack Israel or covenantal violators.[20] Vengeance in the Apocalypse, according to Musvosvi, directly relates to the suffering and persecution of God's covenant people. He argues that in the Old Testament God exercised vengeance on Israel's oppressors as a means of protecting his covenant people.[21]

The martyrs request the vengeance to be directed at the τῶν κατοικούντων ἐπὶ τῆς γῆς ("the inhabitants of the earth").[22] The phrase οἱ κατοικοῦντες ἐπὶ τῆς γῆς denotes the objects of wrath in the Apocalypse (Rev 3:10; 6:10; 8:13; 11:10; 13:8, 14; 17:2, 8). This group is consistently set in juxtaposition to the saints. The inhabitants of the earth are the ones responsible for the execution of the saints (Rev 6:10), and they will subsequently be recipients of God's wrath. With the breaking of the sixth seal, they seek to hide due to their dread and terror of the coming wrath of God and the Lamb (Rev 6:13-17). Nothing in that fear indicates repentance from their wickedness; rather it implies they recognize that their guilt deserves punishment.

This plea for justice through vindication receives an initial answer assuring the martyrs that judgment is coming, but not until the predetermined number of martyrs reaches completion (Rev 6:11). The notion of a set number to reach fulfillment, especially in response to the "how long" question, represents a fairly common theme in Apocalyptic writings (cf.

---

[18]Ibid., p. 47.

[19]Ibid., pp. 47-131.

[20]Ibid., pp. 130-31.

[21]Ibid., p. 149. On page 153, he highlights the common pattern associated with persecution and vengeance: (1) Covenant broken by Israel; (2) God exacts vengeance on the covenant violators, usually by sending foreign armies; (3) the call for and performing of repentance on Israel's part; and (4) God brings vengeance upon those who shed Israel's blood.

[22]Ronald Herms, *An Apocalypse for the Church and for the World: The Narrative Function of Universal Language in the Book of Revelation*, BZNW 143 (Berlin: de Gruyter, 2006), pp. 185-201.

1 En 47:1-4; *4 Ezra* 4:35-37; *2 Bar* 23:4-5a).[23] In this context, the souls must
rest and wait until the remaining number of their brothers in Christ joins
them. By stating that additional believers will surrender their lives in
faithful testimony to Christ, John's audience should realize that they very
well could be included in that number (Rev 12:11; 13:7-10).[24] This corresponds with the theme that the way to victory for believers is the way of the
Lamb via martyrdom.[25] The theme of justice and vindication for the martyred souls resurfaces as a central component in the execution of divine
judgment against the nations—especially as it relates to the trumpet and
bowl judgments (Rev 8:3-5; 16:7).

INITIATING THE DIVINE ANSWER TO THE PLEA FOR JUSTICE (REVELATION 8:1-5)

Revelation 8:1-5 establishes a relationship between the seven seals and the
seven trumpets by means of interlocking.[26] John uses the device of interlocking to transition from the seals to the trumpets, but it also intimately
connects the succeeding trumpet judgments with the preceding seals. The
breaking of the seventh seal immediately results in silence for about half an
hour followed by the introduction of the seven angels and the trumpets
given to them. This scene demonstrates that the ensuing judgments are directly related to the martyrs' plea for vindication in Revelation 6:9-11.

The interconnectedness between the martyrs' plea and the trumpet judgments is made explicit with the emphasis on the altar and the offering up of
the saints' prayers. Revelation 8:1-5 represents the initiation of the sequence
of judgments that will ultimately accomplish the full outpouring of God's
retribution for the blood of his saints. The most obvious connection to the
martyrs of Revelation 6:9-11 is that the altar once again takes center stage.
Due to the lack of any other altar mentioned in the heavenly courtroom,
this seems to be the same one containing the souls of the slain saints.[27]

---

[23]Bauckham, *Climax of Prophecy*, pp. 48-56. See also Giesen, *Die Offenbarung des Johannes*, p. 185.

[24]Pattemore, *The People of God in the Apocalypse*, p. 89.

[25]Caird, *The Revelation to Saint John*, p. 87.

[26]Adela Yarbro Collins, *The Combat Myth in the Book of Revelation* (Eugene, OR: Wipf & Stock, 2001), p. 17.

[27]Charles, *Revelation to St. John*, 1:227.

An angel standing at the altar holding a golden censer is given a large amount of incense for the purpose of offering up the prayers of all the saints. Although these prayers generally include all the prayers offered by every saint throughout history, as indicated by the phrase "all the saints," the only contextual antecedent is the petition of the slaughtered souls. Interestingly, the request of the souls constitutes the only explicit example of prayer in the Apocalypse.[28] The act of offering the prayers indicates that the petition of Revelation 6:10 "is now being formally presented before God with angelic favor and authority."[29]

The answer to the request for vindication is symbolically portrayed in Revelation 8:5. The angel uses a censer that once held the incense to scoop up the fiery coals from the altar to hurl it toward the earth. The use of ἔβαλεν ("he cast out") conveys the sense of a forceful action and evokes a sense of anger and wrath. It is as if the verdict of guilt has been reached and now the angels are permitted to sound their trumpets after an anticipated delay (cf. Rev 7:1-3; 8:1). What follows is a series of successive trumpet blasts with dire consequences for the earth's inhabitants but, remarkably, they still refuse to repent (Rev 9:20-21). The last trumpet signals the consummation of God's wrath in that it introduces the seven bowl judgments that destroy life on earth (Rev 16:1-21). By developing the theme of the prayer for vindication from Revelation 6:9-11, Revelation 8:1-5 explicitly connects the wrath of God with the prayers for vindication from the martyred saints.

GOD'S PEOPLE ENGAGED IN HOLY WAR (REVELATION 12:1–15:8)

An interlude appears between the sounding of the seventh trumpet (Rev 11:15-19) and the introduction of the seven bowls containing the final judgments (Rev 15:5-8). This interlude tells the story of a war between Satan and God via his war against the saints. The dragon, Satan (Rev 12:9), attempts to destroy a beautiful woman in the sky with her unborn child (Rev 12:3-4). The pregnant woman represents Israel through whom the messiah would come.[30] The language used to describe the rule of her son indicates that he

---

[28]Cf. Heil, "The Fifth Seal as a Key to the Book of Revelation," p. 224.

[29]Beale, *Book of Revelation*, p. 455.

[30]On the interpretation of the woman as Israel and/or the messianic community see Stephen S. Smalley, *The Revelation to John: A Commentary on the Greek Text of the Apocalypse* (Downers Grove, IL: InterVarsity Press, 2005), pp. 314-15; Edmondo F. Lupieri, *A Commentary on the*

is Jesus—the Davidic Messiah (cf. Rev 19:15; Ps 2:9). After the child ascends to heaven and the woman flees to the desert for 1,260 days, a war in heaven ensues between Michael and Satan. Michael expels Satan and his rebellious angels out of heaven by casting him down to the earth (Rev 12:7-9). Caird perceptively captures the legal and militaristic nature of this struggle when he remarks, "The real victory of Michael may be a forensic one, the victory of an advocate whose case is wholly dependent on the record of his client; but it takes open war to clinch it."[31]

The conflict between Satan and God's people in Revelation 12:10-17 is a continuation of this war and legal battle. Immediately upon Satan's defeat and prior to his war against the Christians, a loud voice in heaven announces the victory of God and his people in litigation with Satan the accuser (Rev 12:10-12). The point is that victory in war results from victory in God's courtroom.[32] The dragon's identity is confirmed as Satan (ὁ Σατανᾶς) in Revelation 12:9, but in Revelation 12:10 his role is described as the accuser (ὁ κατήγωρ) who brings charges against God's people. The term ὁ Σατανᾶς comes from the Hebrew form of שָׂטָן,[33] which basically carries the sense of a legal "adversary."[34]

Although Satan brings accusations against the saints, in Revelation 12:11 they are assured of certain victory because they overcame him (ἐνίκησαν αὐτόν). The means of their victory is not military might but through faithful testimony to Christ. John states that they overcame Satan on three grounds (διά). First, because the blood of the Lamb (τὸ αἷμα τοῦ ἀρνίου) has re-

---

Apocalypse of John, trans. Maria Poggi Johnson and Adam Kamesar (Grand Rapids: Eerdmans, 1999), p. 189; Osborne, *Revelation*, pp. 457-8; Keener, *Revelation*, p. 314; J. Ramsey Michaels, *Revelation*, IVPNTC (Downers Grove, IL: InterVarsity Press, 1997), p. 148; Mounce, *Revelation*, p. 236; Collins, *Combat Myth*, pp. 106-7. Prigent argues that she represents the church that has "taken root in the history of Israel" (Prigent, *Commentary on the Apocalypse*, p. 378). Beale, however, more correctly identifies her as representative of the faithful community of God's people both before and after the coming of Christ (Beale, *Book of Revelation*, p. 625). For a survey of additional interpretations of the identity of the woman see Aune, *Revelation 6–16*, pp. 679-82. On the relationship between this woman and the New Jerusalem in contrast to the harlot see Paul B. Duff, *Who Rides the Beast?: Prophetic Rivalry and the Rhetoric of Crisis in the Churches of the Apocalypse* (Oxford: Oxford University Press, 2001), pp. 83-96.

[31]Caird, *Revelation of Saint John*, p. 157.

[32]Osborne, *Revelation*, p. 475.

[33]The devil is only called Satan in 1 Chronicles, Job and Zechariah.

[34]Cf. Num 22:22, 32; 11:14, 23, 25; 1 Chron 21:1; Job 1:6-9, 12; 2:1-4, 6-7; Ps 71:13; 109:4, 6, 20, 29; Zech 3:1, 2.

deemed them from their sin (cf. Rev 1:5-6). Second, because they maintained faithful testimony to Jesus (τὸν λόγον τῆς μαρτυρίας αὐτῶν) even while suffering (cf. Rev 6:9; 11:7). The third phrase, "they did not love their lives to the point of death" (οὐκ ἠγάπησαν τὴν ψυχὴν αὐτῶν ἄχρι θανάτου), indicates that their faithfulness to Christ surpassed even their desire for self-preservation. By connecting their testimony with their death, John associates them with the slain souls under the altar making an appeal for true justice (Rev 6:9-10).[35] The point of the proclamation in Revelation 12:10-12, then, reminds John's audience that the way of victory is the way of the slain Lamb.[36]

Once the dragon plummets to the earth he continues with his vehement assault on the people of God (Rev 12:13-17). In his rage, the dragon declares war (ἀπῆλθεν ποιῆσαι πόλεμον) against the rest of the woman's offspring. In Revelation 12:17, John identifies these offspring with two phrases that clearly designate them as Christians. The woman's offspring are those who observe God's commands and have the testimony of Jesus. The dragon enlists the aid of two beasts in order to execute his war against the saints (Rev 13:1-18).[37] The beast from the sea (Rev 13:1-8) may represent the brute force of the political and military power of Rome, but he is commonly recognized as the Antichrist.[38]

The beast was granted the authority to speak blasphemously and to reign for forty-two months. The use of ἐδόθη ("it was given") emphasizes God's sovereignty over the Antichrist and his actions.[39] In Revelation 13:7, the beast is given authority to wage a war against the saints and conquer them (ἐδόθη αὐτῷ ποιῆσαι πόλεμον μετὰ τῶν ἁγίων καὶ νικῆσαι αὐτούς; cf. Dan 7:25; Rev 11:7). Although Revelation 12:11 explicitly states that the saints will ultimately conquer Satan (ἐνίκησαν αὐτὸν), during this time of war they may face physical death (νικῆσαι αὐτούς). This miscarriage of justice continues as all the inhabitants of the earth worship the beast (Rev 13:8) and the false prophet (i.e., the land beast) mandates forced idolatry by executing offenders and instituting economic restrictions (Rev 13:11-17). As Satan pro-

---

[35]Beale, *Book of Revelation*, pp. 665-66.

[36]Osborne, *Revelation*, p. 476.

[37]Giesen, *Die Offenbarung des Johannes*, p. 270.

[38]Bauckham, *Climax of Prophecy*, p. 343. See also Beale, *Book of Revelation*, pp. 682-85; Roloff, *Revelation*, pp. 155-57.

[39]Osborne, *Revelation*, p. 498.

ceeds to execute his war against the saints on earth, the subsequent slaughter of the righteous would make it appear that Satan has indeed triumphed through this injustice.

John inserts a brief prophetic admonition for the saints in Revelation 13:9-10. The unjust and merciless onslaught against believers may tempt them either to retaliate or to conform, but John encourages them to remain faithful as they patiently endure captivity and possible execution (cf. Jer 15:2). By responding to this oppression with patient endurance, they place the judgment of their enemies in the hands of God and the Lamb (cf. Rev 6:10).[40] Revelation 15:3-4 offers a glimpse of their victory with the imagery of a group of the redeemed who overcame (τοὺς νικῶντας) the beast, his image and his number. The redeemed saints, then, worship the rightful Lord and king of the nations because all his ways are "just and true."

Justifying the Severity of Divine Wrath (Revelation 16:4-7; 17:1-6; 18:1-8)

Revelation 16 describes how the seven bowls, containing the wine of God's wrath, are poured out on the inhabitants of the earth. The objects of this wrath are identified as everyone with the mark of the beast that worshiped his image (Rev 16:2). This would most likely include all the inhabitants of the earth in juxtaposition to the people of God (Rev 13:8). The bowls represent the answer to the prayer of Revelation 6:9-11 as explicitly affirmed in the judgment doxology of Revelation 16:5-7.[41]

The pouring out of the third bowl in Revelation 16:4 transforms all fresh water into blood. Although it echoes the first exodus plague (Ex 7:17-21), it represents a far more serious plague due to its global impact. It is a plague that deprives all life on earth from drinkable water and forces them to consume blood out of thirsty desperation. At this point, the pattern of pouring out the bowls is interrupted with brief but profound doxological statements affirming the justice of God inherent in this harsh judgment.

This judgment doxology provides two declarations affirming the justness of God's judgment. The angel of the waters declares God as just/

---

[40]Ibid., p. 161.

[41]So Pattemore, *The People of God in the Apocalypse*, p. 99. He creatively calls this a "progress report" on God's activity regarding his answer to this prayer.

righteous (δίκαιος εἶ).[42] Two ὅτι clauses provide the basis or cause for this declaration.[43] God is just *because* "he judged them" (ταῦτα ἔκρινας). The use of the plural "them" suggests that "waters" are the object of the divine judgment. The angel in charge of the waters acknowledges the righteousness of God's judgment by turning the waters into blood. The second ὅτι clause further explains the reason why this judgment is appropriate by evoking the law of retribution (*lex talionis*). This judgment is just because they (i.e., the earth's inhabitants collectively) have poured out (ἐξέχεαν) the blood (αἷμα) of the saints and prophets. God has avenged the blood (αἷμα) of his witnesses (Rev 6:10) by forcing the inhabitants of the earth to drink blood (cf. Deut 32:43; 2 Kings 19:10; Ps 79:10).[44] The ironic use of ἄξιοί ("worthy," cf. Rev 3:4) indicates that the punishment fits the crime and they got what they deserved.

The second witness to testify to the justness of this judgment is a voice that comes from the altar containing the souls of the martyrs (Rev 16:7).[45] The connection of this judgment with the martyrs' plea for vindication is now made explicit when this voice exuberantly affirms the angel's declaration. The phrase, "true and just" (ἀληθιναὶ καὶ δίκαιαι) constitutes an allusion to the Song of Moses and the Lamb sung by the victorious saints in Revelation 15:3. In that context it specifically describes the ways of God (αἱ ὁδοί σου). It occurs again in Revelation 19:2 (ἀληθιναὶ καὶ δίκαιαι αἱ κρίσεις αὐτοῦ) affirming God's judgments as in Revelation 16:7. Significantly, these declarations come from the mouths of the redeemed saints who now praise God for the acts of retribution accomplished in their behalf.

The next set of images providing justification for the severity and finality of divine wrath relates to the judgment of Babylon. After the last bowl is emptied, one of the angels holding a bowl came to John and invited him to a closer look at the judgment (τὸ κρίμα) of the great prostitute (Rev 17:1-

---

[42]The theme of a holy God who is just and righteous is a major thrust in the Song of Moses (cf. Deut 32:2, 4).

[43]Daniel Wallace, *Greek Grammar Beyond the Basics: An Exegetical Syntax of the New Testament* (Grand Rapids: Zondervan, 1997), p. 674. So Aune, *Revelation 6–16*, p. 856; Beale, *Book of Revelation*, p. 818; Smalley, *Revelation to John*, p. 403.

[44]Paul B. Decock, "The Symbol of Blood in the Apocalypse of John," *Neotestamentica* 38 (2004): 171-78.

[45]The genitive τοῦ θυσιαστηρίου is most likely a partitive genitive meaning that someone from the altar spoke instead of the altar itself speaking. Smalley, *Revelation to John*, p. 404.

2).[46] John, then, beheld a great prostitute sitting astride the seven-headed beast and drunk on the blood of the saints (Rev 17:3-6). She personifies the city Rome with her military might, opulence and allurement.[47] But she may also be more broadly conceived of as the world system evident in all great earthly civilizations like Babylon and Rome.[48]

John paints a verbal portrait of the prostitute city that sparkles with facets highlighting her political power, economic extravagance and religious devotion.[49] In Revelation 17:1-6, he evokes a sense of disgust regarding the lewd and immoral character of Babylon by describing her as a prostitute.[50] She entices the earth's inhabitants to forsake truth, righteousness and justice in order to indulge in her flagrant adulteries consisting of idolatry,

---

[46]John ultimately juxtaposes the destiny of the harlot city Babylon with the bride city of the New Jerusalem. On the use of contrasting feminine imagery, see Gordon Campbell, "Antithetical Feminine-Urban Imagery and a Tale of Two Women-Cities in the Book of Revelation," *TynBul* 55 (2004): 81-108; Barbara Rossing, *The Choice Between Two Cities: Whore, Bride, and Empire in the Apocalypse*, HTR 48 (Harrisburg, PA: Trinity Press International, 1999), pp. 61-165; Daria Pezzoli-Olgiati, "Zwischen Gericht und Heil: Frauengestalten in der Johannesoffenbarung," *BZ* 43.1 (1999): 72-91; Eva Maria Räpple, "The City in Revelation," *TBT* 34 (November 1996): 359-65; Marla J. Selvidge, "Powerful and Powerless Women in the Apocalypse," *Neot* 26.1 (1992): 157-67; J. Edgar Bruns, "The Contrasted Women of Apocalypse 12 and 17," *CBQ* 26 (1964): 459-63.

[47]The personified figure of Rome seated as a queen may correspond to common conceptions of the goddess Roma. See Bauckham, *Climax of Prophecy*, pp. 343-50; Aune, *Revelation 17-22*, pp. 920-22, 929-30; Beale, *Book of Revelation*, p. 854; Osborne, *Revelation*, p. 608; Smalley, *Revelation to John*, pp. 428-31; Prigent, *Commentary on the Apocalypse*, p. 492; Lupieri, *Commentary on the Apocalypse of John*, p. 271; John M. Court, *Myth and History in the Book of Revelation* (Atlanta: John Knox Press, 1979), p. 125; Caird, *Revelation of Saint John*, p. 216; Roloff, *Revelation*, pp. 196-201; Mounce, *Revelation*, p. 310; G. R. Beasley-Murray, *The Book of Revelation*, NCB (Grand Rapids: Eerdmans, 1981), pp. 256-57; Henry Barclay Swete, *Commentary on Revelation* (Grand Rapids: Kregel, 1977), pp. 210-15; Beckwith, *The Apocalypse of John*, p. 698; Adela Yarbro Collins, "Revelation 18: Taunt-Song or Dirge?," in *L'Apocalypse johannique et l'Apocalyptique dans le Nouveau Testament*, ed. Jan Lambrecht (Leuven: Leuven University Press, 1980), p. 200; K. Kuhn, "Βαβυλών," *TDNT*, I:514-17. Contra Ford, *Revelation*, pp. 282-88; Eugenio Corsini, *The Apocalypse: The Perennial Revelation of Jesus Christ*, trans. Francis J. Moloney, GNS (Wilmington, DE: Michael Glazier, 1983), p. 200; D. Holwerda, "Ein Neuer Schlüssel zum 17. Kapitel der johanneischen Offenbarung," *EstBib* 53, no. 3 (1995): 389-91; Iain Provan, "Foul Spirits, Fornication and Finance: Revelation 18 from an Old Testament Perspective," *JSNT* 64 (1996): 81-100.

[48]Judith Kovacs and Christopher Rowland, *Revelation* (Oxford: Blackwell, 2004), pp. 178-89; Ian Boxall, "The Many Faces of Babylon the Great: Wirkungsgeschichte and the Interpretation of Revelation 17," in *Studies in the Book of Revelation*, ed. Steve Moyise (Edinburgh: T & T Clark, 2001), pp. 54-55; M. Eugene Boring, *Revelation*, Interpretation (Louisville: John Knox Press, 1989), p. 184; Kiddle, *Revelation*, p. 187.

[49]Boxall, *Revelation of Saint John*, p. 242.

[50]Keener, *Revelation*, p. 404.

greed and murder.[51] But it is the golden cup in her hand in Revelation 17:4 that provides the most incriminating evidence against her.[52] Her cup symbolically represents her ability to maintain control of and corrupt the world with the wine of her immorality through religious idolatry (Rev 14:8; cf. Rev 16:19). With the wine in this cup, according to Revelation 17:2, she has made all the nations drunk.

The cup is filled with "abominations" (βδελυγμάτων) described as the "filth of her fornication" (τὰ ἀκάθαρτα τῆς πορνείας αὐτῆς). Although the term βδελυγμάτων generally denotes anything abhorrent, it is most commonly associated with pagan practices and worship.[53] This idea is made even more explicit with the use of ἀκάθαρτα ("impurities") especially as it relates to sexual immorality (πορνείας).[54] The religious connotation of the cup's contents conveys an even more sinister and gruesome quality to the wine, for it is apparently mixed with the blood of the saints (Rev 17:6). John indicates that she was drunk on the blood of the saints (ἐκ τοῦ αἵματος τῶν ἁγίων) and the witnesses of Jesus (ἐκ τοῦ αἵματος τῶν μαρτύρων Ἰησοῦ). While this evokes the memory of all the witnesses that were slain for their faith (Rev 2:13; 11:7; 13:7), it more specifically recalls the souls crying out for justice (Rev 6:9-10). Aune remarks that "becoming drunk on blood" was a metaphor in the Old Testament and the ancient world for the blood lust of soldiers in battle.[55] The idea, then, is that Babylon's/Rome's power, wealth and idolatry precipitated and resulted in the senseless slaughter of the faithful saints who refused to commit adultery with her.

One salient feature of this entire scene is that John has saturated this section with material drawn from Old Testament prophetic oracles per-

---

[51]The judgment of Babylon was anticipated in the earlier announcement that Babylon has fallen in Rev 14:8 and 16:19. See also Rossing, *The Choice Between Two Cities*, p. 62.

[52]John draws his imagery of Babylon and the cup from Jer 51:7. Babylon is the cup making the nations drunk. The *Targ.* Jer 51:7 compares the cup with Babylon's sin. See Beale, *The Book of Revelation*, p. 855; Rossing, *The Choice Between Two Cities*, pp. 64-65. For more on possible Old Testament backgrounds see Keener, *Revelation*, p. 405.

[53]See Werner Foerster, "βδέλυγμα," TDNT, 1:600.

[54]It specifically denotes demonic spirits leading people astray in Rev 16:3 and 18:2. See also Mounce, *Revelation*, pp. 310-11; Beale, *Book of Revelation*, pp. 855-56; Osborne, *Revelation*, p. 612; Smalley, *Revelation to John*, pp. 430-31.

[55]David E. Aune, *Revelation 17–22*, WBC 52C (Nashville: Thomas Nelson, 1998), p. 937. Cf. Osborne, *Revelation*, p. 613; Smalley, *Revelation to John*, p. 432.

taining to the judgment of the historical Babylon.[56] John has already alluded to the imagery of Babylon and the cup of judgment from Jeremiah 51:7 in Revelation 17:4. Jeremiah 50–51 essentially provides the *Vorbild* for describing the destruction of the new Babylon. He reworks the oracle of judgment against the historical Babylon in Jeremiah 50–51, however, by drawing from the taunt songs of Isaiah 23–24 and oracles against Tyre in Ezekiel 26–27.[57] John freely rearranges the material and includes oracles of judgment against several pagan cities as well as Jerusalem. This interweaving of allusions creates the effect that Babylon's judgment represents the culmination of God's judgment against all nations in terms of military, political and economic devastation. The reason God destroyed ancient Babylon and predicts the doom of the new Babylon is because the blood of his people has been found within her walls (cf. Jer 51:49; Rev 18:24).

The angelic declaration of Revelation 18:1-3 announces Babylon's fall coupled with a statement about the desolation decreed for her. The announcement of Babylon's fall reiterates Revelation 14:8 and echoes Isaiah 29:1 as an allusion to the destruction of ancient Babylon and its idols.[58] John arrogates the imagery of a desolate city inhabited by demons and carrion birds from prophetic oracles of judgment against Babylon (Is 13:21-22; Jer 50:39; 51:37), Edom (Is 34:11-14) and Nineveh (Zeph 2:14). All of these cities have violated the righteous requirements of God's law and consequently received their due penalty.[59] The new Babylon will not escape the certainty of God's justice.

Once the verdict is announced, another voice from heaven commences with Babylon's sentencing. The sentencing is characterized by a series of imperatives. The first imperative represents a preliminary order for the withdrawal of the people of God from Babylon before the execution of the final judgment. The injunction for God's people to come out of her constitutes an allusion to Jeremiah 51:6 where the prophet urges the Israelites to

---

[56]Aune, *Revelation 17–22*, p. 983; Musvosvi, *Vengeance in the Apocalypse*, p. 252; Jan Fekkes, *Isaiah and Prophetic Traditions in the Book of Revelation: Visionary Antecedents and Their Development*, JSNTSSUP 93 (Sheffield: JSOT Press, 1994), pp. 87-88.

[57]Boxall, *Revelation to Saint John*, p. 254; Keener, *Revelation*, p. 423.

[58]Fekkes, *Isaiah and Prophetic Traditions in the Book of Revelation*, pp. 204-5, 213-14. Cf. Osborne, *Revelation*, p. 635; Mounce, *Revelation*, p. 323.

[59]Osborne, *Revelation*, p. 636.

flee from Babylon because the time has come for God to exact his vengeance (ὅτι καιρὸς ἐκδικήσεως αὐτῆς ἐστιν [LXX]) for its crimes. The purpose (ἵνα) for this command is so they do not share in her sins and receive her plagues. This prophetic appeal not only implies the removal of God's people prior to Babylon's destruction, but it also compels John's audience to abstain from participating in Rome's idolatry, especially for social ease and economic prosperity.[60] An additional ὅτι clause indicates the reason for God's judgment against Babylon (Rev 18:5) in that the sinfulness of Babylon has reached maximum capacity and God must judge her for her crimes.[61] This reason comports well with the biblical notion that God waits until a city or nation reaches the full measure of sin before destruction (Gen 15:16; Jer 51:9).

The second string of imperatives comprises the actual sentence God has decreed for Babylon in accordance with her sins and crimes (Rev 18:6-7a). The imperatives are not voiced to earthly saints but rather to some undesignated agents of God's vengeance (possibly the glorified saints).[62] Four imperatives (ἀπόδοτε, διπλώσατε, κεράσατε, δότε) expressly convey the principle of *lex talionis* and divine retribution.[63] The justice of the sentence is demonstrated in that each command parallels a direct action of Babylon. God administers justice through rendering judgment warranted by the crimes committed (Jer 50:29; Ps 137:8; cf. Is 40:2). The language of paying back double constitutes a metaphor of a judge who renders a full recompense or

---

[60]Cf. Keener (*Revelation*, p. 425) posits, "This warning to flee comes in the same context as the mention that Babylon was an intoxicating cup for the nations and would be mourned ([Jer] 51:7-9). That people are still invited to escape just before the judgment reveals the greatness of God's mercy. God invites his people to leave Babylon because they have a better city."

[61]See also Aune, *Revelation 17-22*, p. 992. Regarding the idea of sins reaching heaven and God remembering as language typically reserved for prayer, Aune observes, "Here that motif is used in an ironic sense, for it is the sins that have reached heaven, analogous to the smoke of sacrifices or incense or the prayers of the worshipers, and have provoked a response."

[62]Mounce, *Revelation*, p. 325; Prigent, *Commentary on the Apocalypse*, p. 504. Contra Aune, *Revelation 17-22*, p. 994. Although he makes a strong case for taking "my people" as the most logical subject for the verbs commanding retributive justice, viewing of saints as the agents of this divine judgment seems unlikely.

[63]Aune (*Revelation 17-22*, p. 993) posits, "The principle of *lex talionis* (i.e., 'proportional retribution') from the Latin legal term *talio*, 'payment in kind' . . . and exemplified by the OT phrase 'an eye for an eye and a tooth for a tooth' . . . is a frequent motif in the prophetic judgment speeches of OT prophets (Is 34:8; 59:18; 65:6-7; Ezek 9:10; 11:21; 16:43; 17:19; 23:31; 23:49; Hos 4:9; 12:2; Joel 3:4, 7 [MT 4:4, 7]; Obad 15-16; see Prov 24:12) and early Jewish literature (Sib. Or. 3.312-14; *Apoc. Abr.* 29.19)."

requital.[64] In this sentencing, the martyrs' prayer for vindication concerning their shed blood (Rev 6:10) has been fully satisfied. Babylon unjustly condemned the saints to death and now God condemns her accordingly.[65]

Interestingly, Revelation 18:20 abruptly ends a series of laments with an imperative call exhorting God's people to rejoice (cf. Rev 12:12). The idea of saints rejoicing over the destruction of Babylon may seem a little mean spirited or vindictive, but in reality it flows out of the concern for God's justice by vindicating his righteous servants.[66] The command to rejoice may echo Jeremiah 51:48, but it is rooted theologically in Deuteronomy 32:43—the climax of the Song of Moses as evidenced by the verbal parallels between Deuteronomy 32:43a (LXX) (εὐφράνθητε οὐρανοι) and Revelation 18:20a (Εὐφραίνου ἐπ' αὐτῇ, οὐρανὲ). Both passages indicate that rejoicing is the proper response to the expressed retribution against the nations for the way they treated God's people.[67] The reason they are commanded to rejoice is because (ὅτι) God has judged her in a manner corresponding to the way she had judged them (cf. Rev 18:6).[68]

Babylon's sentencing concludes with a symbolic act depicting her complete destruction along with a final reassertion of her indictment (Rev 18:21-24). A mighty angel casts (ἔβαλεν) a large boulder the size of a millstone into the sea to demonstrate the expectation that Babylon will be cast (βληθήσεται) from the face of the earth.[69] The future verb form indicates that while there is an imminent expectation of the sentence's execution, the actual judgment will occur with the return of Christ in Revelation 19:11-21.[70]

---

[64]Osborne, *Revelation*, p. 641; Beckwith, *Apocalypse of John*, p. 715; Mounce, *Revelation*, p. 325; Prigent, *Commentary on the Apocalypse*, p. 504.

[65]Caird, *Revelation of Saint John*, pp. 227-48.

[66]Beale (*Book of Revelation*, p. 916) posits rightly that "The focus is not on delight in Babylon's suffering but on the successful outcome of God's execution of justice, which demonstrates the integrity of Christians' faith and of God's just character." Cf. Osborne, *Revelation*, p. 654; Klassen, "Vengeance in the Apocalypse," p. 304.

[67]For more parallels between Deuteronomy 32:43 and Revelation, see Beale, *Book of Revelation*, pp. 393, 666, 917, 928.

[68]Caird (*Revelation to Saint John*, pp. 227-30) argues that verse 20b is best translated as God judging Babylon because of "the sentence she passed on you." In this way, God vindicates the martyrs who were condemned by the Roman courts and it directly relates to the law of the malicious witness (Gen 9:5-6; Deut 19:16-19). Caird describes it as God reversing Babylon's sentence in the final court of appeals. Justice is accomplished when the saints are acquitted and Babylon is condemned.

[69]On the rhetorical use of paronomasia in Revelation 18:21 see Aune, *Revelation 17–22*, p. 1008.

[70]Osborne, *Revelation*, p. 656. The judgment will take place in two eschatological phases: (1) a

The finality of Babylon's destruction is also poetically recounted by the eternal absence of any music, commerce, work, lights and wedding celebrations (Rev 18:22-23a). The reason that these things will never be *found* (εὐρεθῇ) in Babylon again is because the blood of the prophets, saints and all those who have been slain was *found* (εὑρέθη) within her.[71] Not only does God judge Babylon because she has led all the nations astray (Rev 18:23b) and she has slaughtered his people (Rev 18:24a), but also because of all violence and bloodshed perpetrated on earth (Rev 18:24b).[72]

THE RETURNING WARRIOR KING AND JUDGE (REVELATION 19:11-21)

Revelation 19:1-10 functions like a bridge interlocking the preceding courtroom scene regarding the judgment of Babylon (Rev 18:1-24) with the return of Christ who carries out the sentence rendered against her (Rev 19:11-21).[73] The saints praise God for vindicating them because he has judged Babylon and avenged the blood of his servants (Rev 19:2). The heavenly multitude affirms God's judgments as both true and just (ἀληθιναὶ καὶ δίκαιαι αἱ κρίσεις αὐτοῦ), which echoes Revelation 16:7. What is more, their gratitude is warranted because God has completely answered the martyrs' plea for vindication (Rev 6:10).[74] This is confirmed by the lexical parallels (κρίνεις, ἔκρινεν and ἐκδικεῖς, ἐξεδίκησεν) between the request of Revelation 6:10 and the response of Revelation 19:2b. God has avenged the blood of his servants because they were unjustly sentenced to death at Babylon's hand.[75]

The phrase ἐξεδίκησεν τὸ αἷμα τῶν δούλων αὐτοῦ ἐκ χειρὸς αὐτῆς ("he avenged the blood of his servants from her hand") suggests an allusion to 2 Kings 9:7 [LXX], which reads ἐκδικήσεις τὰ αἵματα τῶν δούλων μου τῶν προφητῶν καὶ τὰ αἵματα πάντων τῶν δούλων κυρίου ἐκ χειρὸς Ιεζαβελ

---

civil war between the beast and the harlot (Rev 17:16); and (2) the *Parousia* (Rev 19:11-21).

[71] Collins, "Revelation 18," p. 199.

[72] Fiorenza, *Book of Revelation*, p. 7.

[73] Prigent, *Commentary on the Apocalypse*, p. 517.

[74] Beale, *Book of Revelation*, p. 928.

[75] The phrase ἐκ χειρὸς αὐτῆς represents a Hebraism and could be translated as "from her hand," "by her hand," or "at her hand." The point is that Babylon and its corrupt system was directly responsible for the judicial verdicts that sentenced God's faithful servants to death. Cf. Aune, *Revelation 17-22*, p. 1024; Beale, *Book of Revelation*, p. 928; Smalley, *Revelation to John*, p. 478.

("you will avenge the blood of my servants the prophets and the blood of all
the servants of the Lord from her hand"). In the Old Testament context, a
prophet commissions Jehu to destroy the house of Ahab in order to exact
God's vengeance (ἐκδικήσεις) because Jezebel had ordered the execution of
God's prophets. The allusion effectively combines John's polemic against the
false prophet of Thyatira (Rev 2:20) and the politically oppressive Babylon
(Rev 17:1-6). The notion of God's vengeance on behalf of his people in both
Revelation 19:2 and 2 Kings 9:7 is grounded in Deuteronomy 32:43. Therefore
Revelation 19:1-2 not only represents the culmination of the martyrs' prayer
(Rev 6:10) but, more importantly, it signals the final act of retributive justice.

Now that a judicial verdict has been rendered, Jesus returns to earth to
prosecute the sentence against Babylon. He returns as the rightful king and
divine warrior in this christological culmination of the Apocalypse (cf. Rev
1:14-16; 2:12, 16, 18; 5:6b; 11:15; 12:11; 14:14; 17:14).[76] He returns as a conquering
king who subjugates all the kingdoms of the earth to his control. The imagery of riding a white horse was the common Roman symbol of the emperor who triumphed over his enemies.[77] The multiple diadems (διαδήματα
πολλά) upon his head demonstrates that his cosmic sovereignty surpasses
all other pretentious earthly claims to a throne (cf. Rev 12:3; 13:1).[78] He
comes accompanied by his army of redeemed saints (cf. Rev 1:6). Although
the saints come as a messianic army, Christ alone is the one who executes
the battle. The image of the iron scepter indicates that he alone is the true
messianic king (cf. Ps 2:9; Is 11:4). Finally, the name engraved on his thigh
attests that he is the "king of kings and Lord of lords" (cf. Rev 1:5; 17:14).[79]

He also comes as the divine warrior to dispense justice through judgment
and salvation.[80] The appellative "faithful and true" (πιστὸς καὶ ἀληθινός)
represents the quality of his character denoting authentic justice (cf. Rev 1:5;

---

[76]Osborne, *Revelation*, pp. 678-79. See also Holtz, *Die Offenbarung des Johannes*, pp. 124-131.

[77]Aune, *Revelation 17-22*, pp. 1050-51.

[78]Caird, *Revelation to Saint John*, p. 241; Beale, *Book of Revelation*, p. 954.

[79]This title is used for God in the OT and Jewish writings (cf. Deut 10:17; Ezek 26:7; Dan 2:37;
Ezra 7:12; Ps 136:2; 2 Macc 13:4; *1 En* 9:4; 63:2; 84:2; 1QM4:16; 4Q4910). For the Christological
significance of this designation for Christ see Matthias Reinhard Hoffmann, *The Destroyer and
the Lamb: The Relationship Between Angelomorphic and Lamb Christology in the Book of Revelation*, WUNT 203 (Tübingen: Mohr Siebeck, 2005), p. 185.

[80]On the dual aspect of his judgment as punishment for the wicked but salvation for the righteous, see Smalley, *Revelation to John*, pp. 487-88.

3:14; 6:10).[81] He comes to wage a just war (ἐν δικαιοσύνῃ κρίνει καὶ πολεμεῖ) against the beast's kingdom, to exact vengeance for the unjust war that was waged against the saints (Rev 13:7). The two images from the inaugural vision of Christ reappear to denote judicial insight (blazing eyes) and pronouncements (sword out of mouth).[82] One of the most graphic and violent images depicting Jesus as the divine warrior is his blood-soaked robe (Rev 19:13) from treading the winepress of the fury of God's wrath (Rev 19:15). The winepress used to crush the grapes of wrath was introduced in Revelation 14:19-20. According to this, the wine of God's fury was a metaphor for the massive bloodshed associated with the final battle.[83] The blood on Jesus' robe is that of his victims, as confirmed by the allusion to Isaiah 63:2-6. In the Song of Moses (Deut 32:41-42), God promises to exact vengeance on behalf of his people with very violent and bloody language (cf. Is 42:13; Hab 3:11-14).[84] Jesus, therefore, is the full revelation of the divine warrior from the Old Testament who executes judgment against all the enemies of God and his people.

The great and final battle constitutes a slaughter that ends just as soon as it begins (Rev 19:17-21). Prior to the battle, an angel standing in the sun issues a dinner invitation to all the carrion birds to feast on the corpses of all those in rebellion to Christ (Rev 19:17-18; cf. Rev 18:2). The beast along with all the earth's kings amasses an army in an attempt to revolt against the coming King of kings (cf. Rev 16:13-16).[85] Despite the boasts of the beast and the false prophet, they are quickly captured and tossed immediately into the lake of fire with no hint of a struggle (Rev 19:20). The remaining people all die instantly at the spoken word of Christ (Rev 19:21). The collective use of οἱ λοιποι ("the rest") signals the fate of the kings, their armies and all other inhabitants of the earth aligned against God (cf. Rev 9:20-21; 11:13).[86] The

---

[81]See also Lupieri, *Commentary on the Apocalypse*, p. 303.

[82]Cf. *4 Ezra* 13:9-13. See also Hoffmann, *The Destroyer and the Lamb*, p. 179.

[83]Aune, *Revelation 6–16*, p. 847. Cf. Joel 3:12-13; *1 En* 100:3; *4 Ezra* 15:35-36; Bauckham, *Climax of Prophecy*, pp. 40-48.

[84]Keener, *Revelation*, p. 453.

[85]For the basis of this conception see Ezek 38:14-16; 39:1-6; Joel 3:2; Zech 12:1-9; 14:2; Ps 2:1-3; cf. *1 En* 56:5-6; 90:13-19; 99:4; *2 Bar* 48:37; 70:7; *4 Ezra* 13:33-38; *Jub.* 23:23; *Sib Or* 3.663-68; *Pss Sol.* 2:1-2; 17:22-23; 1QM 1:10-11.

[86]Herms, *An Apocalypse for the Church and for the World*, p. 136; contra Aune, *Revelation 17–22*, p. 1067.

final battle demonstrates the victory of Christ as he conquered all other kingdoms of the earth and subsumed them under his kingdom now established on earth.

CONCLUSION

Is God just to allow his people to be treated unjustly by wicked men, and is he just to exact divine warfare against the earth's inhabitants? In a sense, that is one of the primary questions addressed in the book of Revelation when it is voiced by the souls of martyred saints in Revelation 6:10. The answer to this question is found throughout John's vision amid scenes of judgment, wrath and vindication. The vision unambiguously depicts how the sovereign judge of the universe will render just verdicts that accord with his standards of truth and righteousness. He will hold all of humanity accountable for their sin, but especially for the way they treated his own covenantal people.

The images of vengeance, wrath and warfare in John's Apocalypse are central to the purpose of the book as a means to encourage believers to remain faithful, patiently endure and trust in God's justice. The martyr-witnesses are introduced in Revelation 6:9-11 as those who have been unjustly executed as a result of their Christian testimony. They are initially assured of their innocence and future vindication when they are given white robes, but their full vindication is delayed in anticipation of additional martyrs. The injunction to wait effectively causes the readers *to expect persecution and death* as part and parcel of Christian testimony in a world dominated by a tyrannical beast and intoxicated by a brazenly arrogant prostitute. John's vision encourages his audience to endure faithfully to Christ through their words, worship and witness even if their blood is unjustly spilled by wicked hands. Believers are not only braced for persecutions, but they are encouraged *to bring their case before the ultimate judge through prayers and petitions.* Although believers may not find deliverance from execution, their pleas for justice will not go unanswered. The careful connection made between the prayers of the saints, the altar before the throne and the initiation of God's wrath in Revelation 8:1-5 assuages any doubts that God will avenge the blood of his faithful ones. Finally, believers who overcome through faithful testimony in the midst of persecution, entrusting themselves to the heavenly judge, may *confidently expect full vindication and salvation through resurrection and the right to reign with Christ* (Rev 3:21; 20:4-6).

Theodicy represents a major theological thrust of the Apocalypse providing the reader with a clear sense of God's justice.[87] The martyred souls make a request that directly addresses the question of justice when they inquire in Revelation 6:10, "How long, Sovereign Lord, holy and true, until you judge the inhabitants of the earth and vindicate our blood?" This request echoes the sentiments of countless generations of God's servants who suffer unjustly as the wicked appear to remain unpunished. The Old Testament abounds with the same inquiry pondering when God will take judicial action regarding the mistreatment of his people (e.g., Ps 79:5-10; 94:1-3).[88] The concern in Revelation 6:10 is not why does evil exist in the world or why Christians suffer in general but, specifically, why they are suffering as a consequence of faithfulness to Christ and obedience to the righteous requirements of his commands. The plea for justice and vindication in Revelation 6:9-10 constitutes a theological locus for the theme of theodicy as it relates to the overall message of John's vision to suffering believers. In a sense, the remainder of John's vision seeks to answer this query by demonstrating that God will render true justice in a world filled with evil and injustice.

---

[87]Grant R. Osborne, "Theodicy in the Apocalypse," *TrinJ* 14 (1993): 77.

[88]See also D. A. Carson, *How Long, O Lord?: Reflections on Suffering and Evil*, 2nd ed. (Grand Rapids: Baker, 2006); John N. Day, *Crying for Justice: What the Psalms Teach Us About Mercy and Vengeance in an Age of Terrorism* (Grand Rapids: Kregel, 2005), p. 107; Enrique Nardoni, *Rise Up, O Judge: A Study of Justice in the Biblical World*, trans. Seán Charles Martin (Peabody, MA: Hendrickson, 2004), p. 123.

PART FOUR

Biblical-Theological
Perspectives

7

COMPASSION AND WRATH
AS MOTIVATIONS FOR
DIVINE WARFARE

David Lamb

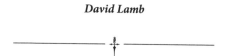

Bıblıcal dıscussıons of dıvıne warfare typically focus on associations with holiness, consequently the term "holy war" is used frequently to describe the phenomenon. Two classic German works on the subject of divine warfare use identical titles that make the connection between warfare and holiness explicit. Schwally's 1901 book appears to be the first to use the term "holy war" (*Der heilige Krieg im alten Israel*).[1] Von Rad's 1958 work, translated into English in 1991 by Ollenburger as *Holy War in Ancient Israel*, has been highly influential in Old Testament discussions on the subject.[2] Kidner's article on Old Testament perspectives on war includes a section discussing "holy war."[3] While Longman and Reid primarily focus on God as warrior, they still frequently use the term "holy war" in their descriptions of divine warfare: "the theme of the divine warrior, however, has a background in the concept of holy war."[4]

However, there are several problems with usage of the term "holy war" in discussions of God and warfare. Despite its frequent usage in scholarly dis-

---

[1]Friedrich Schwally, *Der heilige Krieg im alten Israel* (Leipzig: Deiterich, 1901).
[2]Gerhard von Rad, *Holy War in Ancient Israel*, trans. Ben C. Ollenburger (Grand Rapids: Eerdmans, 1991).
[3]F. Derek Kidner, "Old Testament Perspectives on War," *Evangelical Quarterly* 57 (1985): 99-112.
[4]Tremper Longman and Daniel Reid, *God Is a Warrior* (Grand Rapids: Zondervan, 1995), p. 32.

cussions, the Old Testament never uses the term "holy war," as both Craigie and Ollenburger observe.[5] While Old Testament texts mention the noun "holiness" (קֹדֶשׁ), the adjective "holy" (קָדוֹשׁ) or the related verb "sanctify" (קָדַשׁ) in contexts of divine warfare (e.g., Ex 15:13; Josh 5:15; 6:19; Jer 6:4), in none of these contexts is the warfare itself actually described as holy.[6]

Several scholars (e.g., Smend, Jones, Craigie) even question the validity of referring to warfare as "holy."[7] They suggest speaking of "YHWH war" or "wars of the Lord" which receive more biblical support as a term (e.g., Num 21:14; 1 Sam 18:17; 25:28). Ollenburger notes that Schwally's original use of the term "holy war" comes from the Arabic *jihād*,[8] which is problematic because of negative connotations associated with *jihād*, increasingly so since 9/11.

The scholarly preoccupation with "holy war" has overshadowed other possible associations with and motivations for divine warfare. This preoccupation can be seen with scholars who use the term frequently (e.g., Schwally, von Rad, Kidner, Longman and Reid) as well as with scholars who argue against its usage (e.g., Smend, Jones and Craigie).

Thus, other associations with divine warfare need to be examined. I am not arguing that use of the term "holy war" be avoided or that investigations of holy warfare are invalid but that other possible connections with divine warfare also need to be studied.

The problems extend beyond use of the term "holy war," however. The disturbing behavior of God in the Old Testament in the context of warfare (specifically the Canaanite genocide) has been the focus of much study, as evidenced by recent books by Wright, Seibert, Copan and Lamb.[9] These

---

[5]Peter C. Craigie, *The Problem of War in the Old Testament* (Grand Rapids: Eerdmans, 1978), p. 48; Ben C. Ollenburger, "Introduction: Gerhard von Rad's Theory of Holy War" in von Rad, *Holy War*, p. 5.

[6]The NRSV is quoted throughout this chapter unless otherwise indicated.

[7]For example, see R. Smend, *Yahweh War and Tribal Confederation*, trans. M. G. Rogers (Nashville: Abingdon, 1970); G. H. Jones, "'Holy War' or 'Yahweh War'?" *VT* 25 (1975): 642-58; Craigie, *The Problem of War*, pp. 49-50.

[8]Ollenburger, "Introduction," p. 6.

[9]Christopher J. H. Wright, *The God I Don't Understand: Reflections on Tough Questions of Faith* (Grand Rapids: Zondervan, 2008), pp. 76-108; Eric A. Seibert, *Disturbing Divine Behavior: Troubling Old Testament Images of God* (Minneapolis: Fortress, 2009); Paul Copan, *Is God a Moral Monster? Making Sense of the Old Testament God* (Grand Rapids: Baker, 2011); David T. Lamb, *God Behaving Badly: Is the God of the Old Testament Angry, Sexist and Racist?* (Downers Grove, IL: InterVarsity Press, 2011).

scholars address the troubling questions of God's warlike behavior. Why does YHWH kill so many people? Why does he command Israel to slaughter the Canaanites? These types of questions are wrestled with not only by scholars but also by most readers of the Old Testament. Discussions of divine warfare need to engage the concerns raised by these scholars and propose possible alternative perspectives for understanding how and why God acts as a warrior. This analysis will therefore examine how compassion and wrath motivate divine warfare.

WARFARE, WRATH AND COMPASSION

In their discussion of God as a warrior, Longman and Reid describe the pattern of how God fights both for and against Israel.[10] Their assessment of Israel as "unfaithful" seems appropriate, particularly during the periods when YHWH was handing his people over to the Canaanites in the book of Judges (Judg 2:15; 20–21) or over to the Babylonians and the Assyrians in the book of Kings (2 Kings 17; 24–25).

However, Longman and Reid's description of Israel as "faithful" while YHWH was fighting on their behalf only seems to be partially accurate. YHWH did not fight for them primarily because they were deserving of divine assistance due to their faithful obedience, but because they desperately cried out for help.[11] In their desperation they asked for assistance by appealing to God's compassion, which led him to fight on their behalf (e.g., Ex 2:23-24; Judg 2:18).

While YHWH's wrath toward the enemies of Israel motivated his acts of deliverance, frequently divine wrath is also given as a motivation when YHWH fights against Israel. Thus, two other motivations for divine warfare are seen throughout the Old Testament: anger and compassion. YHWH's wrath leads him to fight both against Israel and against their foes. His compassion toward his people leads him to fight on their behalf.

Within this discussion, an effort also has been made to include selections from diverse biblical contexts (Pentateuch, Prophets, Writings and New Testament narrative). The examination will begin with the book of Exodus

---

[10]Longman and Reid, *God Is a Warrior*, pp. 31-60.
[11]While Longman and Reid may understand faithfulness as humble dependence, it is difficult to say since they do not clarify how they are using the term "faithful."

and then discuss the conquest and judge cycles in Joshua-Judges and the term "LORD of hosts" in contexts of divine anger and compassion in Isaiah. The focus of study will then shift to retellings of Old Testament warfare narratives in the context of two historical psalms (Ps 78 and Ps 106) before moving to the New Testament, specifically Mark's gospel and Stephen's speech in Acts 7.

EXODUS

Since the book of Exodus is foundational to understanding how divine warfare, divine wrath and divine compassion are interrelated, this examination will begin by looking at Exodus in depth before moving on to other Old Testament texts where these themes are found. The theme of warfare permeates the book of Exodus.[12] Within the book's context of conflict, Israel is formed into a nation, and throughout the process YHWH reveals himself to be a warrior who is both wrathful and compassionate. Four texts from the book will be discussed here: (1) the call of Moses (Ex 2:23–4:17), (2) the songs that celebrate deliverance at the sea (Ex 15:1-21), (3) the covenant code laws that protect the marginalized (Ex 22:20-26) and (4) the revelation of YHWH's name (Ex 34:5-12).

The call of Moses (Exodus 2:23–4:17).[13] The catalyst for YHWH's military deliverance for his people in Exodus is divine compassion. Immediately before YHWH appears to Moses at the burning bush, the oppressed Israelites in Egypt cry for help. They groan (אָנַח) and cry out (זָעַק), and their cry (שַׁוְעָה) rises up to God and their groaning (נְאָקָה) is heard by God, so that he takes notice of them (Ex 2:23-25). While the text does not make the connection explicit, the narrative is set up to suggest that YHWH's call for Moses to deliver the Israelites comes as a direct result of YHWH's compassion upon his people for their predicament. Echoes of Israel's cry language appear several places later in the interaction between Moses and YHWH. YHWH informs Moses that he has seen the affliction of his people and has heard their cry and knows their sufferings (Ex 3:7). YHWH also tells Moses to

---

[12]See, for example, the monograph of Thomas B. Dozeman, *God at War: Power in the Exodus Tradition* (New York: Oxford University Press, 1996).

[13]The classic article on call narratives is N. Habel, "The Form and Significance of the Call Narratives," *ZAW* 77 (1965): 297-323. His first section focuses on the calls of Gideon and Moses (pp. 297-305).

inform the people that he has observed their suffering in Egypt and that he promises to bring them out of their affliction (Ex 3:16-17).

While the portrayal of YHWH as a warrior may not be as explicit in Moses' call as it is in the three Exodus texts to be discussed later, several examples can be observed of language used in the call that links to other more explicit divine warrior texts. Several connections are present between Moses' call and the appearance of the commander of YHWH to Joshua. The greeting used by the angel in Moses' call is strikingly similar to the one given to Joshua in his vision before the conquest of Jericho (Ex 3:3; Josh 5:15). In both the recipient is commanded to remove his sandals since the ground on which he stands is holy.[14] In Joshua, the divine warrior imagery is clear as the man confronting Joshua has a drawn sword and identifies himself as the commander of the army of YHWH (Josh 5:13-15).

In Moses' call, language of divine deliverance speaks both of YHWH's compassion and his role as warrior. In response to seeing, hearing and knowing their sufferings, YHWH informs Moses that he has come down to deliver his people from the hand of the Egyptians (Ex 3:8). Elsewhere in the Hebrew Bible the phrase "to deliver from the hand of" frequently appears in contexts of military deliverance (e.g., 1 Sam 7:3; 12:10; 2 Kings 18:29-30; 20:6). YHWH also says he will bring them up to the land of the Canaanites (Ex 3:17) which implies a military conquest. YHWH tells Moses that his mighty hand will be stretched out to strike Egypt to compel them to let his people go (Ex 3:19-20). Thus YHWH makes it clear to Moses that he will fight for them in the near future against the Egyptians and later against the Canaanites.

Over the course of their interaction, Moses gives a series of objections to the divine call (Ex 3:11, 13; 4:1, 10), each of which YHWH takes seriously and responds to patiently. However, after the fifth objection ("O my Lord, please send someone else!"), YHWH becomes angry (Ex 4:13-14). Fortunately for Moses, YHWH's anger here does not lead to bloodshed, but it does effectively motivate Moses to action since he offers no more objections and immediately returns to his father-in-law and tells him he is leaving (Ex 4:18).

YHWH's anger here is significant since this is the first instance in the Hebrew Bible that YHWH is described as angry.[15] It is striking that this initial

---

[14]In Joshua 5, the connection between holiness and warfare is obvious.

[15]Abraham was concerned that YHWH might become angry when he was interceding on behalf

occurrence of divine anger is motivated by compassion. As discussed above, YHWH's call to Moses is connected to their cry for help (Ex 2:23), so Moses' unwillingness to help deliver his own relatives provokes a strong response of anger from God. YHWH was angry that Moses was unwilling to participate in his act of compassion. YHWH was not willing to let Moses' lack of compassion prevent him from delivering Israel from Egyptian bondage.

From Moses' call, we see that divine compassion served as a primary catalyst for the dramatic military deliverance. The themes of YHWH's anger, compassion and military deliverance will continue to reappear at key junctures in the book of Exodus.

The songs that celebrate deliverance at the sea (Exodus 15:1-21). The songs of Exodus 15 include some of the most dramatic examples of divine warrior language in the Hebrew Bible, so it is not surprising that scholars such as Longman and Reid begin their discussion there.[16] To celebrate YHWH's victory over Egypt and Pharaoh at the sea (Ex 14:28), Moses, the people and Miriam sang to commemorate the deliverance.

At the beginning of the first song (of Moses and the Israelites) and at the end of Miriam's song, YHWH is described as throwing the Egyptian horse and rider into the sea (Ex 15:1, 21) forming an inclusio for this prototypical divine warrior section. As singular representatives for the entire Egyptian chariot force which was drowned in the sea (Ex 14:28), the phrase "horse and rider" serves here as a synecdoche. In addition to the horse and rider inclusio, the various aspects of Pharaoh's military are referred to frequently throughout the passage: his chariots (Ex 15:4, 19), his host (Ex 15:4), his officers (Ex 15:4), his sword (Ex 15:9), his horses (Ex 15:19) and his horsemen (Ex 15:19). The hand or arm of YHWH is mentioned four times (Ex 15:6[2], 12, 16) to do things such as "shatter the enemy" (Ex 15:6). However, the clearest example of divine warrior imagery occurs in Exodus 15:3, where we find the "first explicit statement of the warlike nature of God"[17] as Moses declares that "YHWH *is* a man of war" (יְהוָה אִישׁ מִלְחָמָה) (my translation).

The themes of wrath and compassion appear alongside the theme of

---

of Sodom (Gen 18:30, 32), but the text does not describe YHWH as actually becoming angry.

[16]Longman and Reid, *God Is a Warrior*, p. 31. I will primarily focus on the song of Moses, since it is much longer than the song of Miriam and the latter is basically just a repetition of the first verse from the former.

[17]Ibid., p. 32.

YHWH as divine warrior in the song of Moses. While divine anger appears only to be mentioned once in the song in Exodus 15:7, there are compelling reasons to see a second reference in 15:8. YHWH's burning anger (חָרוֹן) is sent out to consume the Egyptians (Ex 15:7). Most English translations render אַף in Exodus 15:8 as "nostrils" (ESV, NAS, NRSV) which makes sense in that context; YHWH's nostrils blast back the waters of the sea (a beautiful image!).[18] However, the word translated as "nostrils" (אַף) should be viewed here as a play on words, since elsewhere the word often connotes "anger" and is translated accordingly (e.g., Ex 4:14; 11:8; 22:23; 32:10; 34:6; Deut 9:10). Additionally, divine anger is mentioned at the end of Exodus 15:7 in a parallel construction to its usage at the beginning of 15:8. Propp observes that the noun אַף in Exodus 15:8a is often used with the verb חָרוֹן ("burning anger") which appears in 15:7b (Gen 30:2; Ex 4:14; 22:23).[19] Durham even translates אַף as "anger" instead of "nostrils" in Exodus 15:8.[20] Thus, אַף appears to be used in Exodus 15:8 as a paronomasia, connoting both divine wind and divine wrath. YHWH's anger at Egypt is therefore repeated twice in the song of Moses, and his warlike nature is linked to his anger. Whereas YHWH's anger earlier in Exodus was directed at Moses, here the target is Israel's enemy, Egypt (Ex 15:6, 7, 9).

In the song, divine compassion is referred to indirectly as a motivation for the deliverance of his people at the sea. Moses and the people call YHWH their "salvation" (Ex 15:2),[21] which recalls their cries for help earlier (Ex 2:23). Also, YHWH led them in his "steadfast love" (חֶסֶד), redeemed them and guided them to his "holy abode" (Ex 15:13).

Military language is used not only to describe the primary context of deliverance from Egypt at the sea; it is used also for the future Canaanite conquest of the land. The Canaanite residents tremble, they are seized by "pangs," they are "dismayed," and "terror and dread" fall upon them because of the greatness of God's arm (Ex 15:14-16). Elsewhere in the song, YHWH's hand is associated with his power, his sword and his destruction of the

---

[18] A similar image appears in 2 Sam 22:16 and Job 4:9.

[19] William H. C. Propp, *Exodus 1-18: A New Translation with Introduction and Commentary* (New York: Doubleday, 1999), p. 520.

[20] John I. Durham, *Exodus* (Waco, TX: Word, 1987), pp. 200-201.

[21] First person singular pronominal forms are used here, so "my salvation," but the context of the song makes it explicit that Moses and the people are singing (Ex 15:1).

enemy (Ex 15:6, 9, 12). Into this context, the song declares that he will bring them in and plant them on his own mountain (Ex 15:17). Thus, the portrayal of God as a compassionate and wrathful warrior is emphasized in the songs of Exodus 15 and, as we will soon see, in other texts in Exodus.

Covenant code: Laws that protect the marginalized (Exodus 22:20-26 [ET 22:21-27]). After traveling away from the sea, Moses leads the people to Mount Sinai and is in the process of receiving the covenant code from YHWH. Within a section of the covenant code, specifically the laws protecting the marginalized (Ex 22:20-26)[22] the three themes we have been examining (warfare, anger and compassion) each reappear. YHWH commands that four types of marginalized people are to be protected: the sojourner (גֵּר; Ex 22:20[2x]), the widow (אַלְמָנָה; 22:21, 23), the orphan (יָתוֹם; 22:21, 23) and the poor (עָנִי; 22:24). After commanding that these marginalized people should not be wronged, oppressed or mistreated, YHWH warns what will happen if they cry out—he will surely hear them, his anger will burn hot and he will kill their oppressors with the sword (Ex 22:22-23).

Several features of this section parallel Israel's own situation in Egypt. The text makes an explicit connection to Israel's earlier predicament—"for you were sojourners in the land of Egypt" (Ex 22:20; cf. Ex 23:9; Lev 19:34)—explaining why they should not mistreat sojourners. Also, the three-part pattern of a human cry, a divine hearing and a divine response is identical to what happened immediately before YHWH called Moses. The verb "cry" (צָעַק) is used three times in this text for the marginalized (Ex 22:22 [2x], 26), and a parallel form of the verb "cry" (זָעַק) is used in the earlier text for the Israelites (Ex 2:23).[23] The verb "hear (שָׁמַע) appears three times in this section as God hears the marginalized (Ex 22:22, 26) just as God previously heard the Israelites (Ex 2:24).

God's response to the heard cry differs here, as he warns Moses and the people that if they mistreat the sojourner, the widow and the orphan his wrath (אַף) will burn hot (חָרָה) and as a result he will kill them with the sword (Ex 22:22-23). So we see God's anger leads to his acting as a warrior

---

[22]For this section of the covenant code, the English text [ET] verse numbers are one higher than the Masoretic Text [MT]. For the remainder of this discussion of Exodus 22 references will only be given to the MT.

[23]Brown, Driver and Briggs lists these two as parallel forms of the same verb (see BDB: 277, 858).

even against his own people because of their lack of compassion. YHWH is willing to kill, or at least threaten to kill, Israelites in order to motivate them to be compassionate toward weaker members of society. While Cole regards the punishment as a "divine application of *lex talionis*" (their wives become widows, their children become orphans),[24] what is being described is presumably more severe than simply "an eye for an eye," since the ones being oppressed were widows and orphans already. Thus YHWH's threatened punishment is meant to be an extreme disincentive for exploiting the weak.

In the beginning of this text, anger motivates God to hear and respond as warrior to the cry of the marginalized, but at the end compassion motivates him to hear and respond: "if he cries to me, I will hear, for I am compassionate [חַנּוּן]" (Ex 22:26 my translation). In an ironic reversal from Exodus 15, where God displayed anger and violence toward Israel's enemy, in Exodus 22 God will display anger and violence toward oppressive Israelites. While this switch may seem shocking (threatening to kill his own people), God's character is consistent throughout each of these incidents. In Exodus 15 and 22, as well as in Exodus 2:24-25, YHWH acts compassionately toward those who are being oppressed (Israelites in Egypt and sojourners among the Israelites). Thus YHWH does not simply fight for Israel against their neighbors, but his anger and his compassion lead him to fight against oppression and for the oppressed.

The revelation of YHWH's name (Exodus 34:5-12). After the covenant code blood sprinkling ceremony (Ex 24:1-8), Moses receives from YHWH the stone tablets and directions regarding the ark, the tabernacle and other cultic objects (Ex 25–31). While they wait for Moses, Aaron and the people construct a golden calf, provoking the wrath of YHWH (Ex 32:1-6). YHWH then informs Moses that he will consume his own people in his anger (Ex 32:7-10), reminiscent of his threat to kill "with the sword" for oppression of the marginalized (Ex 22:23). Moses convinces YHWH to change his mind about the punishment (Ex 32:14), but then Moses and the Levites pull out swords and act as agents of judgment (Ex 32:26-29). After Moses changes YHWH's mind a second time (agreeing to accompany them to the new land), he asks YHWH to show him his glory, which YHWH agrees to do by revealing

---

[24]R. Alan Cole, *Exodus: An Introduction and Commentary* (Downers Grove, IL: InterVarsity Press, 1973), pp. 174-75.

to Moses his name. In the context of YHWH's name revelation the themes of divine compassion, anger and warfare feature prominently.

The compassionate character of YHWH is emphasized in multiple ways as YHWH proclaims his own name to Moses (Ex 34:6): "compassionate" (רַחוּם), "gracious" (חַנּוּן) and abounding in "steadfast love" (חֶסֶד). In the midst of these divine characteristics, YHWH also informs Moses that he is "slow to anger" (literally, "long nosed": אֶרֶךְ אַפַּיִם; Ex 34:6). These two contrasting divine emotions, compassion and anger, thus appear together in the list of primary characteristics in YHWH's own self definition. While YHWH's steadfast love is unlimited and abundant, his anger is restricted and delayed. The compassionate-angry divine dichotomy can be seen in the next verse also, as YHWH forgives iniquity, transgression and sin but does not clear the guilty and visits iniquity on the third and fourth generation (Ex 34:7).

As their interaction continues YHWH reveals to Moses the implications of these divine characteristics in the context of his relationship with Israel. He will perform works before his people that will be marvelous and awesome (Ex 34:10), but exactly what YHWH is referring to is initially unclear. Finally, he says, "See, I will drive out before you the Amorites, the Canaanites, the Hittites, the Perizzites, the Hivites, and the Jebusites" (Ex 34:11). Because of his compassion for his people, YHWH will act as conquering warrior on their behalf, clearing out the nations who currently inhabit the land. Just as earlier in Exodus, YHWH fought for his people to defeat their Egyptian oppressors, now he declares that he will fight for them to defeat the Canaanite people occupying the land.

Before moving to discuss these themes in books outside of Exodus, it will be helpful to trace how the Exodus 34 description of YHWH as both compassionate and slow to anger appears throughout the Old Testament in contexts portraying YHWH as warrior (although not always as motivations for warfare). In an incident similar to Exodus 32, YHWH threatens to wipe out the Israelites because they refuse to enter the land after the report of the spies, so Moses quotes Exodus 34:6-7 to convince him to forgive the people (Num 14:1-19). In his prayer before the people, Ezra the priest speaks of YHWH seeing the Israelites' oppression in Egypt, hearing their cry, performing wonders at the sea against Pharaoh and subduing the Canaanites; in the midst of this he declares that YHWH is "gracious and compassionate, slow to anger and abounding in love" (Neh 9:17). Three psalms (Ps 86; 103; 145) describe YHWH in terms reminiscent of Exodus 34:6-7 as "compassionate, gracious, slow to anger, abounding in steadfast love": in a request for protection from a "band of ruffians" (Ps 86:14-17), in a declaration of YHWH's protection of the oppressed and deliverance of the Israelites (Ps 103:6-8) and in praise for YHWH's awesome deeds and his compassion to all (Ps 145:8). Two minor prophetic books also include a version of the Exodus 34:6-7 characterization of YHWH. In Joel, the portrayal of YHWH "at the head of his army" with a vast host is used alongside an Exodus 34 description of YHWH to motivate the people to repent (Joel 2:11-14). Jonah is upset that YHWH is "gracious and merciful, slow to anger and abounding in steadfast love" (Jon 4:2) since he wants YHWH to wipe out the city of Nineveh.

The pattern of repeating language from Exodus and referring to incidents from Exodus in contexts where YHWH's warlike behavior is associated with divine anger and divine compassion continues into the books of Joshua and Judges.

JOSHUA AND JUDGES

Warfare dominates the first two books of the Deuteronomistic History, and within these contexts compassion and wrath lead YHWH to fight both for and against Israel.[25] In the book of Joshua, because Achan kept certain items from Jericho that should have been destroyed, YHWH was angry at the Israelites (Josh 7:1, 26) and did not help them fight. Consequently they lost badly in the first battle against the city of Ai. The Achan incident is recalled later in the message to the half-tribe of Manasseh and YHWH's anger is twice mentioned (Josh 22:18, 20) as leading to significant loss of life. Joshua also warns the people that if they serve other gods the "anger of YHWH" will be kindled against them and they will perish quickly from "the good land" (הָאָרֶץ הַטּוֹבָה) that YHWH had given them (Josh 23:16). While it is difficult to find many examples of YHWH motivated by compassion in warfare in

---

[25]While the monograph of Kari Latvus on divine anger in Joshua and Judges (*God, Anger and Ideology: The Anger of God in Joshua and Judges in Relation to Deuteronomy and the Priestly Writings* [Sheffield, UK: Sheffield Academic Press, 1998]), might seem relevant to this discussion, his approach is primarily redactional (distinguishing between levels of Deuteronomist redaction and the Priestly source) and not theological. However, his brief description of Hebrew terms for anger (pp. 25-26) is particularly helpful.

Joshua, the theme appears frequently in Judges.

In the book of Judges, YHWH fought *against* Israel in anger against their evil deeds and *for* Israel in compassionate response to their cries for help. The overview of the book of Judges (Judg 2:11-23) lays out the pattern which is followed generally through the various judge cycles. Israel did evil in the eyes of YHWH (Judg 2:11; 3:7, 12; 4:1; 6:1; 10:6; 13:1), so his anger (אַף) was kindled against Israel (Judg 2:14, 20; 3:8; 10:7). YHWH then either "sold" (מָכַר; Judg 2:14; 3:8; 4:2; 10:7) or "gave" (נָתַן; 2:14; 6:1; 13:1) them into the hands of their enemies. The text also says that YHWH's hand was against them and that he would no longer drive out the Canaanite nations (Judg 2:14, 21). Thus in these contexts YHWH either fought against them or no longer for them in his anger.

However, after they were oppressed for an extended period and they cried out to YHWH (Judg 2:18; 3:9, 15; 4:3; 6:6, 7; 10:10), he raised up a military judge-deliverer (Judg 2:16; 3:9, 15; 10:1) and sent his spirit to the judge (Judg 3:10; 6:34; 11:29; 13:25). With divine assistance, the judge would then rescue Israel from their foreign oppression. In the overview at the beginning of Judges, the text provides the reason for the divine deliverance: YHWH "had compassion" (Niphal of נָחַם) because of their groaning (Judg 2:18).

Several points of comparison between Exodus and Judges can be now noted. Just as with Moses, YHWH also called judges to deliver his people in a military context (e.g., Othniel, Ehud, Deborah, Gideon). Whereas in the song of the sea YHWH's anger was directed at Egypt, in Judges divine anger repeatedly targets Israel (similar to the covenant code protection of the marginalized) allowing them to fall into foreign subjugation. Finally, in both Exodus and Judges, YHWH is moved with compassion to fight in response to Israel's cries for help.

ISAIAH

While one might expect divine warrior language to disappear as the discussion shifts from the Deuteronomistic History to prophetic poetry due to the lack of battle narratives in Isaiah that were typical in books like Exodus, Joshua and Judges, this is not the case. Just as a high concentration of these themes appeared in the song of the sea (Ex 15), the poetry in the book of Isaiah portrays YHWH as a warrior motivated by wrath and compassion.

In Isaiah, Yhwh is revealed as the "Holy One of Israel" with twenty-five repetitions of the phrase (e.g., Is 1:4; 5:19, 24),[26] however the title "Lord of hosts" (יְהוָה צְבָאוֹת) or more literally "Yhwh of armies" appears some fifty times, twice as often as the other divine title (e.g., Is 1:9, 24; 2:12; 5:7, 9, 16, 24). Brueggemann suggests that a better translation for the phrase would be "the God of the troops."[27] Elsewhere in the Old Testament the title "Yhwh of armies" is used almost two hundred times, often appearing in prophetic literature in contexts of divine anger (e.g., Jer 11:17; 42:18; 50:25; Zech 7:12; 8:2, 14; 10:3) or divine compassion (e.g., Jer 32:18; 33:11; Zech 1:16; 7:9; Mal 1:9). Thus the frequent repetition of this title emphasizes Yhwh's role as a military leader not only in the book of Isaiah but also in other prophetic books.

Divine wrath is a major theme of Isaiah, occurring over forty times in the book (e.g., Is 5:25 [2x]; 10:4-6, 25; 12:1; 13:3).[28] The first occurrence of divine wrath appears after the "woes" of chapter five in the context of Yhwh's people rejecting the instruction of "Yhwh of armies," so his anger is kindled against them and he stretches out his hand and strikes them (Is 5:24-25). In this context he also calls a warrior nation (Assyria) from far away to come with sharp arrows, bent bows and horses with flint-like hoofs (Is 5:26-28). In his anger, therefore, Yhwh uses the armies of foreign powers to fight his battles for him in an almost mercenary manner.

An oracle against Jacob (Is 9:7-20 [ET 9:8-21][29]) uses the title "Yhwh of armies" twice (Is 9:12, 18) and in these contexts declares four times that Yhwh is angry at his people (Is 9:11, 16, 18, 20). Because of his anger, he raises up adversaries, stirs up enemies and strikes his people (Is 9:10-12). Yhwh is so angry at his own people that, in a reversal of Exodus 22, he refrains from showing compassion on their widows and orphans (Is 9:16).

In an oracle against Babylon (Is 13), Yhwh's wrath features prominently (six times: Is 13:3, 5, 9 [2x], 13 [2x]). A clear expression of Yhwh as divine warrior appears after the first mention of divine anger where "Yhwh of armies" is mustering an army for battle (Is 13:4 my translation). This army

---

[26]See John Goldingay's discussion of "The Holy One of Israel" and descriptive diagram in *Isaiah* (Peabody, MA: Hendrickson, 2001), pp. 7-8.

[27]Walter Brueggemann, *Isaiah 1–39* (Louisville: Westminster John Knox Press, 1998), p. 17.

[28]See Goldingay's discussion of divine anger in the book of Isaiah in *Isaiah*, p. 56.

[29]For the remainder of this discussion of Isaiah 9 references will only be given to the MT.

is described as the "weapons of his indignation" (Is 13:5). People who are caught in the "wrath of YHWH of armies" will be thrust through and fall by the sword (Is 13:13-15 my translation). But at the end of this section of divine anger and warfare, a word of hope is given for his people, as YHWH "will have compassion (רָחַם) on Jacob and will again choose Israel" (Is 14:1).

The final occurrence of the title "YHWH of armies" appears in second Isaiah (Is 54:5) in a context where divine anger is spoken of in the past (Is 54:8, 9) and YHWH is taking his people back to himself. YHWH's compassion toward his people is mentioned three times in only four verses (Is 54:7-10). This song, which speaks of a covenant of peace (Is 54:10), concludes by stating that "no weapon that is fashioned against you shall prosper" (Is 54:17). Thus, in each of these Isaianic oracles YHWH's warlike attributes appear in contexts of divine anger and of divine compassion.

PSALM 78

Whereas the book of Isaiah spoke of divine warfare primarily in Israel's later history (involving Assyria and Babylon), Psalm 78 recounts highlights of Israel's earlier history (involving Egypt), including many of the significant military events from the books of Exodus, Joshua and Judges and describing the phenomenon of divine warfare using similar language.[30] In the psalm Egypt is mentioned by name three times (Ps 78:12, 43, 51), each time in the context of describing YHWH's miraculous works to deliver his people from bondage. The parting of the sea for the Israelites to pass through is also mentioned (Ps 78:13, 53). Divine anger is a major theme of the psalm as "wrath" (אַף), "indignation" (עֶבְרָה) and "burning anger" (חֲרוֹן) are referred to ten times in connection with YHWH (Ps 78:21, 31, 38 [2x], 49 [2x], 50, 58, 59, 62).

War terminology permeates the psalm. YHWH's anger prompts him to kill his own people (Ps 78:31, 34), to strike the firstborn of Egypt (78:51) and to release on the Egyptians a "company of destroying angels" (78:49). The enemies and adversaries of YHWH are overwhelmed and routed (Ps 78:53, 66). YHWH uses weapons in his wrath, giving his people to the sword and allowing their priests to fall by the sword (Ps 78:62, 64). One of the final military images of the psalm describes almost comically how YHWH wakes

---

[30]See the discussion of James Luther Mays on the categorization for the psalm in *Psalms* (Louisville: John Knox Press, 1994), p. 254.

up from sleep like a warrior shouting because of wine (Ps 78:65).

However, because of his "compassion" (רַחוּם) Yhwh's anger is restrained and his wrath is not stirred up, which leads him to forgive Israel's iniquity (Ps 78:38). Thus Yhwh is again described as a warrior who fights both for and against Israel, and motivating his behavior are wrath and compassion.

Psalm 106

Psalm 106 is also a historical psalm and while both Psalms 78 and 106 recount Israel's many sins, the latter has more of a confessional tone as it speaks of divine anger and compassion. The psalm describes how on three occasions the Israelites provoke Yhwh to anger: with their association with Baal of Peor (Ps 106:29; Num 25:1-13), at the waters of Meribah (Ps 106:32; Num 20:2-13) and in a more general manner, perhaps fitting the context of the judge cycles, since Yhwh gives them into the hands of nations who then rule over them (Ps 106:40; Judg 2:14-18). While these first two examples of divine wrath do not necessarily involve God acting as a warrior, the third certainly describes God working in a military context.

Other examples of God as warrior are scattered throughout the psalm. The great works performed by Yhwh in Egypt are mentioned twice (Ps 106:7, 21), and the deliverance from the Egyptians at the sea is mentioned specifically three times (106:7, 9, 22). Yhwh "redeemed" (גָּאַל) Israel from the hand of the enemy (Ps 106:10) and he "delivered" (Hiphil of נָצַל) them from their enemies (106:43). In four places in the psalm Yhwh is associated with saving Israel, and in each instance the same Hebrew root (יָשַׁע) is used: Yhwh "saved" (Hiphil of יָשַׁע) Israel (Ps 106:8, 10), he is called their "Savior" (106:21) and at the end they cry out, "save us" (106:47). While "being saved" often has spiritual connotations today, in the context of ancient Israel it primarily had military connotations, as in "saved from the hand of the foe" (Ps 106:10).

The psalm describes how these works of Yhwh are performed in the context of divine compassion. The psalm begins and ends describing Yhwh's "steadfast love" (חֶסֶד; Ps 106:1, 45), and at the end Yhwh's steadfast love is linked explicitly to his "compassion" (נָחַם; 106:45).[31] The language of

---

[31] Some English versions (ESV, NAS) translate נָחַם here as "relented," but the NRSV's "showed compassion" is reasonable and fits the context well.

YHWH hearing the cry of his people (Ps 106:44) is reminiscent of both Exodus 2–3 and the pattern of the book of Judges. YHWH also caused Israel to be pitied by their captors (Ps 106:46). Thus both Psalm 78 and Psalm 106 reveal how these two divine characteristics, wrath and compassion, motivate YHWH's acts of military deliverance.

MARK

While warfare language is used frequently in the New Testament, in many instances it has spiritual connotations: a king plans to wage war in Jesus' discussion of the cost of discipleship (Lk 14:31-32), "the whole armor of God" will help the Ephesians withstand evil (Eph 6:11-17), and a "two-edged sword" is not as sharp as the word of God (Heb 4:12).

However, Longman and Reid argue that the Gospels, Mark in particular, depict Jesus in the divine warrior tradition in conflicts with demonic powers and in language of a "New Exodus."[32] In Mark, Jesus is frequently motivated by "compassion" (σπλαγχνίζομαι) in contexts of healings and feedings (Mk 1:41; 6:34; 8:2; 9:22), and in one of these healings, the exorcism of a boy with a mute spirit, Jesus acts as a compassionate deliverer (Mk 9:14-29). Into a context full of struggle—arguing, violent convulsing, spiritual oppression and apparent death—the father asks Jesus to enter with compassion and help them, reminiscent of Exodus 2 and Judges 2. Jesus acts compassionately and delivers the boy that the disciples could not heal.

Not only does Jesus fight against spiritual opponents, but many of his battles involve religious leaders. One of Jesus' conflicts with the Pharisees in Mark's Gospel centers on a test of Sabbath observance (Mk 3:1-6), specifically whether or not Jesus will break the Sabbath by healing a man with a withered hand. Jesus acts compassionately toward the man and is "angry" (ὀργή) at the Pharisees for their "hardness of heart" (Mk 3:5), an obvious reference back to the conflict with Pharaoh in Egypt (e.g., Ex 4:21; 7:3; 8:15). Jesus' failure to "pass" the Pharisees' test apparently is interpreted by them as an act of war, as they immediately leave and conspire with the Herodians to kill him (Mk 3:6), the first reference in Mark's Gospel to this theme that dominates the rest of the book.

---

[32]Longman and Reid, *God Is a Warrior*, pp. 91-118.

While warfare narratives typical of the Old Testament do not appear in the Gospels, in Mark's Gospel in particular Jesus is portrayed in constant conflict with spiritual and human opposition. The motivations described for YHWH in the Old Testament, compassion and anger, similarly motivate Jesus.[33]

ACTS 7

Actual warfare is rarely mentioned in the New Testament (outside of Revelation; see Rev 2:16; 11:7; 12:7, 17; 13:7; 17:14; 19:11, 19), except in contexts that recount events from the Old Testament. Stephen's speech in Acts 7 refers to significant Old Testament military events discussed above and therefore will be examined next.

In Acts 7, after being accused of blasphemy by the council, Stephen gives a defense before his martyrdom, in which he recalls the Old Testament narrative. While Stephen's is one of the longer New Testament speeches at fifty-two verses, he is summarizing the entire story of the Old Testament, so he must have been highly selective. Thus only events deemed sufficiently significant or pertinent would have been chosen for this address.

Stephen's first reference to the exodus appears in the context of YHWH's words to Abraham (Gen 15:13-14), "But I will judge [κρίνω] the nation [i.e., Egypt] that they serve" (Acts 7:7). While the divine anger spoken of in Exodus 15 is not mentioned in this context, elsewhere in the New Testament wrath and judgment are almost synonymous. Paul tells the Roman church that rulers do not bear the sword in vain but act as the servant of God to execute wrath on the wrongdoer (Rom 13:4; cf. 1:18). In Luke's Gospel, John the Baptist warns the crowds, "Who warned you to flee the wrath to come?" (Lk 3:7; cf. 21:23).

Divine compassion is, however, emphasized in the context of Stephen's reference to the call of Moses (Acts 7:30-34). In Stephen's words, God tells Moses, "I have surely seen the mistreatment of my people who are in Egypt and have heard their groaning, and I have come down to rescue them" (Acts 7:34; cf. Ex 3:7-8). While many aspects of Moses' extended interaction with YHWH from Exodus 3 and 4 could have been included, the divine com-

---

[33]In Jesus' parable of the wedding banquet, he describes a king who, in his anger, sends his troops to destroy the invited guests who, instead of attending, insult the host king (Mt 22:1-14).

passion motivating the deliverance was selected for inclusion and thus deemed significant.

As a part of this deliverance YHWH's wonders and signs, particularly at the Red Sea, are also mentioned (Acts 7:36). Joshua is mentioned as Stephen speaks of the nations that were dispossessed, which God drove out before their ancestors (Acts 7:45), but no reference to anger or compassion is given for the conquest of Canaan.

While the motivations for divine warfare are not stated as clearly in Stephen's speech as they were in the Old Testament contexts, even brief references to the narratives of the exodus and the conquest still emphasize the themes of the original narrative, specifically that in his anger and compassion YHWH fights for and against Israel.

WARLIKE BEHAVIOR WORTHY OF PRAISE

This examination of divine warrior texts has shown how frequently God's behavior is motivated by anger or compassion. Even in contexts in which the divine motivation is unclear or alternative ones are given, God's military actions are still often associated with his wrath and his compassion. Among the summary texts, Psalms 78 and 106 highlight these motivations more clearly than Acts 7. However, historical reviews will choose to focus only on certain aspects of the narrative to make a point. While the anger and compassion themes emphasized in the book of Exodus are not always given the same prominence elsewhere, the fact that the deliverance from Egyptian bondage—arguably the most important event in Israel's history—is referred to so often throughout the Old Testament and New Testament still serves to highlight God's role as compassionate warrior for his people. Additionally, the repetition of phrasing from the divine name revelation of Exodus 34 throughout the Old Testament in divine warrior contexts reveals the theological significance of YHWH's characterization as both compassionate and slow to anger. This emphasis is also seen in how the title used frequently in Isaiah, "YHWH of armies," is used similarly elsewhere in the Old Testament in contexts of anger and compassion.

This article began by observing problems associated with the use of the term "holy war" (particularly because of associations with *jihād*) and with the behavior of YHWH in contexts of warfare. Readers of the Old Testament may continue to be disturbed by divine warfare texts and the issues these texts raise. However, warfare motivated by compassion and by anger is less problematic than warfare motivated by other motives. A helpful pattern can be observed that fits many, but perhaps not all, of the texts discussed above. In the exodus narrative, the laws protecting the marginalized, the judge-cycles and the psalms, YHWH fights in compassion to defend the oppressed and in anger against the oppressor. Not only is this perspective on God's warlike behavior less problematic, but it is also highly compelling, even worthy of praise.

8

HOLY WAR AND חרם

A Biblical Theology of חרם

Douglas S. Earl

———————— ✝ ————————

THE CONCEPT OF HOLY WAR IS DIFFICULT from various perspectives. From a historical perspective one may ask whether or not Israel actually practiced holy war given the difficulty of, for example, identifying an Israelite conquest of Jericho within the right era for the conquest described in the book of Joshua.[1] From the perspective of comparative religion (and some recent apologetic) one might ask whether Israel simply conducted and narrated warfare just like the people around her, documenting it using similar literary conventions, such as hyperbole.[2] From a moral perspective one might question whether such a practice—or indeed its portrayal, even if fictional—can ever be considered responsible or morally acceptable.[3] In particular, from a Christian perspective one might ask how one could reconcile holy war with Jesus' exhortation to love one's neighbor, whoever that might be, as demonstrated in the parable of the Good Samaritan (Lk 10:25-37).

---

[1]For an introduction to the issues see M. E. Mills, "Joshua and the Conquest of Canaan," in *Historical Israel: Biblical Israel: Studying Joshua to 2 Kings* (London: Cassell, 1999), pp. 13-22. For detailed discussion of the archaeology of Jericho see T. A. Holland and E. Netzer, "Jericho (place)," in D. N Freedman, ed., *The Anchor Bible Dictionary* (New York: Doubleday, 1992), 3.723-40.

[2]Cf. K. Lawson Younger Jr., *Ancient Conquest Accounts: A Study in Ancient Near Eastern and Biblical History Writing*, JSOTSup 98 (Sheffield, UK: JSOT Press, 1990).

[3]See Randall Rauser, "Let Nothing that Breathes Remain Alive: On the Problem of Divinely Commanded Genocide," in *Philosophia Christi* 11, no. 1 (2009): 27-41.

Discussion of these questions has been hindered by the tendency to conflate various depictions of warfare in the Old Testament using this category of "holy war."[4] This conflation causes a number of difficulties. First, Peter Craigie comments on Gerhard von Rad's conception of "holy war" that: "While war was religious by association, it was no more a cultic and holy act than was sheep shearing."[5] So we need to reexamine the assumption that some forms of warfare have (or were perceived to have) an inherent "holiness" that is not inherent in more mundane forms of human activity. Second, "holy war," or its Hebrew equivalent term, is not a category that is used in the Old Testament. What has been described as "holy war," or "Yahweh War," is described in the Old Testament in terms of either war in general (מלחמה) or, perhaps most notoriously, in terms of חרם. These categories are conflated into the scholarly construction of "holy war."[6] Third, scholars have tended to conflate essentially different usages of the concept of חרם in the Old Testament.

However, the virtual absence of חרם from Israel's presentation of her history in Genesis-Exodus, most of Numbers, Judges, Samuel-Kings and Chronicles is striking, suggesting that it is not part of Israel's regular vocabulary of warfare. Moreover, the absence of חרם in the psalms is striking, suggesting that it is not part of Israel's "liturgical" language either. So it is problematic to lump חרם and other stories of warfare into a category like "holy war." For example Genesis 34, which narrates the rape of Dinah and subsequent massacre of the Shechemites, appears to describe something like חרם, but the text does not use the term חרם. This suggests that one ought to proceed cautiously in considering what might be termed "holy war."

---

[4]See Gerhard von Rad, *Holy War in Ancient Israel* (Grand Rapids: Eerdmans, 1991); S Niditch, *War in the Hebrew Bible* (Oxford: Oxford University Press, 1993). G. M. H. Ratheiser, *Mitzvoth Ethics and the Jewish Bible: The End of Old Testament Theology* (London: T & T Clark, 2007), pp. 307-10, offers a recent summary of research on the concept of holy war. E. H. Merrill, "The Case for Moderate Discontinuity," in *Show Them No Mercy: 4 Views on God and Canaanite Genocide*, ed. S. N. Gundry, Counterpoints (Grand Rapids: Zondervan, 2003), pp. 63-106, esp. pp. 64-74 discusses difficulties with the concept of holy war and uses "Yahweh War" instead. This seems to be an improvement but is still problematic in that different categories in the Old Testament's own presentation are conflated.

[5]P. Craigie, *The Problem of War in the Old Testament* (Grand Rapids: Eerdmans, 1978), p. 49.

[6]Note also that Num 21:14 refers to the book of "wars of Yahweh," giving rise to the category "Yahweh War." However, it is a category that the Old Testament does not develop. See the discussions of Chapman and Thomas in this volume.

Having indicated the difficulty in using "holy war" in relation to the Old
Testament, I would like to focus now on the issue of חרם, being the aspect
of Old Testament warfare that raises the most moral and theological difficulties today and being the form of practice that has most affinity with what
one would think of as "holy war." חרם is the term used in Deuteronomy
7:1-5 expressing God's command to Moses to enter the Promised Land and
"utterly destroy" the idolatrous inhabitants. It is the term used throughout
much of Joshua to narrate the fulfillment of this command. The moral difficulties with חרם are clear, with Christian apologetic accounts often seeking
to deal with the issue in terms of the punishment of the extremely wicked
practices of the Canaanites.[7] However, there are difficulties with such an
approach. Can a six month old Canaanite baby or indeed a donkey really be
killed (as demanded by חרם) within a "moral framework of punishment"?[8]
Moreover, the historical difficulties are clear. A significant number of interpreters of the archaeological data gleaned from Palestine have concluded
that there was no Israelite conquest of Canaan.[9] How, then, is one to understand חרם in the Old Testament?

חרם IN THE OLD TESTAMENT[10]

The significance of the use of the verb חרם and the noun חֵרֶם (homonym
I)[11] is difficult to determine, for their usage intersects with various appar-

---

[7]See e.g. Christopher J. H. Wright, "What About the Canaanites," in *The God I Don't Understand:
Reflections on Tough Questions of Faith* (Grand Rapids: Zondervan, 2008), pp. 92-94.

[8]Cf. ibid., and see Rauser, "Let Nothing that Breathes Remain Alive" for discussion of the moral
problems.

[9]See P. R. Davies, *Memories of Ancient Israel: An Introduction to Biblical History—Ancient and
Modern* (Louisville: Westminster John Knox, 2008) for an overview (with bibliography) of the
issues from this perspective. See however J. J. Bimson, *Redating the Exodus and Conquest*, rev.
ed. (Sheffield, UK: The Almond Press, 1981) for an earlier re-evaluation of some of the debates
of the mid-late twentieth century.

[10]This section summarizes my fuller discussion in D. S. Earl, *Reading Joshua as Christian Scripture*, JTISup 2 (Winona Lake, IN: Eisenbrauns, 2010).

[11]The most comprehensive recent study of חרם is Philip Stern's, perhaps replacing that of C. H.
W. Brekelmans as the standard work. (P. D. Stern, *The Biblical Ḥērem: A Window on Israel's Religious Experience*, Brown Judaic Studies 211 [Atlanta: Scholars Press, 1991]; C. H. W. Brekelmans, *De ḥērem in het Oude Testament* [Nijmegen, the Netherlands: Centrale Drukkerij, 1959]).
Other treatments include: H. H. Cohn, "Ḥērem" in *EJ* 8 (1972): 344-56; Y. Hoffman, "The Deuteronomistic Concept of the Ḥērem," in *ZAW* 111, no. 2 (1999): 196-210; N. Lohfink, "Ḥāram"
in *TDOT* V (1986): 180-99; R. D. Nelson, "Ḥērem and the Deuteronomic Social Conscience," in
Deuteronomy and Deuteronomic Literature, ed. J. Lust and M. Verdenne (Leuven: Peeters, 1997),
pp. 39-54; C. Schäfer-Lichtenberger, "Bedeutung und Funktion von Ḥērem in biblisch-hebräischen

ently contradictory categories, as attempts to translate Joshua 6:17 (the razing of Jericho) demonstrate.[12] The root occurs frequently in Deuteronomy and Joshua in relation to the conquest but is rare in the remainder of the Old Testament.

While one might hope to gather extrabiblical evidence from ancient Near Eastern texts that would illuminate חרם in the Old Testament, the evidence is surprisingly sparse. Cognates of חרם occur only in the Mesha Inscription, a ninth-century B.C. Moabite inscription that describes how Mesha, King of Moab, takes Israelite territory; and in a Ugaritic text, "An Incantation Against Infertility" (*KTU* 1.13), where the verb is associated with annihilation.[13] Other parallels have been sought, such as the *assaku* offering in the Mari letters, yet this seems as likely to mislead as to help.[14] The Ancient Near Eastern context is thus unlikely to help significantly.

חרם occurs in three main contexts in the Old Testament. First, in the deuteronom(ist)ic materials it is associated with total annihilation of peoples and their property.[15] In Deuteronomy חרם is used in the injunction to annihilate the inhabitants of Canaan during the conquest (Deut 7:1-5) but also in relation to Israelite settlements where other gods are worshiped (Deut 13:13-19 [Heb]). In both cases it is clearly associated with the problem

---

Texten," in *BZ* 38 (1994): 270-75. Moreover, there are important discussions in חרם in M. Fishbane, *Biblical Interpretation in Ancient Israel* (Oxford: Clarendon, 1985), pp. 200-209; J. Milgrom, *Leviticus 23-27*, AB 3B (New York: Doubleday, 2000), pp. 2417-21, and G. M. H. Ratheiser, *Mitzvoth Ethics and the Jewish Bible: The End of Old Testament Theology* (London: T & T Clark, 2007), pp. 307-15.

Stern distinguishes a "war-חרם" from a "priestly-חרם" (represented in Lev 27), which he argues is a later reinterpretation of חרם in a peaceful cultic setting, but still involving separation, inviolability, holiness and destruction (Stern, *Ḥērem*, pp. 125-6), a distinction that I shall develop. He argues that the earlier war-חרם is deeply rooted in mythic conceptions, with the execution of חרם interpreted as a participation with Yhwh in fighting the forces of chaos to secure order (pp. 220-21).

[12] E.g., "devoted for destruction" (NRSV); "devoted" (NIV); "under the ban" (NAS); "set apart" (NET); "devoted under the curse of destruction" (NJB); "doomed to destruction" (NKJV); "completely destroyed as an offering" (NLT).

[13] For texts see Stern, *Ḥērem*, pp. 5-6 and pp. 55-56.

[14] See Stern, *Ḥērem*, pp. 5-87 for a full discussion of the parallels that have been proposed. More recently L. A. S. Monroe ("Israelite, Moabite and Sabaean War-*ḥerem* Traditions and the Forging of National Identity: Reconsidering the Sabean Text RES 3945 in Light of Biblical and Moabite Evidence," in *VT* 57 [2007]: 318-41) has re-dated RES 3945, placing it in an era relevant for understanding the Old Testament.

[15] For convenience I shall consider deuteronomic (i.e., material relating to the book of Deuteronomy) and deuteronomistic (i.e., materials relating to the so-called Deuteronomistic History) together at this stage.

of idolatry. The root חרם is common in Joshua (occurring twenty-eight times in the book), although idolatry is never explicitly associated with חרם in Joshua, unlike in Deuteronomy 7:1-5, 25-26. Second, in the prophetic literature the verb is used again with reference to annihilation, but in an eschatological/apocalyptic sense to describe the fate of the nations (e.g. Jer 50:21, 26; 51:3) as well as in relation to Israelites (e.g. Is 43:28). Third, the root occurs in the priestly materials, usually to refer to something or someone that is irrevocably dedicated to YHWH (e.g. Lev 27:21-29). Outside these contexts its usage is rare.

While there has been a tendency to seek to understand חרם through the conflation of its usage in these three contexts, reading the concepts from each context into the others introduces problems. In Deuteronomy what is declared חרם is associated with that which is detested and abhorred (שִׁקֵּץ תּוֹעֵבָה, Deut 7:25-26); yet in Leviticus, and in other priestly material, that which is חרם is associated with that which is holy (קֹדֶשׁ; Lev 27; Num 18:14; Ezek 44:29 and perhaps Josh 6:19). So comparison of Leviticus 27 with Deuteronomy 7, texts which offer paradigmatic accounts of חרם in the priestly and deuteronomistic materials, indicates a confusion of categories with the usage of חרם different in each case. However, in Deuteronomy and Joshua, what is חרם is said to be ליהוה ("to YHWH"; e.g. Josh 6:17), resembling the vocabulary associated with offerings, which might connect with priestly conceptualities and usages of the term. Moreover, Deuteronomy 7 and 13 and Joshua 7 (the story of Achan and Ai) in particular, give the impression that objects that are subject to חרם may be viewed as a "contagion" that have "a property of חרם." Again, there are resonances with priestly categories. Yet objects that are declared חרם vary in the deuteronomistic literature (compare Josh 6 with Josh 8), so it is difficult to identify any such inherent property of "herem-ness." Finally, while Deuteronomy 7 uses חרם to interpret the entrance into Canaan, this category is not used in parallel accounts (Ex 23:20-33; Num 33:50-56). This suggests that a divine declaration of people or objects as, or subject to, חרם does not reflect some inherent, irrevocable "property" or "state" of the people or objects that would provide the correct (theological) interpretation of Israel's entrance to Canaan—the Bible can describe Israel's entrance to Canaan without using the term. Thus we must reexamine חרם.

Reexamining חרם *in the deuteronomistic literature.* Is the "priestly" conception of חרם found in Leviticus 27 reflected in the deuteronomistic materials? A few texts have been used to suggest that it is. Joshua 6:19 and 6:24 are perhaps two key texts that might suggest that it is. Here precious metal objects from Jericho are said to be deposited in the "treasury of the Lord" rather than destroyed (cf. Deut 7:5; Josh 6:17-18). Moreover, in Joshua 7, where Israel's crushing defeat at Ai is traced to Achan's disobedience in taking some of the חרם of Jericho (cf. Josh 6:19, 24), it appears that חרם has a "contagious" nature, somehow "contaminating" Israel, resulting in her defeat (Josh 7:11-13). Such a concept might resonate with priestly ideas. Similarly, it has been argued that Deuteronomy 7:25-26 supports such a conception of חרם objects as contagious. Here there is the risk that if an Israelite brings an idol into their house then they, like the idol, will "become חרם." So it has become popular to regard חרם objects as somehow "contagious."[16] For example, Joel Kaminsky suggests that "The sacral character of חרם . . . extends to the effect it has on those who misuse it. It is clear from Deut. 7:25-26 . . . and from Josh. 6:18 . . . that when one misappropriates חרם, one runs the risk of having the tabooed status of the חרם transferred to oneself."[17] However, many scholars suggest that Joshua 6:19 and 6:24 are later priestly or post–priestly additions to Joshua 6, a suggestion that I develop elsewhere.[18] The conception found here is, therefore, not the deuteronomistic concept as such, and is thus not the essential conception of חרם in Joshua 6 but a development of it.

Moreover, חרם is never associated with the vocabulary of "spreading" or "contagion" or "purity" as per priestly categories such as פרש, פשׂה, טמא and טהר. The language of "transmission" for טמא uses the verb נגע (touch), a verb not used in conjunction with חרם anywhere. Furthermore, there is no deuteronomistic conceptual equivalent to such categories with regard to חרם. While Deuteronomy 7:25-26 and 13:12-18 (Heb) might be said to imply such conceptions of the transmission of a "property" of חרם, Deuteronomy

---

[16]See e.g., L. D. Hawk, *Joshua*, Berit Olam (Collegeville, MN: Liturgical Press, 2000), p. 100; R. D. Nelson, *Joshua*, OTL (Louisville: Westminster John Knox Press, 1997), p. 101; J. F. D. Creach, *Joshua*, Interpretation (Louisville: John Knox Press, 2003), pp. 72-74; J. S. Kaminsky, "Joshua 7: A Reassessment of the Israelite Conceptions of Corporate Punishment," in *The Pitcher is Broken: Memorial Essays for Gösta W. Ahlström*, ed. S. W. Holloway and L. K. Handy, JSOTSup 190 (Sheffield, UK: Sheffield Academic Press, 1995), pp. 315-46, esp. p. 331; Lohfink, "*Ḥāram*," p. 194.

[17]Kaminsky, "Joshua," p. 331.

[18]Earl, *Reading Joshua*, pp. 96-97.

13:12-18 uses the language of "cleaving" (דבק), and Deuteronomy 7:25-26 uses the language of "coveting" (חמד), which implies more than a notion of "contagion" *per se*—rather, an "attachment" in some sense is implied. Thus it is difficult to make sense of these texts in "ontological" terms. Rather, it would seem that a better way of making sense of these texts is to read them in terms of rhetoric. The texts are concerned with the avoidance of idols. If one reads the texts in a rhetorical sense, then it would make sense to see חרם symbolically evoking an existential threat. If you are attached to idols or idolatry then you will perish with them. It is idolatry that is presented as the contagion rather than חרם. Then in Joshua 7 the issue is not that Israel is contaminated with חרם and so "becomes חרם," but that Achan's theft of the precious objects of חרם from Jericho represents disobedience to YHWH manifested in lying, stealing, coveting and covenant violation. Indeed, the vocabulary of the story draws attention to Achan's crime by using these categories from the Decalogue (Josh 7:11). So חרם here, building on Joshua 6:18, affords the opportunity to evocatively symbolize such covenant violation.[19]

Finally, is חרם to be construed as something like an "offering" to YHWH? The grammar of חרם as being ליהוה is rare,[20] and the sense of the *lamed* preposition is wide and varied and need not be taken thus.[21] However, the use of כליל in Deuteronomy 13:17 (Heb) in conjunction with חרם is often taken to reinforce further this sacrificial understanding of חרם. כליל is usually taken to mean "whole burnt offering" here, but I suggest that it should be read adverbially, for emphasis: "burn the town and all its spoil with fire **completely for** the LORD your God" (rather than "burn the town and all its spoil with fire, **as a whole burnt offering to** the LORD your God"). This rendering would reflect the more common adverbial usage of כליל, conveying a sense of completeness,[22] especially since it seems odd to offer

---

[19]However, it is interesting that Joshua 7 is read in terms of a priestly conception of חרם in the Dead Sea Scrolls (4Q379 3.2.5-6). Along with the additions of Josh 6:19 and 24, this indicates a tendency to read the differing conceptions of חרם together from a very early stage.

[20]Found only in Josh 6:17 in the deuteronomistic materials and only Mic 4:13 and Leviticus 27 elsewhere.

[21]Cf. e.g., Gen 24:26; Deut 1:41; 16:1; 1 Sam 1:3; 2:8; 3:20; 2 Sam 21:6; 1 Kings 6:1-2; 19:10 and 2 Kings 6:33 for a variety of senses for ליהוה.

[22]It occurs in Ex 28:31; 39:22; Lev 6:15, 16; Num 4:6; Judg 20:40; Is 2:18; Lam 2:15; Ezek 16:14; 27:3; 28:12 in the sense of completeness and Deut 33:10; 1 Sam 7:9 and Ps 51:21 in the sense of offering. Cf. Lohfink, "Ḥāram," p. 184, who questions whether כליל "was perceived as a sacrificial term" here.

that which is associated with detestable (תועבה) practice to Yhwh.

In summary, then, there has been a tendency, first, to understand חרם in deuteronomistic texts in something like ontological terms as a property of people or objects that can "spread" or "contaminate." But it appears to make more sense to understand חרם in imaginative, symbolic and rhetorical terms. Second, there has been a tendency to read conceptions of priestly-חרם into the deuteronomistic accounts of חרם which has led to this skewed understanding of חרם in Deuteronomy and Joshua. Such a conception might have developed "through language," especially via texts such as Micah 4:13 ("Arise and thresh, O daughter Zion, for I will make your horn iron and your hoofs bronze; you shall beat in pieces [דקק] many peoples, and shall devote [חרם] their gain to the Lord, their wealth to the Lord of the whole earth"), and in priestly influenced redactions of the Hexateuch. This tendency began at an early stage, witnessed in redactional glosses in Joshua (6:19, 24) and is developed further in 4Q379 3.2.5-6, a text that rewrites Joshua 7 using allusions to Leviticus 27.

A symbolic approach to חרם **in the Old Testament.** I shall now argue that a symbolic/rhetorical/existential, rather than a literal/ontological/historical, reading of texts involving חרם is appropriate. Outside the priestly conception reflected in Leviticus 27, חרם functions existentially and symbolically in different ways in different contexts. It takes the image of mass annihilation (perhaps stemming from ancient Near Eastern imagery as found in the Mesha Inscription) as its literal or "concrete" sense, a sense that is literal only within the "world of the text." But its significance, especially its theological significance, is discovered elsewhere. חרם is to be appropriated or enacted existentially in another way, through the symbol's opaque or "second-order" sense,[23] and it is in this sense that we discover the significance of חרם as our witness to God, even on the Old Testament's own terms.

First, we shall consider temporal perspectives on חרם to help establish its symbolic, or even "mythical," character before, second, considering what its significance is by studying the way in which its second-order sense was construed and developed according to the witness of various biblical texts, i.e., how חרם as a concept was *used*.

Outside Deuteronomy and Joshua, references to a deuteronomistic con-

---

[23]See Paul Ricoeur, *The Symbolism of Evil* (Boston: Beacon Press, 1969), p. 15, on symbol.

ception of חרם are rare. In Judges, Samuel-Kings and Chronicles it occurs
only occasionally, and mostly in relation to activities that relate to the conquest. The significant exception is in 1 Samuel 15 in relation to Saul's rejection as king, which we shall return to later. But the virtual absence of חרם
from Judges, Samuel-Kings and Chronicles is striking. Leaving aside
1 Samuel 15, חרם only occurs nine times in these books, suggesting that it is
not part of Israel's vocabulary of warfare (Judg 1:17; 1 Kings 9:21; 1 Chron 2:7;
4:41. It is used to narrate actions of non-Israelites in 2 Kings 19:11 [and parallels: 2 Chron 32:14; Is 37:11]; 2 Chron 20:23; 1 Kings 20:42; Judg 21:11.).
Similarly, the absence of חרם from the psalms is significant, indicating that
it is not inherent to Israel's liturgy and worship. Leaving Deuteronomy and
Joshua aside for a moment, taken together, these observations suggest that
חרם is not a category that Israel uses to describe her existence or narrate her
actions *in the present*, suggesting that the application of חרם is "displaced"
from the present. It is primarily related to what is perhaps an "other-worldly
conquest" located in the prototypical past.

Turning to the prophets, חרם is developed and used in an other-worldly
eschatological or future direction as part of the language of poetic prophetic oracles that are replete with metaphor to warn Israel against unfaithfulness, or encourage her regarding the fate of her oppressors (Is 34:2, 5;
43:28; Jer 25:9; 50:21, 26; 51:3; Dan 11:44; Mic 4:13; Zech 14:11). So in the prophetic literature חרם is a concept of the future which provides the contours
for Israel's (or the Christian reader's) existential response in the "here and
now"; do not go after the nations and their ways, and do not worry about
them, for they are doomed (as חרם), as will *you* be if *you* keep following
their gods. Or do not worry, keep persevering, because you will no longer
be subject to destruction from the nations. So it makes sense to see חרם as
having an imaginative, existential and rhetorical rather than "literal" or ontological significance. Indeed, while Israel was prophetically threatened
with חרם in her near future, when such punishment occurred it was not
interpreted using the category of חרם in the canonical narrative books. So
חרם remained rhetorical in nature and was not used to describe what actually happened.[24] So in the prophets, actualization of חרם *per se* is kept in

---

[24]In the prophetic books see e.g. Jer 25:9. However Is 43:28 is an exception, in that חרם is YHWH's
own interpretation of what he did to Jacob. But this is in the context of a poetic oracle replete

an imaginative portrait of the future in the world of the text, displaced from the present, even if—and perhaps this is the main point—it has existential significance in the present.

But returning to Joshua and Deuteronomy, why shouldn't one take these texts as reflecting a factual description of the past recorded in an era that is roughly contemporary with the events narrated? Many scholars consider that Deuteronomy and Joshua were written much later than the events they portray, where the historical status of the narrative content is unclear.[25] Indeed there is evidence in the texts themselves that might point to their genre as being "mythical" in nature—in the sense of the texts being symbolic presentations of an imaginatively constructed prototypical past that are written to shape the worldview of the author's contemporaries, without trying to describe the past. First, Joshua places the portrayal of a "literal חרם" in a past that is most naturally taken as mythological. This is seen through, for example, references to the Anakim and Rephaim in the conclusion of the conquest in Joshua 11 and Joshua 17, mythical giants and ghosts from the distant past that dwelt in the world of Joshua's חרם, a world very different from the Israelites' experienced world.[26] Second, the portrait of entrance to the Promised Land via חרם is only *one* of several portraits of entrance into the land in the Old Testament. The injunctions of Deuteronomy 7 are based upon חרם in a text that reflects both Exodus 23:20-33, which uses כחד ("disappear") and not חרם, and Numbers 33:50-56 which uses ירש ("possess") and not חרם.[27] Moreover, in Leviticus the land is said to vomit (קיא) the locals out so that Israel can possess the land (Lev 18:24-30; 20:22-24), providing another symbolic and rhetorical image of entrance to

---

with metaphor, and such an interpretation of Jacob's punishment is not found elsewhere. Again the concept is rhetorical in focus.

[25]For discussion of trends in research see T. C. Römer and A. de Pury, "Deuteronomistic Historiography: History of Research and related Issues," in *Israel Constructs its History: Deuteronomistic Historiography in Recent Research*, ed. A. de Pury et al., JSOTSup 306 (Sheffield, UK: Sheffield Academic Press, 2000), pp. 24-141. For an introduction to the archaeological issues and a suggestive account of the nature of the texts such as Joshua and Samuel-Kings see Davies, *Memories*.

[26]See discussion in Earl, *Reading Joshua*, pp. 168-70, with further bibliography on the Anakim and Rephaim.

[27]Deut 2–3, cf. Num 21:21ff.; Deut 7, cf. Ex 23:20-33; 34:10-14 and Num 33:50-56. It seems that if there ever was a conquest, it is unlikely that it was interpreted using the category of חרם at the time.

the land without חרם. Furthermore, some scholars have recently traced another portrait of the emergence of Israel in Canaan using the book of
Genesis,[28] a portrait of gradual peaceful emergence that is possibly more
fitting with the archaeological data. Thus חרם forms the basis of one of
several different portraits of the emergence of Israel in Canaan in Scripture,
appearing to reflect a retrospective category that has symbolic significance
in senses that we shall see below. Finally, there are indicators within the
narrative of Joshua that would suggest that it is not appropriate to take
Joshua as a "factual history" in genre. For example, the location of Rahab's
house in the city wall (Joshua 2) does not sit easily with the report of the
collapse of the wall (Joshua 6), an observation that has indeed troubled
rabbis through the centuries. Moreover, portrayals of complete conquest
(Josh 10:40-42; 11:16, 23) do not sit well with reports of incomplete conquest
(Josh 15:63, 16:10; 17:13) in the book. One could regard these examples as
reflecting what Origen described as "stumbling blocks" in the text of
Scripture that point one away from a "literal" reading toward a "spiritual"
reading,[29] an approach that I am seeking to reconstrue here in terms of
symbolic interpretation. Indeed, Origen refused to read Joshua in literal
terms, seeing such an approach as reflective of the errors of Marcion.[30]

In summary then, "literal" חרם only exists symbolically, and in the world
of the text; it is "never now," it is never used to narrate or to interpret contemporary events or experience even if the symbol has a second-order
sense that relates to contemporary life "here and now" in a way that we shall
see. חרם exists in the world of the text in the prototypical past and in the
apocalyptic future, but not in everyday experience, and it is appropriate to
seek its significance in symbolic, existential and rhetorical terms in the construction of a theology of חרם.

The significance of חרם *in Deuteronomy.* Deuteronomy 7:1-5 reflects the
paradigmatic sense of חרם in Deuteronomy. What then is the significance

---

[28]See K. Schmid, "The So-called Yahwist and the Literary Gap between Genesis and Exodus," in
A Farewell to the Yahwist? The Composition of the Pentateuch in Recent European Interpretation,
ed. T. B. Dozeman and K. Schmid, SBL Symposium 34 (Atlanta: SBL, 2006) pp. 29-50, esp. p. 49.
[29]Origen, *On First Principles*, Latin Text, IV.ii.9, in G. W. Butterworth, trans., *Origen: On First
Principles* (Gloucester, MA: Peter Smith, 1973), pp. 285-7.
[30]Homily on Joshua 12.3 (see B. J. Bruce, trans., Origen, *Homilies on Joshua*, FC 105 [Washing-
ton, DC: The Catholic University of America Press, 2002], pp. 123-24).

of חרם in Deuteronomy 7:1-5? Since Joshua is, in some sense, the fulfillment of Deuteronomy 7:1-5, we may find some clues in the conclusion of Joshua (Josh 23–24). From the parallels between the texts, one may see that Joshua 23–24 draws the specific charge to Israel prior to entering the land (Deut 7:1-5) into an ongoing charge to Israel relevant to the life of the reader. But it is noteworthy that Joshua 23–24 does not mention חרם or indeed the destruction of property. Only separation from Canaanites is commanded, something that is in fact implicit in Deuteronomy 7:1-5. Indeed, Deuteronomy 7:1-5 is incoherent if read literally, for the command to kill all the inhabitants of the land is followed by an exhortation against intermarriage with them. In other words, in a "mythological" sense, Deuteronomy 7 itself encourages not so much annihilation of Canaanites as radical separation from them and their idolatrous practices—exactly what Joshua 23–24 exhorts. This suggests Joshua 23–24 might be seen as something as a "commentary" on Deuteronomy 7:1-5. Deuteronomy 7:1-5 is, therefore, best read rhetorically in an existential sense, drawing on חרם as a symbol. Indeed, this sense of separation as the enactment of Deuteronomy 7:1-5 finds support in Ezra 9:1-2 through the explicit use of בדל ("separation"), a text that develops Deuteronomy 7:1-5. By using חרם as a symbol, the sense of conflict with and the need for annihilation of idolatry is evoked in Deuteronomy, comparable perhaps with the use of קיא (vomit) in the priestly materials in relation to the inhabitants of the land and their practices (Lev 18 and 20), evoking a sense of revulsion against idolatry.

Thus in Deuteronomy 7:1-5, and in texts that develop it, the sense of חרם is that of the separation of Israelites from Canaanites, and especially their idolatrous practices. Israel is to avoid Canaanite attachments, symbolized in the world of the text as חרם. Symbolically, חרם demonstrates here in the most dramatic terms that there is no transformation or mediation possible between the categories of "non-Israel" and "Israel." It is "them" and "us," with any attempts to transform or mediate ending in death and destruction.

The Significance of חרם *in Joshua.* As we saw above in regard to Joshua 23, at one level Joshua presents itself as the fulfillment of Deuteronomy 7:1-5. Israel enters the land, destroys the inhabitants (Josh 6–12) and settles in it (Josh 13–21). However, the way Joshua uses the symbol of חרם is actually rather different from the way that it is used in Deuteronomy. It is more subtle and uses the symbol of חרם in Deuteronomy to *qualify* the assumptions and message of Deuteronomy 7:1-5. Joshua challenges the notion of what is an essentially ethnically defined identity for Israel—or at least the notion of an already determined "us" group with rigid boundaries preventing the entrance of others in to the group—even as it reinforces Deuteronomy's injunctions to be separate from idols and obey YHWH, manifested in covenant faithfulness.

In Joshua חרם can be seen as a symbol for "divine action" in the world of the text that demands a response; it forms a test that is reflective of character or identity in a theological sense. How does one respond to חרם? If one responds appropriately (i.e., favorably toward YHWH) it establishes one as essentially "Israelite," whereas an inappropriate response establishes one as "non-Israelite." Rahab, the "quintessential other"—a Canaanite prostitute—behaves as a model Israelite when confronted with the campaign of חרם, offering an exemplary "confession" that is matched only by Moses and Solomon elsewhere in the Old Testament (Deut 4:39; 1 Kings 8:23). Her actions are interpreted in terms of "doing חסד," being what is at the heart of the covenant between YHWH and Israel (Ex 34:6; Deut 5:10; Ps 136; Mic 6:8). Conversely, Achan, the model Israelite genealogically, an observation emphasized through repetition (Josh 7:1, 16-18), when confronted with the campaign of חרם lies, covets and steals, symbolizing disobedience to the covenant as expressed in the Decalogue. Hence Achan is the paradigmatic non-Israelite in terms of character and response to YHWH. Moreover, the stories of Rahab and Achan have Jericho as their intersection, with the extreme חרם of Jericho being required by the narrative to make the stories of Achan and Rahab work. If it was not extreme, Achan would not have exemplified disobedience and Rahab might have lived anyway. Thus the significance of the extreme חרם in Joshua 6 may essentially be literary. The various local kings (especially in Joshua 10-11) are portrayed as reacting with aggression toward Israel when confronted with the campaign of חרם, confirming their status as outsiders, while Joshua, and the Israelites, are completely obedient to commands to conduct חרם (in the world of the text), confirming their Israelite status as those who respond faithfully and obediently to YHWH even in the most demanding circumstances, as symbolized in חרם. Finally there are the Gibeonites, who deceive the Israelites into making a treaty by pretending that they are from afar (cf. Deut 20:10-20, where people from afar are not to be subject to חרם). It is striking that חרם does not occur in their story in Joshua 9, even though there are places that cry out for its use (e.g., Josh 9:24). They behave in a somewhat marginal way and end up in a "liminal" state—they are betwixt and between on the boundary, with the "test" of חרם being unable to establish the nature of their response to God, and hence their identity, clearly. They do not quite have the positive traits of Rahab, but neither do they have the negative traits of the hostile kings. They are on the borders of what constitutes Israel in terms of character.

It is noteworthy that there is so little evaluation in all these narratives in Joshua, probably because they pose a searching challenge to accepted norms of Israelite identity and to Deuteronomy 7:1-5.[31] Moreover, it is noteworthy that so little narrative space is given to depicting annihilation in Joshua, suggesting that the message of the book is not that of annihilation. The majority of Joshua 6–11 focuses on stories of unusual individuals or groups who usually do not fit the pattern expected in Deuteronomy 7:1-5. While Joshua 23–24 confirms that Israel is to be separate from the nations and to abhor idolatry, the rest of the book subtly and searchingly qualifies the nature of this separation from its deuteronomic basis. Canaanites with Israelite character are embraced by Israel whereas Israelites with Canaanite character are ousted. There is no attempt to justify the conquest in terms of the extreme wickedness or idolatry of the Canaanites (unlike Deut 9:5 and Lev 20:22-24[32]). We are simply told that the local inhabitants hardened their hearts to war against Israel (Josh 11:20).

So, rather surprisingly, Joshua represents a qualification of accepted notions of identity and places searching demands upon the faithfulness of "insiders." It does so by encouraging an openness to the "other" based upon their responsiveness to Yhwh as symbolized in response to חרם by skillfully using the very discourse that Joshua seeks to qualify. Although set in the context of conquest, the message of Joshua, and the significance of חרם, is

---

[31] I also argue elsewhere that Joshua 22 qualifies the definition of Israelite identity in terms of land (Earl, *Reading Joshua*, pp. 178-83).

[32] But note that these texts are in the context of urging Israelite faithfulness, not conquest apologetic per se.

not really conquest or annihilation at all. To seek a contemporary analogy, Joshua functions something like a war protest movie. The "them" and "us" of Deuteronomy 7:1-5 is challenged, as reflected in Joshua 5:13-15 which, I suggest, rather than being cryptic or defective, can well be seen as the hermeneutical key to Joshua. Here, a figure with a drawn sword appears to Joshua. Joshua asks what side he is on. The figure then identifies himself as the commander of YHWH's army but refuses to answer Joshua's question on Joshua's terms, simply replying "no." No discussion of warfare or tactics takes place. While ultimately YHWH does fight for Israel (Josh 10:42), here at this crucial stage in the story, before any of the land is possessed, the commander makes it clear that YHWH is not merely co-opted on to the "side" of any people group as they determine themselves. The stories between Joshua 5:13-15 and 10:42 indicate that these notions of "sides" are problematic and cannot be drawn in societal terms. To put it another way, Joshua 5:13–10:42 indicates that God works on the behalf of those who respond faithfully to him. Israel has been demonstrated to be comprised of those who respond faithfully to God rather than simply a sociopolitical entity.

The significance of חרם *in Samuel.* We have seen how חרם in Joshua appears to symbolize divine action in the world (of the text), calling for a response that itself symbolizes response to YHWH. Faithfulness to חרם is faithfulness to YHWH; unfaithfulness to חרם is unfaithfulness to YHWH in a symbolic or mythological sense. It is in this sense that חרם functions in 1 Samuel 15, the other extended and extreme חרם narrative in the Old Testament. Here Saul is confronted with a test of whether he will obey YHWH as symbolized by commands of conducting חרם against the Amalekites. He does not fully obey, keeping back some of the best spoils for himself, rather like Achan, and is rejected as king as a result. He fails the test (1 Sam 15:26).

חרם *outside the Deuteronomistic materials.* We have touched briefly upon חרם in the priestly and prophetic materials. As the priestly conception of חרם does not relate to the question of "holy war," I do not wish to say more about this conception here, although there is an interesting inversion of the symbol—that which is חרם is now holy (קדש) rather than detestable (תועבה) as per Deuteronomy 7.

חרם is used in several different ways in the prophetic literature. In Isaiah 34:2, 5 and Jeremiah 50:21, 26 and 51:3 חרם is used as a verb in an eschato-

logical/apocalyptic context to describe what Yʜwʜ will do to the nations
(Isaiah) or Babylon (Jeremiah). Jeremiah makes more explicit the association between sins and חרם but, again, חרם clearly refers to widespread destruction. Second, in Isaiah 43:28, Jeremiah 25:9 and Zechariah 14:11 the
verb is used, in slightly different ways, with respect to Jacob, Judah or Jerusalem. It is understood in terms of Yʜwʜ's punishment and functions as
either a warning or encouragement for Israel. In Zechariah it is used in an
eschatological context, where Jerusalem will suffer חרם no more. In Daniel
11:44, חרם appears in an apocalyptic context, but it is one of the kings in
Daniel's vision that is the subject of the verb, and it is simply "many people"
that is the object as a result of this king's great rage. Finally, in Micah 4:13,
חרם appears in an apocalyptic/eschatological vision, but it is the "unjust
gains" of the nations that are the object of the verb חרם and are said to be
חרם "to Yʜwʜ." The usage here is thus slightly ambiguous, occupying a
position that resonates both with the "war-חרם" and the "priestly-חרם."

The symbolic and rhetorical use of the category of חרם in a way that is
existentially relevant to the reader in the present is demonstrated. The literal
sense of the symbol—radical annihilation on a massive scale—is used in
places to warn Israel against idolatry and in other places to evoke a sense of
assurance and confidence amid suffering and confusion amid those who
would persecute, oppress or worship idols. Although this shares the imagery with the deuteronomistic materials, it has a different symbolic significance and, as we saw above, it is not used to interpret actual destruction.
It is used as an imaginative, mythological image of the future to help the
reader live hopefully and appropriately in the present and thus shape their
future well.

חרם IN THE NEW TESTAMENT

There is no clear trajectory or development of חרם as such in the New Testament.[33] There is no development of Deuteronomy 7:1-5, although there are
general exhortations to avoid idolatry. Joshua finds remarkably little development in the New Testament, with its use centering on the positive qual-

---

[33]H. D. Park, however, has attempted to find developments, but these seem unconvincing. See
Park, *Finding Herem? A Study of Luke-Acts in the Light of Herem*, LNTS 357 (London: T & T
Clark, 2007).

ities of Rahab—she is an exemplar of faith (Heb 11:31) or works (Jas 2:25).

However, it is common to seek to trace the trajectory of certain forms of warfare in the Old Testament into Revelation in particular in order to find an eschatological or spiritual continuity of such ideas. For example, Merrill seeks to trace a trajectory from "Yahweh War" (which encompasses חרם for Merrill) into Revelation.[34] Although there is certainly a trajectory of the imagery of warfare from the Old Testament prophets into Revelation, there is perhaps no explicit trajectory of חרם into Revelation. However, by general association one might say that the prophetic concept of חרם finds resonance in Revelation, through the imagery of widespread annihilation in the future, intended to evoke existential encouragement or challenge to suffering or complacent Christians. This is a reflection of its existential and rhetorical significance in the Old Testament. But perhaps this is not a development of חרם as such. Thus the New Testament does little to guide our appropriation or theology of חרם in any direct or explicit way.

חרם IN THE CHRISTIAN TRADITION

It is interesting to consider the Christian reception of the relevant Old Testament texts.[35] I demonstrate elsewhere that Deuteronomy 7 has surprisingly little significance and use in the Christian context.[36] Origen's reading of Joshua appears paradigmatic for much of the history of the church, with Rahab's story being especially important. Joshua was a significant Old Testament book probably owing largely to the etymology of the names Joshua and Jesus—they are identical in Greek, and so one would expect to discover important typology or allegory. Thus crossing the Jordan and entrance to the Promised Land became a type for Christian baptism and entrance to new life in Christ;[37] the inheritance of the land typifies the Christian inheritance of the kingdom;[38] the fall of Jericho in Joshua 6 typifies the fall of

---

[34]Merrill, "Moderate Discontinuity," pp. 88-90.

[35]In particular see J. R. Franke, ed., *Joshua, Judges, Ruth, 1-2 Samuel,* Ancient Christian Commentary on Scripture, Old Testament IV (Downers Grove, IL: InterVarsity Press, 2005) for a summary indicating the kinds of ways that Joshua has been read. See further discussion in Earl, *Reading Joshua*, pp. 120-96.

[36]See Douglas S. Earl, "The Christian Significance of Deuteronomy 7," in *JTI* 3, no. 1 (2009): 41-62.

[37]E.g., Origen, *Homilies on Joshua* 4.1; Gregory of Nyssa, *Against Those Who Put off Baptism* (*PG* 46.421A).

[38]E.g. Calvin, *Inst.* II.11.1.

the kingdoms of the world or of one's former way of life.[39] But it is interesting that Origen is dismissive of those who want to take the accounts of the battles with the hostile kings in Joshua 10 in a literal sense, arguing that such a hermeneutic simply does not fit with a Christian hermeneutic or *regula fidei* perhaps. Rather, for Origen the trajectory of the significance of texts like these is found in Ephesians 6 in the spiritual warfare of the Christian.[40] Indeed, as I argue in "Joshua and the Crusades" in this volume, Joshua was not used to support or to discuss earthly conflicts in much of the history of the church.[41]

An interesting way of understanding חרם in the Christian context that draws upon all its various Old Testament resonances is provided by Richard Hess. Hess discusses חרם in terms of "holy war" and suggests that, as well as there being a development of this theme in Revelation (Rev 1–2; 12; 14; 18–22) in which Jesus battles against all earthly and heavenly opponents and demonic forces in particular (as seen in the synoptic gospels), "Christ takes upon himself the sin of the world and becomes the victim of the holy war that God wages against sin (2 Cor 5:21)."[42] This might be said to draw upon prophetic, priestly and deuteronomistic conceptions of חרם. Jesus, the holy one, is separated from Israel by being disowned and scorned even though he is set apart by God. He bears the sins of the world, becoming an abomination subjected to annihilation, inaugurating the eschaton.

However, it is interesting that there is little discussion of חרם per se in the Christian tradition. And in particular Hess's sort of association was not made despite extensive imaginative allegorical and typological reading of the Old Testament. Perhaps this is because the early Christian church generally read the Old Testament in Greek (the LXX) and not Hebrew, and so it was interpretation from the Greek rather than the Hebrew text that was foundational and would become normative for exegesis and theology in the centuries to come. The LXX renders חרם in Joshua 6:17 as ἀνάθεμα, which is a crucial interpretive move that sets up all sorts of resonances and allu-

---

[39]E.g., Origen, *Homilies on Joshua* 6.4; Gregory of Nyssa, *Against Those Who Put off Baptism* (PG 46.421A).

[40]Origen, *Homilies on Joshua* 12.1.

[41]The one exception is the regular use of Joshua 8 in relation to the question of whether it is legitimate to use ambush in warfare. See Douglas S. Earl, "Joshua and the Crusades."

[42]R. S. Hess, *Joshua*, TOTC (Leicester, UK: Inter-Varsity Press, 1996), p. 46.

sions that are not present in the Hebrew, whilst losing other important ones.[43] Canonically, one might expect the use of ἀνάθεμα in Galatians 3:13 (citing Deut 21:23, being applied to the crucifixion) to set up a resonance with its use in Joshua in the Greek, which, on reverting to Hebrew, might form the basis for a typology in which חרם could be said to be "fulfilled" by Jesus on the cross, in that he takes the "חרם of the world" onto himself, rather like Hess suggests. But there is no evidence of this sort of interpretative move being made in the early Christian tradition.

Contemporary readings such as Hess's and ancient readings such as Origen's indicate that texts of חרם such as Joshua do not find their Christian significance in terms of the plain or literal sense of the text. But I have tried to show that they were never intended to be read in their plain or literal sense, too, and that to attempt to do so is to fail to respect the genre of the text. However, the difficulty with readings such as Hess's and Origen's is that they represent a tendency to extract atomistically the more peripheral parts of a symbolic concept without also taking the core meaning and sense, and its narrative context, into the Christian context. If my readings of Deuteronomy 7, Joshua and 1 Samuel 15 above are roughly along the right lines, then it seems that a Christian biblical theology of חרם should consider the concepts of radical separation from idolatry by refusing attachments with "outsiders" and "outside influences" (Deuteronomy 7); a qualification of who it is that constitutes "outsiders" in Joshua in which חרם symbolizes divine action that calls for a response so as to demonstrate identity and thus challenge accepted constructions of identity; and existential encouragement or challenge in relation to future fate and hope. It will, however, be necessary to consider how these ideas are refracted through the New Testament.

TOWARD A BIBLICAL THEOLOGY OF חרם

There are a number of difficulties in trying to construct a biblical theology of חרם and in the Christian hermeneutics of the relevant texts.

First there is, perhaps, a tendency to assume that Scripture speaks with a unified and clear voice—witness attempts to harmonize the Gospels. But scholars have recently become more aware of the diversity of voices within

---

[43]A similar problem occurs with translating חרם into English. Rendering it as "destroy" shifts the meaning of the term, for Hebrew has other words for destroy (e.g. שׁמד) distinct from חרם.

Scripture, even though such diverse voices may be regarded as testimonies to the same reality. We have seen that Joshua and Deuteronomy speak with different voices using the very symbol of חרם to urge and to develop different ideological/theological outlooks, even as the books share much in common in terms of the worship of Yhwh through the covenant. How then does one adjudicate between different voices?

Second, there is a tendency to assume that "history-like" narratives in Scripture must be historically accurate and referential in the plain sense in order to be true or trustworthy. Texts such as Deuteronomy 7:1-5, Joshua 6:1-27 and Joshua 10:40-42 have been taken to reflect what God actually said, what Joshua and Israel actually did. The interpretation of the events in the narrative is seen as accurate, being divinely inspired interpretation of history. Likewise prophetic texts (e.g., Is 34:2) are sometimes taken as actually referring to what God will do, as if they were like film clips of the future made available in the present. From this deductions of the metaphysical character and nature of God are made. But if my reading of the texts is correct, this approach is flawed. As Paul Ricoeur has argued, texts of "poetic discourse," which I suggest is what texts such as Joshua or the prophets are, are referential but in a different sense than narratives that claim to be historically referential in nature.[44] This is not to detract from their value and nature as inspired revelatory texts but rather to rethink the way in which they are revelatory—to rethink their genre and thus how and what we can learn from them. In other words, narratives such as Joshua evoke a response to God from which something of the character of God can be inferred, but the response evoked is one of, for example, challenging assumptions of the ethnic or sociopolitical definition of the people of God and how this is worked out in daily life. The theological inferences are then rather different from those arising from questions about Canaanite genocide which arise when one attempts to read the narrative as history, either actual or as Israel might have wished it to be.

To put it in more traditional Christian theological terms, the assumption has been roughly that scriptural texts such as Joshua relate to the knowledge of God in the sense that they are understood primarily as making direct

---

[44]Paul Ricoeur, "The Narrative Function," *Semeia* 13 (1978): 177-202.

referential claims about history, God and God's "acts in history" (as proposi-
tional truth, perhaps). These claims have implications for practical living, but
this is rather different from seeing the texts primarily as exciting stories that
shape in indirect and symbolic ways our practical living before God, with
the texts thus relating to the character of God only opaquely and indirectly.
This distinction (that perhaps I have exaggerated somewhat for clarity) has
some resonances with the distinction between "speculative science" (*scientia
speculativa*)—knowledge referring directly to and being about God—and
"practical science" (*scientia practica*), relating to actions and living. Thomas
Aquinas develops the use of these categories and related questions, such as
whether *sacra Scriptura* should employ symbol and metaphor and the nature
of the senses of Scripture, in the very first question of the *Summa Theologiae*.
He concludes that theology is both speculative and practical in orientation,
that the use of symbol is fitting and that Scripture has multiple senses.[45] His
framing of the *Summa Theologiae* in these terms seems to afford the possibility from within the Christian tradition of reframing our approach to the
task of biblical theology by recognizing that the nature of the balance between *scientia speculativa* and *scientia practica* might look different from
what has often been assumed. One might suggest that the nature of Scripture,
and how and in what terms it speaks to us, may be faithfully and fruitfully
considered using various recent anthropological approaches to narrative
and myth in particular that stress the role of symbol, such as those of Paul
Ricoeur, Victor Turner or Seth Kunin. These approaches, if appropriate,
would imply that one cannot simply read the message of Scripture off the
surface in what is apparently its "plain sense" to make deductions about the
nature of God, the acts of God or what is morally acceptable or paradigmatic
or historically accurate.[46] This was recognized by the early fathers in their
preference for the spiritual sense but is something that has become neglected.
Moreover, it is common to seek to interpret Scripture primarily in the sense
of *scientia speculativa* rather than *scientia practica*. We need a subtler herme-

---

[45]See e.g. T. Gilby, trans., *St Thomas Aquinas Summa Theologiae Volume 1 (1a. 1): Christian Theology* (Cambridge: Cambridge University Press, 2006), pp. 15-17, 33-41. He privileges the "literal sense" but construes it fairly broadly.

[46]See Earl, *Reading Joshua*, pp. 14-48. See especially Victor Turner, "Myth and Symbol," in *International Encyclopedia of the Social Sciences*, ed. D. L. Sills (London: Macmillan, 1968), 10:576-81,
on the nature and significance of the portrayal of immoral behavior in myth.

neutic that recognizes where each of these categories is most appropriate for reading particular texts. It would seem appropriate, if one is to respect the genre of the text, to read Joshua and the חרם it portrays in its symbolic sense primarily in terms of *scientia practica* rather than *scientia speculativa*. So while Joshua 10:40-42 has been taken to be paradigmatic of the message of Joshua and all that is problematic about God in moral terms (or, some might say, the Old Testament perception of God), in fact the locus of the message of Joshua, and what might be inferred about God, might be found in the apparently cryptic Joshua 5:13-15. Joshua's question relating to God as taking sides that are sociopolitically determined is shown to be problematic, as we saw above. In light of the stories of Rahab and Achan, the question is not, "Whose side is God on?" but rather, "Who can faithfully worship and serve God, and what is involved in this?" The stories of Rahab and Achan begin to answer this. Thus the issue that we face is not considering what a literal practice of חרם might say about the nature of God. This is simply not how חרם is functioning in Scripture.

Third, Nicholas Lash suggests that hermeneutics relates to considering how one might re-express what was once achieved, intended or shown in the biblical texts in terms of concrete expressions of human practice and behavior today. Thus the question that we are moving toward is not that of how one should "practice חרם today" or, as we saw above, that of what חרם says about the nature of God, but rather that of how one can express the practices and behavior that חרם (rhetorically, symbolically and existentially) evokes today. In other words, how can one faithfully re-express practices of radical separation from idolatry (Deut 7), of challenging certain forms of identity construction (Josh), of evoking response to divine action in the world as reflective of identity construction (Josh; 1 Sam), and of encouraging suffering Christians (Is 34:2; Zech 14:11) or challenging complacent Christians (Achan in Josh 7; Jer 25:9)? In our world, deeply troubled by religiously motivated violence, it is likely that a symbol using widespread annihilation is no longer a wise or appropriate choice for such practices. If John's Gospel (in particular) can be understood as portraying Jesus as the supreme embodiment of divine action in the world, along with patterns of various responses to such divine action, then it would seem that a good development or recontextualization of the idea of response to חרם is that of response to Jesus. How one responds to Jesus says something crucial about character and identity, causing us to rethink questions of inclusion/exclusion and the nature of idolatrous attachments.

Finally, we must remember that we are dealing with Old Testament texts, which might urge caution in simply trying to "apply" the points above. On the one hand, as Christians we cherish these texts, respect them and read them with full seriousness. But on the other hand, we view these texts as in some sense (that requires clarification) provisional, being refracted through the New Covenant and the fullness of revelation of God in Christ. So, for example, one may wish to develop the story of Rahab and the observation that it was her "steadfast love/faithfulness" (חסד) that brought her into fellowship with Israel as a response to חרם (Josh 2:10); but, conversely, one might not wish to develop the observation that Achan discovered death (i.e., symbolic exclusion) rather than forgiveness on confession of sin (Josh 7:20-26). Thus we might expect that some trajectories of the symbolism will develop and find a fuller significance while others will wane. This problem is acute with חרם, certainly as expressed in Deuteronomy 7:1-5, not necessarily because of the imagery of annihilation, but because the concept is symbolically expressive of the impossibility of mediation or transformation between the categories of "non-Israel" and "Israel." In the Christian context, if one develops the natural trajectory of the concept, it would suggest that there is no transformation possible between "non-Christian" and "Christian." In other words, the symbol as used in Deuteronomy 7:1-5 when read in a Christian context effectively denies the possibility of Christian mission and conversion! This clearly does not express a Christian conception. This is not because of the imagery of warfare but because of the fundamental contradiction to the Christian call to mission and conversion (Mt 28:18-20). In other words, חרם is a concept used in Deuteronomy 7:1-5 to reflect the inherent nature of the Old Covenant and not the New, rather like circumcision and dietary laws express the Old Covenant. Thus although the Christian might develop the call to the separation from idolatry in Deuteronomy 7 that חרם evokes, there are difficulties with developing its full meaning and sense here.[47] Indeed Christians have instead developed the story of Rahab.

---

[47]See Douglas Earl, "The Christian Significance of Deuteronomy 7."

CONCLUSION

We have seen that the significance of חרם even on the Old Testament's own terms is not that of a report of or call to genocide. The difficulty for the Christian is not, then, what חרם construed in its literal sense might say about a violent God or Israel and the associated moral problems. For חרם imaginatively symbolized a variety of concepts: separation from idolatry and exclusivist construction of identity (Deut); response to divine action in the world, and rethinking notions of the identity and nature of God's people (Josh); comforting and encouraging oppressed Israel (Is 34:2; Zech 14:11); and challenging complacent Israel (Josh 7; Jer 25:9). One might say that there are a number of "theologies of חרם" in the Old Testament, none of which is really developed explicitly or directly in the New, or in the Christian tradition.

The challenge for the Christian today in constructing a "theology of חרם" is a case of developing the theology of a symbol. One might say that the task is first that of considering what forms of separation "from the world" the Christian life demands and what forms of living embody this, as balanced by a call to mission and involvement in the world. Second, it is a case of considering what other trajectories there are of its symbolic aspects and how these may be re-expressed today in suitable symbols that evoke concrete practices of faithfulness, challenge, encouragement and worship as response to our Lord Jesus Christ.

PART FIVE

Ethical and
Philosophical Perspectives

9

CRUSADE IN THE
OLD TESTAMENT AND TODAY

Daniel R. Heimbach

THERE IS NO MORE ACUTE CHALLENGE to the moral understanding
of Christians than comes with handling the record of the Hebrew Bible
concerning Israel's practice of "holy war," a sort of war now more specifically designated "Yahweh war."[1] This is because Israel's God, being understood as not just a tribal deity but the one true Creator of the universe, is
recorded as himself commanding the wholesale slaughter of women,
children, the elderly, the infirmed and even animals, as well as soldiers; and
as ordering the complete destruction of cities, idols and temples, as well as
military fortifications. This study will assess the contemporary relevance of
the ethic employed in the Yahweh wars of Israel, that ethic being a divinely
sanctioned version of crusade war.

War was a topic of great importance in the life and history of ancient
Israel. Of the thirty-nine books in the Hebrew Bible, war is directly mentioned in all but two—Ruth and the Song of Songs—and even in these, war
is in the near background. Ruth is identified as the great-grandmother of
David, Israel's most famous warrior-king (Ruth 4:17), and soldiers armed
and experienced in battle escort the king in the Song of Songs (Song 3:7-8).

---

[1]See Rudolf Smend, *Yahweh War and Tribal War*, trans. Max Gray Rogers (Nashville: Abingdon,
1970); G. H. Jones, "The Concept of Holy War," in *The World of Ancient Israel: Sociological,
Anthropological, and Political Perspectives*, ed. R. E. Clements (New York: Cambridge University
Press, 1989); and J. P. U. Lilley, "Understanding the *Herem*," *Tyndale Bulletin* 44 (1993): 169-77.

As Helmut Thielicke well observed, "the Old Testament is full of wars and rumors of wars."[2] War was ubiquitous in the ancient landscape. But most war activity recorded in the Old Testament is not a matter of war in general, but rather of "holy war" and is not just a matter of any "holy war," but rather of a particular sort pertaining to Israel's special status with God. While the ethic by which this sort of war operated is foreign to modern thinkers and is for that reason especially hard to grasp, doing so is essential for understanding some very important biblical concepts, including the character of God and the development of salvation history, to say nothing of the nature and coherence of divinely established moral order.

The task of analyzing the ethic of Yahweh war is complex and immense, so it is not surprising to find that doing so raises many important issues. These issues include whether the Old Testament supports any coherent view on the ethics of war at all; and, if so, whether the close connection of religion and war in the Old Testament means that any ethic justifying war is necessarily in some sense a matter of "holy war"; and, if so, whether there is in the religiously connected war thinking of the Old Testament only one, or possibly two, different ethics (both a religiously connected just war ethic and a religiously connected crusade ethic); and, if so, whether either or both of the religiously connected war ethics in the Old Testament is in fact compatible with the character of a loving and merciful God; and, if so, whether either or both religiously connected war ethics in the Old Testament is continuous with ethical teaching in the New Testament; and, if so, whether either of the religiously connected war ethics of the Old Testament—but especially whether the crusade ethic of Yahweh war—is a viable option for the understanding and practice of war today.

These questions are given special urgency by the all too real threat now posed by the reappearance of militant Islam as an actor on the world stage, and that is because the war ethic of militant Islam is in ways very like the ethic employed in the Yahweh wars of ancient Israel. This underscores both the relevance and importance of the topic at hand. What mattered formerly to only a few scholars now affects national security, and analyzing the ethics of crusade war in the Hebrew Bible now bears on directions in global leadership.

---

[2]Helmut Thielicke, *Politics*, vol. 2 of *Theological Ethics*, ed. William H. Lazareth (Grand Rapids: Eerdmans, 1979), p. 453.

This study focuses narrowly and will assume and not dispute positions on a number of related questions well defended elsewhere. We will assume and not dispute the standard ordering of approaches to the ethics of war in three mutually exclusive, internally coherent systems of moral thought, these being pacifism, just war and crusade.[3] We will assume and not dispute the possibility of finding and studying a coherent crusade war ethic within the Old Testament record.[4] We will assume and not dispute the notion that any ethic justifying war is religious in some broad sense and is therefore in that sense also a sort of "holy war."[5] We will assume and not dispute that there is in the Old Testament more than one identifiable and coherent ethic of war—both a crusade ethic and a just war ethic—and that while both are given to Israel by God they are not the same.[6] We will assume and not

---

[3]While Glen Stassen disputes these categories, I am following the standard categories well explained and defended by Roland Bainton in *Christian Attitudes Toward War and Peace* (Nashville: Abingdon, 1960). With all due respect, I believe Stassen is wrong to conflate the crusade war ethic with just war and is wrong, as well, to suggest just peacemaking can be a separate paradigm for the ethics of peace and war contrasting with just war. For Stassen's case see *Just Peacemaking: Transforming Initiatives for Justice and Peace* (Louisville: Westminster John Knox, 1992); and also *Just Peacemaking: The New Paradigm for the Ethics of Peace and War* (Cleveland: Pilgrim, 2008). In my estimate, just peacemaking cannot be a "new paradigm" because it is not (and cannot be) an operational ethic for all matters of war and peace but only confuses standard moral distinctions by alleging the very different and mutually exclusive definitions of "peace" employed by pacifists and just war proponents are neither different nor mutually exclusive. I base this on a personal conversation I have had with Stassen concerning his method and intentions. Beyond Bainton, my claim that most scholars accept crusade as a distinctly different ethic from just war is verified, for example, by the work of Karl Barth, who insisted there are crucial differences between war justified on just war terms and "a crusade or . . . war of religion." Karl Barth, *A Letter to Great Britain from Switzerland* (London: Sheldon Press, 1941), p. 21.

[4]Peter Craigie disputes the presence of any coherent war ethic in the Old Testament. See Peter C. Craigie, *The Problem of War in the Old Testament* (Grand Rapids: Eerdmans, 1978). But coherence is supported by Gerhard von Rad, *Holy War in Ancient Israel*, ed. and trans. Marva J. Dawn and John H. Yoder (Grand Rapids: Eerdmans, 1991); Bainton, *Christian Attitudes Toward War and Peace*; Helmut Thielicke, *Politics*; Tremper Longman III and Daniel Reid, *God Is a Warrior* (Carlisle, PA: Paternoster, 1995); and Eugene Merrill, "The Case for Moderate Discontinuity," in *Show Them No Mercy: 4 Views on God and Canaanite Genocide*, ed. Stanley N. Gundry (Grand Rapids: Zondervan, 2003).

[5]This view is held in one form by Glen Stassen (verification based on personal conversation) and in another form by Roland Bainton, *Christian Attitudes Toward War and Peace*. It was earlier, and perhaps first, articulated by Max Weber, *Ancient Judaism*, trans. and ed. Hans H. Gerth and Don Martindale (Glencoe, IL: Free Press, 1952), a work composed of articles first published 1917–1919.

[6]Rudolf Smend, in *Yahweh War and Tribal War* (Nashville: Abingdon, 1970), first published as *Jahwekrieg und Stämmebund: Erwägungen zur ältesten Geschichte Israels* (Göttingen: Vanderhoeck & Ruprecht, 1963), distinguishes Yahweh war from "holy war" in general (Smend, *Yahweh War*, pp. 36-37). This does not go the whole way but does support thinking there must be a

dispute the Old Testament record of crusade war employed by God as something that is indeed consistent with his character.[7] And we will assume and not dispute the logic of thinking that the unchanging moral character of God (Num 23:19; Ps 102:27; Mal 3:6; Heb 1:12; 13:8; Jas 1:17) strongly suggests continuity of moral order between the Old and New Testaments.[8]

This study aims to show that, *even when conceived as fully consistent with the unchanging moral character of God, and even when taken as part of a unified moral order applicable in both the Old and New Testaments, there are nevertheless good reasons to conclude that the crusade ethic evident in the Yahweh wars of ancient Israel is not, and never has been, allowable as an option for human decision in matters of war.* We will first discuss what makes crusade a separate ethic of war not to be confused with the just war approach toward defining and restraining the practice of war on moral grounds. We will then review features specifically characterizing divinely sanctioned crusade in the Yahweh wars of Israel. We will go on to survey efforts by theologians who have sought to explain divinely sanctioned crusade in the wars of Israel, and will then develop three specific reasons that keep divinely sanctioned crusade in the Yahweh wars of Israel from making crusade a viable option in today's world.

WHAT DISTINGUISHES CRUSADE FROM JUST WAR?

There has been much confusion among scholars as to whether crusade exists and, if so, what makes it an ethic of war to itself identifiably different from pacifism and just war. From a pacifist perspective crusade seems a rather more extreme version of the just war ethic, a case of justifying war

---

different sort of ethical justification involved beyond what applies only to Yahweh war. Texts that support a God-given just war ethic in the Hebrew Bible are Deuteronomy 20:10-15 and Amos 1:3–2:3.

[7]This has been defended in some degree by many different Bible scholars. For a recent example see Merrill, "Moderate Discontinuity," pp. 80-88. For defenders earlier in history see Augustine, c. *Faustus* 22.74-78; *Letters*, 138.2. 14; *City of God*, 1.21; Martin Luther, *Whether Soldiers Too, Can Be Saved*; John Calvin, *Institutes of the Christian Religion*, 4.20.31.

[8]Many defend this position in some form. For a recent example see Merrill, "Moderate Discontinuity." The strongest opposition to this position has been expressed always and most consistently by proponents of Christian pacifism. On this see Daniel R. Heimbach, "The Problem of Universal Ethics for Christian Pacifists," *Journal of Faith and War* (2009), also delivered as a paper at the annual meeting of the Evangelical Theological Society, 2008. Available at http://faithandwar.org/index.php?option=com_content&view=article&id=67%3Areligious-perceptions-of-the-just-war-and-military-ethics&catid=42%3Agod-and-human-nature&Itemid=58.

without modifying conditions. Even from a just war perspective crusade may not seem that far removed from merely articulating just war in religious terms. Consequently one finds respected scholars treating crusade war in completely contrary ways, with some confusing aspects of just war with crusade and others confusing forms of crusade with just war.[9] It is therefore important first to clarify what in general makes crusade an ethic to itself and then to clarify more particularly what distinguishes crusade from just war. And, since the latter depends on the former, we shall proceed in that order.

Roland Bainton clearly explains why crusade is not merely a version of the just war approach but must be an ethic to itself, distinguished not only from pacifism but just war as well. For Bainton, "holy war" covers all treatment of war on religious terms, and he acknowledges that principles of the just war tradition are often conceived in religious terms. What makes crusade as an ethic to itself is not mere concern for some conception of justice. Were that so, crusade could not be distinguished from either just war or pacifism, since one is as deeply concerned with justice as the other. Neither is reliant on religious authority or meaning enough to make crusade a uniquely different ethic, since that also characterizes versions of both just war and pacifism.

According to Bainton, what makes crusade a separate ethic is not merely that it justifies war at all (*pace* pacifism and *per* just war), nor that it pursues justice (*per* just war and pacifism in different ways), nor even that it concerns religion (also *per* just war and pacifism in different ways). Rather, what makes crusade ethic a separate ethic is the *manner* in which crusade thinking employs religion (or what functions religiously). Bainton explains, "The crusade went beyond the holy war in the respect that it was fought *not so much with God's help as on God's behalf,* [and] *not for a human goal which God might bless but for a divine cause which God might command.*"[10] He observes that among

---

[9]For example, Harold O. J. Brown, "The Crusade or Preventive War," in *War: Four Christian Views,* ed. Robert G. Clouse (Downers Grove, IL: InterVarsity Press, 1981), pp. 153-68, treats war to recover wrongly taken territory, a traditional part of the just war tradition, as a matter of crusade; and John Kelsay, in *Islam and War: The Gulf War and Beyond* (Louisville: Westminster John Knox, 1993), treats Islamic holy war as no more than a variety of the just war moral tradition claiming that "Islamic conceptions of war" entail a "more inclusive just war tradition" and not a different ethic of war altogether. Kelsay, *Islam and War,* pp. 54-55.

[10]Bainton, *Christian Attitudes Toward War and Peace,* pp. 44-45. My emphasis.

the ancients, "the just war, to be sure, was not devoid of religion, and to disregard its conditions would be to incur the displeasure of the gods, but it was fought for mundane objectives, albeit with a religious sanction, whereas the crusade was God's war."[11] Thus Bainton shows that while the just war ethic may be, and often has been, conceived religiously, wars fought on just war terms are never fought on God's behalf or for a divine cause. And while the pacifist ethic is often conceived religiously as well, pacifism never justifies war under any circumstance, not even at God's direction or for a cause he commands.

Building on this fundamental distinction, it is possible to identify twelve features marking crusade as an ethic unique to itself. These are:

1. Crusade treats war as the ultimate means for eliminating evil and imposing ideal social good.

2. Crusade fights by divine command, or on behalf of whatever is conceived as the source of ultimate authority and truth. The ethics of war therefore transcends human law.

3. Crusade requires no declaration of war. War commanded by God requires no ratification by any human authority.

4. Crusade is fought for a divine purpose or social ideal conceived on a universal scale. War is not viewed in terms of limited goals on less than a cosmic scale.

5. Crusade accepts no restrained use of force against the opposition. Anything done for good is justified and nothing resisting good is worthy of tolerance or respect. Crusade war is always a matter of "total war" conducted with "no holds barred" and "no quarter given."

6. Crusade does not spare enemies and takes no prisoners. It accepts conversion but not surrender.

7. Crusade does not compromise with opponents except if viewed as a stage toward eventually achieving the ideal for which war is fought.

8. Crusade seeks to conquer, to punish and either to convert or destroy the enemy.

---

[11] Ibid., p. 44.

9. Crusade opposes the entire social order, belief system or religion of enemy people and therefore has no basis for distinguishing combatants from noncombatants.

10. Those fighting in wars of crusade fight as volunteers out of zeal (for God, for the divine cause, for the social ideal). They are not conscripts fighting out of duty and rarely consider themselves to be professionals.

11. Those fighting in wars of crusade fight a double war: one that is material (a war of flesh and blood) and one that is spiritual or ideological.

12. Crusade wars would end by achieving the ideal for which they are fought; but since no ideal is ever fully realized, crusade wars never really cease.

Having clarified what makes crusade a separate ethic, we turn now to consider particular differences distinguishing crusade from just war ethics.[12] First, whereas crusade treats war as the ultimate means for eliminating evil and imposing ideal social good, just war treats war as a last resort; while war may be a necessary means for resisting evil, to some degree just war does not employ forces of war to impose ideals but only to correct specific acts of injustice. Second, whereas crusade fights by divine command or on behalf of whatever is conceived as the source of ultimate authority and truth, and therefore transcends human law, just war treats war as an instrument of civil government fought where necessary for limited human goals and never above but always under the auspices of established law. Third, whereas crusade requires no declaration of war, just war requires a declaration of war be made by the authority of whatever human government is concerned.

Fourth, whereas crusade is fought for a divine purpose or social ideal conceived on a universal scale, war conceived on just war terms is fought on human terms and for human goals that are limited to restoring specific infractions of justly established social order. Fifth, whereas crusade neither tolerates nor respects engaging enemy opposition with anything less than maximum effort with maximum force for maximum effect, just war never allows more force than is minimally necessary, and the entire

---

[12]For more see, Daniel R. Heimbach, "Distinguishing Just War from Crusade: Is Regime Change a Just Case for Just War?" in *War in the Bible and Terrorism in the Twenty-First Century*, ed. Richard S. Hess and Elmer A. Martens (Winona Lake, IN: Eisenbrauns, 2008), pp. 79-92.

just war ethic is composed of principles of moral restraint. Sixth, whereas crusade does not accept surrender but seeks either to convert or destroy enemies, just war spares those who surrender and recognizes basic human rights for enemy combatants held as prisoners of war. Seventh, whereas crusade does not negotiate with opposing forces except as a strategy for achieving unconditional results, just war prefers to negotiate any compromise less costly than continuing a war that becomes more costly than the cause originally justifying war is worth.

Eighth, whereas crusade aims to conquer, punish and destroy, just war seeks only to rectify a specific infraction of justice and no more. Ninth, whereas crusade opposes the entire social order, belief system or religion of an enemy people and therefore does not distinguish combatants from noncombatants, just war only seeks to rectify specific actions and is careful to distinguish combatants from noncombatants. Tenth, whereas crusaders fight out of zeal for achieving some universal ideal, soldiers in a just war fight out of duty to protect the weak from oppression or preserve the security of an established political order. Eleventh, whereas crusaders fight a double war, one material and the other ideological, soldiers fighting a just war only fight on material terms. And twelfth, whereas wars of crusade never really cease, just war hostilities cease as soon as whatever specific action that led to war is corrected.

CRUSADE IN THE YAHWEH WARS OF ISRAEL

Having shown why crusade is a separate ethic not to be confused with just war, we shall now examine how the crusade ethic of war is employed in the Old Testament, paying special attention to its use in the Yahweh wars of ancient Israel. The ethic of Israel's Yahweh wars is not the only instance of crusade in the Bible, since just about every nation with which Israel fought operated on crusade terms as well.[13] The Philistines, Midianites, Moabites and Edomites all fought on crusade terms, as did the Egyptians, Assyrians and Babylonians. And nowhere is this more apparent than in the war taunt

---

[13]I disagree with Bainton who says crusade as "God's war . . . could scarcely have originated in antiquity save among the Jews," and alleges "before the Maccabees one may doubt whether a crusade ever really took place in Israel" (Bainton, *Christian Attitudes Toward War and Peace*, pp. 44-45).

delivered by the Rabshakeh on behalf of Sennacherib,[14] king of Assyria, when addressing the people of Jerusalem under King Hezekiah. As recorded by Isaiah, the Assyrian Rabshakeh said,

> This is what the great king, the king of Assyria, says: On what are you basing this confidence of yours? . . . have I come to attack and destroy this land without the LORD? The LORD himself told me to march against this country and destroy it. . . . Do not let Hezekiah mislead you when he says, "The LORD will deliver us." Has the god of any nation ever delivered his land from the hand of the king of Assyria? (Isaiah 36:4, 10, 18).[15]

Nor is the biblical record on crusade war limited only to the Old Testament, for New Testament prophecy indicates that the last battles fought on earth after Jesus Christ returns to impose absolute rule at every level will be fought on crusade and not merely on just war terms (Rev 19:17-21; 20:7-10).

The special interest moral theologians and biblical ethicists have in studying the Yahweh wars of Israel does not come from thinking they were unprecedented or even unusual, but rather from how in the Yahweh wars of Israel we have recorded in sacred Scripture instances in which using the crusade ethic of war was sanctioned by God, therefore suggesting it would be morally allowed in equivalent circumstances. It also is the case that, while divinely sanctioned moral use of crusade also occurs in Revelation, the subject is covered in far greater detail in the Old Testament history of Israel as compared to anything in the New Testament corpus.

When it comes to studying the actual history of "holy war" in the life and practice of ancient Israel, no one has yet surpassed the work of Gerhard von Rad in *Holy War in Ancient Israel*.[16] While some have clarified aspects of his work,[17] and others have disputed points,[18] von Rad's treatment remains definitive on this topic. Gerhard von Rad identified a number of key elements as distinctive of the way Israel conducted war at the direction of Yahweh. Com-

---

[14]"Rabshakeh" is the title of a senior military commander in the Assyrian army.
[15]All Scripture references are quoted from the NIV 1984, unless otherwise noted.
[16]von Rad, *Holy War*.
[17]For example: Smend, *Yahweh War*; Jones, "The Concept of Holy War"; Lilley, "Understanding the *Herem*"; Bainton, *Christian Attitudes Toward War and Peace*; Longman and Reid, *God Is a Warrior*; and Merrill, "The Case for Moderate Discontinuity."
[18]Craigie, *The Problem of War*.

pared to the features we covered earlier that define crusade war in general, the elements von Rad identifies as particular to Israel's practice of holy war do not so much define what makes crusade an ethic of war as such but are better understood as procedures by which the people of Israel knew they were fighting the sort of crusade war ordered by the one true Creator of the Universe.

According to von Rad,[19] the conditions and practices by which the people of Israel knew they were participating in Yahweh-authorized crusade war are as follows:

1. God summoned the people to battle by ordering a trumpet call (Num 10:9; Josh 6:8-9; Judg 3:27; 6:34; 1 Sam 13:3-4).

2. Men were consecrated for battle (Josh 3:5). Men were circumcised (Josh 5:4-8) and abstained from sex (1 Sam 21:4-5; 2 Sam 11:11).

3. Weapons were consecrated for battle (1 Sam 21:5; 2 Sam 1:21).

4. Vows were made (Num 21:2; Judg 11:36; 1 Sam 14:24).

5. The camp of the assembled army was ceremonially purified (Deut 23:9-14).

6. Israel offered sacrifices to God (1 Sam 7:9; 13:9-10, 12).

7. An oracle came from God with directions and/or assurance of victory (Judg 20:13, 18; 1 Sam 7:9; 14:6-12, 14:37; 23:2, 4, 9-12; 28:6; 30:7-8; 2 Sam 5:19, 23).

8. God leads/goes before the army into battle (Judg 4:14; 5:4; Deut 20:4).

9. The number of troops and amount of equipment is not considered important because God does not need Israel to win but rather commands Israel to fight on his side (Judg 7:2-25; 1 Sam 14:6; 17:45, 47).

10. God is the one who fights both on behalf of (miraculously) and through (empowering) the men of Israel (Ex 14:14; Deut 1:30; Josh 10:14, 42; 23:10; 1 Sam 14:23).

11. The men of Israel are charged not to fear but to believe (Ex 14:13-14; Deut 20:3; Josh 8:1).

---

[19]The elements of Yahweh-approved holy war isolated by von Rad are listed in different ways by different authors. This listing follows my own reading of von Rad but benefits from careful consideration of similar summaries made by Roland Bainton in *Christian Attitudes* and Eugene Merrill in "The Case for Moderate Discontinuity." For von Rad see, *Holy War*, pp. 41-51. For Bainton see, *Christian Attitudes Toward War and Peace*, pp. 44-48. For Merrill see, "Moderate Discontinuity," p. 69.

12. God sends divine terror over the enemy who is often far superior in number and equipment (Ex 23:27; Deut 7:23; Judg 7:22-25; 1 Sam 14:15-23).

13. The taking of spoils (enemy possessions) is strictly controlled on God's terms by means of the "ban" or *ḥērem* (Deut 20:1-18; Josh 6:18-19; 1 Sam 15:3).

14. The army is officially dismissed from service (2 Sam 20:1; 1 Kings 12:6).

UNDERSTANDING APPROVED CRUSADE IN YAHWEH WAR

It is one thing to argue the presence of crusade in the Old Testament and to identify various conditions associated with the practice of divinely approved crusade in the Yahweh wars of Israel. It is another thing entirely to address the morality of doing so. And the moral challenge involved in assessing Yahweh war is especially challenging for Christians who accept the biblical record as properly crediting God with burning up enemies, showing no mercy and directing Israel to destroy everything and spare no one.

Most difficult to assess are passages portraying God as a bloodthirsty warrior—"I will make my arrows drunk with blood, while my sword devours flesh" (Deut 32:42)—or as burning with anger so ruthless it consumes the enemy "like stubble" (Ex 15:7). Also troubling are passages ordering the Israelites to "carry out the LORD's vengeance" (Num 31:3); to "kill all the boys" and "kill every woman who has slept with a man" (Num 31:17); to "make no treaty with them, and show them no mercy" (Deut 7:2); to "not leave alive anything that breathes" (Deut 20:16); so that the Israelites "left no survivors" (Deut 2:34; Josh 10:39). In one passage the people are told, "you must certainly put to the sword all who live in that town. Destroy it completely, both its people and its livestock. Gather all the plunder of the town into the middle of the public square and completely burn the town and all its plunder as a whole burnt offering to the LORD your God" (Deut 13:15-17); and in another "They devoted the city to the LORD and destroyed with the sword every living thing in it—men and women, young and old, cattle, sheep and donkeys" (Josh 6:21). This was all in obedience to instructions issued by God prior to a battle.

Scholars taking a non-supernaturalist approach to biblical interpretation dismiss such passages as expressing ancient prejudice, later abandoned when human understanding advanced to higher levels.[20] But these passages cannot be so easily dismissed by scholars who believe with the apostle Paul that "all Scripture is God-breathed and is useful for teaching, rebuking, correcting and training in righteousness" (2 Tim 3:16). For us, these passages on Yahweh approved wars of crusade must be taken as fully consistent with the unchanging moral character of God and must be accepted as morally instructive along with the rest of divinely inspired Scripture. Our conclusion must be that because God never sins and is himself the measure of moral perfection, and because God defines morality for us and not the other way around, it must therefore be that God acting as a bloodthirsty warrior is sometimes morally justified; and it must also be that at those times fighting on God's side on crusade terms, allowing no surrender, showing no mercy and sparing no one, is also entirely justified. But if so, how can this be explained, especially in view of all the Bible also says about love and mercy even for enemies?

The first and most important answer is that God of course owes no explanation for anything he does. If God truly exists and is no mere figment of human imagination, then he it is who evaluates us and we have no standing to evaluate him. On this Isaiah says, "Woe to him who quarrels with his Maker. Woe to him who is but a potsherd among the potsherds on the ground. Does the clay say to the potter, 'What are you making?'" (Is 45:9). And when Job questioned God's moral judgment, God challenged him by asking, "Would you discredit my justice? Would you condemn me to justify yourself?" (Job 40:8).

Theologians through history have stressed this point in treating the crusade ethic applied in the Yahweh wars of Israel. Augustine held that a man is "blameless who carries on war on the authority of God, of whom everyone who serves Him knows that He can never require what is wrong,"[21] that men who fight wars "by a special intimation from God Himself" are not "implicated in the guilt of murder,"[22] and that "undoubtedly that type of war is also just [is morally warranted] which God orders, in whom there is no

---

[20]For example see, Bainton, *Christian Attitudes Toward War and Peace*; and Marion J. Benedict, *The God of the Old Testament in Relation to War* (New York: Teachers College, 1927).

[21]Augustine, *c. Faustus* 22.75.

[22]Augustine, *City of God* 1.21.

iniquity and who knows what ought to happen to each person."[23] In the case of what is now called Yahweh war, Augustine believed that "the commander of the army or the populace itself should be judged [morally innocent, being] not so much the author of the war, as the agent [assigned by God] of it."[24] Luther maintained that "God's hands are not bound so that he cannot bid us make war against those who have not given us just cause, as he did when he commanded the children of Israel to go to war against the Canaanites," and that is because "in such a case God's command is necessity enough."[25] And Calvin argued that, "both Moses (Ex 32:27-28) and David (1 Kings 2:5-6, 8-9), in executing the vengeance committed to them by God, by this severity sanctified their hands, which would have been defiled by leniency."[26]

But while God owes no explanation for anything he does, this does not keep us from analyzing what God has revealed about his character and purposes through the history of Israel. This process has led scholars to offer secondary insights aimed at trying to explain why God may have approved Israel's use of crusade war. Of these secondary and admittedly speculative insights, major attention has been given to linking Yahweh war with maintaining the holiness of Israel as a unique people, chosen of God to reflect his character and fulfill his plan for saving the world.[27]

This leads Helmut Thielicke to suggest that Yahweh war is in a unique moral category "related to the special nature of the situation of Israel," a category wherein they are "a chosen people" with "a privileged position in salvation history."[28] Similarly, Eugene Merrill asserts that "a comprehensive theological overview yields the conclusion that Israel must be holy because Yahweh is holy and that one of the major purposes of Yahweh war was to protect that holiness."[29] Elaborating further, Merrill argues that "The extreme measure of Yahweh war was necessary for at least four reasons: (1) the irremediable hardness of the hearts of its victims; (2) the need to protect Israel against spiritual corruption; (3) the destruction of idolatry; and (4)

---

[23]Augustine, *qu. Heptateuch* 6.10.
[24]Ibid.
[25]Martin Luther, *Whether Soldiers, Too, Can Be Saved.*
[26]John Calvin, *Institutes* 4.20.10.
[27]For example see Ex 19:6; Deut 7:6; 14:2, 21; 26:19; 28:9.
[28]Thielicke, *Politics*, p. 453.
[29]Merrill, "Moderate Discontinuity," p. 81.

the education of Israel and the nations as to the character and intentions of the one true God."[30]

Beyond this, other attempts to justify divine approval of crusade ethics in the prosecution of Yahweh war have included "righteous retribution" in which God gave "to all what they deserved"[31]; the need of God to "rebuke, humble, or crush the pride of man"[32]; the affliction of "mercy" by which God suppressed "those vices . . . which ought . . . to be extirpated";[33] and the value of "cut(ting) off all wicked doers from the city of the Lord."[34]

WHY GOD'S APPROVED CRUSADE IS NOT FOR US

The most difficult moral question for Christian understanding of crusade in the Yahweh wars of Israel does not concern whether it was properly sanctioned by God but rather concerns whether divine approval in the Old Testament makes employing the crusade war ethic legitimate in today's world. While Pope Urban II called eleventh-century Christians to oppose Islamic crusade in like fashion,[35] most theologians have firmly denied that divinely approved crusade in the wars of ancient Israel makes crusade an option for others. So, for example, Calvin says, "though the correction of tyrannical domination is the vengeance of God, we are not, therefore, to conclude that it is committed to us, who have received no other command than to obey and suffer."[36] Thielicke sees nothing in the Old Testament "which can help to fix a theological position with respect to war as such."[37] And Merrill denies "any possible justification for modern genocide for any reason."[38] But these are conclusions, and we must consider why this is or is not the case.

The moral relevance of approved crusade in the Yahweh wars of Israel can be denied in three ways: (1) by rejecting its moral legitimacy altogether; (2) by rejecting continuity with the moral order in which it was legitimate; or (3) by identifying conditions precluding relevance in other situations.

---

[30]Ibid., p. 85.
[31]Augustine, c. Faustus 22.74.
[32]Ibid., 22.75.
[33]Augustine, Letters 138.2.14.
[34]Calvin, Institutes, 4.20.10.
[35]Zoé Oldenbourg, The Crusades, trans. Anne Carter (New York: Random House, 1966), p. 78.
[36]Calvin, Institutes, 4.20.31.
[37]Thielicke, Politics, p. 453.
[38]Merrill, "Moderate Discontinuity," p. 93.

Marion Benedict, Gerhard von Rad and Peter Craigie all take the first approach—but for different reasons; Christian pacifists take the second approach; and Helmut Thielicke, Tremper Longman III and Eugene Merrill all take the third approach. After documenting each, I will explain and defend a form of this third approach.

Benedict, von Rad and Craigie each deny the relevance of crusade in the Old Testament by rejecting original legitimacy—but all for different reasons. Marion Benedict does so by dismissing original worthiness under any alleged circumstance. According to Benedict, early Old Testament depictions of Israel's God as a God of crusade are records of a "God whose power is not yet joined to good-will and moral responsibility, but rather to caprice and jealousy and terrifying destructiveness."[39] Gerhard von Rad does so by dismissing transcendence, suggesting that the holy war literature of Israel is to be understood as something produced by writers far removed from the events depicted, who shaped Israel's history to meet their own needs and were not recording how an actual God truly acted on their behalf.[40] And Peter Craigie does so by attacking coherence and doubting whether any ethic of war can be derived from alleging divine presence in various war activities.[41]

A second way of denying the relevance of crusade war in the history of Israel is an approach most closely associated with Christian pacifism, which is to reject continuity with the moral order applicable in Yahweh war. Proponents of this approach do not attack the legitimacy, transcendence or coherence of the crusade war ethic employed in the Yahweh wars of Israel, but only argue that it describes a moral order that either is discontinued or at least does not apply to the followers of Jesus Christ. Thus Tertullian held that, even though Moses and Joshua led the people of God in war, "still the Lord [Jesus] . . . in disarming Peter, unbelted every soldier."[42] The Swiss Brethren maintained that while "the sword is ordained of God outside the perfection of Christ," nevertheless Christians may not in this life "employ the sword against the wicked [even] for the defense and protection of the good."[43] William McGrath, representing what Amish and Mennonite Chris-

---

[39]Benedict, *God of the Old Testament*, p. 15.
[40]von Rad, *Holy War*, pp. 81-93.
[41]Craigie, *The Problem of War*, pp. 41-49.
[42]Tertullian, *On Idolatry*, p. 19.
[43]Swiss Brethren, Article VI: "Concerning the Sword," *The Schleitheim Confession*.

tians believe, states that it is plainly "mistaken" to think "what was right then [in the Old Testament] must be alright [sic] now, too."[44] And Richard Hays writes that while "the Old Testament obviously validates the legitimacy of armed violence by the people of God," it is now the case for Christians that "Jesus' explicit teaching and example of nonviolence reshapes our understanding of God and the covenant community." As for the moral contrast this involves, Hays simply states, "the New Testament vision trumps the Old Testament."[45]

The third way by which the current relevance of divinely sanctioned crusade can be denied involves identifying prerequisite conditions unique to Old Testament Israel that preclude its application in other circumstances. Those taking this approach accept the legitimacy, transcendence and coherence of crusade in the Yahweh wars of Israel. Yet, while accepting these terms, proponents nevertheless reject contemporary moral relevance for reasons having to do with the nature of Yahweh war understood on its own terms and within the original biblical-historical context in which the Yahweh wars of Israel are reported to have occurred.

As there are variations among proponents of the first approach, there are variations among proponents of this third approach as well. For example, Thielicke and Merrill effectively deny the universality of the biblical ethic by maintaining the Yahweh wars of Israel are in a moral category unique to the role and mission of Israel and so never did and never will apply to others. They do not believe moral standards have evolved or changed, but rather deny the universality of Israel's war ethic by relegating it to a category that only applies to a single, nonrepeatable circumstance.

Concerning the ethic of Israel's Yahweh wars, Thielicke says "they constitute a special category" related to Israel's "privileged position in salvation history" whereby they were "not just a nation politically" but were "also a chosen people."[46] So Thielicke concludes, "the situation in Israel is without analogy."[47] Similarly, Merrill argues that, "because only Israel was authorized to carry it out in Old Testament times. . . . [T]he ramifications of this

---

[44]William R. McGrath, *Why We Are Conscientious Objectors to War* (Carrollton, OH: Amish Mennonite Publications, 1980), p. 18.

[45]Richard Hays, *The Moral Vision of the New Testament* (San Francisco: Harper, 1996), p. 336.

[46]Thielicke, *Politics*, p. 453.

[47]Ibid.

for the issue of war in general and war conducted under the guise of divine direction in particular are immense." And therefore Merrill decides, "if no case could be made for Yahweh war without Israel's participation in Old Testament times, surely none can be made today whether done in the name of Christ, Allah, or any other authority."[48]

Tremper Longman takes this third approach. But rather than dispute the universality of Israel's war ethic, Longman instead denies its continuing *material* relevance while affirming ongoing relevance, not only for Israel but the world, in a *nonmaterial spiritual* sense. Thus Longman argues that "there is both continuity and discontinuity between the Old and New Testaments on the issue of *ḥērem* warfare"; that "the war against the Canaanites was simply an earlier phase of the battle that comes to its climax on the cross and its completion at the final judgment"; and that "the Bible makes it clear that we are still involved in *ḥērem* warfare; but rather than being directed toward physical enemies, it is a spiritual battle."[49] Longman therefore concludes that while "it is now a betrayal of the gospel to take up arms to defend or promote the interests of Christ. . . . The spiritual battle that has been waged throughout history" is still a matter of "*ḥērem* warfare."[50]

I agree with Thielicke, Merrill and Longman in denying that divine approval of a crusade ethic in the Yahweh wars of ancient Israel makes employing crusade war an option human beings may choose today. And with them I arrive at this conclusion in a way that accepts the Bible as trustworthy and coherent, accepts the reality of transcendence in moral order, accepts the worthiness of divinely sanctioned crusade in the Yahweh wars of Israel and accepts the continuity of moral order between the Old and New Testaments. But I do not think Thielicke and Merrill are right to reduce the crusade ethic of Yahweh war to nonuniversal status; I do not think Longman is correct to restrict moral continuity to the nonmaterial. Rather I take the position that because God's moral character never changes (Num 23:19; Ps 102:27; Mal 3:6; Heb 1:12; 13:8; Jas 1:17) and nothing other than God's character limits what he does, this means the only possible basis for precluding the relevance of crusade as a morally acceptable option for wars

---

[48]Merrill, "Moderate Discontinuity," p. 85.
[49]Tremper Longman III, "The Case for Spiritual Continuity," in *Show Them No Mercy*, pp. 184-86.
[50]Ibid., p. 187.

must be located in prerequisite conditions applying as much to others as to Israel, and applying as much today as at the time of Israel's Yahweh wars.

I believe three conditions did apply and continue to apply in the same way now as they did before. These prerequisites are: (1) that approved crusade always had *to be initiated by God* and never by anyone else; (2) that approved crusade always had *to be led by God* and never by anyone else; and (3) that approved crusade always had to be initiated and led by God *in a manner that could be verified* by those called to participate.

The first of these conditions is evident where God orders Israel to "Go in and take possession of the land that the LORD swore he would give to your fathers" (Deut 1:8); where God orders Israel "to conquer and possess" the land of the Amorites under King Sihon, so that Israel "left no survivors" (Deut 2:31, 34); where God orders Israel to attack Og king of Bashan saying, "Do to him what you did to Sihon king of the Amorites" (Num 21:34; Deut 3:2); where God commands Israel to "Take vengeance on the Midianites" (Num 31:2); where God commands Israel to attack the occupants of the Promised land, ordering that Israel "must destroy them totally. Make no treaty with them, and show them no mercy" (Deut 7:2); and where God orders faithful Israelites to attack any of their own towns that starts worshiping other gods saying, "you must certainly put to the sword all who live in that town. Destroy it completely, both its people and its livestock" (Deut 13:15).

This first condition is mentioned by Longman and Reid where they say "holy war was always initiated by Yahweh, never Israel"[51] and by Merrill where he says "God initiated the process by singling out those destined to destruction, empowering an agent (usually his chosen people Israel) to accomplish it."[52] Merrill also says, "if anything is clear . . . it is that such war was conceived by God."[53] So even though Longman and Merrill rely on other reasons for denying the continued relevance of crusade war, they both recognize this one prerequisite that alone is sufficient to disqualify treating crusade as an option for human decision.

The second condition limiting approved crusade is present in passages

---

[51]Longman and Reid, *God Is a Warrior*, p. 33.
[52]Merrill, "Moderate Discontinuity," p. 65.
[53]Ibid., p. 80.

where troops going into battle are told "the LORD your God is the one who goes with you to fight for you against your enemies to give you victory" (Deut 20:4); where Moses tells Israel "the LORD your God himself will cross over ahead of you. He will destroy these nations before you" (Deut 31:3); where on the verge of entering the Promised Land Israel is told, "Do not be afraid or terrified because of them, for the LORD your God goes with you; he will never leave you nor forsake you" (Deut 31:6); where after the conquest of Canaan God makes sure that Joshua knows it was God alone who "gave them into your hands," it was he who "drove them out before you," and "[y]ou did not do it with your own sword and bow" (Josh 24:11-12); and where Deborah the prophetess assures the commander of Israel's army of victory by asking him rhetorically, "Has not the LORD gone ahead of you?" (Judg 4:14).

But the critical nature of this second condition is revealed most clearly in what took place just before the battle of Jericho. While surveying the future battlefield, Joshua "saw a man standing in front of him with a drawn sword in his hand" (Josh 5:13). When Joshua challenged this figure's allegiance, the figure did not answer on Joshua's terms but instead reversed his challenge by declaring himself to be "commander of the army of the LORD" (Josh 5:14), meaning that he was, of course, Yahweh himself. Joshua immediately assumed a posture of total and complete submission and, rather than question God's allegiance, he asked instead what orders God wished to assign him. The point of all this was to make clear to Joshua, as most senior human commander of Israel's army, that a divinely sanctioned crusade not only had to be authorized by God but also had to be led by God. The army of Israel was to follow God himself into battle. They were following his lead on his terms, not the other way around. And the whole business of losing the next battle to Ai, after victory over Jericho, was about the same point in reverse (Josh 7:10-12).

Merrill also mentions this second condition where he recognizes that Yahweh war was not only "conceived by God" but also "commanded by him," and where he notes that Yahweh war was not only always "initiated" but also always "led" by God himself.[54] But, while Merrill notes this second

---

[54]Ibid., pp. 80-81, 85.

condition, he again does not seem to realize its value for disqualifying crusade as an option for wars initiated by human leaders and led by human generals.

The third prerequisite essential to Yahweh approved crusade war in the Old Testament is that it always had to be initiated and led by God in a manner that could be verified by those called to participate. It is always possible for some charlatan to allege divine orders in a dream, vision or trance, or even to maliciously claim the mantle of divine authority in calling others to war. And it is possible even to claim divine leadership by alleging the presence of some invisible deity. But that is not what happens in the biblical record of crusade in the Yahweh wars of Israel. Rather what happens is that when Yahweh does, in fact, initiate crusade and does, in fact, himself lead Israel into battle on crusade terms, he does it in a way that participants can verify.

The people of Israel were able to verify that God did indeed speak to Moses, giving him detailed instructions for leading their nation out of Egypt and into the Promised Land. They saw the plagues God poured out on Egypt (Ex 7–11). As they "went up out of Egypt armed for battle" (Ex 13:18), they could literally see how "by day the LORD went ahead of them in a pillar of cloud to guide them on their way and by night in a pillar of fire to give them light, so that they could travel by day or night" (Ex 13:21). When "Pharaoh, his chariots and his horsemen" approached them on the shore of the Red Sea, they saw how "the angel of God, who had been traveling in front of Israel's army, withdrew and went behind them" and "the pillar cloud also moved from in front and stood behind them, coming between the armies of Egypt and Israel" (Ex 14:19-20) and saw how Yahweh parted the sea "and turned it into dry land" after "Moses stretched out his hand over the sea" (Ex 14:21) and saw—and most likely also heard—God order Moses to "[s]tretch out your hand over the sea so that the waters may flow back over the Egyptians and their chariots and horsemen"; and they saw how when Moses obeyed "the LORD swept them into the sea" drowning "the entire army of Pharaoh that had followed the Israelites into the sea" so that "not one of them survived" (Ex 14:26-28).

Later they heard God delivering instructions to Moses at Sinai (Ex 20:1-21) and saw and experienced many other miraculous evidences supporting the fact that Moses was receiving directions directly from God himself. So it was they had every reason to believe Moses did indeed have orders directly from God when he told them Yahweh was commanding they "go to war against the Midianites and to carry out the LORD's vengeance on them" (Num 31:3). So also, when preparing for the conquest of Canaan on crusade terms, the warriors of Israel followed instructions each already had verified came from God (Deut 31:1-6). And beyond that, when entering the Promised Land to fight on crusade terms, they did so under Joshua whose role in succeeding Moses they saw verified in crossing the Jordan "on dry ground" (Josh 3:17).

CONCLUSION

Many have analyzed the ethic of Yahweh war in the Hebrew Bible and have reached different conclusions, but no serious scholar currently maintains that divinely sanctioned use of crusade in the wars of ancient Israel makes employing crusade a legitimate option in today's world. Nevertheless, while those who deny the reality of Israel's God or who claim the Bible is just a human book can dismiss it as ancient prejudice superseded by more enlightened moral thinking, those who believe Israel's God truly exists, and who accept the Bible as the inerrant Word of God, cannot dismiss Israel's ancient war ethic in that manner. They too may deny the contemporary relevance of Old Testament crusade but must find other grounds for doing so.

While denying along with others that crusade war is a proper option for human initiative and leadership, I have taken and defended a position that goes farther than most in affirming the accuracy, worthiness and continuity of God's moral order revealed in the Old Testament. I have done this not by limiting Israel's ancient war ethic to something absolutely unrepeatable, or less than timeless, or less than universal or now relevant only in a nonmaterial spiritual sense. Rather I have argued that, taken as presented in the Bible itself, legitimate application of crusade in the wars of ancient Israel always had to meet three prerequisite conditions, and these conditions are as applicable now as they were then. In effect I have argued that, taking the biblical record on its own terms, the crusade ethic sanctioned in the Yahweh wars of Israel is not an option for human decision now because it never was in the first place. Yet I realize that in taking this position I am also suggesting that, should these conditions be satisfied once more, then crusade war would be as morally legitimate again as it was in the Yahweh wars of Israel.

So if what is prophesied in Revelation 19:11-21 comes to pass and God again initiates war on crusade terms, and God again leads such a war in person, and God again does it in a manner all can verify—then the crusade ethic of Yahweh war will again apply. But only on those conditions and those conditions alone. Until and unless all three prerequisite conditions are satisfied together, the crusade ethic of war must be resolutely rejected and opposed, because *it never has been and never will be a legitimate option for human initiative, human leadership or even human imagination of divinely sanctioned war.*

10

THE ETHICS OF "HOLY WAR"
FOR CHRISTIAN MORALITY
AND THEOLOGY

Paul Copan and Matthew Flannagan

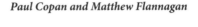

ONE OF THE MOST PERPLEXING ISSUES facing Christian believers is a series of jarring texts in the Old Testament. After being liberated from slavery in Egypt, the Israelites arrived on the edge of the Promised Land. The book of Deuteronomy records that God then commanded Israel to "destroy . . . totally" (Deut 7:2) the people occupying these regions (the Canaanites), to "not leave alive anything that breathes" (Deut 20:16).[1]

The book of Joshua records the carrying out of this command. In the sixth chapter it states, "they devoted the city to the LORD and destroyed with the sword every living thing in it—men and women, young and old, cattle, sheep and donkeys" (Josh 6:21). A few chapters later, the text affirms that Joshua "left no survivors. He totally destroyed all who breathed, just as the LORD, the God of Israel, had commanded" (Josh 10:40). The text mentions city after city where Joshua, at God's command, put every inhabitant "to the sword,"[2] "totally destroyed,"[3] the inhabitants and "left no survivors."[4]

---

[1]All quoted Scripture is from the NIV unless otherwise stated.
[2]Josh 10:28, 30, 32, 35, 37, 39; see also Josh 11:11, 12, 14.
[3]Josh 10:1, 28, 35, 37, 39, 40; see also Josh 11:11, 12, 14, 20, 21.
[4]Josh 10:28, 30, 33, 34, 37, 39, 40; see also Josh 11:9, 22.

Similarly, in 1 Samuel God commanded Saul to "utterly destroy" and to "not spare" the Amalekites: "put to death both man and woman, child and infant, ox and sheep, camel and donkey" (1 Sam 15:3). If one takes these passages literally, they record the divinely authorized commission of a "holy war"—a total war fought at God's command—not only against enemy combatants but also against noncombatants such as women and children. In light of this, critics of Christian theism often ask, "How could a good and loving God command the extermination of the Canaanites?"

In this article we will address this question. In part one we will set out the moral problem these texts create. In part two we will look at one popular response to this problem, which holds that "holy wars" are permissible if they are commanded by God. In part three we will call into question the strict literal reading of the relevant texts this question presupposes; we will defend a hagiographical hyperbolic understanding of them. Part four will look at the question of whether the texts create obvious moral problems even if we take them hyperbolically. Finally, part five will address two objections that have been raised for this position.

THE MORAL PROBLEM OF BIBLICAL "HOLY WARS"

The problem the texts create is put forcefully by Raymond Bradley. Bradley contends that these passages show "the falsity of the theistic theory of ethics."[5] He formulates principle P1 this way: "P1: It is morally wrong to deliberately and mercilessly slaughter men, women, and children who are innocent of any serious wrongdoing."[6]

Bradley cites two cases from the Old Testament which, *prima facie*, are in conflict with P1. In the book of Joshua, God "commanded Joshua to kill old and young, little children, maidens, and women."[7] Also in 1 Samuel 15, God commands Saul to "strike Amalek and utterly destroy all that he has, and do not spare him; but put to death both man and woman, child and infant." In

---

[5]Raymond Bradley, "A Moral Argument for Atheism," in *The Impossibility of God*, eds. Michael Martin and Ricki Monnier (Amherst, NY: Prometheus Books, 2003), p. 144. In this article Bradley developed two arguments, one against the existence of God, the other against "Theistic Ethics." This article criticizes the second of these arguments.

[6]Ibid., p. 132.

[7]Ibid., p. 134.

light of this, Bradley contends a Christian theist is committed to an "inconsistent tetrad":[8]

(1) Any act that God commands us to perform is morally permissible.

(2) The Bible is an authoritative revelation of what God commands.[9]

(3) It is morally impermissible for anyone to commit acts that violate principle P1.

(4) The Bible tells us that God commands us to perform acts that violate moral principle P1.

Bradley is not alone in pointing out this tetrad. Recently, Wes Morriston,[10] Randal Rauser,[11] Evan Fales,[12] Edwin Curley,[13] Michael Tooley,[14] Walter Sinnott-Armstrong[15] and Louise Antony[16] have each made the same basic line of argument. Given that (1)–(4) entail a contradiction, it is not possible for one to rationally affirm them all. So which one should we reject? These authors argue that the only defensible response is to deny (1) or (2).[17] Here

---

[8]Ibid., p. 144.

[9]Ibid. Bradley's original formulation of (2) is, "The Bible reveals to us many of the acts that God commands us to perform." On the face of it, this states that many things God commands are revealed in the Bible; however, the claim that the Bible accurately reveals many of God's commands is entirely compatible with the claim that it inaccurately records others; and hence, is not inconsistent with (1), (3) and (4). Elsewhere in the same article Bradley makes it clear that he has in mind a robust view of biblical authority in (2). So we have reworded (2) to reflect this.

[10]Wes Morriston, "Did God Command Genocide? A Challenge to the Biblical Inerrantist," *Philosophia Christi* 11, no. 1 (2009): 8-26.

[11]Randal Rauser, "Let Nothing that Breathes Remain Alive: On the Problem of Divinely Commanded Genocide," *Philosophia Christi* 11, no. 1 (2009): 27-41.

[12]Evan Fales, "Satanic Verses: Moral Chaos in Holy Writ," in *Divine Evil? The Moral Character of the God of Abraham*, ed. Michael Bergmann, Michael J. Murray and Michael C. Rea (New York: Oxford University Press, 2011), pp. 91-108.

[13]Edwin Curley, "The God of Abraham, Isaac and Jacob," in *Divine Evil?* pp. 58-78.

[14]Michael Tooley, "Does God Exist?" in Michael Tooley and Alvin Plantinga, *The Knowledge of God* (Malden, MA: Blackwell, 2008), pp. 73-77.

[15]Walter Sinnott-Armstrong, "Why Traditional Theism Cannot Provide an Adequate Foundation for Morality," in *Is Goodness without God Good Enough? A Debate on Faith, Secularism and Ethics*, eds. Robert K. Garcia and Nathan L. King (Lanham, MD: Rowman & Littlefield, 2008), p. 110.

[16]Louise Antony, "Atheism as Perfect Piety" in *Is Goodness Without God Good Enough?* p. 73.

[17]An exception is Randal Rauser. In a later follow up presentation, Rauser appears to suggest solving the problem by modifying (2) so inerrancy is not attributed to the human author but to the divine author alone and then rejecting (3) using canonical criticism and *sensus plenior*. From his "Three Theses on Devotional Child Killing," a paper presented at the panel discussion "Is Yahweh a Moral Monster?" at the Evangelical Philosophical Society section of the annual meeting of the Society of Biblical Literature, Atlanta, Georgia (November 21, 2010).

we will argue that this is mistaken, as the Christian theist can plausibly deny either (3) or (4).

ARE HOLY WARS PERMISSIBLE IF THEY ARE COMMANDED BY GOD?

One response is to deny (3) and contend that it is not *always* morally impermissible to commit acts which violate P1. This view was proposed by Augustine of Hippo:

> [T]here are some exceptions made by the divine authority to its own law, that men may not be put to death. These exceptions are of two kinds, being justified either by a general law, or by a special commission granted for a time to some individual. And in this latter case, he to whom authority is delegated, and who is but the sword in the hand of him who uses it, is not himself responsible for the death he deals. And, accordingly, they who have waged war in obedience to the divine command, or in conformity with His laws, have represented in their persons the public justice or the wisdom of government, and in this capacity have put to death wicked men; such persons have by no means violated the commandment, "Thou shalt not kill."[18]

Augustine affirms we have a *prima facie* duty to not kill. "A particular *prima facie* duty is objectively true and exceptionless, but it may be overridden by a weightier duty in a particular circumstance, such as lying to save the life of an innocent person."[19] In this instance, the *prima facie* duty to not kill is overridden when God commands the contrary. This is not implausible. In situations where a just and loving person, aware of all the relevant facts, could endorse killing noncombatants, it is hard to see how such killing could be wrong.[20]

Philip Quinn notes Augustine's conclusion can be defended within the context of a divine command theory of ethics.[21] According to a divine

---

[18]Augustine, *City of God,* 1:21.

[19]Mike Austin, "Moral Difficulties in the Bible: The Concessionary Morality Response." Paper presented at the annual meeting of the Evangelical Philosophical Society, Atlanta, Georgia (November 18, 2010). See also "Is It Okay to Lie to Nazis?" in Paul Copan, *When God Goes to Starbucks* (Grand Rapids: Baker, 2007).

[20]What is questionable is not the claim that *if* a loving and just fully informed person endorses killing noncombatants, this is permissible, but rather that a loving and just fully informed person *would* endorse such killing. We address this second claim in our discussion of Robert Adams.

[21]Philip L. Quinn, "The Recent Revival of Divine Command Ethics," *Research Philosophy and Phenomenological Research* 50 (Fall 1990): 345-65.

command theory, wrongness is constituted by the property of being contrary to God's commands.[22] If God has issued a command to all people to refrain from *P*, then engaging in *P* has the property of being wrong. However if, in a specific situation, God commands a specific person to do *P*, then *P* is no longer contrary to God's commands for that person; as such, *P* no longer has the property of being wrong *for that person*.

This divine command theorist appropriation of Augustine has a long history and is suggested by Bernard of Clairvaux[23] and Aquinas,[24] as well as fourteenth-century divine command theorists such as Andreas de Novo.[25] Contemporary defenders of this position are Philip Quinn[26] and William Lane Craig.[27] Despite sophisticated advocacy, several objections have been raised to this approach. Here we will examine two.[28]

---

[22]Robert M. Adams, "Moral Arguments for Theism," in *The Virtue of Faith*, ed. Robert M. Adams (New York: Oxford University Press, 1987), p. 145.

[23]Bernard of Clairvaux, *On Precept and Dispensation*, III.6.

[24]Thomas Aquinas, *Summa Theologica*, I-II q. 100, a. 8, ad 3.

[25]Andrea de Novo Castro, *Primum Scriptum Sententiarum*, d. 48, q. 2, a. 2 concl. 2. I.

[26]Quinn, "The Recent Revival of Divine Command Ethics," pp. 345-65.

[27]William Lane Craig, "Does the Christian God Exist? A Debate between William Lane Craig and Edwin Curley," at the University of Michigan (Ann Arbor), February 5 1998. Available at http://www.leaderu.com/offices/billcraig/docs/craig-curley12.html. Accessed November 17, 2010.

[28]In this paper we will address objections based on the idea of God commanding a violation of P1. There are, of course, several objections against a divine command theory per se that have nothing to do with the issue of "holy war." Defenses of divine command theories against such objections can be found in Robert M. Adams, "Divine Command Meta-Ethics Modified Again," *Journal of Religious Ethics* 7, no. 1 (1979); Robert M. Adams, *Finite and Infinite Goods* (New York: Oxford University Press, 1999); John E. Hare, *God's Call: Moral Realism, God's Commands and Human Autonomy* (Grand Rapids: Eerdmans, 2001); John E. Hare, *God and Morality: A Philosophical History* (Oxford: Blackwell, 2007); William Alston, "Some Suggestions for Divine Command Theorists," in *Christian Theism and the Problems of Philosophy*, ed. Michael Beaty (Notre Dame, IN: University of Notre Dame Press, 1990); William Lane Craig, "This Most Gruesome of Guests," in *Is Goodness Without God Good Enough?* p. 172. See also William Lane Craig and J. P. Moreland, *Philosophical Foundations of a Christian Worldview* (Downers Grove, IL: InterVarsity Press, 2003), pp. 529-32; C. Stephen Evans, *Kierkegaard's Ethic of Love: Divine Commands and Moral Obligations* (New York: Oxford University Press, 2004); Philip Quinn, *Divine Commands and Moral Requirements* (Oxford: Oxford University Press, 1978); Philip Quinn, "An Argument for Divine Command Theory," in *Christian Theism and the Problems of Philosophy*, ed. Michael Beaty (Notre Dame, IN: University of Notre Dame Press, 1990), pp. 289-302; Philip Quinn, "The Recent Revival of Divine Command Ethics," *Philosophy and Phenomenological Research* (Fall 1990): 345-65; Philip Quinn, "The Primacy of God's Will in Christian Ethics," *Philosophical Perspectives* 6 (1992): 493-513; Philip Quinn, "Divine Command Theory," in *The Blackwell Guide to Ethical Theory*, ed. Hugh Lafollette (Oxford: Blackwell, 2000), pp. 53-73; Philip Quinn, "Theological Voluntarism," in *The Oxford Handbook of Ethical Theory* (New York: Oxford University Press, 2006), pp. 63-90; Edward Wierenga, *The Nature of God: An Inquiry into the Divine Attributes* (Ithaca, NY: Cornell University Press, 1989), pp. 215-

Nihilism objection. Bradley argues that denying (1) would be to "Ally oneself with moral monsters like Ghenghis Khan, Hitler, Stalin, and Pol Pot. It would be to abandon all pretense to a belief in objective moral values. Indeed, if it is permissible to violate . . . [P1], . . . then it isn't easy to see what sorts of acts would *not* be permissible. [It would be] tantamount to an embrace of moral nihilism."[29]

This does not follow.[30] If a specific individual is commanded to kill on a specific occasion, then it is only permitted for *that particular individual* to perform *that particular act* on *that particular occasion.* Hence this view is compatible with contending that these actions are generally and, in most cases, wrong. Moreover, nothing about this view requires a person to believe that God ever issued such commands to anyone apart from the specific instances mentioned. Nor does it require a person to accept any and every claim made by any would-be killers that God has commanded them to act as they do.[31]

People who hold this view can, and typically do, think that cases in which God commands such things are extremely rare and that any claim that God has commanded such an action today is unlikely.[32] In fact, they may have theological reasons for thinking that such commands would not occur outside of the events recorded in salvation history.[33] Adopting this view, one

---

27; Edward Wierenga, "Utilitarianism and the Divine Command Theory," *American Philosophical Quarterly* 21 (1984): 311-18; Edward Wierenga, "A Defensible Divine Command Theory," *Nous* 17 (1983): 387-408; Janine Marie Idziak, "Divine Commands are the Foundation of Morality," *Contemporary Debates in Philosophy of Religion* (Oxford: Blackwell, 2004), pp. 290-98; William Wainwright, *Religion and Morality* (Aldershot, UK: Ashgate, 2005); William Mann, "Theism and the Foundations of Ethics," in *The Blackwell Guide to Philosophy of Religion,* ed. William Mann (Oxford: Blackwell, 2005); Thomas L. Carson, *Value and the Good Life* (Notre Dame, IN: University of Notre Dame Press, 2000); Alvin Plantinga, "Naturalism, Theism, Obligation and Supervenience," available at www.ammonius.org/grant_topics.php#0708; Matthew Flannagan, "The Premature Dismissal of Voluntarism," *Colloquium: The Australian and New Zealand Theological Review* (August 2010).

[29]Bradley, "A Moral Argument for Atheism," p. 136.

[30]Bradley here appears to conflate the claim that killing the innocent is not always wrong with the claim that killing the innocent is never wrong. This is not the same thing. A person can, for example, claim that there are certain situations where lying is not wrong (such as concealing a Jewish fugitive from the Gestapo) without contending that every lie is justified.

[31]Philip Quinn, *Divine Commands and Moral Requirements* (Oxford: Clarendon Press, 1978), p. 55.

[32]Ibid.

[33]Consider, for example, the cessationist view that prophetic utterances ceased in the Apostolic period, held by people like B. B. Warfield, J. Gresham Machen, F. N. Lee, Richard B. Gaffin Jr., John F. MacArthur and Daniel B. Wallace.

could even accept that such actions are for practical purposes absolutely wrong. All this position entails, then, is that in specific, rare and probably never to be repeated occasions, these actions have been permitted.

Robert Adams' objection. A more substantive objection comes from Robert Adams. Adams persuasively reasons that (1) is true only if God is understood as perfectly good, in the sense of being loving, just and so on. If God were evil or morally indifferent, then it would be possible for him to command wrongdoing and so (1) would be false. This means that a person who accepts (1) must presuppose that God is good.[34] However, we have some grasp of what goodness is and what kinds of things a good person does not command. Therefore God cannot coherently be called good if what he commands is contrary to "our *existing* moral beliefs."[35] To do so would be "playing word games which are intellectually dishonest,"[36] depriving "the word 'holy' of its ordinary meaning and make it a synonym for 'evil.'"[37] But one of our existing moral beliefs is P1; so we cannot coherently attribute a command that conflicts with P1 to a loving and just God.

Adams' argument needs qualifying. It is true we have some grasp of what goodness is, but this is mitigated by two factors. First, our moral judgments are fallible. While God does not command wrongdoing, it is likely that a perfectly good omniscient being would command something contrary to what *we think* is wrong. To say otherwise dogmatically assumes we are such good judges of morality that God could never disagree with us.

Second, our moral concepts are subject to revision. We change our opinions about the goodness and rightness of certain things without "playing word games which are intellectually dishonest" or depriving "the word 'holy' of its ordinary meaning and make it a synonym for 'evil.'" If this were not the case, one could *never* honestly or rationally change one's mind on an ethical issue.

Consequently, Adams' argument does not show that we cannot attribute

---

[34]Robert M. Adams, *Finite and Infinite Goods: A Framework for Ethics* (New York: Oxford University Press, 1999), p. 250.

[35]Ibid., p. 256.

[36]Raymond Bradley's opening statement in "Can a Loving God Send People to Hell?"—a debate between Raymond Bradley and William Lane Craig (Vancouver, BC: Simon Frasier University, 1994). Available at www.reasonablefaith.org/site/News2?page=NewsArticle&id=5301.

[37]Bradley, "A Moral Argument for Atheism," p. 143.

to God commands contrary to "our *existing* moral beliefs"; rather we cannot coherently ascribe to "God a set of commands that is *too much* at variance with the ethical outlook we bring to our ethical thinking." Adams allows for "the possibility of a conversion in which one's whole ethical outlook is revolutionized, and reorganized around a new center," but argues that "we can hardly hold open the possibility of anything too closely approaching a revolution in which, so to speak, good and evil would trade places."[38]

The problem is that a command to violate P1 is compatible with these qualified claims. Many ethicists contend that while P1 is correct as a general rule, it can be overridden in rare circumstances of *supreme emergency*,[39] when the alternative to killing noncombatants is to tolerate significantly greater evils, such as world occupation and domination by the Nazis.

Whatever one thinks of this position, it cannot be dismissed as conceptually incoherent. If a proponent of an absolutist position on killing noncombatants examined the arguments and concluded that in rare circumstances of supreme emergency, killing noncombatants was not wrong, then it is implausible to suggest their concept of goodness was so radically at odds with prior beliefs that "good and evil would trade places" and that their position consisted of mere word games. Consequently, a person can coherently believe a good person can endorse actions that violate P1.

THE CASE FOR A HYPERBOLIC READING OF "HOLY WAR" TEXTS

We have established that a Christian can coherently reject (3).[40] This brings us to our second line of argument: Is a person who accepts (1), (2) and (3) rationally required to accept (4)? Can a person accept that whatever God commands is permissible, that it is wrong to violate P1, that the Bible is the Word of God and yet plausibly deny that the Bible commands acts which violate P1?

---

[38] Adams, *Finite and Infinite Goods*, p. 256.

[39] Michael Walzer, *Just and Unjust Wars: A Moral Argument with Historical Illustrations*, 3rd ed. (New York: Basic Books, 2000), esp. chap. 16. See also Igor Primoratz, "The Morality of Terrorism," *Journal of Applied Philosophy* 14 (1997): 221-33.

[40] For fuller elaboration of the arguments in Part III see Matthew Flannagan, "Did God Command Canaanite Genocide?" in *Come Let Us Reason: New Essays in Christian Apologetics*, ed. Paul Copan and William Lane Craig (Nashville: B & H Academic, 2012); and Paul Copan, *Is God a Moral Monster? Making Sense of the Old Testament God* (Grand Rapids: Baker Books, 2011), chaps. 15-17.

It is worth noting that (4) is based on a strict literal reading. Since the patristic era, many theologians have claimed Old Testament Yahweh war passages should not be read in a strict literal fashion. Recently, several Protestant scholars have suggested a hyperbolic reading of the relevant passages.[41] They suggest language such as "destroy totally," "do not leave alive anything that breathes," destroy "men and women, young and old," and so on should be understood more as we understand what a person means who yells, in the context of watching Lennox Lewis in a boxing match, "knock his block off! Hand him his head! Take him out!" or hopes that the All Blacks will "annihilate the Springboks" or "totally slaughter the Wallabies." Now, the sports fan does not actually want Lennox Lewis to decapitate his opponent or for the All Blacks to engage in mass homicide. The same could be true here; understood in a nonliteral sense, the phrases probably mean something like, "attack them, defeat them, drive them out; not literally kill every man, woman, child donkey and the like."[42]

Perhaps the most detailed defense of this position is proposed by Nicholas Wolterstorff:

> The Book of Joshua has to be read as a theologically oriented narration, stylized and hyperbolic at important points, of Israel's early skirmishes in the Promised Land, with the story of these battles being framed by descriptions of two great ritualized events. The story as a whole celebrates Joshua as the great leader of his people, faithful to Yahweh, worthy successor of Moses. If we strip the word "hagiography" of its negative connotations, we can call it a hagiographic account of Joshua's events.[43]

---

[41]Alvin Plantinga, "Comments on Evan Fales' Satanic Verses: Moral Chaos in Holy Writ." Presented at "My Ways Are Not Your Ways: The Character of the God of the Hebrew Bible" Conference at the Center for Philosophy of Religion, University of Notre Dame, September 11, 2009, available at www.nd.edu/~cprelig/conferences/documents/HBprogram_006.pdf; Paul Copan, "Yahweh Wars and the Canaanites: Divinely Mandated Genocide or Corporate Capital Punishment," *Philosophia Christi* 11, no. 1 (2009); Copan, *Is God a Moral Monster?*; Christopher Wright, *The God I Don't Understand: Reflections on Tough Questions of Faith* (Grand Rapids: Zondervan, 2008), pp. 87-88. In his latest discussion on the issue, William Lane Craig states, "I've come to appreciate that the object of God's command to the Israelites was not the slaughter of the Canaanites, as is often imagined. The command rather was primarily *to drive them out of the land.* The judgment upon these Canaanite kingdoms was to dispossess them of their land and thus destroy them as kingdoms." See "Question 147: Divine Command Morality and Voluntarism." Available at www.reasonablefaith.org/site/News2?page=NewsArticle&id=7911.

[42]Ibid.

[43]Nicholas Wolterstorff, "Reading Joshua," in *Divine Evil? The Moral Character of the God of*

Wolterstorff's argument. Wolterstorff's contention is that "a careful reading of the text in its literary context makes it implausible to interpret it as claiming that Yahweh ordered extermination."[44] It is important to note what he means by context. Here it is clear that Wolterstorff is advocating a *canonical* approach. "Joshua as we have it today was intended as a component in the larger sequence consisting of Deuteronomy, Joshua, Judges, I and II Samuel, and I and II Kings," he writes. "I propose that we interpret the Book of Joshua as a component within this larger sequence—in particular, that we interpret it as preceded by Deuteronomy and succeeded by Judges."[45]

Joshua comes after Numbers[46] and Deuteronomy and before Judges. These books should be read as a single narrative. However, when one does this several issues become apparent. First, Joshua 6–11 summarizes several battles and concludes, "So Joshua took the entire land, just as the LORD had directed Moses, and he gave it as an inheritance to Israel according to their tribal divisions. Then the land had rest from war" (Josh 11:23). Scholars readily agree that Judges is literarily linked to Joshua.[47] Yet the early chapters of Judges which, incidentally, *repeat* the death and burial of Joshua, show a different picture:

Abraham, ed. Michael Bergmann, Michael J. Murray and Michael C. Rea (New York: Oxford University Press, 2010), pp. 252-53.

[44]Ibid., p. 249.

[45]Ibid.

[46]In light of the command to "kill all the [Midianite] men" in Num 31:7.

[47]Joshua and Judges should be read as a connected literary unit. For example, Joshua 24:28-31 mentions Joshua's death and burial place at Timnath-serah "in the hill country of Ephraim," and then Judges 2:6-9 refers to Joshua's death and burial place at Timnath-heres "in the hill country of Ephraim." That is, Joshua and Judges are literarily connected in their mention of Joshua's (a) death and (b) burial. (a) Both books state that "Joshua the son of Nun, the servant of the LORD, died" at the age of "one hundred and ten" (Josh 24:29; Judg 2:8). (b) Then a deliberate literary connection is made on the burial place of Joshua, using the Hebrew letter-substitution cipher known as *atbash*, in this case reversing the first and last consonants of the burial place from "-serah" to "-heres." Compare "they buried him in the border of his inheritance in *Timnathserah*, which *is* in mount Ephraim, on the north side of the hill of Gaash" (Josh 24:30, NASB, my emphasis) with "they buried him in the territory of his inheritance in *Timnath-serah*, which is in the hill country of Ephraim, on the north of Mount Gaash (Judg 2:9, NASB, our emphasis). Not only this, Judges connects to 1 (and 2) Samuel (the next book in the Hebrew canon) with its reference to "the hill country of Ephraim." (Note this phrase in Josh 17:15; 19:50; 20:7; 24:30; 24:33; then in Judg 2:9; 3:27; 4:5; 7:24; 10:1; 17:1, 8; 18:2, 13; 19:1, 16, 18; and then in 1 Sam 1:1; 9:4.) The linkage of Judg 17:1 and 19:1 with 1 Sam 1:1 is connected by the general threefold pattern of (a)"There was a (certain) man . . . " (b)"from the hill country of Ephraim" (c)"and his name was _____."

> After the death of Joshua, the Israelites inquired of the LORD, "Who shall go
> up first for us against the Canaanites, to fight against them?" The LORD said,
> "Judah shall go up. I hereby give the land into his hand." Judah said to his
> brother Simeon, "Come up with me into the territory allotted to me, that we
> may fight against the Canaanites; then I too will go with you into the territory
> allotted to you." So Simeon went with him. Then Judah went up and the LORD
> gave the Canaanites and the Perizzites into their hand; and they defeated ten
> thousand of them at Bezek. (Judg 1:1-4 NRSV)

Taken literally, the book of Joshua states that Joshua conquered the
whole land, yet Judges states that much of the land was unconquered. Similarly, Joshua affirms he exterminated all the Canaanites in this region. Repeatedly the text states that Joshua left "no survivors" and "destroyed everything that breathed" in "the entire land" and "put all the inhabitants to the
sword." Alongside these general claims the book of Joshua identifies several
specific places and cities where Joshua exterminated everyone and left no
survivors. These include Hebron (Josh 10:36-37), Debir (Josh 10:38), the hill
country and the Negev and the western foothills (Josh 10:40). Yet in the first
chapter of Judges, we are told that the Canaanites lived in the Negev, in the
hill country (Judg 1:9), in Debir (Judg 1:11), in Hebron (Judg 1:10) and in the
western foothills (Judg 1:9). Moreover, they did so in such numbers and
strength that they had to be driven out by force. These are the same cities
where Joshua 10 tells us Joshua had annihilated and left no survivors.[48]

Likewise, Joshua 11:23 asserts that "Joshua took the entire land" and then
"gave it as an inheritance to Israel according to their tribal divisions." Note
the conquered region is the *same land* that is later divided between the Israelite tribes. Only a chapter later, when the text turns to give an account of
these tribal divisions, the allotments begin with God telling Joshua, "You are
very old, and there are still very large areas of land to be taken over" (Josh
13:1). Moreover, when one examines the allotment given to Judah, we see
Caleb asking permission to drive the Anakites from the hill countries (Josh

---

[48]In addition to these general claims about exterminating populations, Joshua 11:21-22 declares
that "Joshua came and wiped out the Anakim from the hill country, from Hebron, from Debir,
from Anab, and from all the hill country of Judah." This happened after Joshua is already said
to have killed the inhabitants in these areas in Joshua 10:30-40. Joshua 11:21 states that no
Anakites were left living in Israelite territory after this campaign. Yet in Judges 1:21 the text
explicitly states that *Anakites* are in Hebron.

14:11). We also read how Caleb has to defeat Anakites living in Hebron and, after this, march against the people "living in Debir" (Josh 15:13-19). Similarly, it is evident with several of the other allotments that the people have yet to drive out the Canaanites entrenched in the area. It is further evident that the Israelites were not always successful in doing this. Tribe upon tribe is recorded as having failed to drive out Canaanites (Josh 13:13; 15:63; 16:10; 17:12-13, 18). Joshua asks seven of the tribes, "How long will you put off entering to take possession of the land which the LORD, the God of your fathers, has given you?" (Josh 18:3). Joshua went on to warn Israel to not mention, swear by, serve or bow down to their gods (Josh 23:7, 12-13; Judg 2:10-13). Many of the Canaanites were still around "until this day" and many of these would become forced laborers in Israel (Josh 15:63; 16:10; 17:12-13; Judg 1:19, 21, 27-35).

Finally, the account of what God commanded differs in the two narratives. Joshua states, "He left no survivors. He totally destroyed all who breathed, just as the LORD, the God of Israel, had commanded" (Josh 10:40) and "exterminat[ed] them without mercy, as the LORD had commanded Moses" (Josh 11:20b). However, when this command is retroactively referred to in Judges 2:1, there is no mention of genocide or annihilation. Instead we read of how God had promised to drive them out and of his commands to the Israelites not to make treaties with the Canaanites and to destroy their shrines. This silence is significant in the context. If God had commanded genocide, then it is odd that only instructions concerning treaties and shrines were mentioned. Therefore, taken as a single narrative and taken literally, Joshua 1–11 gives a different account of events than that narrated by Judges—not to mention events narrated in the later chapters of Joshua itself.

Wolterstorff adds:

> Those whose occupation it is to try to determine the origins of these writings will suggest that the editors had contradictory records, oral traditions, and so forth to work with. No doubt this is correct. But those who edited the final version of these writings into one sequence were not mindless; they could see, as well as you and I can see, the tensions and contradictions—surface or real—that I have pointed to. So what is going on?[49]

49Wolterstorff, "Reading Joshua," p. 251.

Wolterstorff's point is that, regardless of what sources or strata of tradition are alleged behind the final form of Joshua, the redactors who put these books into a single narrative would have been well aware of the obvious contradictions mentioned above. Moreover, these redactors were not stupid. They obviously would not want to affirm that both accounts were true literal descriptions of what occurred. Yet they chose to put in the canon, next to Joshua, a book which began with a narration at odds with a literal reading of the early chapters of Joshua, and they chose to juxtapose the picture of Joshua 1–11 with the later chapters I mentioned above. The redactor cannot therefore be asserting that both accounts are literally true.

Wolterstorff is correct here. However, his position could be strengthened on theological grounds. Remember we are asking whether a person who accepts (1), (2) and (3) can defensibly deny (4). In other words, assuming Scripture is God's Word, is it plausible to claim it teaches that God commands us to perform acts that violate moral principle P1? In *Divine Discourse: Philosophical Reflections on the Claim that God Speaks*, Wolterstorff provides an interesting and rigorous analysis of the notion that Scripture is the Word of God. Central to his analysis is that "an eminently plausible construal of the process whereby these books found their way into a single canonical text, would be that by way of that process of canonization, God was authorizing these books as together constituting a single volume of divine discourse."[50]

This understanding of Scripture provides the theological justification for reading the text as a single series. By examining what was affirmed in Judges and in later passages of Joshua, one can determine what the author of the early chapters of Joshua intended.[51] Moreover, if the primary author of

---

[50]Nicholas Wolterstorff, *Divine Discourse: Philosophical Reflections on the Claim That God Speaks* (Cambridge: Cambridge University Press, 1995), p. 295. See also Nicholas Wolterstorff, "Unity behind the Canon," in *One Scripture or Many? The Canon from Biblical, Theological, and Philosophical Perspectives*, ed. Christine Helmer and Christof Landmesser (New York: Oxford University Press, 2004), pp. 217-32.

[51]Alvin Plantinga notes in *Warranted Christian Belief* (New York: Oxford University Press, 2000), "an assumption of the enterprise is that the principal author of the Bible—the entire Bible—is God himself (according to Calvin, God the Holy Spirit). Of course each of the books of the Bible has a human author or authors as well; still, the principal author is God. This impels us to treat the whole more like a unified communication than a miscellany of ancient books. Scripture isn't so much a library of independent books as itself a book with many subdivisions but a central theme: the message of the gospel. By virtue of this unity, furthermore (by virtue of the

Scripture is God then the primary author of the final canonical text is unlikely to have deliberately (or accidentally) authored an obviously contradictory narrative. Hence even if the contradictions were not obvious to the
redactors, I think Wolterstorff is correct that these apparent contradictions
would have been evident to God.[52] Given that the redactors' incorporating
these books into a single canonical text constitutes God's authorizing them,
this process cannot have involved the redactors affirming as literally true
two contradictory accounts.

At this point Wolterstorff raises a further issue about the type of literature
Joshua appears to be. He notes that the early chapters of Judges, by and large,
read like "down-to-earth" history.[53] However, anyone who reads "the Book of
Joshua in one sitting cannot fail to be struck by" certain stylistic features in
the narrative. One is "the highly ritualized character of some of the major
events described."[54] "The book is framed by its opening narration of the ritualized crossing of the Jordan and by its closing narration of the equally ritualized ceremony of blessing and cursing that took place at Shechem; and the
conquest narrative begins with the ritualized destruction of Jericho."[55] A related ritualistic feature is "the mysterious sacral category of *being devoted to
destruction*."[56] Most significant is the use of formulaic language:

---

fact that there is just one principal author), it is possible to 'interpret Scripture with Scripture.'
If a given passage from one of Paul's epistles is puzzling, it is perfectly proper to try to come to
clarity as to what God's teaching is in this passage by appealing not only to what Paul himself
says elsewhere in other epistles but also to what is taught elsewhere in Scripture (for example,
the Gospel of John)" (p. 385).

[52] In the question and answer time following his "Reading Joshua" paper, Nicholas Wolterstorff
notes that the phrase "he killed all the inhabitants with the edge of the sword" occurs at least
fifteen times in Joshua 6–11 in close succession. This is "hammered home with emphasis" then
followed a chapter later with the claim that Joshua had not conquered the whole land. In the
next five chapters, it is stressed repeatedly that the land is not yet conquered. This is followed by
the opening chapters of Judges, which affirms eight times in a single chapter that the Israelites
had failed to conquer the land or the cities finishing with the Angel of Bokim rebuking them for
failing to do so. These are not subtle contrasts. They are, in Wolterstorff's words, "flamboyant";
it is unlikely that an intelligent redactor would have missed this. Presented at the "My Ways Are
Not Your Ways: The Character of the God of the Hebrew Bible" conference at the Center for
Philosophy of Religion, University of Notre Dame. September 12, 2009. Available at www.nd
.edu/~cprelig/conferences/documents/HBprogram_006.pdf.

[53] Wolterstorff, "Reading Joshua," p. 253.

[54] Ibid., pp. 251, 252.

[55] Ibid. The ritualized nature of the narration is also stressed by Duane L. Christensen, *Deuteronomy 1:1–21:9* (Nashville: Thomas Nelson, 2001).

[56] Wolterstorff, "Reading Joshua," p. 252. That the word ḥērem, translated as "devoted to destruction," often serves a figurative or rhetorical function is also noted by other scholars. See the

> Anyone who reads the Book of Joshua in one sitting cannot fail to be struck by the prominent employment of formulaic phrasings. . . . Far more important is the formulaic clause, "struck down all the inhabitants with the edge of the sword."
>
> The first time one reads that Joshua struck down all the inhabitants of a city with the edge of the sword, namely, in the story of the conquest of Jericho (6:21), one makes nothing of it. But the phrasing—or close variants thereon—gets repeated, seven times in close succession in chapter 10, two more times in chapter 11, and several times in other chapters. The repetition makes it unmistakable that we are dealing here with a formulaic literary convention.[57]

The early chapters of the book of Joshua appear to be something other than a mere literal description of what occurred. In light of these facts, Wolterstorff argues that Judges should be taken literally whereas Joshua should be taken as hagiographic history. He provides the example of North American morality tales of the noble Puritan and Washington crossing the Delaware. These function as rhetorical hyperbolic accounts of what occurred; their purpose is to teach theological and moral points. They are not precise accounts of what actually occurred.

Ancient Near Eastern conquest accounts. Wolterstorff's position gains support from research into ancient Near Eastern (ANE) historical records. In a comprehensive comparative study of ANE conquest accounts, Old Testament scholar K. Lawson Younger concludes that the book of Joshua employs the same stylistic, rhetorical and literary conventions of other war reports of the same period. Younger notes such accounts are "highly figurative"[58] and narrate military events via a common transmission code.

What is noteworthy is the hyperbolic nature of the "transmission code."

---

discussion on the use of the term under the heading "The argument applied to the Amalekites."

[57]Wolterstorff, "Reading Joshua," p. 251.

[58]K. Lawson Younger Jr. points out: "As the ancient historian (whether Near Eastern, biblical, or otherwise) reconstructed 'historical' referents into a coherent description, he produced a figurative account, a 're-presenting representation.'" Younger suggests such an historian functions as "a literary artist." He adds: "Ancient Near East conquest accounts are figurative in three ways: (1) the structural and ideological codes that are the apparatus for the text's production; (2) the themes or motifs that the text utilizes; and (3) the usage of rhetorical figures in the accounts." In "Judges 1 in Its Near Eastern Literary Context," in *Faith Tradition and History: Old Testament Historiography and Its Ancient Near Eastern Context*, ed. A. R. Millard, J. K. Hoffmeier and D. W. Baker (Winona Lake, IN: Eisenbrauns, 1994), p. 207.

Many ANE conquest accounts hyperbolically describe battles taking place in one day; the numbers of armies and enemy casualties can also be rhetorically exaggerated. The literary motif of divine intervention is another example. Both *The 10 Year Annals of Mursilli* and *Sargon's Letter to the God* record a divine intervention when the god sends hailstones on the enemy.[59] Tuthmosis III has a similar story regarding a meteor.[60] Younger notes these accounts are very similar to parallel accounts in Joshua 10.

Similarly, Younger notes in many ANE texts "one can discern a literary technique in which a deity is implored to maintain daylight long enough for there to be a victory,"[61] which has obvious parallels to Joshua 10:13-14. Richard Hess notes that Hittite conquest accounts describe the gods knocking down the walls of an enemy city in a manner similar to that described in the battle of Jericho.[62] The fact that similar events are narrated in multiple different accounts suggests they are "a notable ingredient of the transmission code for conquest accounts";[63] that is, they appear to be part of the common hyperbolic rhetoric of warfare rather than descriptions of what actually occurred.

However, and most important, part of this "transmission code" is that victories are narrated in an exaggerated hyperbolic fashion in terms of total conquest, complete annihilation and destruction of the enemy, killing everyone, leaving no survivors, etc. For example:

- Egypt's Tuthmosis III (later fifteenth century) boasted that "the numerous army of Mitanni was overthrown within the hour, annihilated totally, like those (now) not existent"; in fact, Mitanni's forces lived on to fight in the fifteenth and fourteenth centuries.

- Hittite king Mursilli II (who ruled from 1322–1295 B.C.) recorded making "Mt. Asharpaya empty (of humanity)" and the "mountains of Tarikarimu empty (of humanity)."

---

[59]Ibid., pp. 208-11.

[60]Ibid., p. 217.

[61]Ibid., p. 219. For further discussion of the relationship between Joshua's long day and other ANE texts see John Walton, "Joshua 10:12-15 and Mesopotamian Celestial Omen Texts," in *Faith, Tradition, and History*, pp. 181-90.

[62]Richard Hess, "West Semitic Texts and the Book of Joshua," *Bulletin for Biblical Research* 7 (1997): 68.

[63]Younger, "Judges 1 in its Near Eastern Literary Context," p. 211.

- The "Bulletin" of Ramses II narrates Egypt's less-than-spectacular victories in Syria (around 1274); nevertheless, he announces that he slew "the entire force" of Hittites—indeed "all the chiefs of all the countries," disregarding the "millions of foreigners," which he considered "chaff."

- In the Merneptah's Stele (ca. 1230 B.C.), Rameses II's son Merneptah announced, "Israel is wasted, his seed is not"—another premature declaration!

- Moab's king Mesha (840/830 B.C.) bragged that the Northern kingdom of "Israel has utterly perished for always," which was over a century premature. The Assyrians devastated Israel in 722 B.C. In the same stele, Mesha rhetorically describes victories in terms of his fighting against a town, taking it and then killing all the inhabitants of the town.

- The Assyrian ruler Sennacherib (701–681 B.C.) used similar hyperbole: "The soldiers of Hirimme, dangerous enemies, I cut down with the sword; and not one escaped."[64]

Numerous other examples could be provided. The hyperbolic use of language similar to that in Joshua is strikingly evident.[65] It is equally evident that histories of this sort are, as Wolterstorff notes, highly stylized and often used exaggeration (for what could be called hagiographic purposes) so as to commend the kings as faithful servants of the gods. The

---

[64]Taken from Kenneth A. Kitchen, *On the Reliability of the Old Testament* (Grand Rapids: Eerdmans, 2003), pp. 173-74; K. Lawson Younger Jr., *Ancient Conquest Accounts: A Study in Ancient Near Eastern and Biblical History Writing* (Sheffield, UK: Sheffield Academic Press, 1990), pp. 227-28, 245. And though we disagree with the postmodern themes, see Lori K. Rowlett's documentation of this rhetoric in *Joshua and the Rhetoric of Violence: A New Historical Analysis* (New York: Continuum, 1996), especially chapter 5. See also James K. Hoffmeier, *Israel in Egypt: The Evidence for the Authenticity of the Exodus Tradition* (Oxford: Oxford University Press, 1997), pp. 41-43.

[65]In addition, both Kitchen and Younger note that such hyperbolic language is used in several places within the book of Joshua itself. In Joshua 10:20, for example, it states Joshua and the sons of Israel had "finished destroying" and "completely destroyed" their enemies. Immediately, the text affirms that the "survivors went to fortified cities." In this context, the language of total destruction is clearly hyperbolic. Similarly, the account of the battle of Ai is clearly hyperbolic. After Joshua's troops feign a retreat the text states that "all the men of Ai" are pressed to chase them. "Not a man remained in Ai or Bethel who did not go after Israel. They left the city open and went in pursuit of Israel." Joshua lures the pursuers into a trap "so that they were caught in the middle with Israelites on both sides. Israel cut them down, leaving them neither survivors nor fugitives." Then it immediately goes on to assert, "When Israel had finished killing all the men of Ai in the fields and in the desert where they had chased them, and when every one of them had been put to the sword, they went to the city of Ai and killed all the men in it" (Josh 8:24).

purpose was not to provide literal descriptions of what occurred;[66] they constitute "monumental hyperbole."[67] The language is typically full of bravado and generally depicts total devastation. The knowing ANE reader recognized that this was massive hyperbole and the accounts were not understood to be literally true.[68]

On realizing this, we see three things are evident. First, taken as a single narrative, and taken literally, Joshua 1–11 gives a contradictory account of events as that narrated by Judges and also by the later chapters of Joshua itself. Second, "those who edited the final version of these writings into one sequence were not mindless," particularly if God speaks through them. Third, while Judges reads more like "down-to-earth" history, a careful reading of Joshua reveals it to be full of ritualistic, stylized accounts and formulaic language. This third point is supported by research into ANE conquest accounts. Such studies show such accounts are hyperbolic, hagiographic, figurative and follow a common transmission code. Comparisons between these accounts and the early chapters of Joshua suggest Joshua is written according to the same literary conventions and transmission code; part of this transmission code involves hyperbolically portraying a victory in the absolute terms of "totally destroying the enemy" or in terms of miraculous divine intervention. "Such statements are rhetoric indicative of military victory"[69] and not literal descriptions of what occurred.

These three points taken together provide compelling reasons for thinking that one should interpret the text as a hyperbolic, hagiographic

---

[66]Thomas L. Thompson examines several different ANE conquest accounts of this type and notes they have a hagiographic function. See his "A Testimony of the Good King: Reading the Mesha Stele," in *Ahab Agonistes: The Rise and Fall of the Omri Dynasty*, ed. Lester L. Grabbe (New York: T & T Clark, 2007).

[67]John Goldingay gives yet another example from within the Bible itself: "While Joshua does speak of Israel's utterly destroying the Canaanites, even these accounts can give a misleading impression: peoples that have been annihilated have no trouble reappearing later in the story; after Judah puts Jerusalem to the sword, its occupants are still living there 'to this day' (Judg. 1:8, 21)." In "City and Nation" in *Old Testament Theology, Volume 3: Israel's Life* (Downers Grove, IL: InterVarsity Press, 2009), p. 570.

[68]Christopher J. H. Wright, *Old Testament Ethics for the People of God* (Downers Grove, IL: InterVarsity Press, 2004), pp. 474-75; Iain Provan, V. Philips Long and Tremper Longman III, *A Biblical History of Israel* (Louisville: Westminster John Knox Press, 2003), p. 149.

[69]K. Lawson Younger Jr., "Joshua" in John H. Walton, Victor H. Matthews and Mark W. Chavalas, *The IVP Bible Background Commentary: Old Testament* (Downers Grove IL: InterVarsity Press), p. 227.

and figurative account of what occurred. In light of these factors it seems sensible to conclude that the accounts of battles in Joshua 6–11 are not meant to be taken literally.

Two implications. Two implications follow from this conclusion. First, Joshua's "utter destruction" of the Canaanites is exactly what "Moses the servant of the LORD had commanded":

- "Joshua captured all the cities of these kings, and all their kings, and he struck them with the edge of the sword, and utterly destroyed them; just as Moses the servant of the LORD had commanded" (Josh 11:12 NASB).

- "All the spoil of these cities and the cattle, the sons of Israel took as their plunder; but they struck every man with the edge of the sword, until they had destroyed them. They left no one who breathed. Just as the LORD had commanded Moses his servant, so Moses commanded Joshua, and so Joshua did; he left nothing undone of all that the LORD had commanded Moses" (Josh 11:14-15 NASB).

- "that he might destroy them, just as the LORD had commanded Moses" (Josh 11:20 NASB).

Joshua's comprehensive language echoes Moses's sweeping commands to "consume" and "utterly destroy" the Canaanites, to not "leave alive anything that breathes";[70] Scripture clearly indicates that Joshua fulfilled Moses' charge to him. So *if* Joshua did just as Moses commanded and *if* Joshua's described destruction was really massive hyperbole common in ANE warfare language and familiar to Moses, *then* clearly Moses himself did not intend a literal, comprehensive Canaanite destruction. He, like Joshua, was merely following the literary convention of the day.[71]

A second implication of Wolterstorff's position is that Joshua does not assert that Israel engaged in divinely-authorized violation of P1:

---

[70]Deuteronomy 7:2 declares: "when the LORD your God has given them up before you and you have struck them, you shall utterly destroy them" (our translation). Similarly, Deuteronomy 20:16-17 commands: "do not leave alive anything that breathes. Completely destroy them." In Joshua 10 one sees the formulaic language of "and the LORD gave [the city]" and he/they "struck it and its king with the edge of the sword" until "there was no one remaining" (NRSV). The chapter is summarized with the phrase, "So Joshua defeated the whole land . . . he left no one remaining, but utterly destroyed all that breathed" (Josh 10:40 NRSV). The similar phraseology is evident.

[71]Wolterstorff, "Reading Joshua," p. 252.

[W]hen a high school basketball player says his team slaughtered the other team last night he's not asserting, literally now, that they slaughter the other team. What is he asserting? Not easy to tell. That they scored a decisive victory? Maybe, but suppose they barely eked out a win? Was he lying? Maybe not. Maybe he was speaking with a wink of the eye hyperbole. High school kids do.[72]

In the same way, when one realizes that Joshua is hagiographic and highly hyperbolic in its narration of what occurred, the best one can conclude from the accounts of "killing everyone that breathed" is that "Israel scored a decisive victory, and once you recognize the presence of hyperbole it is not even clear how decisive the victories were. Joshua did not conquer all the cities in the land nor did he slaughter all the inhabitants in the cities he did conquer. The book of Joshua does not say that he did."[73]

Canonical factors force the same conclusion. In Judges and Exodus the command is expressed in terms of avoiding treaties and driving the Canaanites out. In Joshua and Deuteronomy the command is expressed in the language of "utterly destroying them." The conclusion we have reached is that the latter is figurative language and the former is literal. If this is the case, then the command was to drive them out and not to literally exterminate them.

Further considerations. In addition to the above arguments regarding the Canaanites, we could include further considerations frequently overlooked by the critic. First, as briefly noted above, the dominant language of "driving out" and "thrusting out" the Canaanites indicates that "extermination" passages are hyperbolic (Ex 23:28; Lev 18:24; Num 33:52: Deut 6:19; 7:1; 9:4; 18:12; Josh 10:28, 30, 32, 35, 37, 39; 11:11, 14). Israel would "dispossess" the Canaanites of their land (Num 21:32; Deut 9:1; 11:23; 18:14; 19:1, etc.). Just as Adam and Eve were "driven out" of the garden (Gen 3:24) or Cain into the wilderness (Gen 4:14) or David from Israel by Saul (1 Sam 26:19), so the Israelites were to "dispossess" the Canaanites. "Driving out" or "dispossessing" is different from "wiping out" or "destroying." Clearly utter annihilation was not intended.

---

[72]Nicholas Wolterstorff, "Reply to Antony," in *Divine Evil?* p. 263.
[73]Wolterstorff "Reading Joshua" presented to "My Ways Are Not Your Ways"; this paragraph was in the paper presented at the conference but was omitted from the published version.

Second, the biblical language of the Canaanites' destruction is identical to that of Judah's destruction in the Babylonian exile—clearly not utter annihilation or even genocide. Indeed, God threatened to "vomit" out Israel from the land just as he had vomited out the Canaanites (Lev 18:25, 28; 20:22). In the context of the Babylonian invasion and Judah's exile (sixth century B.C.), God said he would "lay waste the towns of Judah so no one can live there" (Jer 9:11). Indeed God said, "I will completely destroy them and make them an object of horror and scorn, and an everlasting ruin" (Jer 25:9). God threatened to "reach out and destroy you" (Jer 15:6; cf. Ezek 5:16)—to bring "disaster" against Judah (Jer 6:19). The biblical text, supported by archaeological discovery, suggests that while Judah's political and religious structures were ruined and that Judahites died in the conflict, the "urban elite" were deported to Babylon while many "poor of the land" remained behind.[74] Clearly Judah's being "completely destroyed" and made an "everlasting ruin" (Jer 25:9) was a significant literary exaggeration—which reinforces our point about the Canaanites.

Third, archaeology confirms the biblical account of a gradual infiltration rather than a massive military assault against the Canaanites; this was a development that took over two centuries to accomplish. This being the case, all tangible aspects of the Canaanites' culture—buildings and homes— would have remained very much intact (cf. Deut 6:10-11: "cities which you did not build"). Preserving such structures would have been a very sensible move if Israel was to settle down in the same region. Archaeologists have discovered that by 1000 B.C. (during the Iron Age), Canaanites were no longer an identifiable entity in Israel. Around this time also, Israelites were worshiping a national God whose dominant personal name was Yahweh. An additional significant change from the Late Bronze to the Iron Age was that town shrines in Canaan had been abandoned but not relocated elsewhere—say, to the hill villages. This suggests that a new people with a distinct theological bent had migrated here, had gradually occupied the territory and eventually become dominant.[75]

---

[74]Provan, Long and Longman, *A Biblical History of Israel,* pp. 281-85.
[75]Alan R. Millard, "Were the Israelites Really Canaanites?" in *Israel: Ancient Kingdom or Late Invention?* ed. Daniel I. Block (Nashville: B&H Academic, 2008), pp. 156-68; cf. Copan, *Is God a Moral Monster?* pp. 182-84.

Thus the critic's strategy of emphasizing literal Canaanite annihilation at the expense of literal Canaanite survival simply cannot be sustained. Consider the following:

- If the critic believes that Israel really wiped out the Canaanites militarily, will he reject archaeological discovery that stands against this suggestion?

- If the critic claims that Israel engaged in literal annihilation of the Canaanites, why does he not take literally passages within the same texts that reveal an abundance of survivors?

- If the critic believes that Moses commanded the literal annihilation of the Canaanites, why not treat literally the claim that Joshua obeyed "all that Moses commanded" (Josh 11:12, 14-15, 20), which includes leaving plenty of survivors?

- If the critic claims that God literally commanded Israel to "completely destroy" the Canaanites, then what are we to make of the language of God's "completely destroying" Judah under the Babylonians (Jer 25:9)— something that didn't literally happen?

- If the critic believes that the Old Testament does not use hyperbole and rhetoric in warfare texts, then what does he do with clear indications of rhetorical exaggeration in other ancient Near Eastern war texts?

The argument applied to the Amalekites. An analogous line of argument applies to the holy war reported in 1 Samuel 15. We read of God telling Saul to "utterly destroy [*ḥāram*]" and to "not spare" the Amalekites, but to "put to death men and women, children and infants, cattle and sheep, camels and donkeys" (1 Sam 15:3). By the end of the chapter, Saul has apparently killed all the Amalekites except King Agag and a lot of livestock. Saul did not obey God fully and the prophet Samuel had to step in and finish off Agag himself. Because Saul did not carry out God's command completely, God rejected him as king.

When one reads this passage as part of the broader narrative, features similar to those of Joshua 1–11 become apparent. The 1 Samuel 15 story appears to be a clear-cut case of complete obliteration. The text appears to state that no Amalekites remain; but in 1 Samuel 27:8 we see, "David and his men went up and raided the Geshurites, the Girzites and the Amalekites." The "utterly destroyed" Amalekites appear to have risen again, but this is not the end of them either.[76] They pop up again in 1 Samuel 30 where the Amalekites made one of their infamous raids (1 Sam 30:1). David pursued them to get the Israelites and the booty the Amalekites had taken back and four hundred of them escaped (1 Sam 30:18). So contrary to the common impression, Saul *did not* wipe out all the Amalekites, something 1 Samuel itself makes clear. Even David did not complete the job. The Amalekites were *still* present during King Hezekiah's time 250 years later (1 Chron 4:43).

During the time of Esther, when Jews were under the rule of the Persian king Ahasuerus/Xerxes (486–465 B.C.) we encounter Haman "the Agagite" (Esther 3:1). Like *King Agag*, the Amalekite from 1 Samuel 15:8, *Haman was an Amalekite* who continued the Amalekite tradition of aggression against God's chosen people. An "enemy of the Jews" (Esther 3:10), Haman mounted a campaign to destroy the Jews as a people (Esther 3:13).

Again, as with Joshua, whoever "edited the final version of these writings into one sequence"[77] juxtaposed two accounts; one of which, if taken literally, describes Saul and Samuel annihilating the entire population while the second affirms that the Canaanites were not annihilated. Assuming this person was not "mindless" he cannot have intended to affirm both as literally true.

Similarly, while David's battle with the Amalekites reads more like "down-to-earth" history, 1 Samuel 15 appears highly hyperbolic and contains obvious rhetorical exaggeration.[78] Saul's army was said to be 210,000 soldiers strong, larger than any army known at this time in antiquity.[79] Moreover, "Saul attacked the Amalekites all the way from Havilah to Shur"

---

[76]Compare the record of Saul's "holy war" (or Yahweh war) in 1 Samuel 15:7-9 and 21 with David's campaign in 1 Samuel 27:8-9. Not only do these texts affirm the Amalekites still exist, but the reference to Egypt and Shur states they exist in the *same* area that Saul attacked in the previous passages. Moreover, David killed Amalekite men and women living in his area and took sheep and cattle as plunder. However, these are the very things Saul was said in 1 Samuel 15 to have eradicated.

[77]Wolterstorff, "Reading Joshua," p. 251.

[78]Ralph W. Klein, *1 Samuel*, Word Biblical Commentary 10 (Waco, TX: Word Books, 1983), p. 147.

[79]On the exaggeration of numbers in the ancient Near East and Old Testament, see Daniel M. Fouts, "A Defense of the Hyperbolic Interpretation of Numbers in the Old Testament," *Journal of the Evangelical Theological Society* 40, no. 3 (1997): 377-87.

(1 Sam 15:7). Shur is on the edge of Egypt, and Havilah is in Saudi Arabia. This is an absurdly large battle field.[80] Similarly, the language of "totally destroying [*ḥāram*]" populations "with the sword," which is used hyperbolically in Joshua, parallels the language used in the Mesha Stele. Thomas Thompson notes that such motifs "are clearly part of the totalitarian rhetoric of holy war rather than historical considerations."[81] Similarly, Christopher Wright states that this rhetoric of "total destruction [*ḥērem*]" was "proudly claimed, elsewhere. But we must also recognize that the language of warfare had a conventional rhetoric that liked to make absolute and universal claims about total victory and completely wiping out the enemy."[82] And likewise there was the stock phrase, "men and women, young and old, cattle, sheep and donkeys."[83] "Men and women" occurs seven times in the Old Testament: Ai (Josh 8:25); Amalek (1 Sam 15:3); Saul at Nob (1 Sam 22:18);[84] Jerusalem during Ezra's time (Neh 8:2); and Israel (2 Sam 6:19; 2 Chron 16:3). Each time, except at Nob, where Saul killed the entire priestly family, except one (1 Sam 22:19-20), the word "all [*kol*]" is used. The expression "men and women" or similar phrases appear to be *stereotypical* for describing all the inhabitants of a town or region "without predisposing the reader to assume anything further about their ages or even their genders."[85] Such stereotypical language is very similar to the hyperbolic description of military defeat in 2 Chronicles 36:16-20, where Jewish *defeat and exile* to Babylon was described in similar language.[86]

---

[80]"It's impossible to imagine the battle actually traversed the enormous distance from Arabia almost to Egypt," Klein, *1 Samuel*, p. 150.

[81]Thomas L. Thompson, writing on the use of *ḥērem* in the Mesha Stele, in "Mesha and Questions of Historicity," *Scandinavian Journal of the Old Testament* 22, no. 2 (2007): 249.

[82]Christopher Wright, *The God I Don't Understand*, pp. 87-88.

[83]Richard Hess points out that the phrase is actually "from men to women, from young to old, from cattle, sheep to donkeys" in "Yahweh Wars"—a panel presentation ("Is Yahweh a Moral Monster") at the annual meeting of the Society of Biblical Literature, Atlanta, Georgia (November 21, 2010).

[84]Only here are children explicitly mentioned.

[85]Richard S. Hess, "The Jericho and Ai of the Book of Joshua," in *Critical Issues in Early Israelite History*, ed. Richard S. Hess, Gerald A. Klingbeil and Paul J. Ray Jr. (Winona Lake, IN: Eisenbrauns, 2008), p. 39.

[86]Compare to the language of God's command to "not spare" the Amalekites, "put to death both man and woman, child and infant, ox and sheep, camel and donkey" with the hyperbolic account of Judah's defeat to the Babylonian's in 2 Chronicles 36:16-17. This was written to a postexilic audience, who knew full well that not everyone had been killed, that Judah had been exiled and later restored under Cyrus, a fact pointed out only a few verses later. The same passage

Again in 1 Samuel 15, we see the author juxtaposing two accounts—one in fairly realistic terms, claiming the Amalekites continue to live in the land as a military threat, and another that is clearly hyperbolic, using exaggerated stereotypical language and stock phrases about Saul wiping them all out at God's command. Assuming the author is an intelligent person, we are at least owed an argument as to why the literal reading is preferable in this context.[87]

It is important to note that the crucial issue is whether the hyperbolic interpretation is *more* plausible than a literal one. Wes Morriston has argued that 1 Samuel 15 must be taken literally because in 15:19 Saul is condemned for not taking the command literally.[88] Morriston's objection is that a hyperbolic reading is mistaken because it appears to contradict part of the narrative whereas a literal account coheres better with this part. However, even if a literal interpretation of the passage fits better with 1 Samuel 15:19, it does not follow that a literal reading is more plausible than a hyperbolic one. We have argued above that a literal reading creates massive incoherencies in the text; it puts the whole account of 1 Samuel 15 in contradiction with the rest of the Samuel narrative, particularly 1 Samuel 27–30. It also puts the account in contradiction with 1 Chronicles 4:43 and the book of Esther. These are fairly massive inconsistencies. It is hard to believe the author of the final form was meticulously careful to avoid making a minor incoherence in 1 Samuel 15:19 and yet was oblivious to these gaping contradictions. Taking 1 Samuel 15 as a highly hyperbolized account creates a much more coherent narrative. It is far more plausible to think the author was careful to avoid massive inconsistencies but was willing to allow some minor incoherencies in a narrative that is not supposed to be literally true

---

also juxtaposes "He carried to Babylon all the articles from the temple of God, both large and small, and the treasures of the LORD's temple and the treasures of the king and his officials" with "They set fire to God's temple and broke down the wall of Jerusalem; they burned all the palaces and destroyed everything of value there."

[87]Richard Swinburne notes that if the idea that the author is speaking literally is more absurd given the context than the idea the author intended to speak figuratively, then one should adopt the figurative reading. Hence, to rebut the argument that these texts are hyperbolic, the critic then needs to show that it is *less absurd* to claim the author of the final form is intending to speak literally than that he intended to speak hyperbolically. Richard Swinburne, *Revelation: From Metaphor to Analogy*, 2nd ed. (Oxford: Oxford University Press, 2007).

[88]Wes Morriston suggested this response in online correspondence with Matthew Flannagan, http://prosblogion.ektopos.com/archives/2009/09/thoughts-from-t.html, accessed 18 May 2011.

in its details anyway. In short, the "holy war" narratives appear to be highly hyperbolic accounts of victory which the author quite candidly affirms are not literally true descriptions elsewhere in the text.

Our discussion has given reason for thinking that (4)—that the Bible tells us that God commands actions that are in violation of P1—is questionable. It is not clear that the text affirms that God commanded acts which violate P1. James K. Hoffmeier notes that such a reading commits "the fallacy of misplaced literalism . . . the misconstruction of a statement-in-evidence so that it carries a literal meaning when a symbolic or hyperbolic or figurative meaning was intended."[89]

The argument applied to the Midianites. Wolterstorff's approach may also shed light on some other troubling texts, such as the apparent genocide of the Midianites in Numbers 31. After the Israelites "fought against Midian, as the LORD commanded Moses, and killed every man" (Num 31:7), Moses commanded them to "kill all the boys. And kill every woman who has slept with a man, but save for yourselves every girl who has never slept with a man" (Num 31:17-18). Taken in isolation, this text affirms that every Midianite was killed and only female virgins survived so they could be assimilated into the Israelite community. However, read in its literary context, as part of a single narrative—a connected literary unit—similar textual features arise to those we identified as occurring in Joshua.

First, Numbers 31 is one part of a broader context; it is both part of the Pentateuch and also part of a larger canonical sequence. The Pentateuch contains the Torah or Law. Normally in the Torah when Moses utters a command on God's behalf the passage begins with "The LORD commanded Moses." This preface is absent from the commands in Numbers 31. The passages merely state that God commanded them to make war on Midian. Numbers 31:7 states, "They fought against Midian, *as the LORD commanded Moses*, and killed every man" (emphasis added). This suggests the Israelites fulfilled this command. Moses's command to kill women and children occurs after this and appears to be on his own authority.[90] If one reads the laws of war that are elaborated in the book of

[89]Hoffmeier, *Israel in Egypt*, p. 42.
[90]Alvin Plantinga, "Comments on Satanic Verses in Holy Writ," in *Divine Evil?* p. 110. Plantinga

Deuteronomy, which follows Numbers, God commanded Israel not to kill noncombatants, such as women and children. He condemns the kind of conduct Moses commands here.

If one looks at the larger canonical sequence, the proceeding narrative states quite emphatically that the Midianites were not, in fact, literally wiped out. In Judges 6 and 7 the Midianites invade Israel in numbers said to be "like swarms of locusts. It was impossible to count them or their camels" (Judg 6:5). Israel was so overrun with Midianites that they fled to "mountain clefts, caves and strongholds" (Judg 6:2). Unable to win in open battle, Gideon was forced to use deception to defeat them. This is not congruous with the Midianites having been "utterly destroyed."

Second, these tensions in the text are fairly obvious. As with Joshua, whoever "edited the final version of these writings into one sequence"[91] juxtaposed several accounts which, if taken literally, describe Israel, at Moses's command, annihilating the entire population of Midian (including noncombatants). Yet several other accounts affirm that God prohibits the killing of noncombatants and that the Midianites were not annihilated. Assuming this person was not "mindless," he cannot have intended to affirm both claims as literally true.

Third, the genre and style of the accounts suggests Numbers 31 is the nonliteral account. Numbers 31 appears highly hyperbolic; it contains obvious rhetorical exaggeration.[92] The Israelite army is said to have killed every Midianite man in battle without a single Israelite fatality (Num 31:49). Moreover, the spoil from the battle is said to be 32,000 maidens, 675,000 sheep and goats—this is astronomically and absurdly large.[93] Daniel Fouts notes that exaggerated numbers are common forms of hyperbole in ancient

is responding to Evan Fales, who based his reading on the mistaken reading of the verse "kill all the women but save for yourselves every girl who has never slept with a man" as commanding rape—a reading he also ascribes to Deuteronomy 21. In fact, a glance at the immediate context shows that the reference to a woman not sleeping with a man in the former passage was mentioned to distinguish the women in question from those who had seduced Israelite men into idolatry; it is not there to emphasize their availability for sex. Deuteronomy 21, in fact, protects female captives from being raped or sold as concubines. See Paul Copan, *Is God a Moral Monster?* pp. 118-21, 180.

[91]Wolterstorff, "Reading Joshua," p. 251.

[92]Jacob Milgrom, *Numbers: The Traditional Hebrew Text with the New JPS Translation* (Philadelphia: Jewish Publication Society of America, 1990), pp. 490-91.

[93]Ibid., p. 490.

Near Eastern battle accounts.[94] Wolterstorff suggests, "These are all hyperbolic descriptions of battles that took place."[95]

So if we read the text in the literary context of the broader canon we again see the author juxtaposing two accounts. One claims that God prohibits killing noncombatants and that the Midianites continued to live in the land as a serious military threat. Another account, using rhetoric known to be used hyperbolically in military contexts, states that Israel, at Moses' command, wiped them all out. Assuming the author was an intelligent person,[96] we are at least owed an argument as to why one should read these texts as literally claiming that God commanded genocide.

Modifying the Tetrad to Take Hyperbole into Account

Alvin Plantinga suggests a response to the above argument. Suppose one grants that the commands meant something like "attack them, defeat them, drive them out; not literally kill every man, woman, child, donkey and the like."[97] This leaves open the question: "was it just of God to drive these people out, to dispossess them . . . [or] to war against them?"[98] Louise Antony contends this question has a negative answer: "Sometimes [in the text], there is not even a pretext that the doomed people are at fault: The only 'crime' committed by the Canaanites was living in a land God wanted for his people."[99]

This response suggests a modification of Bradley's tetrad. Consider principle P2:

P2: It is morally wrong to forcibly dispossess men, women and children from their homes merely because you want their land.

---

[94]Fouts, "Defense of the Hyperbolic Interpretation," pp. 377-87.

[95]Personal correspondence between Nicholas Wolterstorff and Paul Copan (May 2, 2011).

[96]One again needs to remember the dialectical context here. The skeptic who claims that God commanded genocide is offering a *reductio ad absurdum*. She starts by assuming that whatever God commands is right and that Scripture is the Word of God; she then derives from these assumptions the absurd conclusion that genocide is not wrong. The question then is whether, *granting these assumptions*, such a conclusion does, in fact, follow; hence, one is quite entitled, in this context, to assume the author was an intelligent person.

[97]Alvin Plantinga suggested this in the Q&A during the presentation of "Comments on Evan Fales' Satanic Verses."

[98]Ibid.

[99]Louise Antony, "Atheism as Perfect Piety," in *Is Goodness Without God Good Enough?* p. 79.

The revised tetrad is:

(1) Any act that God commands us to perform is morally permissible.

(2) The Bible is an authoritative revelation of what God commands.

(3*) It is morally impermissible for anyone to commit acts that violate principle P2.

(4*) The Bible tells us that God commands us to perform acts that violate moral principle P2.

We contend that (4*) is false. An examination of the biblical text shows the command occurred in a certain context in which there existed good reasons for dispossessing the Canaanites. The text elaborates four such reasons.

First, the Canaanites were occupying land Israel had legitimate title to. Deuteronomy 20 limits "holy war" to the "cities of the nations the LORD your God is giving you as an inheritance" (Deut 20:16). God *prohibited* Israel from conquering other neighboring nations. These nations were Moab and Ammon (Deut 2:9, 19) and Edom (Deut 2:4; 23:7), despite the fact that Edom had earlier refused to assist the Israelites (Num 20:14-21; Deut 2:6-8). The reason stated was that those peoples, and not the Israelites, had legitimate title to their lands.

The granting of title is elaborated in the Genesis narrative, which precedes these texts. After the protohistory of fall, flood, Babel and so on, the story of Israel's history proper begins in Genesis 12 with Abram being called by God to leave Ur of the Chaldees to go to an unknown land (later identified as Canaan). Abram was given several promises that ultimately promised the renewal of all nations on earth. The text states, "The LORD had said to Abram, 'Leave your country, your people and your father's household and go to the land I will show you. I will make you into a great nation and I will bless you; I will make your name great, and you will be a blessing'" (Gen 12:1-2).

Here Abram was told by God that he would be the father of an entire nation, one that would have its own country. The reference to "make you into a great nation" parallels the hubristic boast of the builders of Babel in Genesis 12. This promise was reiterated in several other encounters between God and Abram. The point is that Abram was given this land as a means to bless the whole world and reverse the curse of Babel.

In the next chapter Abram and Lot had reached Canaan and Abram had amassed considerable wealth. Disagreement over land and resources led to "quarrelling . . . between Abram's herders and Lot's" (Gen 13:7). Abram diplomatically solved the dispute by allowing Lot to take his pick of the land, promising that his men would go elsewhere: "Lot *looked around* and saw that the whole plain of the Jordan toward Zoar was well watered, like the garden of the LORD,[100] like the land of Egypt. . . . So Lot chose for himself the whole plain of the Jordan and set out toward the east" (Gen 13:10-11, emphasis added).

Despite having been promised the land of Canaan in Genesis 12, Abram rather generously gave it to Lot. In response God told Abram: "*Look around* from where you are, to the north and south, to the east and west. All the land that you see I will give to you and your offspring forever. . . . Go, walk through the length and breadth of the land, for I am giving it to you" (Gen 13:14-17, emphasis added).

The reference to "look around" was an allusion to the conduct of Lot a few verses earlier. Because of his generosity and willingness to share the land with others, Abram and his offspring were given *eternal* title to the land.[101] Gary Anderson notes, "Abraham only receives the land of Canaan as an *eternal* patrimony after he has shown himself willing to part with its most valuable acreage. The making of a great name is predicated on an act of generosity rather than legal entitlement."[102]

Second, this title, while necessary, is not sufficient. In Genesis 15 "the word of the LORD" came to Abram "in a vision." Abram's response was, "You have given me no children; so a servant in my household will be my heir." God's answer was emphatic: "This man will not be your heir, but a son coming from your own body will be your heir." The text continues, "He took him outside and said, 'Look up at the heavens and count the stars—if indeed you can count them.' Then he said to him, 'So shall your offspring be.'" And this is followed by an important addendum:

---

[100]The reference to the garden of the Lord here is an allusion to the Garden of Eden.
[101]Gary Anderson, "What About the Canaanites?" in *Divine Evil?* p. 289. Anderson notes that "walking across the territory in such a fashion" was the "legal custom of formally taking possession"; hence, in this passage Abram gains legal possession of Canaan (ibid.).
[102]Ibid., p. 281.

> Know for certain that for four hundred years your descendants will be
> strangers in a country not their own and that they will be enslaved and mis-
> treated there. But I will punish the nation they serve as slaves, and afterward
> they will come out with great possessions. You, however, will go to your an-
> cestors in peace and be buried at a good old age. In the fourth generation
> your descendants will come back here, for the sin of the Amorites has not yet
> reached its full measure. (Gen 15:13-16)

Despite having legal title to the land, Abram and his descendents could
not take immediate occupation of the land. They had to wait until the "sin
of the Amorites" had "reached its full measure." Anderson notes, *"Even if the
land of Canaan will become part of the eternal patrimony of the descendants
of Abraham it is not a land that God can simply hand over at will. The rights
of the citizens who presently reside upon it must be respected.* God will not
evict them until their immoral ways justify such a punishment."[103]

This was reiterated in Israel's Torah, which centuries later authorized
Israel to take the land because the Amorite iniquity was then complete.
Deuteronomy states that Israel could drive the nations out "on account of
the wickedness of these nations" (Deut 9:5). The most exhaustive list of the
kind of wickedness meant comes from Leviticus 18, which chronicles
incest, adultery, bestiality, ritual prostitution, homosexual acts and, most
significantly, child sacrifice. The last item on the list, infant sacrifice, was
particularly singled out (Deut 12:29-31) and a repeated polemic against
ritual infant sacrifice followed in the Prophets, Psalms and historical books
(Jer 7:31-32; 19:5-6; Ezek 16:20-21; 20:31).[104] It is worth noting that most of
these practices are illegal today, even in modern western nations, and no
religious group that practiced incest, prostitution, bestiality and human
sacrifice would be tolerated even in contemporary liberal societies with
freedom of religion laws.

A third reason that Israel was allowed finally to occupy the land was that
they entered into a covenant involving promises not to engage in these
practices; if they were to breach this covenant they, like the Canaanites,
would lose possession of the land. As we have seen the very language of "ut-

---

[103]Ibid., p. 280.
[104]Kings who engage in it are criticized in the historical books. 2 Kings 23:10 and Psalm 106:38
　condemn it as murder.

terly destroy [*ḥāram*]" could be applied equally to Israel (Deut 13:16).[105] The
catalogue of sins mentioned in Leviticus 18 finishes with this command:

> Do not defile yourselves in any of these ways, because this is how the nations
> that I am going to drive out before you became defiled. Even the land was
> defiled; so I punished it for its sin, and the land vomited out its inhabitants.
> But you must keep my decrees and my laws. The native-born and the for-
> eigners residing among you must not do any of these detestable things, for all
> these things were done by the people who lived in the land before you, and
> the land became defiled. And if you defile the land, it will vomit you out as it
> vomited out the nations that were before you. (Lev 18:24-28)

If one pays attention to the remaining narrative one will see that it documents throughout the Deuteronomic history and the Prophets how Israel
did not obey the terms of the covenant. Centuries after the Exodus the Israelites were exiled and dispossessed of the land. The biblical narrative makes
it clear that Israel's possession of Canaan *was* subject to the same conditions
as the Canaanites' possession was.[106]

A fourth reason the text laid down was the corrupting influence of the
Canaanite religion. Deuteronomy 20 warned if the Israelites did not dispossess the Canaanites, "they will teach you to follow all the detestable
things they do in worshiping their gods, and you will sin against the LORD
your God" (Deut 20:18). They "will turn your children away from following
me to serve other gods" (Deut 7:4); they will be "a snare" (Deut 7:16). Exodus
was explicit: "Do not let them live in your land or they will cause you to sin
against me, because the worship of their gods will certainly be a snare to
you" (Ex 23:33). Also, "Be careful not to make a treaty with those who live in
the land; for when they prostitute themselves to their gods and sacrifice to

---

[105] As mentioned earlier, the language of the *ḥērem* was applied to Judah hyperbolically. For example, in Jeremiah 25:9 God promises, "I will bring them against this land and its inhabitants
and against all the surrounding nations. I will completely destroy them and make them an
object of horror and scorn, and an everlasting ruin." The text goes on to state that the inhabitants who have been "completely destroyed [*ḥāram*]" will be restored from exile after seventy
years.

[106] This addresses Louise Antony's further objections. In a later writing Antony grants that "various apologists have argued" that the Canaanites were "morally corrupt." She then rejoins, "But
this hardly distinguishes them from the Israelites themselves, against whom God is constantly
fuming and whom he is constantly threatening to destroy." See her "Comments on Reading
Joshua," in *Divine Evil?* p. 262.

them, they will invite you and you will eat their sacrifices. And when you choose some of their daughters as wives for your sons and those daughters prostitute themselves to their gods, they will lead your sons to do the same" (Ex 34:15-16).

So (4*) is false. The Canaanites were not driven out merely because the Hebrews wanted the land in question. The command occurred in a context in which the four conditions above jointly held. Taken jointly the force of these conditions is best illustrated by examining an analogy Wes Morriston uses:

> If the President of the United States were to announce that God had told him to use the vast military power at his disposal to obliterate, say, the nation of Iran, "saving alive nothing that breathes," people would assume that he was mad and he would speedily be dismissed from office. No one—well, almost no one—would take seriously the idea that God had instructed him to do this terrible thing.[107]

The above discussion shows the significant dissimilarity between the case expounded in the biblical narrative and that expounded in Morriston's example. Suppose one modifies his example by reflecting on our discussion in part three so that the phrases "obliterate" and "saving alive nothing that breathes" are a hyperbolic way of describing the United States using military force to drive inhabitants from their territory. Then imagine the case differs in the following ways.

First, the land in question is not Iran but a piece of land the federal government has legally inherited; they had been bequeathed the land by the generosity of previous administrations for the specific purpose of benefiting the entire community. So here we are not talking about a foreign country but state-owned territory.

Second, the current occupant is a religious sect whose rituals involved criminal activities such as incest, bestiality and burning children alive as a sacrifice. For centuries, previous administrations have turned a blind eye to their activities and have refused to evict the tenants.

Third, a group of US citizens want to take up occupancy and have signed a contract committing themselves and their families to working for the purpose for which the land was bequeathed and have agreed that they will

---

[107]Morriston, "Did God Command Genocide?" p. 8.

not engage in the criminal activities of the sect. They also agree that should they breach these conditions their right to occupancy will be made void, and they can be evicted by force if necessary.

Fourth, imagine that the religious culture of this sect has become so pervasive in the area that almost any person who lives there cannot help but get caught up in it and that CNN is reporting that more and more people are becoming involved in the commission of the sorts of crimes the sect commits as part of their beliefs, pictures of baby burnings are appearing on the Internet and so on.

Finally, suppose that the sectarians who occupy the area are heavily armed and will not leave unless they are evicted by force. Now, if the US president authorized the military to use force in evicting the current occupants from the land under these conditions, is it really obvious that people would assume he was mad or a warmonger and that he ought to be dismissed from office? Is it really the case that no one would take seriously the idea that such an eviction was permitted by the law of God?[108]

In a more recent article Morriston has focused his attention on the Amalekite case. He writes,

> The prophet Samuel instructs King Saul to exterminate the Amalekites. "Now go and smite Amalek, and utterly destroy all that they have; do not spare them, but kill both man and woman, infant and suckling, ox and sheep, camel and ass" (1 Samuel, 15.5). Why? Here is the answer: "Thus says the LORD of hosts, I will punish what Amalek did to Israel in opposing them on the way, when they came up out of Egypt" (1 Samuel, 15.3). According to the best Bible

---

[108]It is worth noting that Morriston's analogy is also flawed in another respect, in that there are American and British presidents who have ordered obliterations of whole populations who have not been considered "mad." The bombing of Hiroshima and Nagasaki at the end of World War II and the aerial bombing of German civilian centers by Churchill were done by leaders who enjoyed significant support and admiration from their constituents. Moreover, whatever one thinks of these actions, it is indisputable that their morality remains a matter of significant debate among ethicists. To take Morriston's "Iran" analogy, one does not have to think terribly hard to imagine situations in which a decision of the sort Morriston suggests would not be *obviously* a "moral outrage." Suppose, for example, credible intelligence from multiple sources verifies that Iran has produced a nuclear weapons silo. Suppose similarly, the best, most credible intelligence suggests they plan to launch a nuclear attack on Israel in a matter of days. Further suppose the weapons silo is so deeply entrenched in a civilian center that the only realistic way of destroying it is by a tactical nuclear strike. Under such conditions it is not *obvious* that an attack on an Iranian civilian center would be a "moral outrage," which a perfectly good being would not, in the situation, endorse.

arithmetic, the crime for which the Amalekites—men, women, children, and animals—are to be punished was committed some 400 years previously (see Deuteronomy 25.17–19).[109]

Morriston assumes the literalistic reading we critiqued above to be correct. However, even taking the hyperbolic interpretation into account, his comment suggests a further modification of Bradley's tetrad:

P3: It is morally wrong to go to war against another nation for aggressive actions and war crimes that nation committed centuries earlier.

(1) Any act that God commands us to perform is morally permissible.

(2) The Bible is an authoritative revelation of what God commands.

(3**) It is morally impermissible for anyone to commit acts that violate principle P3.

(4**) The Bible tells us that God commands us to perform acts that violate moral principle P3.

Many find (3**) to be intuitively very plausible. Why is this? We suggest the reason is that any criminal or immoral activities committed by the parents were not committed by the children. The children did not do it; the parents did. If the children had committed the parent's crimes then things would be different, but they have not. The children are innocent of the parents' sins and cannot be punished for them. However, this suggests an ambiguity in (3**). There might be two separate situations being confused here:

(a) The nation engaged in aggressive activities and war crimes centuries earlier and subsequent generations have turned away from these kinds of actions and no longer engage in them

Or

(b) The nation engaged in aggressive activities and war crimes centuries earlier and subsequent generations have not turned away from these actions; they have chosen to continue engaging in the same activities themselves.

---

[109]Wes Morriston, "What if God Commanded Something Terrible? A Worry for Divine-Command Meta-Ethics," *Religious Studies* 45 (2009): 265.

If one envisages (a), then (3**) is plausible. However, if one envisages (b) it is not clear that (3**) is plausible. In the case of the Amalekites the children have continued in the same conduct and essentially appropriated their parents' crimes as their own. If we reflect on why it is unjust to punish children for the sins of the parents, the intuition we have is that it is unjust because the children did not do the crime. But in situation (b) this is not true; it is only true in situation (a).

If (3**) is only plausible if (a) is envisaged, then the further modified tetrad is only plausible if (4**) also envisages (a) and if (4**) is affirming that the Bible teaches that the Amalekites had engaged in aggression centuries earlier but subsequent generations rejected such activities and turned away from them. If what the biblical text portrays is situation (b), then any attempt to derive a contradiction from the modified tetrad will commit the fallacy of equivocation.

When one examines the biblical text, it is clear that (b) and not (a) is envisaged. The Amalekites were Israel's enemies since the Red Sea crossing (Ex 17). Weary and unprepared to fight, Israel faced a fierce people who showed no concern for the vulnerable Israelite population. This is the incident Morriston refers to in the quote above. What he fails to note is that subsequent generations of Amalekites were relentless in their aim to destroy Israel and they continued to be a thorn in Israel's side for generations (i.e., Judg 3:13; 6:3-5, 33; 7:12; 10:12, etc.). Continued aggressive activity of this sort is evident from the Samuel narrative itself.[110]

It is true that 1 Samuel 15:2 states, "I will punish the Amalekites for what they did to Israel when they waylaid them as they came up from Egypt"; however only a few lines later in 1 Samuel 15:18, Samuel summarizes the same command as, "Go and completely destroy those wicked people, the Amalekites; wage war against them until you have wiped them out." Here the present wickedness of the current Amalekites is the issue.

A few verses later when Samuel executes the Amalekite king Agag he states, "As your sword has made women childless, so will your mother be

---

[110]As noted earlier in 1 Samuel 30, the Amalekites made one of their infamous raids (v. 1); David pursued them to get back the captured Israelites and the booty the Amalekites had taken (v. 18).

childless among women."[111] Samuel put Agag to death because of his personal involvement in aggressive wars. Consequently, when the account of Saul and the Amalekites is taken in context, looking at the entire narrative up until this point and also taking both what Samuel says in 1 Samuel 15:2-3 ("go strike Amalek and utterly destroy . . . ") and what he says after this passage in the same chapter, the picture is clearly one of (b) not (a). It is not just that the Amalekites' parents had engaged in aggression and war crimes centuries earlier but that the subsequent and current generations had continued in these crimes themselves.

It follows then that further modifying the tetrad in terms of P3 fails to provide a cogent objection. If P3 is referring to (a), then while (3**) might be plausible, (4**) is false. If, on the other hand, P3 envisages a situation like (b), then (4**) is plausible but (3**) ceases to be obviously correct.[112]

Two Objections

In parts two, three and four we have argued that (4) is false and that attempts to reconstruct the tetrad that take into account the hyperbolic and hagiographic nature of the text also fail. Before concluding, we will briefly address two common objections to a hyperbolic interpretation of the text.

The first is that God, by allowing his divine discourse, the Bible, to be mediated through the literary conventions of ANE military history writing, should have foreseen that future generations would misinterpret it. This, of course, is correct. It is unclear why this means that the text should be taken literally. After all, it seems any language through which God mediates his Word, whether literal or figurative, will have this implication. A message mediated through the more literalistic conventions of twenty-first century English, history or moral philosophy would be misunderstood by numerous people and nonwestern cultures to which such conventions are quite alien. This seems to be more a problem with verbal revelation than any particular interpretation of the revelation. Peter van Inwagen notes

---

[111]Note this passage seems to suggest that Amalek's mother was alive at the time of the execution—hence, again the suggestion that the Amalekites were not literally exterminated.

[112]Remember, as discussed in part one, the issue is whether the command is contrary to a moral belief central to our concept of goodness or is just that it revises our concept of goodness. It is quite plausible that God's commands will contradict some debatable moral claims that some individuals think are correct.

[T]he Bible has not been translated into more languages than any other book, *only* because missionary societies believe it to be the inspired word of God; another important part of the explanation is that missionaries know from experience that the Bible is one of their most effective tools. They know that those to whom they preach "take to it" with very little prompting or preparation. They know it captures their attention. They know people of most cultures will listen to the words of the cloud of witnesses who speak to them across the millennia from its pages. And quite possibly—who is in a position to deny this—a version of, or replacement for, the Bible that a secular reader of our culture would find more appealing (or less appalling) than the actual Bible would have very little meaning for the peoples of most times and most cultures.[113]

The second objection is a slippery slope worry: if one takes the commands to exterminate the Canaanites and Joshua figuratively, then why not take the rest of the text figuratively as well? Why not claim, for example, that the resurrection of Christ is figurative or hyperbolic? This kind of argument relies on the peculiar assumption that if one grants that one part of a text is not literal, then one cannot, without acting arbitrarily, take any other part of the text as literal. This assumption is false. Consider Bradley's argument for the tetrad. In a later defense of this argument he states his tetrad "puts God in a logical straight-jacket."[114] Now obviously he does not literally mean that God exists and is in a straight-jacket made of logic; Bradley is speaking metaphorically. Does this fact mean we cannot take any of what Bradley says literally, that we must take his whole argument as a figure of speech?

As to these particular texts, we have argued there is compelling *textual* evidence both from within the text itself and also via comparisons between Joshua and other ANE texts to suggest that it is hyperbolic. We are advocating taking a *closer* look at these texts rather than *glossing over* them! These parallels and textual considerations are not present with the resurrection accounts nor is it a given, without argument or substantiation, that

---

[113]Peter van Inwagen, "Reply to Curley," in *Divine Evil?* p. 84.
[114]From Raymond Bradley's opening statement in a debate between Raymond Bradley and Matthew Flannagan: "Is God the source of morality? Is it rational to ground right and wrong in commands issued by God?" This was held in Auckland, New Zealand, University of Auckland (August 2, 2010). Available at www.mandm.org.nz/2010/08/raymond-bradleys-opening-statement-bradley-v-flannagan-debate.html.

they are present in other biblical texts. Some other biblical texts contain hyperbole, others do not. One determines this by examining those texts and their respective genres—*not* by invalidly inferring that because *some* biblical texts are hyperbolic, it follows *all* are.

CONCLUSION

The commands to "destroy totally" the Canaanites, the conquest account in Joshua 6–11 and Saul's campaign against the Amalekites in Samuel 15, if taken literally, pose a challenge to the theist who accepts the Bible as the Word of God. The challenge can be formalized as an inconsistent tetrad to which Christians are allegedly committed.

We have argued Christians are not committed to this tetrad. A person can coherently accept that, in rare circumstances, a perfectly good being can command the killing of noncombatants. Moreover, such a position takes seriously the fallibility and revisability of our moral judgments. Furthermore, the contexts in which these texts occur, as well as the literary motifs they use, make it unlikely they are intended to be read literally. One can sensibly deny that the Bible teaches that God commanded the "slaughter [of] men, women, and children" who were "innocent of any serious wrongdoing."

11

THE PROPHETS' CALL
FOR PEACEMAKING PRACTICES

Glen Harold Stassen

———————— ✝ ————————

RABBI MARC GOPIN (MY FRIEND) has published a wonderful book, *Holy War, Holy Peace: How Religion Can Bring Peace to the Middle East.*[1] He spends no time discussing when it is right, or not right, to make war. He points his message toward how faithful persons can avoid war and work for peace.

Rabbi Jesus of Galilee (also my friend, and more) stood where Marc and I once stood, on the Mount of Olives, and there he wept over Jerusalem because they did not know the practices that make for peace (Lk 19:41-42). Not only on that occasion but many times in his teaching, Jesus spent less time discussing when it is right to make war, or not, than pointing his message toward practices that can bring peace. These practices include forgiveness, loving your enemy, putting up your sword, taking the log out of your own eye, going to make peace with a brother or adversary when there is anger and seeking first God's delivering justice and reign rather than piling up money for yourself. He warned that not knowing the practices that make for peace and instead practicing resentment toward Rome would lead to destruction of the temple whose remains everyone can see from the Mount of Olives—where Jesus once stood and Marc and my students and I

---

[1] Marc Gopin, *Holy War, Holy Peace: How Religion Can Bring Peace to the Middle East* (New York: Oxford University Press, 2002).

stood twenty centuries later. Jesus' prophecies came true in A.D. 66–70. The rebellion that Jesus saw fomenting began in A.D. 66, and Rome destroyed the temple and Jerusalem in A.D. 70, as Jesus had prophesied.

My purpose is to call our attention to practices that make peace and avoid unholy war by calling attention to an important book that Old Testament scholars I know speak highly of and that deserves to be more widely known. The book is Norman Gottwald's *All the Kingdoms of the Earth*.[2] Like my two rabbi friends, Marc Gopin and Jesus of Galilee, it focuses on practices that do or do not lead to peace. It studies the foreign policies of the prophets, and the result is a call to repentance for placing too much trust in horses and chariots—weapons of war—and not enough trust in God's will for practices of peace. It focuses on practices that lead to peace and ways to avoid the destruction of war. I will also occasionally supplement my attention to Gottwald with some of my own observations on the teachings of the prophets.

Gottwald does mention limits to war-making based on the "holy war tradition." When Syria sent a band of troops to capture Elisha, YHWH struck them blind at Elisha's request. In Samaria, the band's sight was restored but Israel's king wanted to kill the Syrian (or Aramean) troops on the spot (see 2 Kings 6:21). However, as Gottwald notes, "Elisha reminded him of the terms of holy war, i.e., non-Canaanite captives are to be killed only when they belong to forces which have resisted an ultimatum to surrender (Deut 20:12-14)."[3] Still, the prophets focused much more on how to avoid war and make peace, and so Gottwald does likewise.

Gottwald also frees us from Plato's cave where all we see is unreal—mere shadows on the wall in front of us, while the light comes from a fire behind us that we cannot see because our heads are tied—and the truth is like the sun outside the cave, high ideals far removed from the actual life we live. The long reach of Plato through European civilization has caused us to think in dualisms, separating religion into a realm of high ideals and life into this realm of practical considerations. Separating mind into a realm of disembodied rational deductions and body into a realm of temporary passions that occlude our perceiving what matters marginalizes Jesus' way as

---

[2] Norman Gottwald, *All the Kingdoms of the Earth: Israelite Prophecy and International Relations in the Ancient Near East* (New York: Harper & Row, 1964).

[3] Ibid., p. 75. See also pp. 66-68, 81-83, 372-73.

high ideals. Separating faith into a disembodied spirit realm and weekday
life into a rat race blocks us from celebrating God's mustard-seed break-
throughs in the midst of our lives. Separating idealism into a Platonic realm
and realism into a secular realm of calculations of how we can get ahead
leads to idolatrous "me-ism." Gottwald writes:

> We must now attempt to trace the political facets of the totality experience of
> the prophet so that we may ground his "politics" precisely where it is at home,
> i.e., in the unified field of the knowledge of God and man. We must make a
> particular effort to avoid the misleading [Platonic] dichotomies (subject/object,
> cause/effect, utopian/prudential, ideal/real, religion/politics) which have re-
> peatedly lured interpreters into one-sided or superficial reconstructions.[4]

Think of a prophet in the temple meditating on God as holy and lifted up
but thinking he has unclean lips and is surrounded by a people of unclean
lips, a people who are seeking security while surrounded by powerful and
greedy neighbors. Think of him or her as well-informed about the history
of relations with other nations, well informed about the moral lives and
passionate loyalties of the people and well informed about the historical-
theological ethics of Israel's covenant traditions. So when that prophet is
meditating, it is not a "spiritual" inspiration that he receives dissociated
from knowledge of the historical realities of politics or isolated from the
Yahwistic traditions of Israel. The inspiration he or she receives comes in
the midst of this historical awareness. This is not a life of mystical contem-
plation in which the prophet makes his mind empty of all concerns, but a
historically located Word of God in the midst of all those concerns and
traditions. This is simultaneously spiritual and realistic. This is biblical realism. And it is what Gottwald shows the prophets doing. Each prophet is
"well informed about international affairs and generally shows a realistic
understanding of the balance of power in the ancient world."[5]

Think of you or me or our fellow church members engaging in a similar
practice of listening prayer. A vision comes to us of a church that really is
committed to following the way of Jesus, and that makes a difference for
peacemaking. Think of a vision of a nation that really does seek the un-

---

[4]Ibid., p. 363.
[5]Ibid., pp. 145-46.

alienable human rights of life, liberty and dignity in community of all persons—all persons in our nation and in Somalia, Burma, Palestine and Israel. Think of that vision being spiritual not in the sense that it is empty of historical reference but in the sense of being well informed about the prophetic tradition from Moses to Jesus and well informed about the injustices being practiced by the Slork government in Burma, of the Al Shabbab forces in Somalia, of the dictatorial Assad government in Syria, and of the United States with all its power biases and recent war-making in addition to its historical commitment to human rights for all. Our vision of a church really committed to making a difference for Jesus' call to peacemaking will include our sense that our nation could be more committed to peacemaking. Jesus' call to peacemaking will not be marginalized into some Platonic otherworldly realm but will lead us to ask whether our government is doing what it could be doing for avoiding the terrible destruction of war—a destruction that almost killed my own father and several of my students. It is about the real world.

Gottwald works through the prophets' interpretations with situated sensitivity of how to avoid the destruction and judgment of war and exile. He pays attention to the increasing knowledge scholars are giving us of the actual history of relations between Israel and Judah with Assyria, Egypt and Babylon and other neighbors, living there on that land bridge where powerful empires made smaller states into vassals who had to pay tribute, and where those empires would sometimes fight wars, and where Judah and Israel were tempted to engage in wars and military alliances that would bring the power drives of competing empires down on their heads. He shows that the prophets were remarkably well informed also about the actual power realities and the actual tendencies of the various empires that surrounded them. They took these historical realities into account as they fashioned their prophecies. They were no Platonic philosophers, deducing their oracles from ideals in their heads; they paid attention to the empirical evidence from the actual history of international relations and to the actual tradition of Israel seeking faithfulness to God's way. They were, in other words, situated—aware of historical context. What they saw on the walls of the cave was real. Though it was not a cave; it was a land bridge between power-driving empires.

But do not think of them as mere pragmatists, calculating how they could get the most advantageous results. They were also situated in the heritage of Yahwistic traditions, with faith in God and God's trustworthy will. Do not think of Yahwistic traditions as Platonic ideals, deduced from the logical speculations of philosophers who yearned to be philosopher-kings over the ordinary people who lacked their intelligence. The Yahwistic traditions concerned God's trustworthiness revealed in the history of slavery in Egypt, of exodus from Egypt, of covenants of justice on which community needed to be based, of the occasional wisdom but frequent corruption and pride and folly of kings. In other words, the Word of God was not somewhere outside the cave in an ideal realm while we live in an unreal shadow realm. The Word of God came in the midst of the drama of real history, with its empirical evidence about pride and wars of adventure that lead to destruction.

If I have a criticism of Gottwald's book, it is that I would want stronger attention to the prophets' theology of God as deliverer with compassion, as covenant maker with faithfulness, who demands our faithfulness in response. I would want stronger attention to God as God of delivering justice who demands that we practice delivering justice, of God as present Spirit calling for our repentance from false loyalties that blind us to historical realities and make us foolish, silly like a dove. I am not saying Gottwald is impervious to this theology; I just want more. He is writing of the prophets in their interpretation of international relations not a theology of God, such as Eichrodt or Brueggemann write. Yet he does emphasize that "*The prophet lives his life in communion with the God of Israel. His life in God is analogous to Israel's life in God.* The community and its leaders maintain distinct identities but they receive their entire vitality and meaning in close personal association with God."[6] He continues, "*The prophets adopted neither a purely practical nor a purely utopian attitude toward the relations of nations; their position was instead an experiential and contextual one, provided that 'experience' and 'context' are interpreted in the light of the historic Yahwistic traditions and the overpowering apprehensions of God experienced by the*

---

[6]Ibid., p. 365. I am writing of the Gottwald of his earlier period, in *All the Kingdoms of the Earth*, and not of the later Gottwald of *The Tribes of Yahweh*, which raises other complex questions that I cannot deal with here.

prophets."[7] This is not Platonic idealism; it is prophetic realism.

Gottwald analyzes utopian thinking as working with "two fixed dualities, the lower constantly trying to shape itself by the example of the higher but with no real basis for communication between the two inasmuch as the principles of the higher world cannot formatively penetrate the unreceptive real world." By contrast, in the prophets, "*The whole visible life of people and prophet is a context within which to receive and to embody God's calling.*"[8]

It is not that in call and covenant they first learn from God and subsequently apply it to life. God and God's covenants are already part of the life of the people. They can recognize what God is doing now by their understanding in faith of God's previous dealings with them. God is now acting in ways that are new but are faithful to who God is as they have come to know God.[9] Because our thought has been corrupted by the long reach of Platonic idealism and, by contrast, American pragmatic consequentialism, I want to drive the point home with two extensive quotations from Gottwald:

> Nevertheless the prophets did not select their counsels by balancing the elements of the situation in terms of consequences. *It is true that the prophet was "prudential" in his resolute openness toward what God was actually forming in the social and political life, but that is better described as "theological pragmatism."* . . . *The alternative to rigid utopianism, which would have compelled prophets to prejudge events, was not a heterogeneous bundle of prudential factors, which added together formed a certainty no stronger than the motives were individually strong.* It is of course probable . . . that many elements and factors grasped within prophetic realism's field of vision coincided formally with a calculating political outlook. The prophets saw clearly, for example, the devastating domestic effects of wars and alliances which drained the land of means and manpower and fostered barbarism and vanity in men. Yet all these were ingredients of the total experience of what God was doing among men and what he required of them.[10]
>
> *We may speak of a prophetic pattern or style for ascertaining the will of*

---

[7] Ibid., p. 389. Here and throughout, when quotations are italicized, the italics are in Gottwald's text.

[8] Ibid., pp. 367-78.

[9] Ibid., p. 369.

[10] Ibid., p. 371.

God—a style which involved an oscillation between the depths of psychic communion with God and the manifold communal traditions. For Isaiah this meant that his profound shuddering before the holiness of God was associated with the long-standing tradition of God's judgment of his people, and especially of his city Zion, because of the righteousness that lies insistently at the heart of divine holiness.[11]

Gottwald also makes clear that the biblical prophets had not allowed themselves to be hijacked by partisan political ideologies as some churches have been tempted to do or, indeed, have succumbed to doing. He writes in italics: "*The prophets were well informed about political issues but they were informed largely as intelligent laymen. Some were close advisers of kings or officials, such as Isaiah and Jeremiah, but none was an official in the sense that he had to take responsibility for political decisions.*"[12] They all maintained the independence to speak prophetic words of criticism where they were needed. They were not "kept prophets."

We must make allowances for exaggerated rhetoric. "When we can check their 'predictions,' however," Gottwald explains, "the prophets scored rather well, chiefly because they knew the power realities and had a sense of the tides of political feelings, the rise and fall of morale, the impact of propaganda and terror."[13]

THE FIRST PEACEMAKING PRACTICE IS JUSTICE

Shalmanezer V of Assyria conquered Israel in 722 or 721 B.C. This ended the Northern Kingdom of Israel and left Judah alone and more vulnerable without protection from Israel. The prophet Hosea says the failure of Judah and Israel to treat each other with justice was a cause of the downfall of Israel. Israel sought an alliance with Assyria against Judah (Hos 5:13 and 8:9). In the reign of Menahem, king of Israel from 752 to 742 B.C., justice was neglected and instead there was harsh repression of internal opposition (Hos 10:4). "You have plowed wickedness, you have reaped injustice" (Hos 10:13).[14] "The LORD has an indictment against the inhabitants of [Israel]. . . .

---

[11]Ibid., p. 375.
[12]Ibid., p. 388.
[13]Ibid.
[14]All Scripture references are from the New Revised Standard Version, unless otherwise noted.

Swearing, lying, and murder, and stealing and adultery break out; bloodshed follows bloodshed" (Hos 4:1-2). So Hosea pronounced judgment: "Shall not war overtake them in Gibeah?" (Hos 10:9); "they shall fall by the sword" (Hos 13:16).[15] Instead of doing justice and being faithful to God, they made sacrifices as a cover up: "I desire steadfast love and not sacrifice, the knowledge of God rather than burnt offerings" (Hos 6:6). "The knowledge of God" according to Jeremiah 22:16, is to do justice, and I think this is what Hosea means when he says the LORD desires "the knowledge of God rather than burnt offerings." Hosea says, "But as for you, return to your God, hold fast to love and justice" (Hos 12:6).

Assyria deported many Israelis in 720 B.C. and replaced them with people from other lands that Assyria had conquered. Many Israelites who remained in Israel intermarried with these immigrants. After the takeover of the northern kingdom of Israel, now called Samaria, the hostility of the southern kingdom of Judah against them not only continued but intensified. Jesus repeatedly taught and enacted peacemaking toward Samaritans (Lk 9:55-56; 10:30-37; 17:11-18; Jn 4:7, 40-42; Acts 1:8).[16]

Gottwald says Hosea saw these events "with an objectivity that was not matched by the succession of rulers who bought and fought their way to the throne" in Judah.[17]

> Israel has wronged Judah in its savage attack upon Jerusalem and, for this, Israel has suffered the double blow of a Judean counter-thrust and an Assyrian invasion from the north. At the same time Judah exceeded her warrant of chastisement against Israel and sought self-aggrandizement by invading Ephraim, and she too will suffer the consequences. *Hosea sees, as it were, a complicated network of political sin and punishment, one nation's wrong giving rise to a counter-wrong. Yet neither nation can excuse its political sins by blaming them upon the enemy.*[18]

Similarly, Gottwald says Isaiah of Jerusalem prophesies that "Because the leaders have not listened to the demands of Yahweh for social justice, he will

---

[15]Gottwald, *All the Kingdoms of the Earth*, p. 125.
[16]Donald R. Potts, "Samaria, Samaritans," in *Holman Bible Dictionary*, ed. Trent C. Butler (Nashville: Holman Bible Publishers, 1991), pp. 1224-25.
[17]Gottwald, *All the Kingdoms of the Earth*, p. 123.
[18]Ibid., pp. 126-27.

teach them by the harsher methods of men who do not speak Hebrew at all, but their lesson will be clear enough in the end (28:11-22)."[19] Furthermore, "The only 'rest' possible for Judah is a security won by 'giving rest to the weary' (i.e., the wronged poor of Judah)—in other words by an internal social revolution in which the covenant terms are honored by faithful administration of justice. The king who will do this has no need for a covenant with death for he will build upon the one sure foundation stone of faith in Yahweh and he will not be agitated by each sudden shift in the tide of international affairs."[20]

Considering the book of the prophet Isaiah as a whole, I identify seventeen passages that prophesy God's deliverance—often from war or from exile caused by war (Is 9:1-7; 11; 24:14-25:12; 26; 29:17-24; 31:1-32:20; 33; 35; 40; 42:1–44:8; 49; 51:1-52:12; 52:7–53:12; 54; 56; 60; 61; 62). Fourteen of these passages say that when God brings deliverance, God brings peace; and sixteen of the passages say the deliverance is connected with justice (*mišhpāt*, *ṣĕdāqâ*, or *mišhpāt* and *ṣĕdāqâ*).

Defining the rich meaning of these two Hebrew terms by simply establishing an etymological derivation, as if the terms mean the same thing throughout the Old Testament as what an original derivation meant, produces an inaccurate and thin result. For example, some dictionaries say *ṣĕdāqâ* means "straight," like a ruler. It means far more than that in the actual use of the prophets. A functional rather than etymological approach, asking how the terms function in a particular prophet, produces a richer and more accurate understanding. What kinds of injustice is the prophet pointing to in his use of the terms? What kinds of action or relationship characterize justice?

When we examine Isaiah's use of *mišhpāt* and/or *ṣĕdāqâ* in these seventeen deliverance passages, we find that his proclamation of justice incorporates four dimensions: (1) deliverance of the poor and powerless from economic deprivation by the greedy; (2) lifting the foot of domineering power off the neck of the dominated and oppressed; (3) restoring the outcasts, the Gentiles, the exiles, the immigrants and the refugees to community; (4) establishing peace and nonviolence rather than the violence of

---

[19]Ibid., pp. 160-61.
[20]Ibid., p. 162.

persecution and war. Justice delivers from greed, domination, exclusion and violence. Justice is delivering justice, community-restoring justice, restorative justice.[21]

Most often *ṣĕdāqâ* is translated in our Bibles as "righteousness." But in our culture of possessive individualism, people read "righteousness" as an individualistic virtue that we possess—as self-righteousness. This is far from the relational, community-restoring, delivering action that *ṣĕdāqâ* points to biblically. It points to action that delivers from greed, domination, exclusion and violence. *ṣĕdāqâ* is very often used in synonymous parallelism with *mišhpāt*, and it clearly had a justice meaning, as delivering justice. So in what follows, I shall translate *ṣĕdāqâ* that way—as delivering justice—meaning justice that delivers people from their beat-down situation.

In Isaiah 11:3b-9, peace follows justice:

> He shall not judge by what his eyes see,
> > or decide by what his ears hear;
> But with delivering justice he shall judge the poor,
> > and decide with equity for the meek of the earth;
> he shall strike the earth with the rod of his mouth,
> > and with the breath of his lips he shall kill the wicked.
> Delivering justice shall be the belt around his waist,
> > and faithfulness the belt around his loins.
> The wolf shall live with the lamb,
> > The leopard shall lie down with the kid,
> The calf and the lion and the fatling together,
> > and a little child shall lead them.
> The cow and the bear shall graze,
> > their young shall lie down together;
> > and the lion shall eat straw like the ox.
> The nursing child shall play over the hole of the asp,
> > and the weaned child shall put its hand on the adder's den.

---

[21]*Ṣĕdāqâ* is a relational term that regularly points to action of deliverance, and as Gerhard von Rad's *Old Testament Theology*, vol. 1 (Edinburgh: Oliver and Boyd, 1962) says, it is never a term of punishment, though of course punishment does happen in the Old Testament, described by other terms. I recommend Moshe Weinfeld, *Social Justice in Ancient Israel and the Ancient Near East* (Minneapolis: Fortress, 1995). And for the New Testament, Christopher Marshall, *Beyond Retribution: A New Testament Vision for Justice, Crime, and Punishment* (Grand Rapids: Eerdmans, 2001).

They will not hurt or destroy on all my holy mountain;
  for the earth will be full of the knowledge of the LORD
as the waters cover the sea. (Is 11:3-9 NRSV with author's translation
    of ṣĕdāqâ)

We notice that *judge* and *decide* (a function of *mišhpāt*, judging justice)
are parallel in Isaiah 11:3, and *ṣĕdāqâ* (delivering justice) and *equity* are parallel, as *the poor* and *the meek* are parallel. This fits the frequent pattern in
the Hebrew Scriptures: *ṣĕdāqâ* and *mišhpāt* have parallel meaning, and both
concern deliverance for the poor, meek, dominated, excluded, and violated.
Walter Brueggemann[22] comments on this passage:

> The king is to practice righteousness and equity that are not based on
> surface appearances or on what is said, because a discerning ruler is not
> to be influenced by gestures of the wealthy or swayed by the manipula-
> tions of the powerful. The poetry here taps into a deep and primal con-
> viction . . . that the royal government is *The Equalizer*, to intervene on
> behalf of the poor and the vulnerable (widows, orphans, and immi-
> grants—or aliens) who are unable to supply their own social leverage.
>
> The public responsibility of the king for justice and righteousness ex-
> ercised in fidelity requires that . . . government should have at its disposal
> leverage for sanctions, penalties and punishments for those who violate
> the vision. The positive power to create social good requires the capacity
> for curbing "the wicked." Thus [in Isaiah 11:4] the king has the capacity to
> [strike] and [kill] the wicked, who are here seen to be those who prey
> upon, exploit, and abuse the meek, vulnerable, and poor. This "theory of
> government," articulated in lyrical fashion, is pivotal for discerning Is-
> rael's prophetic notion of what is possible. . . . Insofar as this text, with its
> clear messianic flavor, can be drawn upon as an illumination of Jesus, it is
> a reminder that Jesus cannot be reduced to privatistic salvation or to sac-
> ramental operations, but that Jesus was received, celebrated, and even-
> tually crucified precisely for his embodiment and practice of this vision
> of social possibility.

Isaiah 26:2-10 confirms the meaning of righteousness as (1) requiring
justice for the poor, (2) confronting the powerful who dominate; and (3)
intimately related to peace:

---

[22]Brueggemann, *Isaiah 1–39* (Louisville, KY: Westminster John Knox, 1998), pp. 100-101.

> Open the gates, so that the righteous nation that keeps faith may enter in.
> Those of steadfast mind you keep in peace—in peace because they trust you.
> Trust in the LORD forever, for in the LORD GOD you have an everlasting rock.
> For he has brought low the inhabitants of the height; the lofty city he lays low.
> . . . The foot tramples it, the feet of the poor, the steps of the needy. The way of
> the righteous is level; O Just One, you make smooth the path of the righteous.
> . . . For when your judgments are in the earth, the inhabitants of the world
> learn delivering justice. (Is 26:2-10, NRSV with author's translation of *ṣĕdāqâ*)

Isaiah 32:1 and 32:6-7 again show that the meaning of righteousness (delivering justice) parallels the meaning of justice (judging justice), and that they especially concern meeting the needs of the hungry and the poor and confronting the power of the domineering: "See, a king will reign in delivering justice, and princes will rule with justice (32:1)"; "For fools speak folly, and their minds plot iniquity . . . to leave the craving of the hungry unsatisfied, and to deprive the thirsty of drink. The villainies of villains are evil; they devise wicked devices to ruin the poor with lying words, even when the plea of the need is right" (32:6-7).

Furthermore, Isaiah 32:16-18 shows not only the parallel meaning of justice and righteousness, but also the intimate causal relation to peace:

> Then justice will dwell in the wilderness,
> 　　and delivering justice abide in the fruitful field.
> The effect of delivering justice will be peace,
> 　　and the result of delivering justice, quietness and trust forever.
> My people will abide in a peaceful habitation,
> 　　in secure dwellings, and in quiet resting places. (Is 32:16-18 NRSV with
> 　　　author's translation of *ṣĕdāqâ*)

Again Isaiah 33:5 and 33:15 connect *mišpāt* (judging justice) and *ṣĕdāqâ* (delivering justice) as parallel, assert their confrontation of oppression and greed and connect them with peace as opposed to bloodshed: "The LORD is exalted, he dwells on high; he filled Zion with judging justice and delivering justice" (Is 33:5); "Those [can live] who walk righteously and speak uprightly; who despise the gain of oppression, who wave away a bribe instead of accepting it, who stop their ears from hearing of bloodshed" (Is 33:15).

Isaiah 42:1-7 is of crucial importance. All three synoptic gospels tell us that when the Holy Spirit descended from heaven on Jesus at his baptism, the words the Spirit spoke were those of Isaiah 42:1 (Lk 3:22; see also Mt 3:17; Mk 1:11). Furthermore, the account of Jesus' reading from Isaiah 61 in Luke 4:18-21 includes Jesus' reference to "precisely those elements which are emphasized in the Aramaic Targum for Is. 42:3, 7."[23] We notice how strongly this crucial passage for Jesus' mission emphasizes the centrality of justice for the servant's mission. And it confirms the intimate connection of justice with peace and nonviolence: the servant will not break even a half-broken reed or quench a barely burning wick. Furthermore, it adds a fourth theme to the three we have already noticed: (4) justice not only for Israel but inclusively for all the nations: "justice for the nations," "justice in the earth," "a covenant to the people" and "a light to the nations." Here is this magnificent passage, definitive of Jesus' mission at his baptism:

> Here is my servant, whom I uphold,
>   my chosen, in whom my soul delights;
> I have put my Spirit upon him;
>   he will bring forth justice to the nations.
> He will not cry or lift up his voice,
>   or make it heard in the street;
> a bruised reed he will not break,
>   and a dimly burning wick he will not quench;
> he will faithfully bring forth justice.
> He will not grow faint or be crushed
>   until he has established justice in the earth. . . .
> I am the LORD, I have called you in delivering justice;
>   I have taken you by the hand and kept you;
> I have given you as a covenant to the people,
>   a light to the nations,
>   to open the eyes that are blind,
> to bring out the prisoners from the dungeon,
> from the prison who sit in darkness. (Is 42:1-7 NRSV with author's
>   translation of ṣĕdāqâ)

The intimate connection of justice and peace is announced again in Isaiah 60:17-21:

---

[23]Bruce D. Chilton, *The Isaiah Targum: Introduction, Translation, Apparatus and Notes*, vol. 11, *The Aramaic Bible* (Wilmington, DE: Michael Glazier, 1987), p. 83.

> I will appoint Peace as your overseer
>> and Delivering Justice as your taskmaster,
> Violence shall no more be heard in your land,
>> devastation or destruction within your borders.
> You shall call your walls Salvation,
>> and your gates Praise. . . .
> The LORD will be your everlasting light,
>> and your days of mourning shall be ended,
> Your people shall all be righteous;
>> they shall possess the land forever. (Is 60:17-21 NRSV with author's
>> translation of *ṣĕdāqâ*)

Gottwald says Jeremiah "admired Josiah as defender of the rights of the poor, as one who executes justice and righteousness." But in Jeremiah 5:4-5, 26-29 the prophet criticized failures in administering justice.[24] After a temporary lifting of the siege against Jerusalem, Judah re-enslaved their slaves that they had freed, and so Jeremiah prophesied the sword and famine for them—the outcome of war that would come upon them because of their practices of injustice.[25] Jeremiah called for justice and prayer, not temple and sacrifice.[26]

The prophets of Israel announce repeatedly that if Israel does not repent and do justice, war will come and Israel will be driven into exile. Some, influenced by Christian Zionism, claim that God's covenant with Israel includes a promise that the land is theirs eternally. But the prophets could not be clearer that possession of the land depends on doing justice, not injustice, to the aliens in the land, to those over whom they have power. Paying attention to the message of the prophets can lead Israel to the repentance that restores Israel to the purpose, vision and practice that we all should hope and pray for Israel. Because of that false claim, here I begin to display only some of the key passages in the prophet Jeremiah, with references to other similar passages in that one prophet. Similar passages can be seen in other prophets.

Jeremiah says again and again that great destruction will result from injustice by Israel: "This city must be punished; it is filled with oppression. . . .

---

[24]Gottwald, *All the Kingdoms of the Earth*, pp. 241-42.
[25]Ibid., p. 276.
[26]Ibid., p. 301.

Violence and destruction resound in her. . . . Take warning, O Jerusalem, or I will turn away from you and make your land desolate so no one can live in it" (Jer 6:6-8 NIV). The result of injustice and idolatry will be exile from the land: "Their houses will be turned over to others, together with their fields and their wives" (Jer 6:12 NIV). "They do not defend the rights of the poor" (Jer 5:28 NIV; see also 2:18-19; 5:17, 20-31; 6:13). Elsewhere he proclaims, "if you truly act justly one with another, if you do not oppress the alien, the orphan, and the widow, or shed innocent blood in this place, and if you do not go after other gods to your own hurt, then I will dwell with you in this place, in the land that I gave of old to your ancestors forever and ever" (Jer 7:5-7).[27] See also Jeremiah 7:15: "I will thrust you from my presence, just as I did the people of Ephraim" (NIV). "Wherever I banish them, all the survivors of this nation will prefer death to life" (Jer 8:3 NIV). "Therefore I will give . . . their fields to new owners. From the least to the greatest, all are greedy for gain" (Jer 8:10 NIV). "It is because they have forsaken my law, which I set before them. . . . I will scatter them among nations" (Jer 9:13-16 NIV). "Gather up your belongings to leave the land, you who live under siege. For this is what the LORD says: 'At this time I will hurl out those who live in this land; I will bring distress on them, so that they may be captured'" (Jer 10:17-18 NIV). "So I will throw you out of this land into a land neither you nor your ancestors have known (Jer 16:13 NIV; see also Jer 15:1-2, 14; 16:13; 20:4-6; 22:13-17; 24:1-10; 25:8-11).

> Thus says the Lord,
>> Execute justice in the morning,
>>> and deliver from the hand of the oppressor
>>> anyone who has been robbed,
>> or else my wrath will go forth like fire,
>>> and burn, with no one to quench it,
>>> because of your evil doings. (Jer 21:12)

> "[Your father] did what was right and just,
>> so all went well with him.

---

[27]Gary Burge, *Who Are God's People in the Middle East?* (Grand Rapids: Zondervan, 1993), p. 86, emphasizes this passage as he points out that God's covenant of the land for Israel is conditional on their doing justice to the aliens, the people of other nations, in the land. In many passages, Jeremiah makes this point.

He defended the cause of the poor and needy,
   and so all went well.
Is that not what it means to know me?"
      declares the Lord.
"But your eyes and your heart
   are set only on dishonest gain,
on shedding innocent blood
      and on oppression and extortion."
"I will hurl you and the mother who gave you birth into another country,
      where neither of you was born, and there you both will die." (Jer
   22:15-17, 26 NIV)

This is what the prophet Jeremiah says, and parallels exist in other prophets.
We can claim that the Bible says God has a permanent covenant with Israel,
but not that this covenant promises they will remain in the land even if they
do injustice to those less powerful. If the truth of the prophets still applies,
then true friends of Israel will encourage Israel to do justice to the aliens
and to those over whom they have power, not to practice greed, domination,
exclusion and violence. True friends of Palestinians will encourage them to
practice nonviolence and to focus on building their own society and edu-
cating their people rather than focusing on powerless resentment against
Israel. Many Christian Palestinians have been encouraging exactly such
practices of just peacemaking and, at the time of this writing, Palestinians
on the West Bank and in the Palestinian Authority have finally adopted
such a focus. Hamas has not, and Gaza under Hamas is stuck in self-defeating resentment and occasional attempts at violence. Israel then responds with ten times the killing.

PLACING IDOLATROUS TRUST IN MILITARY WEAPONS LEADS TO FOOLISH WAR-MAKING

Gottwald shows that several of the prophets identified placing trust in horses
and chariots, or in military alliances with Assyria or Egypt, as idolatry. This is
a false trust in what does not deliver. It makes us foolish because in our false
trust in military weapons and military alliances we rely on false promises and
venture into war that will lead to our destruction. "Ephraim has become like
a dove, silly and without sense; they call upon Egypt, they go to Assyria. As

they go, I will cast my net over them; I will bring them down like birds of the air. . . . They turn to that which does not profit; they have become like a defective bow; their officials shall fall by the sword because of the rage of their tongue. So much for their babbling in the Land of Egypt" (Hos 7:11-16).[28]

Hosea prophesies of Israel, "Because you have trusted in your power and in the multitude of your warriors, therefore the tumult of war shall rise against your people, and all your fortresses shall be destroyed. . . . The sword rages in their cities, it consumes their oracle-priests, and devours because of their schemes" (Hos 10:13-14 and 11:6). "Ephraim (Israel) herds the wind . . . they make a treaty with Assyria, and oil is carried to Egypt" (Hos 12:1). Gottwald writes of the foolishness of trust in arms:

> *The confidence in arms and fortifications is strangely incongruous and pitiable.* Israel has "forgotten his Maker" and regarded the laws of Yahweh "as a strange thing"; instead he has preferred sacrifice (Hosea 8:12-13) and has trusted in palaces (8:14a) and in the latest military equipment (14:3a). But this is all to no avail for . . . upon Judah's fortified cities Yahweh will "send a fire . . . and it shall devour his strongholds (8:14b).[29]

Amos and Hosea are well informed about international affairs and show a realistic understanding of the balance of power in the ancient world and of the foolishness of seeking entanglement in that competition for power. Hosea and Isaiah criticized Israel's attack on Judah and Judah's counterattack as false trust in their own military might, which would divide them against each other when they needed each other's support against potential enemies. The prophets also opposed alliances against Assyria, and alliances with Assyria, both of which would draw Assyria in to destroy Israel. "Assyria is an essentially unpredictable and humanly uncontrollable power which Ahaz invokes to his own detriment."[30]

Hosea counsels Judah not to place their trust in military might and alliances that would only draw powerful nations into swallowing them; instead they should place trust in Yahweh and do justice to one another and other nations: "I will have pity on the house of Judah, and I will save them by the LORD their God; I will not save them by bow, or by sword, or by war, or by

---

[28]Gottwald, *All the Kingdoms of the Earth*, pp. 130, 141-43.
[29]Ibid., p. 132.
[30]Ibid., pp. 145-46 and 152.

horses, or by horsemen" (Hos 1:7). Yahweh declares to Judah, "I will abolish the bow, the sword, and war from the land, and I will make you lie down in safety. . . . I will take you for my wife in righteousness and in justice, in steadfast love, and in mercy" (Hos 2:18-19).

Gottwald says Isaiah prophesied similarly against trusting in alliances with Egypt and his predictions were basically right:

> An Egyptian relief force was defeated by Sennacherib at Eltekeh, not far from the Philistine cities. Sennacherib devastated the Judean countryside, received a heavy tribute from Hezekiah, but did not actually enter Jerusalem or turn it into an Assyrian province. *Two articles of Isaiah's expectations were borne out: First, Judah suffered severe devastation.* Many of its cities . . . were destroyed and their citizens deported. . . . Second, the Assyrians did not capture Jerusalem or turn it into a provincial capital, although Hezekiah remained at least the nominal vassal of Sennacherib.[31]

And elsewhere he says of Isaiah, "*The oracle which comes closest to providing the key to Isaiah's attitude toward the Syro-Ephraimite crisis is 8:11-15.* Yahweh 'will become a sanctuary' [for those few who believe] and a stone of stumbling and a rock of stumbling [for the majority who do not believe] to both houses of Israel."[32]

The key is to place trust in Yahweh "so that in obedience to him Judah will 'not fear what they fear,' i.e., will not fear the Assyrian which has so frightened Pekah and Rezon [*sic*]."[33] And further, he says of Isaiah:

> The chief sin of man, his restless and excessive pride, is nowhere more blatantly expressed than in the nation as epitomized in vain monarchs who take insufficient account of their own limits and who rationalize their crimes by committing them in the name of their people. Yet all this pride, symbolized in the most advanced military technology, in horses and chariots, is merely "flesh."[34]

Isaiah was realistic in analyzing the pride of leaders and nations. They "forget their limits and are inclined to throw restraints to the wind in their quest for power." They are "driven to fight one another in bloody strife" and struggle for power. They

---

[31]Ibid., p. 185.
[32]Ibid., p. 156.
[33]Ibid., p. 157.
[34]Ibid., p. 204.

have plundered the property and goods and dislocated the populations of weaker nations. One and all rely upon power above morality and honor. The strong jealously guard and multiply their strength. The weak seek company in other powers and plan for the day of reprisal against the strong. . . . Each tries to rise above history or at least to secure a permanent place within history. Yet all of them—including the Yahweh-worshiping states of Palestine—will be impaled by the weapons in which they trust.[35]

The most thorough study of biblical attitudes toward kingship that I know of—by Frank Crüsemann—shows at best an ambivalence toward monarchy, with the militaristic drive for aggrandizement being a major cause for the negative criticisms.[36] Isaiah was direct and pointed in his criticism of placing idolatrous trust in military weapons:

Oh, rebellious children, says the LORD,
who carry out a plan, but not mine;
who make an alliance, but against my will.
    adding sin to sin;
who set out to go down to Egypt without asking for my counsel,
to take refuge in the protection of Pharaoh,
    and to seek shelter in the shadow of Egypt;
Therefore the protection of Pharaoh shall become your shame,
    and the shelter in the shadow of Egypt your humiliation.
For . . . everyone comes to shame
    through a people that cannot profit them,
that brings neither help nor profit,
    but shame and disgrace (Is 30:1-5).
Alas for those who go down to Egypt for help
    and who rely on horses,
who trust in chariots because they are many
    and in horsemen because they are very strong,
but do not look to the Holy One of Israel
    or consult the LORD! . . .
The Egyptians are human, and not God;

---

[35]Ibid., p. 205.
[36]Frank Crüsemann, *Der Widerstand gegen das Königtum: Die antiköniglichen Texte des Alten Testamentes und der Kampf um den frühen israelitischen Staat* (Neukirchen-Vluyn, Germany: Neukirchener, 1978).

their horses are flesh, and not spirit.
When the LORD stretches out his hand,
the helper will stumble, and the one helped will fall,
and they will all perish together. (Is 31:1-3)[37]

"Jeremiah showed a remarkable detail and accuracy in his prophecies. He predicted the defeat of Egypt at Carchemish, the seventy-year dominion of Babylon in the ancient Near East, the impending death of his prophet opponent, Hananiah, the execution of two Jewish prophet-agitators by Nebuchadnezzar, and the temporary nature of the lifting of the siege of Jerusalem."[38] Jeremiah's poetic prophecy about the broken cisterns is well known:

Be appalled, O heavens, at this,
be shocked, be utterly desolate, says the LORD,
for my people have committed two evils:
they have forsaken me,
the fountain of living water,
and dug out cisterns for themselves,
cracked cisterns
that can hold no water. (Jer 2:12-13)

Much less well known is that in these verses Jeremiah is prophesying about idolatrous trust in military alliances with Egypt and Assyria:

Moreover, the people of Memphis and Tahpanhes
have broken the crown of your head.
Have you not brought this upon yourself
by forsaking the LORD your God,
while he led you in the way?
What then do you gain by going to Egypt,
to drink the waters of the Nile?
Or what do you gain by going to Assyria,
to drink the waters of the Euphrates? (Jer 2:16-18)

Jeremiah was right; "Jehoiachin's pro-Egyptian policy came to a disastrous end."[39]

---

[37]It is idolatrous trust. Gottwald, *All the Kingdoms of the Earth*, pp. 179-80.
[38]Ibid., p. 299.
[39]Ibid., p. 256.

Gottwald says the evidence shows that like Amos, Hosea, Isaiah and Jeremiah, Ezekiel was also very well informed. He described Israel as a silly dove, a lone ass, an overheated oven, placing false trust in its own might. Ezekiel also charged Tyre with the sin of

> nationalistic egocentricity, which leads to an excessive self-regard, an insensitivity to her own limitations and impermanence, and a callousness toward other peoples in distress. . . . An originally desirable and admirable talent for trade has been corrupted by a people who forgot its place among the nations and even came to boast in effect: "I am a god" (Ezekiel 28:2, 9). *The prophetic sense of evil as rebellion and arrogance rather than utter depravity and malevolence is superbly expressed.*[40]

Respect for International Law

The prophet Amos begins by naming transgressions against other nations by Damascus (Syria), Gaza, Tyre (today's Lebanon), Ammon and Moab (today's Jordan) and Israel. Amos can speak of these wrongs because he believes there is "some sort of consensus among nations as to what it is 'to do right.'" Hence the nations can assemble as witnesses to criticize each other and to criticize Israel.[41]

> Probably the more immediate impulse to such a bold assertion of Yahweh's lordship over the nations came from elements of "universalism" which had already taken root in ancient Yahwistic tradition, such notions as are expressed in the Yahwist's use of Genesis 1–11 and the call of Abraham in Genesis 12:1-3. These insights . . . were vigorously activated by Amos and given alarming freshness by the specification of particular peoples with whom Israel was then engaged. . . . In addition, the prophet's view of the natural world with its harsh reign of violence taught him of a God whose justice does not observe national and ethnic boundaries any more than do rain-filled clouds or marauding beasts.[42]

Gottwald says it is logical to see in Amos solid intellectual foundations for the development of natural law and a genuine religious universalism which forms the matrix of international law.

---

[40]Ibid., pp. 302-3, 315-16.
[41]Ibid., p. 110.
[42]Ibid., pp. 118-19.

Isaiah shows yet more internationalism than Amos. He sees Yahweh's call not only for Israel's internal affairs but as a call to be a light to the nations. His controlling principle is that Yahweh is judge of all national prides.[43] Furthermore, he gives us the vision that the United Nations has etched on its own entrance, of God judging between the nations and arbitrating for many peoples: "They shall beat their swords into plowshares, and their spears into pruning hooks; nation shall not lift up sword against nation, neither shall they learn war any more" (Is 2:4).

Gottwald explains that this vision is based on Yahweh as God over all nations. The vision is not about a utopia in which other nations are all converted to Yahwism but about the need of nations for a law to govern their mutual relations. It leaves their internal relations to be governed by their own internal traditions and institutions.[44] Isaiah knows that war is learned, and nations can be more prone to war or more prone to peace depending on their own wisdom and their own respect for the growth of customs and laws that make relationships more regular and more peaceful.

> War is not an unalterable institution in human life but rather one that has developed from a body of habits which can be replaced by another set of habits better serving the interests of nations. . . . He does not hold that the eradication of war will bring about an eradication of evil in human nature or, vice versa, that the elimination of armed conflict requires first the complete removal of evil from the human heart. Apparently the confederated nations will continue to suffer the tensions of conflicting claims but they will at last see that the settlement of these claims by judicial means is preferable to bloodshed. . . .
>
> The lash of history may still teach even the cruelest and blindest of peoples that the way of lawlessness and violence among the nations is a way of mutual death. And even Yahweh's people may learn that their future greatness is not to conquer the world . . . , but rather to introduce an order among the nations derived from obedience to the minimal "natural law" which applies to the several nations of the then-known world.[45]

---

[43]Ibid., p. 147.
[44]Ibid., p. 200.
[45]Ibid., pp. 202-3; cf. p. 228.

Zephaniah parallels Isaiah's international perspective. He speaks of "nations," "kingdoms," "lands of the nations," "peoples," "peoples of the earth" and "inhabitants of the earth."[46]

Of course Amos had already asked if Israel is any better than Calneh, Hamath or Gath of the Philistines (Amos 6:1-2). He measured Israel and the nations by the plumb line of justice (Amos 7:8-9). "'Are you not like the Ethiopians to me, O people of Israel?' says the Lord. 'Did I not bring Israel up from the land of Egypt, and the Philistines from Caphtor and the Arameans from Kir?'" (Amos 9:7).

Throughout the prophets, the call is for loyalty to Yahweh, who is above all nations, whose justice is the norm by which all nations are judged, who created the stars of the universe and all that is, and who is now the ruler of history of all the nations. It may be that Isaiah says this most clearly; and it is Isaiah whom Jesus cited and quoted by far the most. Followers of Jesus are likewise called to obedience to God above any particular nation.

Repentance and Turning, or Returning, to God

The call to repentance, to acknowledging our own idolatry and disloyalty to God and to turning our ways toward obedience of God, echoes through all the prophets. Amos says:

Alas for those who lie on beds of ivory,
 and lounge on their couches,
and eat lambs from the flock,
 and calves from the stall;
who sing idle songs to the sound of the harp,
 and like David improvise on instruments of music;
who drink wine from bowls,
 and anoint themselves with the finest oils,
 but are not grieved over the ruin of Joseph!
Therefore they shall now be the first to go into exile,
 and the revelry of the loungers shall pass away (Amos 6:4-7).

Here we see that the warning to repent proclaims that those who do not repent will go into exile, which of course will come as the result of war. Throughout the prophets the warning of war coming is a call to repentance,

---

[46]Ibid., p. 220.

and the warning that we need to repent is a key to avoiding the destruction of war. Jeremiah 4 reads as if it is describing the destruction after a nuclear war. We all know that the prophets call for us to repent; therefore I need not amass the evidence here. Furthermore, we all know that the prophets warn of war's destruction if we do not repent. Therefore, we can see that the prophets are in effect calling us to repentance, with its call to humility rather than arrogance and with its call to faithfulness to God, as a practice of peacemaking, a practice that we need if we are to avoid war. The message runs throughout the prophets.

Conclusion: Practices of Just Peacemaking

Surprisingly, our study of the prophets has now arrived at most of the practices of the new paradigm for the ethics of peace and war: just peacemaking.[47] Two of the practices of just peacemaking are practices of justice—"advance democracy, human rights and religious liberty" and "foster just and sustainable economic development." One of the just peacemaking practices is "reduce offensive weapons and the weapons trade." This is avoiding placing idolatrous trust in military weapons, which leads to foolish warmaking, as the prophets declare, and as many of us think our nation has engaged in. Two practices of just peacemaking are "work with emerging cooperative forces in the international system" and "strengthen the United Nations and international efforts for cooperation and human rights." These are the practices of international law that the prophets call for. Another just peacemaking practice is to "acknowledge responsibility for conflict and injustice, and seek repentance and forgiveness." This is the prophetic practice of repentance and humility rather than defensive arrogance. Missing are the three just peacemaking practices of transforming initiatives, which Norman Gottwald did not notice in the prophets, but which we could find in Jacob's practice of independent initiatives of gift-giving as he was returning to meet his estranged brother, Esau, and in Judah's call for Joseph to talk and practice conflict resolution (Gen 32:3–33:19; 44:14–45:6) and elsewhere in the Old Testament. Thus we find in the prophets, and in the Old

---

[47]Glen Stassen, ed., *Just Peacemaking: The New Paradigm for the Ethics of Peace and War* (Cleveland: Pilgrim, 1998); Susan Thistlethwaite, ed., *Interfaith Just Peacemaking* (New York: Palgrave Macmillan, 2012). See www.justpeacemaking.org.

Testament, not only debates about the limits on war-making. We find the basic practices of peacemaking that have now become known as the new paradigm of just peacemaking.

The ethic of just peacemaking was developed by Christians, many of whom are just war theorists and others of whom are pacifists. They do not agree on when war is justified or not or on "holy war." But they reached agreement on the new paradigm of just peacemaking. Just peacemaking specifies the practices that are biblically grounded and that are, in fact, working to prevent many wars.

Since these practices have begun to be implemented, the average number of persons killed in war has been reduced from 3.8 million per year in the first half of the twentieth century to 0.8 million per year in the second half of the century.[48] As we began by differentiating prophetic realism from Platonic dualism or utopianism, we now see that the practices of just peacemaking are not merely ideals. Each is actually being practiced by people's movements such as in the nonviolent Arab Spring that brought democracy to Tunisia and Egypt; and previously in East Germany as the people toppled the dictator and the Berlin Wall; in the Philippines as they toppled Marcos, and in many other places. Each of the ten practices of just peacemaking is preventing some wars, and together they are preventing numerous wars. They deserve our support. We have the opportunity to turn churches into followers of Jesus' call to peacemaking.

We have now seen that the just peacemaking practices receive strong support from the prophets of Israel. And examining the Old Testament guided by the hermeneutical question of just peacemaking, "What practices prevent wars?" rather than being stuck with the well-worn question of whether and when wars are justified has enabled us to see major dimensions of what the prophets are calling for. The older question caused us to miss much of what the Old Testament has to teach us. The just peacemaking question opens our eyes to new insights. Let it open our practices to new faithfulness.

---

[48]John Horgan, "Wars Are Decreasing," *Slate Magazine*, August 4, 2009. Nicholas Kristoff, "Are We Getting Nicer?" *New York Times*, November 23, 2011.

12

"Holy War," Divine Action and the New Atheism

Philosophical Considerations

Robert Stewart

*The God of the Old Testament is arguably the most unpleasant
character in all fiction: jealous and proud of it; a petty, unjust, unforgiving,
control freak; a vindictive, bloodthirsty, ethnic cleanser; a misogynistic,
homophobic, racist, infanticidal, genocidal, filicidal,
pestilential, megalomaniacal, sadomasochistic,
capriciously malevolent bully.*

RICHARD DAWKINS, *THE GOD DELUSION*

MY CONCERN IN THIS ESSAY IS TO ASSESS philosophically how
biblical examples, particularly Old Testament examples, of "holy war"
might be used to argue against theism by the so-called "New Atheists." In
surveying the writings of Richard Dawkins, Christopher Hitchens, Sam
Harris and Daniel Dennett, the four major authors identified as New
Atheists by Gary Wolf in his seminal *Wired* magazine article,[1] I found no

---

[1]Gary Wolf, "The Church of the Non-Believers," www.wired.com/wired/archive/14.11/atheism_
pr.html.

"argument" against belief in God from Old Testament Holy War (OTHW). To be sure I found a good bit of Bible-bashing but nothing that resembled a formal argument. Let me be clear about what I am saying. I do not mean that I had to look very far in the writings of the New Atheists to find statements concerning OTHW. They are easy enough to find. But statements do not arguments make. Arguments consist of a set of "statements"[2] that logically lead to a conclusion. Given this definition of an argument, arguments against belief in God's existence are apparently nonexistent in the writings of New Atheists.

So what do we find in their writings? We find something like the partisan political rhetoric one reads in books written by the more zealous in either party, intended primarily for those of their own persuasion. In other words, they are preaching to the choir. I could simply end now by saying that the New Atheists make no significant argument against theism from OTHW. But given that many people, especially many Christians, are deeply bothered by passages like Deuteronomy 7:2, which states, "when the LORD your God delivers them before you and you defeat them, then you shall utterly destroy them," or Deuteronomy 20:16, where God commands his people to "not leave alive anything that breathes," it seems that a response is called for even if the New Atheists themselves make no such (formal) argument.[3] Couple this with the fact that even though they make no formal argument from OTHW, they clearly expect their disparate statements about OTHW to influence people toward atheism.

The so-called principle of charity will figure prominently in this essay. The principle of charity states among other things that we must treat an argument or an idea as charitably as possible before critiquing it. In order to do so we must clarify what the argument or idea is and state it as clearly and precisely as possible. Failure to state an argument clearly often results in refuting arguments or ideas that are neither made nor held by those with whom we disagree. To misrepresent another's position is never a good thing. Sometimes this is done unintentionally and, in such cases, is either under-

---

[2]Statements are sentences that are either true or false, i.e., they have a truth value. Questions, commands, exclamations, etc., are sentences but they are not statements. See C. Stephen Layman, *The Power of Logic*, 3rd ed. (New York: McGraw Hill, 2005), pp. 1-3.

[3]All biblical references are from the New American Standard (NASB), unless otherwise noted.

standable or forgivable, or both. Someone may misrepresent a position unintentionally because she naively believes that her initial understanding is accurate or because she is not trained in the field within which she is working. At other times, a position is misrepresented because of laziness, i.e., not working hard enough to understand what is actually believed or meant. Sometimes, though, the misrepresentation is intentional, and thus is scholastically, if not relationally, unforgivable.

Frankly, the New Atheists frequently are guilty of presenting a position as "Christian," "biblical" or "theistic," that is none of those things properly understood—or at best represents a fringe position within Christian and theistic circles or a simplistic understanding of the biblical text. This may be the result of a lack of theological, biblical or philosophical training, a lack of concern to understand what Christians or theists actually believe or simply because it is easier to attack the position stated than what is actually held to be the case. It frequently appears to me that the New Atheists have chosen not to read the best theistic or Christian thinkers on a subject. When this is found to be the case, they have violated the principle of charity.

The principle of charity also means among other things that, when necessary, we must revise or strengthen an argument in order to be certain that we are dealing with the strongest possible form of an argument. In this case, I will have to find or construct an argument that the New Atheists might make for their position and then assess it as to what it might prove and see how well it fares—and, consequently, how well belief in God fares in light of this argument. As stated above, in reading the New Atheists I found a general rhetorical pattern that works much like political rhetoric. The goal in much political rhetoric is not to convince one that a certain policy *cannot* be correct or that it is likely not the best policy, but rather that *no respectable person would want to be identified with such a viewpoint* or with those who hold such opinions—or at the very least to create some doubt as to the candidate's qualifications to hold office by calling his or her character into question. The goal is not to persuade readers that an argument is invalid, unsound, weak or uncogent, but rather to create enough existential anxiety that readers are unwilling to commit to such a person or position. In other words, people thinking seriously about OTHW are not faced so much with a logical problem as they are with an existential problem. Or dare I say an existential crisis?

A second observation concerning the New Atheists is in order. They frequently equivocate between arguing against theism per se and Christianity, Judaism or Islam in particular. Logically this is mistaken. At the heart of such equivocation is a failure to understand the difference between contradictory and contrary statements. Two statements are *contradictory* if the relationship between them (considered at the same time and in the same sense) is such that one of them must be true and the other must be false. Statement (A) "God exists" and statement (B) "God does not exist" are contradictory. If (A) is true, then necessarily (B) is false and vice versa. More significantly, if (A) is false, then necessarily (B) is true and vice versa. On the other hand, two statements are *contrary* if the relationship between them (considered at the same time and in the same sense) is such that both of them cannot be true but they may both be false. Statement (C) "Christianity is true"[4] and statement (B) "God does not exist" are contrary statements. Both cannot be true at the same time and in the same sense. If (C) is true, then (B) is false. Similarly, if (B) is true, then (C) is false. But it is not the case that if either (C) or (B) is false, then necessarily the other is true. Yet the New Atheists often seem to argue as though it were the case. They frequently mix and match general statements about theism per se with particular statements about Christianity, Judaism or Islam—and seem to think that in asserting that one of the particular religions is absurd they have demonstrated that belief in God is absurd.[5] Such is simply not the case. Logically speaking, Christianity may be false but that does not prove that God does not exist. The upshot of this is that no argument from OTHW can prove that belief in God is irrational.

Putting all this aside for the moment, I did find some arguments from OTHW against biblical inerrancy, though not from the New Atheists. A recent edition of the journal *Philosophia Christi* included a symposium on

---

[4]I recognize the difficulties that entail in speaking of a religion or a belief *system* as true but am using such shorthand language in the hope that my readers will understand the point that I am making despite my lack of precision. The three religions mentioned contain individual statements that are contrary, even if they also contain statements that are not. (C) entails "Jesus is the divine Son of God," a statement that neither Muslims nor Jews would affirm.

[5]I am not saying that they actually demonstrate the absurdity of any of these religions but that they attempt to do so. My point is that even if they were successful in doing so, they would not logically accomplish their goal of proving atheism to be true.

the question: "Did God Mandate Genocide?" Two of the authors taking part in the symposium argued that Christians today should not believe that God mandated genocide even if the Old Testament says that he did. Randal Rauser (a Christian) constructed a logical argument to make his case. The first part of which is:

(1) God is the most perfect being there could be.

(2) Yahweh is God.

(3) Yahweh ordered people to commit genocide.

(4) Genocide is always a moral atrocity.

(5) A perfect being would not order people to commit a moral atrocity.

Rauser notes after premise (5), "As the new atheists would have it, we ought to conclude from this that there is no perfect being."[6] This argument is supposed to demonstrate that God, a perfect being (1) cannot exist as (3) and (4) contradict (5). But is one forced to conclude that God does not exist on the basis of this argument? Certainly not.

Plausible responses fall into several categories. They are: (1) broadly theistic responses; (2) classical theistic responses; (3) non-inerrantist Christian responses; and (4) inerrantist Christian responses.

A "BROADLY" THEISTIC RESPONSE

A theist in the "broad" sense would believe "in the existence of some sort of supernatural being or reality"[7] without necessarily believing that there is a supremely good, omnipotent, omniscient, eternal being who created the world. In other words, this sort of God would not be a perfect being. A theist in this sense would not believe in either the God of classical theism or the Christian, Jewish or Islamic God. More importantly for my purposes this being would not fit Richard Dawkins's description of Einstein or Spinoza's god, i.e., a god that Dawkins has no concern to deny.[8] This would not be a *natural* god. William Rowe lists Paul Tillich as an example of one

---

[6]Randal Rauser, "Let Nothing that Breathes Remain Alive: On the Problem of Divinely Commanded Genocide," *Philosophia Christi* 11, no. 1 (2009): 29.

[7]William L. Rowe, "The Problem of Evil and Some Varieties of Atheism," *American Philosophical Quarterly* 16, no. 4 (October 1979): 335.

[8]Dawkins, *The God Delusion*, pp. 11-20.

holding this sort of theistic belief.[9] The late Antony Flew probably also fell into this category. C. S. Lewis refers to something akin to this position in *A Grief Observed*: "Not that I am (I think) in danger of ceasing to believe in God. The real danger is of coming to believe such dreadful things about Him. The conclusion I dread is not 'So there's no God after all,' but 'So this is what God's really like. Deceive yourself no longer.'"[10] Therefore, the New Atheist argument fails with respect to broad theism. Still, this is hardly reassuring for conservative Christians.

A CLASSICAL THEISTIC RESPONSE

Classical theism *does* conceive of God as a perfect being. But a classical theist is *not required* to identify Yahweh, the God of the Bible, as God. If one distinguishes between God, the perfect being, and Yahweh, the God of the Bible, then there is no charge that could possibly be leveled against the existence of God on the basis of anything in the Bible. Like the broad theistic response above, this response will not be satisfying to the traditional Christian. My point in briefly offering these two options is simply to point out that even should one take as dim a view as possible of the Old Testament narratives involving OTHW, *one is not logically compelled* to deny the existence of God on the basis of OTHW.

A NON-INERRANTIST CHRISTIAN RESPONSE

After noting that, on the above argument, the New Atheists would conclude that God does not exist, Rauser continues his argument: "The Christian however could instead reason in the following direction":[11]

(6) Therefore, a perfect being would not order people to commit genocide. (4, 5)

(7) Therefore, Yahweh did not order people to commit genocide. (1, 2, 6)[12]

The upshot of Rauser's position is not only that one is not required to abandon belief in God but also that one is not required to reject Christian

---

[9]Rowe, "The Problem of Evil and Some Varieties of Atheism," p. 335.
[10]C. S. Lewis, *A Grief Observed* (San Francisco: HarperCollins, 1996), pp. 6-7.
[11]Rauser, "Let Nothing That Breathes Remain Alive," p. 29.
[12]Ibid.

belief. One is only required not to believe the Old Testament narratives in which God commands OTHW. One can therefore be a traditional Christian, even a *broadly* evangelical Christian.[13] This argument simply does not logically lead to denying Christianity, much less the existence of God.

In the same issue of *Philosophia Christi* non-Christian philosopher Wesley Morriston writes:

> The proper conclusion, then, is that Christians should take seriously the possibility that God did not in fact command the genocidal attacks reported in various OT books. His perfect goodness, when combined with the weakness of the case for the morality of these commands, thus yields a very strong *prima facie* reason for rejecting biblical inerrancy.[14]

Morriston also states:

> I do think that the difficulty of reconciling belief in God's perfect goodness with the biblical passages in which God commands genocide constitutes quite a strong *prima facie* reason for Christians to adopt a more flexible view of the OT—one on which the most problematic passages reflect the (comparatively low) level of moral development of the human authors, and not the acts of a perfectly good God.[15]

In fact, as serious a Christian as C. S. Lewis states:

> The human qualities of the raw materials show through. Naivety, error, contradiction, even . . . wickedness are not removed. The total result is not "the Word of God" in the sense that every passage, in itself, gives impeccable science or history. . . . [T]he value of the Old Testament may be dependent on what seems to be its imperfection. It may repel one use in order that we may be forced to use it in another way—to find the word in it, not without repeated and leisurely readings nor without discriminations made by our conscience and our critical faculties, to re-live, while we read, the whole Jewish experience of God's gradual and graded self-revelation, to feel the very material through which it works.[16]

---

[13]A "broadly" evangelical Christian would affirm: that Jesus was truly divine and truly human; the Trinity; the saving death and resurrection of Jesus; and the need for a personal saving relationship with Christ; but deny the inerrancy of Scripture.

[14]Wesley Morriston, "Did God Command Genocide?: A Challenge to the Biblical Inerrantist," *Philosophia Christi*, 11, no. 1 (2009): 25.

[15]Ibid., p. 26.

[16]C. S. Lewis, *Reflections on the Psalms* (San Diego: Harcourt Brace Jovanovich, 1958), pp. 114-15.

AN INERRANTIST CHRISTIAN RESPONSE

To this point I've argued that the above argument from OTHW clearly does not prove atheism in either a broad or narrow sense. Neither does it disprove Christianity, though it might disprove biblical inerrancy. But as a biblical inerrantist, this is not entirely satisfying to me. So far we have considered what would follow from the argument above. The argument form certainly is valid. But are the premises true? Bracketing (6) "Therefore, a perfect being would not order people to commit genocide" and (7) "Therefore, Yahweh did not order people to commit genocide," I have no wish to question (1) "God is the most perfect being there could be," (2) "Yahweh is God" or (5) "A perfect being would not order people to commit a moral atrocity." But (3), "Yahweh ordered people to commit genocide," and (4), "Genocide is always a moral atrocity," seem open to question. Accepting the biblical accounts, there is no doubt that Yahweh ordered his people to war with the Canaanites.[17] But the appropriateness of the term "genocide" is open to question. Aside from the fact that "genocide" is a needlessly pejorative term, it may not be the correct term to describe what Scripture records. Old Testament scholar Christopher J. H. Wright holds that the correct term is "a war of Yahweh." The main feature of "a war of Yahweh" was that it was the Lord, not Israel, who declared war against the enemy and it was the Lord who guaranteed the victory.[18] Yahweh commanded Israel to destroy the Canaanites not for ethnic or racial reasons, as would be the case with genocide, but for moral reasons (Gen 15:16). It is clear that Yahweh did not demand that all those of other religions should be destroyed. But some religions were evil, as was the case with the Canaanites. This is hardly genocide as the term is usually understood. In fact, it is clear that not all the Canaanites were eradicated, as would be the case in genocide, because the command to leave nothing alive was restricted to a particular geographic region and a particular time. The upshot of all this is that if Yahweh did not command "genocide," the argument fails altogether.

Additionally, several Old Testament scholars have maintained that the

---

[17]Throughout this essay I will use the term "Canaanites" as a shorthand designation to refer to all the people groups that Israel was commanded to defeat in taking the promised land. I recognize that in places the text distinguishes between different groups that inhabited the land.

[18]Christopher J. H. Wright, *The God I Don't Understand: Reflections on Tough Questions of Faith* (Grand Rapids: Zondervan, 2008), p. 87.

language found in the passages that speak of wars of Yahweh is not to be taken literally but is in fact common Ancient Near East warfare rhetoric, i.e., exaggeration and hyperbole. K. A. Kitchen, K. Lawson Younger, Jr. and Lori L. Rowlett document how widespread this sort of rhetoric was by showing that it existed among the Egyptians, the Hittites, the Moabites and the Assyrians.[19] Moreover, it is clear that such language was not meant to be taken literally in that there are several Old Testament passages that contradict the claims of total annihilation. This is not to say that the biblical authors lied, but to insist that they followed the literary conventions of their day when writing about war.

Furthermore, the Old Testament is clear that Yahweh held Israel to a similar but stricter standard of morality and that when Israel fell into idolatry and immorality, Yahweh raised up other nations to conquer Israel. In other words, Yahweh judged Israel as well as her neighbors. This is not genocide but rather justice rightly applied.

Some might object that substituting the term "a war of Yahweh" for "genocide" is simply a semantic difference; whatever term we use, Yahweh commanded Israel to annihilate the Canaanites. I do not have space to respond to this objection in detail. Suffice it to say that if Yahweh commanded genocide, then the argument against biblical inerrancy *might* go through, but if he did not, then (4) is false and any argument including (4) obviously is unsound.

Nevertheless, even accepting—for the sake of argument—that Yahweh commanded genocide, premise (4), namely, that *genocide is always a moral atrocity*, is subject to doubt. Clearly the annihilation of a group of people is *generally* immoral, but is it the case that such is *always* immoral? Particularly, is it the case that God, who created all other living beings, does not have the right to take back the life that he has given? To insist that God does not have this right appears to be an example of failing to observe the "principle of relevant difference." The principle of relevant difference is closely related to the fallacy of special pleading. Special pleading is the fallacy of

---

[19]See K. A. Kitchen, *On the Reliability of the Old Testament* (Grand Rapids: Eerdmans, 2003), pp. 173-74; K. Lawson Younger Jr., *Ancient Conquest Accounts: A Study in Ancient Near Eastern and Biblical History Writing* (Sheffield, UK: Sheffield Academic, 1990), pp. 227-28, 245; Lori L. Rowlett, *Joshua and the Rhetoric of Violence: A New Historicist Analysis* (New York: Continuum, 1996), pp. 197-237.

making an exception to a rule for ourselves or some privileged party when there is no relevant difference between ourselves or the privileged party and others for whom we do not make such an exception. But one is justified in making an exception when there is a relevant difference. For instance, police officers sometimes have to break the legal speed limit in the performance of their duty. But they are not entitled to this special privilege when they are off duty. The relevant difference is "in the performance of their duty."

The significant question here is, Is there a relevant difference between God and humans with reference to the taking of life? There is an enormously important difference between God and human beings in this regard. The difference is *qualitative* in nature. There can be no greater difference than that between the Creator and the created. It is wrong for human beings to take another human's life without divine permission because humans, being made in the image of God, are equal to one another in terms of worth and dignity. But God is the ontological ground of all creation; no creaturely life exists apart from the will of God. As such God has a right to do as he sees fit with any or all of his creation. We might label failing to recognize a relevant difference as the fallacy of general pleading.

Furthermore, there is abundant evidence in the Old Testament that even when Yahweh had decided to act against a group that he was willing to relent from such an action if the group that he had targeted repented. Consider the narrative of Jonah. Jonah reluctantly went to Nineveh and prophesied calamity against the people of Nineveh. But when the Ninevites repented, God was merciful and did not follow through on the calamity Jonah had announced to them. Most telling of all, however, is Jonah 4:2, where we read Jonah's complaint to God after Nineveh is spared:

> He prayed to the LORD and said, "Please LORD, was not this what I said while I was still in my *own* country? Therefore in order to forestall this I fled to Tarshish, for I knew that You are a gracious and compassionate God, slow to anger and abundant in lovingkindness, and one who relents concerning calamity."

Jonah's complaint has to do with God's nature, not simply with the willingness of the Ninevites to repent. Note also that nowhere in Jonah do we find Jonah saying something like, "if you don't repent, calamity will come upon you."

Additionally, one of the passages often thought to present a vengeful God is in fact quite probably doing the opposite when properly understood. Exodus 34:6-7 reads:

> Then the LORD passed by in front of him and proclaimed, "The LORD, the LORD God, compassionate and gracious, slow to anger, and abounding in lovingkindness and truth; who keeps lovingkindness for thousands, who forgives iniquity, transgression and sin; yet He will by no means leave *the guilty* unpunished, visiting the iniquity of fathers on the children and on the grandchildren to the third and fourth generations."

Contemporary readers typically place the stress on the statement that the Lord will visit the iniquity of the fathers on the children and grandchildren to the third and fourth generations of those who hate him. But the text actually stresses that the Lord keeps lovingkindness to *thousands of generations*—but that he will not overlook evil. He is far more patient and loving than he is wrathful but, at the end of the day, he will execute justice and all that entails. The upshot of this is that it is reasonable to infer that if the Canaanites had repented, then God would have relented in their case as well.

Above and beyond all this, there is biblical testimony that God was exceedingly patient before ordering a war of Yahweh. In Genesis 15:16 we read that Yahweh waited over four hundred years before ordering the destruction of the Amorites (a Canaanite people) because their iniquity was "not yet complete."

Theologians refer to the sort of statement we find in Jonah 3:4 ("Yet forty days and Nineveh will be overthrown") as a conditional prophecy even though the condition is not explicitly stated. Logicians refer to such statements, whether prophetic or otherwise, as elliptical statements because they are incomplete, i.e., they lack some words that nevertheless are intended by the speaker. An example of an elliptical statement would be: "The United States consists of fifty states." It is elliptical because it does not state the point in history that is referenced. As it stands the statement would be true today in 2011 or at any point since August 21, 1959, and before the point in time when a new state(s) is added to or a state(s) is removed from the Union, but it would be false at any point prior to August 21, 1959. Most of the statements that people use regularly are elliptical, but we generally understand what we and others mean in spite of the fact that we are not speaking with the utmost precision. There is good reason to think that the command to annihilate the Canaanites was also elliptical in nature. In other words, it would have been understood that had they repented of their wickedness, then they would have been spared God's judgment, as was the case with Rahab and her family (Josh 6:17). If this is the case, then the upshot is that the Canaanites bear some responsibility for their fate.

Another philosophical consideration that may be significant related to this issue is that of speech-act theory. In speech-act theory a distinction is made between (1) the locutionary act; (2) the illocutionary act; and (3) the perlocutionary act. In overly simple terms, the *locutionary* act is the act of stating a word or term. It is the utterance of a sound or sounds to form a word or term that *means* something or *refers* to some state of affairs. The *illocutionary* act is the act of intending the locutionary act to accomplish something beyond what the locutionary act means or the state of affairs to which it refers. An example of the difference between a locutionary and il-locutionary act would be when a husband leaves the house in the morning for work and says to his wife, "I love you." He is not intending to commu-nicate to her new information. She already knows that he loves her. He is performing an act of affection. Or, if he has made her angry or disappointed, he may be trying to repair their relationship—perhaps with flowers and a card, as well. Regardless, a statement may mean more or less than the infor-mational content of a locution. Finally, the *perlocutionary* act concerns the effect of the statement. An illocutionary act may or may not accomplish what the speaker intends. Therefore, the locutionary, the illocutionary, and the perlocutionary acts may each be different from either of the other acts.[20] The reason I mention speech-acts is that sometimes one may make a

---

[20]For more on speech-act theory, see John L. Austin, *How to do Things with Words*, 2nd ed. (Cambridge, MA: Harvard University Press, 1962); John R. Searle, *Speech Acts: An Essay in the Philosophy of Language* (Cambridge: Cambridge University Press, 1969); Richard S. Briggs, *Words in Action: Speech Act Theory and Biblical Interpretation* (New York: T & T Clark, 2001); Timothy Ward, *Word and Supplement: Speech Acts, Biblical Texts, and the Sufficiency of Scrip-ture* (Oxford: Oxford University Press, 2002); Donald Evans, *The Logic of Self-Involvement: A Philosophical Study of Everyday Language with Special Reference to the Christian Use of Lan-guage about God as Creator* (London: SCM Press, 1963); Nicholas Wolterstorff, *Divine Dis-course: Philosophical Reflections on the Claim That God Speaks* (Cambridge: Cambridge Univer-sity Press, 1995).

statement (locutionary act) intending something quite different from what the content of the statement taken alone at face value would indicate (illocutionary act). Is it not possible that Yahweh intended something other than the locutionary content of his command to annihilate the Canaanites? Might it not be possible that an omniscient being who knew that Israel would not completely obey him (whatever command he gave in this regard) would command more than he actually intended (illocutionary act) in order to achieve or more nearly achieve the result he intended (perlocutionary effect)? Couple this with the fact that Yahweh is generally seen as omniscient, i.e., he would know perfectly the perlocutionary effect of his speech-act, and does this not become even more plausible? I am not insisting that this is the case. I am asking if this might not be the case. I am trying to be as charitable as possible when reading these texts.

As I've stated above, the argument from OTHW clearly cannot prove what the New Atheists would like for it to prove. In this most recent section I have briefly outlined multiple reasons to think that it doesn't even disprove biblical inerrancy.

EXISTENTIAL CONCERNS

On the surface this seems to settle the issue. There is no compelling argument for atheism from OTHW. But the New Atheists are not overly concerned with putting forward tight, logical proofs of God's non-existence. Their reasons for not believing in God are not primarily logical in nature, and therefore they are not concerned to provide strictly logical arguments for others. They seem to be primarily irreligious (and particularly non-Christian) and only secondarily atheistic. They thus seek to make use of any means at hand to dissuade the religious from their commitments and to convince their fellow non-believers to act on their beliefs or unbelief, as they might state it. Their writings seem then to be more concerned with provoking atheistic beliefs than they are with supplying arguments to justify such beliefs. And their works accordingly are more concerned with rhetorical and psychological issues than with philosophical and logical details. Their basic orientation and motivation is, as I've stated above, more like those of political activists than academic philosophers. Their goal with respect to Christians and theists is to provoke doubt. In short, they want to bring their believing readers to a point of existential crisis that leads to the abandonment of belief in God. As Richard Dawkins forthrightly declares in *The God Delusion*, "If this book works as I intend, religious readers who open it will be atheists when they put it down."[21]

In the final section of this paper, I will briefly take up the question of whether OTHW calls into question God's goodness sufficiently to keep one from making an existential commitment to the Christian God. Despite the logical analysis, some nagging questions may still remain. What if none of these possible explanations is sufficient to absolve God of culpability for OTHW? What if all of them taken together fail as well? What if I'm not satisfied with dealing only with the logical problem of OTHW? What if I can't bring myself to trust in a broadly theistic being/reality or even the god of Classical Theism? What if I am of such a mind that I cannot bring myself to commit to the Christian God if I cannot be certain that the Bible is entirely true in all it intends to state? What if I am deeply troubled by the thought that God commanded OTHW? Or even if I'm not sure that I believe that he did such a thing, what if I'm haunted by the fear that he *might* have done so? How can I make the kind of personal commitment that Christianity calls for?

These are legitimate concerns. One may accept some or all of what I've posited and still be bothered by such fears. And no amount of bare logic will remove these sorts of fears. Simply put, these are *existential* concerns. In the face of such questions one needs a *reason* to believe. In fact, as mysterious as the process of human belief formation is, it seems *prima facie* that to believe without some positive evidence is irrational, or at the very least, existentially irresponsible.[22] And this is precisely what the New Atheists are banking on. As primarily irreligious people their desire is to destroy the trust of believers. Simply put, despite all their talk of rationality and science, at the end of the day the primary aim of the New Atheists is existential in nature.

These sorts of existential questions are far more important than anything I've dealt with up to this point. These sorts of fears are found not only in the head but also in the heart; they touch not only the intellect but also the

---

[21]Dawkins, *The God Delusion*, p. 5.
[22]I am not arguing that belief in God *cannot* be rational without evidence, but it does seem that belief in God with evidence is *generally preferable* to belief in God without evidence.

emotions. The New Atheists are at their strongest at this very point. Existentially and emotionally the New Atheists are not required to show that my logic or possible explanations or possible, plausible, mitigating points concerning OTHW are invalid or false—they have only to plant a seed of doubt about OTHW and then let fear or anxiety take over. Their rhetoric is like a thing that goes bump in the night. We hear it and are troubled by it.

So do I have anything to add that might assuage these fears? In fact I do. Simply put, the New Atheists have not told their readers the entire story. They have cherry-picked the Bible and misrepresented the narrative of the acts of God found in the Bible by focusing on select texts to the neglect of others. OTHW is an important issue that evangelical Christians must deal with, but it is not the only theme we find in Christian Scripture. Given that the New Atheists draw from Scripture in raising this objection to Christian faith—and this objection is primarily, if not entirely, directed toward Christians—it seems only fair and reasonable to hear the rest of the Christian story and to see if it in any way lessens the charge. Some may object that I am now getting "theological" and that doing so is inappropriate in defending the existence of God. But given that the objection itself is "theological," it only seems fair; after all, what's good for the theological goose is good for the theological gander.

So what themes have the New Atheists ignored? First and foremost one must note that the Christian God is not only the Creator of all else, he is also a *Father*. Jesus taught us to pray, "Our *Father* who is in heaven" (Mt 6:9, emphasis added). Luke's genealogy tells us that God was the father of Adam (Lk 3:38). This leads to the conclusion that the Christian God is the Father of all human beings in all places at all times.[23] Fathers suffer when their children suffer. This was made experientially apparent to me when my youngest daughter fell ill at eleven weeks of age. We submitted her to a series of painful medical procedures because we loved her and desired the best for her, but we also wept as we did. And as we put her through her medical ordeal, we knew that there was no way that we could explain to her why we were putting her through this ordeal. The idea of an unmoved, un-

---

[23]I know that some believers might object that God is not the Father of unbelievers, and I grant that there is a difference in how God relates to Christians but still maintain that he is the Father of every human being *via creation* but the Father of believers *via redemption*.

feeling god is not a biblical idea—it is a Greek idea. Because the Christian God is supremely relational, he is invested in the lives of his creatures and has thus suffered more than any or all of his creatures.

Second, there is the suffering of God the Son to consider. The prophet Isaiah tells us that:

> He was despised and forsaken of men, a man of sorrows and acquainted with grief; and like one from whom men hide their face. He was despised, and we did not esteem Him. Surely our griefs He Himself bore, and our sorrows He carried; yet we ourselves esteemed Him stricken, Smitten of God, and afflicted. But He was pierced through for our transgressions, He was crushed for our iniquities; the chastening for our well-being *fell* upon Him, and by His scourging we are healed (Is 53:3-5).

The sinless Son of God suffered and died on a cross for sinners. He took upon himself the punishment for our sins. "At the ninth hour Jesus cried out with a loud voice, 'Eloi, Eloi, lama sabachthani?' which is translated, 'My God, My God, why have You forsaken Me?'" (Mk 15:34). "He made Him who knew no sin *to be* sin on our behalf, so that we might become the righteousness of God in Him" (2 Cor 5:21). Far more than the physical pain of the crucifixion was the sense of separation he experienced from his Father. A movie like Mel Gibson's *The Passion of the Christ* may portray the physical torment in graphic detail. But there is no way to show the spiritual pain Jesus felt. For the first time in all eternity, the Father turned away from the Son. Christ does more than merely understand our sufferings; he feels our suffering with us. He has been hurt and rejected. He has been blameless and suffered through no fault of his own. He is able for this reason to come to the aid of those who suffer. And as suffering people, we may draw close to him without fear of being misunderstood. The late John Stott stated it well:

> I could never myself believe in God, if it were not for the cross. The only God I believe in is the One Nietzsche ridiculed as "God on the cross." In the real world of pain, how could one worship a God who was immune to it? I have entered many Buddhist temples in different Asian countries and stood respectfully before the statue of the Buddha, his legs crossed, arms folded, eyes closed, the ghost of a smile playing round his mouth, a remote look on his face, detached from the agonies of the world. But each time after a while I have had to turn away. And in imagination I have turned instead to that

lonely, twisted, tortured figure on the cross, nails through hands and feet, back lacerated, limbs wrenched, brow bleeding from thorn-pricks, mouth dry and intolerably thirsty, plunged in God-forsaken darkness. That is the God for me! He laid aside his immunity to pain. He entered our world of flesh and blood, tears and death. He suffered for us. Our suffering becomes more manageable in the light of his. There is still a question mark against human suffering, but over it we boldly stamp another mark, the cross which symbolizes divine suffering.[24]

Third, the New Atheists fail to mention anything the Bible says about the comfort of the Spirit. The Holy Spirit is, in Jesus' words, a *comforter*. He comes alongside us and joins us in our pain. Jesus said, "I will ask the Father, and He will give you another Helper, that He may be with you forever; *that is* the Spirit of truth, whom the world cannot receive, because it does not see Him or know Him, *but* you know Him because He abides with you and will be in you. I will not leave you as orphans; I will come to you" (Jn 14:16-18). The apostle Paul writes to the Romans: "The Spirit Himself testifies with our spirit that we are children of God, and if children, heirs also, heirs of God and fellow heirs with Christ, if indeed we suffer with *Him* so that we may also be glorified with *Him*. For I consider that the sufferings of this present time are not worthy to be compared with the glory that is to be revealed to us" (Rom 8:16-18). God's Spirit translates suffering into a means of glory. Please note that this is a *uniquely trinitarian* view of God in relation to suffering—and particularly suffering that is divinely initiated.

Fourth, there is the resurrection to consider. I am not speaking of the resurrection of Jesus, as significant as that is, but the general resurrection of the dead. Paul writes to the Corinthians:

> Now I say this, brethren, that flesh and blood cannot inherit the kingdom of God; nor does the perishable inherit the imperishable. Behold, I tell you a mystery; we will not all sleep, but we will all be changed, in a moment, in the twinkling of an eye, at the last trumpet; for the trumpet will sound, and the dead will be raised imperishable, and we will be changed. For this perishable must put on the imperishable, and this mortal must put on immortality. But when this perishable will have put on the imperishable, and this mortal will

---

[24]John R. W. Stott, *The Cross of Christ* (Downers Grove, IL: InterVarsity Press, 1986), pp. 335-36.

have put on immortality, then will come about the saying that is written, "Death is swallowed up in victory. O death, where is your victory? O death, where is your sting?" The sting of death is sin, and the power of sin is the law; but thanks be to God, who gives us the victory through our Lord Jesus Christ. (1 Cor 15:50-57)

Paul tells Timothy, "Remember Jesus Christ, risen from the dead, descendant of David, according to my gospel, for which I suffer hardship even to imprisonment as a criminal; but the word of God is not imprisoned. For this reason I endure all things for the sake of those who are chosen, so that they also may obtain the salvation which is in Christ Jesus *and* with *it* eternal glory" (2 Tim 2:8-10).

Fifth, the Bible is clear that in the end God will set all things right. In the last book in the Bible, we read:

Then I saw a new heaven and a new earth; for the first heaven and the first earth passed away, and there is no longer *any* sea. And I saw the holy city, new Jerusalem, coming down out of heaven from God, made ready as a bride adorned for her husband. And I heard a loud voice from the throne, saying, "Behold, the tabernacle of God is among men, and He will dwell among them, and they shall be His people, and God Himself will be among them, and He will wipe away every tear from their eyes; and there will no longer be *any* death; there will no longer be *any* mourning, or crying, or pain; the first things have passed away." And He who sits on the throne said, "Behold, I am making all things new." (Rev 21:1-5)

What we find in Scripture is a complex mix of themes and descriptions of God and his actions—just as is the case in describing any person. The biblical God judges and executes wrath. He also loves the unlovable and extends mercy to those who don't deserve mercy. He gives life and he takes it as well.

These biblical themes do not remove all the difficulties that attend to OTHW passages, but they do serve to round out the biblical narrative and to offer us a more complete picture of the Christian God. The question is not will we ever have an explanation that addresses each and every concern we might have related to OTHW but rather do we have *enough positive testimony* to justify a wholehearted existential commitment? How exactly does one determine whether there is enough positive testimony to justify a wholehearted commitment? It's tempting to say that 100 percent commitment requires 100 percent certainty. But this is clearly wrong. I often ask my students if they expect their spouses to be faithful to their marriage vows. Invariably they answer that they do. Then I ask them how they could ever be certain that their spouses were faithful or that a prospective spouse would be. After all they cannot be certain that their spouses are because they cannot be with them at all times. In other words, they cannot have 100 percent certainty as to their spouse's faithfulness, but marriage requires a 100 percent commitment. There is no such thing as 88 percent married. Nevertheless, none of us believes that everyone who gets married and expects their spouse to be faithful is behaving irrationally. In a criminal trial, even one where the death penalty can be applied, the burden is not that the prosecution must demonstrate the defendant's guilt beyond all doubt but rather beyond a reasonable doubt.

So how exactly do we determine whether or not we should commit ourselves to God? This is a question to which I cannot give a precise answer, nor can anyone else, I suspect. But fortunately I don't need to know the answer to this question. Please note, however, that this is a different question than the one we began with. This is a question concerning whether I can trust God, or whether I can radically commit myself to God, not whether I can rationally believe that some sort of God exists.

At the end of the day, it seems that we are faced with this question: Can we commit to a person about whom we do not know each and every detail or understand why he has acted as he has in each and every circumstance? I know that I often have done so in my personal relationships with my spouse, my parents, my brother, my children, some of my colleagues and some fellow believers. Sometimes I have even said to others, "You just have to take my word for it," or "I'm asking you to trust me." And I have also "just trusted" others because I knew them well enough or knew enough about them to believe that they were trustworthy in spite of the fact that not all my questions were answered or all my concerns addressed as fully as I would like. It does not seem unreasonable to do so also with God. In fact, it would seem unreasonable to think that I could understand God in each and every way.

So are all my questions about OTHW answered? No. But am I satisfied that God exists and that he is the sort of being to whom I can commit all my life? Absolutely! In summary, there is no argument from OTHW that leads logically to denying the existence of God, even the Christian God. Nor does OTHW create such an existential crisis that I find I cannot trust my whole self into God's hands and believe that he will deal justly with me. I may fear him because he is perfectly righteous and wholly other. I do not fear that he will deal wickedly with me or anyone else.

PART SIX

Theological Perspectives

13

THE UNHOLY NOTION
OF "HOLY WAR"

A Christian Critique

Murray Rae

———————— ✝ ————————

$\mathbf{A}$T FACE VALUE, THE NOTION OF A "HOLY WAR" seems, from a
Christian point of view, to be an oxymoron. The counsel that Jesus offers
against violence, along with his instruction to love one's enemies, leaves
little scope, one might think, for the proposition that war might be engaged
in as an act of obedience to the God made known in Jesus and on whose
behalf Jesus undertook his ministry of teaching, healing and reconciliation.
I will take it, for the purposes of this essay, that the adjective "holy" when
ascribed to anything other than God himself, designates something that is
distinguished by divine blessing and use and appointed to the working out
of God's purpose. That war and its inherent violence could be so distinguished appears to contradict those well-known sayings of Jesus in which
his disciples are instructed to turn the other cheek in the face of provocation (Mt 5:39), to love their enemies, to pray for those who persecute
them (Mt 5:44; cf. Lk 6:27), and to put away the sword (Mt 26:52). It was the
widely held conviction of early Christians—up until the time of Constantine—that such teaching as this constituted an unequivocal prohibition
of any Christian involvement in war.

I

Evidence for early Christian resistance to violence and warfare comes in several forms, notably in the writings of theologians directly opposed to Christian involvement in warfare, in the taunts of opponents who deride Christians for their pacifist stance, and in the documented cases of Christians who paid with their lives for their opposition to violence. Christian opposition to war gets underway very early in the tradition. Justin Martyr, for example, writing circa A.D. 150–160 claimed on behalf of Christians that "we who formerly used to murder one another now refrain from even making war upon our enemies."[1] The basis for this cessation of violence, Justin contended, lay in the fulfillment through Christ of the prophecy from Isaiah:

> For out of Zion shall go forth instruction,
>   and the word of the LORD from Jerusalem.
> He shall judge between the nations,
>   and shall arbitrate for many peoples;
> they shall beat their swords into plowshares,
>   and their spears into pruning hooks;
> nation shall not lift up sword against nation,
> neither shall they learn war any more. (Is 2:3-4)[2]

Shortly after Justin, Clement of Alexandria (c. 150–215) took up the same theme: "As simple and quiet sisters, peace and love require no arms. For it is not in war, but in peace, that we are trained."[3] A pacifist stance was for Clement a universal imperative of Christian discipleship: "Above all," he wrote, "Christians are not allowed to correct with violence the delinquencies of sins."[4] Likewise, Hippolytus of Rome (c. 170–236) insisted on the incompatibility of military service and Christian discipleship.

> A soldier of the government must be told not to execute men; if he should be
> ordered to do it, he shall not do it. He must be told not to take the military
> oath. If he will not agree, let him be rejected. A military governor or a magis-

---

[1]Justin Martyr, "First Apology XXXIX," in *The Ante-Nicene Fathers*, vol. 1, ed. A. Roberts and J. Donaldson (Grand Rapids: Eerdmans, 1979), p. 39.

[2]All biblical quotations are taken from the New Revised Standard Version (NRSV).

[3]Clement of Alexandria, "The Instructor," in *The Ante-Nicene Fathers*, vol. 2, ed. A. Roberts and J. Donaldson (Grand Rapids: Eerdmans, 1986), pp. 234-35.

[4]Maximus, "Fragment of Sermon 55," in *The Ante-Nicene Fathers*, vol. 2, ed. A. Roberts and J. Donaldson (Grand Rapids: Eerdmans, 2001), p. 581.

trate of a city who wears the purple, either let him desist or let him be rejected. If a catechumen or a baptised Christian wishes to become a soldier, let him be cast out. For he has despised God.[5]

The injunctions of these theologians were taken seriously, at least by some. Toward the end of the same century in which Hippolytus wrote, a young Christian from Numidia became the patron saint of conscientious objectors. "Called up for military service (his father had been a Roman soldier) Maximilianus told the Roman proconsul that, as a Christian, 'I cannot serve as a soldier; I cannot do evil.' He was executed for his persistence."[6]

Christian opposition to military service was prompted not only by opposition to violence and warfare but also by resistance to the obligation upon enlisted soldiers to participate in the cult of emperor worship. The opposition to both aspects of military service among Christians was widespread enough to prompt the complaint from Celsus, a second-century Epicurean philosopher, that "if all were to do the same as you, there would be nothing to prevent [the emperor's] being left in utter solitude and desertion, and the affairs of the earth would fall into the hands of the wildest and most lawless barbarians."[7] In his reply, the Christian theologian Origen contended that if, "in the words of Celsus, *'they do as I do'*" then it is evident that even the barbarians, when they yield obedience to the word of God, will become most obedient to the law, and most humane."[8] And further "if all the Romans, according to the supposition of Celsus, embrace the Christian faith, they will, when they pray, overcome their enemies; or rather, they will not war at all."[9] Echoing Justin Martyr's appeal to Isaiah 2:4, Origen contended on behalf of Christians that "we no longer take up '*sword against nation*,' nor do we '*learn war any more*,' having become children of peace, for the sake of Jesus, who is our leader."[10]

---

[5]Hippolytus, *The Treatise on the Apostolic Tradition of St Hippolytus of Rome*, ed. G. Dix (London: Society for Promoting Christian Knowledge, 1937), pp. 26-27.

[6]The story is told by Jean Bethke Elshtain, *Women and War* (New York: Basic Books, 1987), p. 125.

[7]Origen, "Contra Celsum," in *The Ante-Nicene Fathers*, vol. 4, ed. A. Roberts and J. Donaldson (Peabody, MA: Hendrickson, 1994), p. 665.

[8]Ibid.

[9]Ibid., p. 666.

[10]Ibid., 5.XXXIII, p. 558. The biblical references are drawn from Joel.

While the theologians of the period generally spoke with one voice on the matter, opposition to military service was not embraced by all Christians. There is evidence from that same period (A.D. 170–180) of the participation of Christians in the so-called Thundering Legion under Marcus Aurelius.[11] Then at the beginning of the third century, the theologian Tertullian considered it necessary to rebuke Christians who voluntarily enlisted in the military. Referring to Jesus' instruction to Peter to put away his sword, Tertullian wrote, "Christ in disarming Peter ungirt every soldier." Elsewhere he asks,

> Is it likely we are permitted to carry a sword when our Lord said that he who takes the sword will perish by the sword? Will those who are forbidden to engage in a lawsuit espouse the deeds of war? Will a Christian who is told to turn the other cheek when struck unjustly, guard prisoners in chains, and administer torture and capital punishment?[12]

Clearly Tertullian thinks that the answer will be no! Thus he reports approvingly the instance of a soldier who, on becoming a Christian, withdrew from the military.[13] Others apparently were expelled. Galerius Maximianus, for example, attempted around A.D. 300 to weed Christians out of his forces.[14]

In 325, the ecumenical council of bishops meeting at Nicaea roundly condemned Christians who, having cast aside their soldiers' girdles, later attempted to return to the military "like dogs returning to their own vomit."[15] The Bishops prescribed a rigorous program of repentance for such offenders. This official declaration of the church's position confirmed over two hundred years of tradition. That the bishops at Nicaea should set military service alongside Arianism (the principal concern of the council), as a serious threat to the church, is indicative of a growing conviction among the populace that Christian discipleship and military service might not be incompatible after all. The "conversion" of Constantine little more than a decade earlier was the principal cause of this change of heart. Constantine, the well known story

---

[11]See Roland H. Bainton, *Christian Attitudes Toward War and Peace: A Historical Survey and Critical Re-Evaluation* (Nashville: Abingdon Press, 1960), p. 68.

[12]Tertullian, *De Corona*, XI.

[13]Tertullian, *De Corona*, I.

[14]Eusebius, *Historia Ecclesiastica*, VIII, cited in Bainton, *Christian Attitudes Toward War and Peace*, p. 274.

[15]Council of Nicaea, Canon XII.

goes, was engaged in battle at the Milvian Bridge when he looked to the heavens for inspiration and saw there a cross of light with the words in Greek, "By this Conquer." Constantine had the Christian *chi rho* symbol inscribed upon the shields of his soldiers and went on to win the battle. The victory constituted evidence, for some, that the Christian God favored Constantine in battle. Thus began the conviction among some Christians, but opposed at Nicaea, that soldiers engaged in battle might be legitimate instruments of God's purpose. Here too may be found the roots of a tradition which legitimized in Christian thought the idea of a "holy war," a war waged on God's behalf by *milites Christi* (knights of Christ) and by *fideles sancti Petri* (the faithful of Saint Peter). Such were the titles applied to those engaged in the Crusades during the twelfth and thirteenth centuries.

Despite the protestations of the bishops at Nicaea, the Christian pacifist tradition became in the ensuing centuries a minority position among Christians. As the Roman empire morphed into the *Holy* Roman Empire, Christians offered little objection to some of their number wielding on their behalf the instruments of state power, particularly the shield and sword. It became the norm thereafter, and remains so today, that Christian opponents of "holy" or "just" war, along with "conscientious objectors" to military service, have been required to bear the burden of proof that war, as it is commonly engaged in, is not a legitimate means of promoting the purposes of God and cannot therefore be holy. Throughout the era known as Christendom, a pacifist stance grounded in theological principles was maintained largely by sectarian groups and had little impact upon the "mainstream" Christian church. Notable among them, however, have been the Waldensians who in the late Middle Ages and early Reformation period recovered something of the earlier Christian pacifist tradition and practiced nonviolence in the face of persecution. In Britain a group known as the Lollards emerged under the leadership of John Wycliffe. Adherence to a strict "Law of Christ" led the Lollards to oppose papal violence and to petition the English parliament to desist from warmongering. They were persecuted for their trouble. Such fledgling movements as the Waldensians and the Lollards inspired in Europe a series of more enduring traditions including the Moravian Brethren, the Anabaptists and, within the Anabaptist tradition, the Mennonites founded in Holland by a former priest,

Menno Simons. Each of these movements is known for its advocacy of a pacifist position based on the teachings and example of Christ. The Quakers who emerged in England in the seventeenth century and have subsequently spread, though in relatively small numbers, throughout the Western world, represent an enduring, independent tradition of Christian pacifism. It is fair to say, however, that especially since the Second World War pacifism as an intentional Christian stance has re-entered the main-stream Christian traditions and is less sectarian in character. Recent evidence of this development is the leading role played by churches in nuclear disarmament campaigns around the world and again in Britain in opposing the invasion of Iraq in 2003.

The theological basis for the pacifist tradition in Christian thought remained reasonably constant in the early church, both through the sectarian movements that kept it alive through the Middle Ages and into the modern era, and in the contemporary groundswell of pacifist concern in mainline churches. The commitment to nonviolence and to peacemaking, it is argued, is the straightforward application of Jesus' teaching and example. Those who would follow Jesus are enjoined to turn the other cheek in the face of provocation (Mt 5:39) and to love their enemies (Mt 5:44), while those who are peacemakers will be called children of God (Mt 5:9). More sophisticated theological arguments are also available and we will encounter them as we proceed, but the plain sense of Jesus' teaching is likely to endure as the most compelling reason for Christians to oppose the notion that war may be holy, that it may somehow conform to the purpose of God and be a legitimate expression of Christian discipleship.

II

Having been widely accepted as the straightforward implication of the Christian gospel among theologians of the early patristic period, the pacifist position has been sustained in the church as a minority tradition bearing the burden of proof against the predominant assumption that Christians may legitimately participate in acts of war. There have been, however, a number of theologians who, while defensive of this predominant position, have nevertheless accepted the need to offer theological reasons for engaging in war or who have offered a theological critique of the pacifist position. Among such theologians whose arguments deserve careful consideration are Reinhold Niebuhr and Karl Barth, whose reflections on the subject were prompted by the rise of Nazi Germany, and Oliver O'Donovan, whose writings offer a more general defense of the principle of legitimate military action.

We begin with Niebuhr who published in 1940 a widely influential essay, *Why the Christian Church Is Not Pacifist*.[16] Niebuhr opposes the pacifist position principally because, he alleges, it does not take the fact of human sin seriously enough. It trusts too much in the capacity of human beings to make things right, to usher in the kingdom in virtue of their pacifist and loving ways. But, Niebuhr contends, the historical realities of life give no support to this utopian vision. It is instead heretical to suppose that sin can be overcome through human effort.[17] We will have reason below to dispute the claim that Christian pacifism must involve such an assumption but for now we will pursue further Niebuhr's argument.

While there is no contesting the "law of love," the injunction to love our neighbor and even our enemy, the Christian gospel, Niebuhr says, cannot be equated simply with the law of love. According to Niebuhr, the law of love as commended by Jesus expresses the final norm of human conduct, but the gospel is concerned centrally with the fact of sin. "The good news of the Gospel is not the law that we ought to love one another. The good news of the Gospel is that there is a resource of divine mercy which is able to overcome a contradiction within our own souls, which we cannot ourselves overcome." Niebuhr writes further: "Christianity measures the full seriousness of sin as a permanent factor in human history." The gospel does not end sin; it proclaims the mercy of God for sinners. The pacifist position is heretical, Niebuhr contends, in supposing that sin can be overcome through obedience to the law of love. Christianity is not primarily a challenge to obey the law of Christ but "a religion which deals realistically with the

---

[16]Reinhold Niebuhr, *Why the Christian Church Is Not Pacifist* (London: SCM Press, 1940).

[17]Niebuhr was not the first Christian theologian to argue that pacifism is heretical. The Spanish scholastic Francisco Suárez claimed that it is heretical to assert that war is intrinsically evil and contrary to charity. He calls upon Augustine in support of this claim. See Francisco Suárez, *De triplici virtute theologica*, Disputation XIII. Reproduced in translation in *The Ethics of War: Classic and Contemporary Readings*, ed. Gregory M. Reichberg, Henrik Syse and Endre Begby (Oxford: Blackwell, 2006), pp. 339-70.

problem presented by the violation of this law." Niebuhr concedes at this point that a Christian pacifism is possible that does not rest on the assumption that human moral effort can deal with the problem of sin. But such pacifism is not set forth as a political alternative. It does not labor under the illusion that the sinfulness of political life could be overcome if only we obeyed the law of love. Rather, in striving to achieve a standard of perfect love in individual life, the pacifism proposed by Menno Simons, for example, seeks only to offer a symbol of the Kingdom of God. It seeks to remind the Christian community "that the relative norms of social justice, which justify both coercion and resistance to coercion, are not final norms, and that Christians are in constant peril of forgetting their relative and temporal character and of making them too completely normative." "There is thus," Niebuhr writes, "a Christian pacifism which is not a heresy":[18]

> Yet most modern forms of Christian pacifism are heretical. Presumably inspired by the Christian Gospel, they have really absorbed the Renaissance faith in the goodness of [humanity], have rejected the Christian doctrine of original sin as an outmoded bit of pessimism, have reinterpreted the Cross so that it is made to stand for the absurd idea that perfect love is guaranteed a simple victory over the world, and have rejected all other profound elements of the Christian Gospel as "Pauline" accretions which must be stripped from the "simple gospel of Jesus."[19]

To believe that human sin can be overcome by a more persuasive preaching of the law of love is "to believe something to which experience does not conform." The belief that human beings are essentially good at some level of their being conforms, Niebuhr contends, "neither to the New Testament's view of human nature nor yet to the complex facts of human experience."[20]

Note here Niebuhr's appeal to "the relative norms of social justice which justify both coercion and resistance to coercion." The fallen nature of this world makes it necessary for us to conduct ourselves under norms that clearly fall short of those that pertain to the kingdom of God. Coercion—more specifically war and forceful suppression of injustice—are justified in

---

[18]Ibid., pp. 9-12.
[19]Ibid., p. 12.
[20]Ibid., pp. 13-15.

the sinful world in which we now live. They are justified by the imperative to oppose sin in the name of social justice.

In proposing the need for an interim ethic, Niebuhr does not deny the uncompromising and absolute nature of Jesus' ethic. The injunctions to love one's enemy, to turn the other cheek, to put away the sword, cannot be watered down or relativized. The ethic of Jesus is "finally and ultimately normative" and yet, Niebuhr contends, it is "not immediately applicable to the task of securing justice in a sinful world." Sinful human beings operate under "prudential and relative standards" and "must achieve tentative harmonies of life which are less than the best." "It is because [human beings] are sinners that justice can be achieved only by a certain degree of coercion on the one hand, and by resistance to coercion and tyranny on the other hand."[21] A distinction must be made, therefore, "between the ethic of the 'Kingdom of God,' in which no concession is made to human sin, and all relative political strategies which, assuming human sinfulness, seek to secure the highest measure of peace and justice among selfish and sinful [human beings]."[22] The pure ethic of love and nonviolence promoted by Jesus is not practical in the world that yet falls short of the kingdom of God and so must be moderated by a pragmatic ethic that accepts the need to choose the lesser of two evils.

Niebuhr thus advances what might be termed a "realpolitik," a political ethic based on practical considerations resulting in acceptance of the need to employ coercive and even violent political strategies in a world marred by sin. In the third section of this essay I will offer a critique of this claim, as also of Niebuhr's contention that Christian pacifism is naïve, idealistic and heretical. Before doing so, however, let us consider the claim Karl Barth made, like Niebuhr's, in the face of the tyranny of the Third Reich, that Christians must take up arms against such evil.

In 1941, at the invitation of A. R. Vidler and J. H. Oldham, Karl Barth wrote a letter to his fellow Christians in Great Britain in which he urged them to cooperate in the conduct of the war against Germany. The war against Hitler, said Barth, must be waged "with determination and vigour"[23]

---

[21]Ibid., pp. 16-17, 23.
[22]Ibid., p. 19.
[23]Karl Barth, *A Letter to Great Britain from Switzerland* (London: Sheldon Press, 1941), p. 5.

not because it is simply a necessary evil, but because it is a "righteous war, which God does not simply allow, but which he commands us to wage." Although, Barth says, "we long from the bottom of our hearts for conditions which will allow us [human beings] to exist and to live *for* one another, without being forced to exist and to live *in conflict with* one another," and although "we deeply deplore that war must be waged today ... we must not overlook the fact that this war is being fought for a cause which is worthy to be defended by all the means in our power—even by war; and, further, that this cause could no longer be defended by any other means than war."[24] Barth is clearly suggesting here that the war against Hitler's Germany was a war to be fought in obedience to God. It was, he says, a "righteous" war (*einen rechten Krieg*).[25] Barth does not come lightly to this position. He accepts the force of the pacifist argument in most other cases:

> Theoretically both governments and peoples could always settle their national, territorial, economic and strategic aspirations and claims by other than military action; and probably most of the wars which in the past have been waged for such reasons were not necessary—the war of 1914–18 included. But the war which was declared in September, 1939, is not being waged about such things, and it could not therefore be avoided. It is this that renders the pacifist argument unrealistic.[26]

The decisive difference in 1939 and the threat that had to be opposed under the command of God, "was the attempt by Adolf Hitler to force his 'New Order' on Central Europe to-day, on the whole of Europe tomorrow, and on the whole world the day after tomorrow. The essence of this 'New Order' is the assertion of the sovereignty of the German race and State, which in practice is that of the German Führer."[27] The basic question in this war, Barth continues, "was and is the very simple and practical one: Is it right or wrong to exalt, or even to admit, 'the Revolution of Nihilism' as the

---

[24]Ibid., pp. 4-5.

[25]The German original is available at The Digital Karl Barth Library, which takes the text in turn from *Ein Brief aus der Schweiz nach Großbritannien, 1941* in *Eine Schweizer Stimme: 1938–1945* (Zurich: Theologischer Verlag, 1985).

[26]Barth, *A Letter to Great Britain from Switzerland*, p. 5. Barth's respect for the pacifist position *in most cases* is reiterated in *Church Dogmatics*, III/4 §55.2, "The Protection of Life" (Edinburgh: T&T Clark, 1961).

[27]Barth, *A Letter to Great Britain from Switzerland*, p. 6.

ruling principle of conduct." When Christians are confronted with the question of whether they ought to defend the right against this wrong, "we can only answer 'Yes.'" "[I]t is the clear will of God that we should recognize the true nature and power of the movement, in order to combat it with all our strength. The obedience of the Christian to the clear will of God compels him to support this war."[28] In a letter addressed to "the French Protestants" in 1939, Barth wrote, "Our generation would be answerable before God and before men if the attempt were *not* made to put an end to the menace of Hitler."[29]

Having asserted the divine imperative to engage in the war, Barth proceeds to outline the basis for his certainty. He begins precisely where all Christian ethics should begin, with the resurrection of Jesus from the dead. The resurrection establishes a new order. It signals the defeat of sin and death and the disarming of the principalities and powers. The resurrection means that sin and death and demonic power have no future. The world "has not been given up to the devil" but has been consecrated to God's purpose. The present age, says Barth, "is the time of God's long-suffering until the day when . . . Jesus Christ shall come again in His glory."[30] The completion of God's purpose is, however, assured precisely because the forces of evil gathered at Calvary could not defeat the divine verdict that the creature shall have life.[31] To allow, then, the evil powers to advance unrestrained, to allow the forces of death to hold sway, would be to grant them a power that they do not have, and this, says Barth, would be a denial of the lordship of Christ and of God's victory over death in the resurrection of Christ. "It is precisely Christian thought which insists that resistance should be offered."[32]

This is a very powerful argument with considerable theological merit. But the question arises, what form should resistance take? Can it be theologically defensible to resist evil by inflicting death and destruction upon the enemy? Can we human beings take the power of life and death into our hands? Are

---

[28]Ibid., pp. 7-9.

[29]Ibid., p. 33. The letter to the French Protestants is published as an appendix in *A Letter to Great Britain from Switzerland*.

[30]Ibid., p. 9.

[31]This affirmation is taken from Oliver O'Donovan, but I think it serves well here as a paraphrase of Barth's view. See O'Donovan, *Resurrection and Moral Order: An Outline for Evangelical Ethics* (Grand Rapids: Eerdmans, 1986), p. 14.

[32]See Barth, *A Letter to Great Britain from Switzerland*, pp. 10-11.

there times when we must transgress against the commandment, "you shall not kill"? Barth does not address this question directly in his letter to Great Britain. He argues, however, that the state, in whom is vested the power of the sword, is a legitimate instrument of God's purpose charged with defending "the bounds between Right and Wrong by the threat and by the actual use of the sword."[33] Drawing on Romans 13, particularly verses 4 and 6, Barth contends that God has instituted the state and has entrusted it with the sword precisely to guard against the chaos into which sin threatens to plunge us. Respecting this divine appointment of the state, Christians are bound "to pray that the State may be a righteous one," and they "must work wholeheartedly to this end."[34]

Specific and extensive reflection on the commandment "Thou shalt not kill" is offered by Barth in *Church Dogmatics* III/4. He begins with the fundamental affirmation that, "Human life—one's own and that of others—belongs to God. It is His loan and blessing. For God has unequivocally and fully accepted it in Jesus Christ, in the incarnation of His Word. Therefore respect is due to it, and, with respect, protection against each and every callous negation and destruction."[35]

Immediately, however, Barth offers a qualification. The life to be protected under the injunction of the commandment is temporal life. "It is not divine life but creaturely. It is not the eternal life promised to [human beings]." The life with which we are concerned here "has no absolute greatness or supreme value" in itself. The imperative to protect human life, therefore, does not arise from some absolute value or quality of the life itself but rather from the command of God. Barth continues,

> since human life is of relative greatness and limited value, its protection may also consist *ultima ratione* in its surrender and sacrifice. In certain circumstances, should the commanding of God so will it, it may have to break and discontinue the defense of life in which it should present itself until this boundary is reached. This will be the case only, but then in all seriousness, when God as the Lord of life so wills it.[36]

---

[33]Ibid., p. 14. The same point is made in the letter to the French Protestants: "It is the command of God that justice be done on earth: it is precisely for this purpose that God has instituted the State and given to it the sword" (p. 34).

[34]Ibid., pp. 13-14.

[35]Barth, *CD* III/4, p. 397.

[36]Ibid., pp. 397-98.

Barth here contends *against* the principle that human life is to be protected at all costs. Many of us will be willing to accept this point, at least in some cases, notably, for instance, in the case of a terminally ill patient who could be kept alive by medical interventions of various kinds, some of them painful, unpleasant and undignified, but for whom the withdrawal of such life-protecting mechanisms may be judged the most humane and merciful course of action.[37] Protection of life "at all costs" in such cases would seem to violate rather than uphold God's good purposes for the person concerned. We may, instead, gratefully surrender such a life into the hands of God. If we are to concede the principle that in some *exceptional* cases life should not be protected "at all costs," then we must pay careful and prayerful attention to the question, In which other particular circumstances might the relinquishing of our responsibility to protect life lead to a greater good in conformity with the purpose of God and thus, perhaps, be commanded by God? Taking up arms against Hitler was argued by Barth to be one such case. He emphasizes, however, that such a course can be taken only in the most exceptional cases "with the greatest reserve" and "on the exhaustion of all other possibilities."[38]

Barth is clear too that war is terrible. There is no point in concealing the fact, he says, "that the soldier i.e., the fighting civilian, stands in direct proximity to the executioner." And further, "The fact is that war is for most people a trial for which they are no match, and from the consequences of which they can never recover." War, in other words, does irreparable damage not only to those who are defeated in war but also to those who triumph. "Since all this is incontestable," Barth says, "can [war] and should [war] nevertheless be defended and ventured?"[39] He responds to begin with, "All affirmative answers to the question are wrong if they do not start with the assumption that the inflexible negative of pacifism has almost infinite argu-

---

[37]This is my example, not Barth's, but Barth himself, after stating his unequivocal opposition to euthanasia (*CD* III/4, pp. 423-27), does concede that the withholding of life-prolonging medical interventions might be an exceptional case, allowing us to relinquish the responsibility to protect life.

[38]Ibid., p. 398. One of the critiques offered against Barth by John Howard Yoder is that "there is no written evidence to show [that all other possibilities had been examined] when Barth decided that war was necessary in 1939 and 1940." See John Howard Yoder, *Karl Barth and the Problem of War* (Nashville: Abingdon, 1970), p. 87.

[39]Barth, *CD* III/4, p. 454.

ments in its favour and is almost overpoweringly strong."[40] For Christians, Barth seems to be saying, the pacifist position must be the norm. The burden of proof rests upon those who contend in particular circumstances that war is now the required last resort. The church and theology is responsible for again and again making clear that war can never be the norm; it can only ever be an exceptional last resort, justifiable only in the very darkest of days.[41]

The one case in which war may be justified, Barth contends, is "when a state has to defend within its borders the independence which it has serious grounds for not surrendering." Or, "when a state which is not itself directly threatened or attacked considers itself summoned by the obligation of a treaty or in some other way to come to the aid of a weaker neighbour which does actually find itself in this situation." To put this more plainly, a state is justified in going to war when its independence is under threat from an evil and demonic order directly in conflict with the new order established by the resurrection of Jesus from the dead. Such a threat was present, Barth argued, in the case of Nazi Germany. There are serious theological grounds, based on the resurrection of Jesus from the dead, for a state's refusing to surrender its independence to such an order. "At such a time Christian ethics can no longer be absolutely pacifist."[42] But it must remain pacifist until the very last hour, until all other options have been exhausted, and until nothing more, other than war, can be done to resist the threatening evil. Barth puts it thus:

> The Church which does not give any easy sanction to war, which constantly seeks to avert it, which is studious to avoid any general or institutional approval in principle, which proclaims peace alone as the will of God both internally and externally, which testifies to the very last against unjust reasons for war—this Church is able in a true emergency, or in the rare case of a just war, to tell men that, even though they now have to kill, they are not murderers, but may and must do the will of God in this *opus alienum* of the state.[43]

---

[40]Ibid., p. 455.
[41]Ibid., p. 456. We should note well the question by which John Howard Yoder qualifies his own critique of Barth: "Is it fair . . . to put the question, 'How can Barth justify war?' when Barth's main point is that war is almost never justifiable?" John Howard Yoder, *Karl Barth and the Problem of War*, p. 19.
[42]Barth, *CD* III/4, p. 462.
[43]Ibid., p. 464.

It is individuals, however, who must make the final decision concerning their participation or not in war. Barth defends conscription because it makes clear that the state is constituted by the participation of its citizens. The state is not an alien entity that exists over and above the individual and for which the individual bears no moral responsibility. Conscription makes clear, and properly so, that the state is a vehicle for the implementation of the citizens' collective will. Conscription forces the individual to decide one way or another whether his or her loyalty to the state, that is, to the collective sum of one's fellow citizens, must take the form of military service or conscientious objection.[44] In time of war, no one of mature age is absolved of this responsibility. The Christian is charged with upholding and defending the new order of things established in the resurrection of Jesus and with opposing any demonic order that threatens to overwhelm it. In case of war, the Christian must decide whether the state as the vehicle of the citizen's collective will is undertaking this task or not, whether it is acting in accordance with or in opposition to the purposes of God. Of course human action will always bear the mark of our fallenness. There are no pure motives, nor is there any perfect execution of our responsibility to serve the purpose of God; but *in extremis* and as a last resort, a decision had to be made that, for the sake of God's ordering of things, Hitler, for example, had to be opposed. From a Christian point of view, Barth is right; there can be no doubt about the need to oppose evil. The question is whether the bloody and destructive reality of war can ever be regarded as a legitimate and holy instrument of such opposition.

The principle to which Barth appeals, that the state has divinely bestowed authority to uphold justice and peace, has been taken up much more recently by Oliver O'Donovan in his defense of the principles of "Just War." In *The Just War Revisited* (2003), O'Donovan contends that the state has a responsibility before God to seek justice and peace and that its responsibility has sometimes to be exercised by taking up arms. Like Barth, and in contrast to Niebuhr who takes human sin as the basic fact to be reckoned with, O'Donovan begins by affirming a more fundamental fact than that of our sinfulness, namely, that "the will of God for humankind is peace." Three further propositions flow from this.

---

[44]Ibid., pp. 466-70.

First, God's peace is the original *ontological* truth of creation. We must deny the sceptical proposition that competition and what metaphysicians call "difference" are the fundamental realities of the universe, a proposition which the creation, preservation and redemption of the world make impossible to entertain. Secondly, God's peace is the goal of *history*. We must deny the supposed cultural value of war, its heroic glorification as an advancement of civilisation . . . Thirdly, God's peace is a practical demand laid upon us. We must deny any "right" to the pursuit of war, any claim on the part of a people that it may sacrifice its neighbours in the cause of its own survival or prosperity. For the gospel demands that we renounce goods that can only be won at the cost of our neighbour's good.[45]

The rejection of war, O'Donovan contends, is a "distinctively *evangelical* rejection"; that is to say, it is founded upon what God has accomplished in the death and resurrection of Christ. "Antagonistic practice was superseded by the climax of salvation-history." The reconciliation accomplished in Christ demands a revolutionary counter-praxis "revealing the unifying order of the kingdom of God." We may note here a further similarity with Barth's approach to the matter. The resurrection of Christ establishes a new order that demands of us a new praxis, the praxis of peace-making or, more particularly, "the praxis of winning peace out of opposition."[46] Then comes a crucial turn in O'Donovan's argument. "This counter-praxis," he says, "has more than one theatre":

Staged against the supportive backdrop of the community of belief and worship, it takes a pastoral shape as mutual forgiveness, by which enemies who believe the Gospel are made enemies no longer. But it must also be staged missiologically against a backdrop of unbelief and disobedience, and here it assumes the secular form of judgement — not final judgement, but judgement as the interim provision of God's common grace, promising the dawning of God's final peace. This too, is a word (not the first or last word, but an interim word) of evangelical proclamation: God has provided us a *saeculum*, a time to live, to believe and to hope under a régime of provisional judgement; here, too, it is possible to practice reconciliation, since God's patience waits, and preserves the world against its own self-destruction.[47]

---

[45]Oliver O'Donovan, *The Just War Revisited* (Cambridge: Cambridge University Press, 2003), pp. 1-2.
[46]Ibid., p. 5
[47]Ibid., p. 6.

The primary agent of this secular form of judgment allowed and, indeed, provided for under God's grace, is the state, or more particularly, its government. Because Christ reigns in heaven, and because he alone is worthy of our absolute loyalty and worship, governments, Christianly understood and in contrast to the cult of the emperor in former times, have only the responsibility of exercising judgment in conformity with the reign of Christ who alone is Lord and King.[48] Governments are established and called upon to exercise judgment in the affairs of human communities and must do so in the face of criminal action, including war. Armed conflict may be seen as an "extraordinary" extension of ordinary acts of judgment; it must be subject to the limits and disciplines of ordinary acts of judgment, and its outcome, when successful, must be "a law, which regulates relations between the parties and provides the measure for their future peace."[49] O'Donovan is here crafting a defense of the practice of "just war," although the practice proposed here is so different from the crime of war that the term war, he argues, is hardly usable. The armed conflict legitimately undertaken by governments is "a provisional witness to the unity of God's rule in the face of the antagonistic praxis of *duellum*. Yet it is no less true in this form than in any other that judgement has only the same material means available to it as crime. Armed conflict is the means it requires, because armed conflict is the means by which the crime of war is practised."[50] Just war thinking is a Christian effort to convert these material means "to the service of law-bound and obedient judgment."[51]

Employing the terminology that we have used earlier, governments are appointed on an interim basis to strive for and uphold the new order of things established in the resurrection of Christ, an order, we may say, in which the poor hear good news, the blind see, captives are freed and so on. Governments are held to account, in other words, by divine standards of justice and righteousness.[52] Governments are therefore responsible for op-

---

[48]O'Donovan attributes this idea to St. Paul. See O'Donovan's "Government as Judgment" in Oliver O'Donovan and Joan Lockwood O'Donovan, *Bonds of Imperfection: Christian Politics, Past and Present* (Grand Rapids: Eerdmans, 2004), pp. 207-24.

[49]O'Donovan, *The Just War Revisited*, p. 6.

[50]Ibid., p. 7.

[51]Ibid.

[52]O'Donovan develops this idea more extensively in *The Desire of the Nations: Rediscovering the Roots of Political Theology* (Cambridge: Cambridge University Press, 1996).

posing every demonic threat to the divine order, including the crime of war. A criminal war, I take it, is one waged with the intent of depriving others of their legitimately held territory or resources, of imposing an alien culture or rule upon others or of extending the scope of a nation's own power. In short, a criminal war is any war fought for the sake of imposing an order on others that is in conflict with God's good ordering of things revealed and established in the resurrection. In the case of criminal war, O'Donovan argues, governments either singly or collaboratively, such as may be attempted under the authority of the United Nations,[53] are called to exercise judgment against such a threat and may legitimately engage in armed conflict in order to suppress it. They must do so, however, "within a framework of human lawfulness" where such a framework is itself determined by and accountable to God's authority and God's good ordering of things. The Christian responsibility in respect of war, O'Donovan thus contends, is to ensure that war is undertaken lawfully in the service of peace rather than for selfish or demonic ends. That criterion undoubtedly rules out much of the war-making that so-called Christian nations have engaged in, but it does allow military action in opposition to the bellicose pursuit of evil ends. Like Niebuhr, O'Donovan dismisses the pacifist position as a "utopian dream" and as insufficiently attentive to the finitude and sinfulness of human life. "To demand everything," he says, "is to get nothing. We must make those gains for peace that are open to us to make. 'For God is not a God of disorder, but of peace' (1 Cor. 14:33)."[54]

III

Although none of the three theologians considered here denies that God is a God of peace or that the peaceful coexistence of God with his creatures is a defining characteristic of the promised kingdom of God, each has argued that in the context of human history peace has sometimes to be sought through non-peaceful means, that is, by taking up arms in opposition to human sinfulness and demonic ambition. War may be waged righteously, they agree, and sometimes *must* be waged in faithful service to the pur-

---

[53]On which, see Oliver O'Donovan, *The Ways of Judgment* (Grand Rapids: Eerdmans, 2005), pp. 224-27.

[54]Ibid., pp. 226, 227.

poses of God. Of the three, Barth comes most reluctantly to this view, and it is he who gives most credence to the pacifist position. War for him is clearly a departure from what is normally required of Christians. The only thing that could justify war, therefore, is not some pragmatic calculus in the midst of human history, such as is offered by Niebuhr and is favored by the just war tradition, but an extraordinary command of God.[55]

Niebuhr is, to my mind, the least persuasive of the theologians whose arguments we have considered and for three reasons: first, because of the problematic nature of Neibuhr's claim that the kingdom ethic of Jesus must be set aside in favor of a realist ethic for a sinful world; second, because of Niebuhr's misrepresentation of what a Christian pacifism entails; and third, because of a contradiction arising from his failure to follow through the implications of his claim that we live in a sinful world. Each of these problems derives from Niebuhr's point of departure. His ethical deliberations do not begin with the resurrection of Jesus from the dead, from the place where Christian ethics ought to begin, but rather from the persistent reality of human sinfulness and evil.

As we have noted, Niebuhr seeks at one level to uphold the ethic of Jesus. The injunctions to put away the sword, to love one's enemy and to turn the other cheek constitute an ethic of the kingdom of God "in which no concession is made to human sin," but, says Niebuhr, such an ethic "is not immediately applicable to the task of securing justice in a sinful world."[56] We must adopt a pragmatic and realist ethic instead. The difficulty with this position is that there is not the least support for it in the teaching of Jesus himself, nor in the strategies that Jesus adopted in opposition to evil. It suggests that the teaching of Jesus has no relevance to life in the world now and implies that Jesus himself had little awareness of the conflicted nature of our present human existence. It encourages us to delay taking up the cross, for the instruments of justice appropriate to this world are the sword and the shield. It entails that no change to our human reality has come about through the life, death and resurrection of Christ. The course of world

---

[55]John Howard Yoder claims, however, that when asked to explain how the command of God may be heard, Barth too resorts to a "pragmatic political judgment." See Yoder, *Karl Barth and the Problem of War*, pp. 113-15.

[56]Niebuhr, *Why the Christian Church Is Not Pacifist*, p. 16.

history is to be determined after all, not by the Word of God, but by the word of sinful human beings. This is not a Christian ethic, but the abandonment of Christian ethics.

A second problem is Niebuhr's misrepresentation of what Christian pacifism entails. It is, he claims, both naïve and heretical to suppose that the law of love, albeit commanded by Christ, can overcome human sinfulness. That is so far correct; human sin is not overcome by our loving more consistently. But Christian pacifism, insofar as it is Christian, does not and should not claim that if only we were more loving, evil would be brought to an end. The Christian pacifist strives to love his or her enemies and to oppose evil with love, not because "perfect love is guaranteed a simple victory," as Niebuhr alleged, but because God commands it. There is no law of historical cause and effect that will guarantee success for those who love their enemies and seek to forgive. The example of Christ, who refused the temptation of political or armed power and accepted that it would cost him his life, is to be followed not because a more satisfactory outcome is thereby assured but because it is not our will but God's that should be done. Christian obedience trusts not in a supposed law of history but in the faithfulness of God.

The third concern with Niebuhr's position is the contradiction arising from his failure to take seriously his own claim about the sinful nature of human existence. Pacifists are criticized for supposing that human action, the actions of love, can overcome evil, a supposition that Niebuhr claims is heretical; and yet he proceeds to argue that because the command of Christ is impossible to realize, we must take matters into our own hands. "It is because [human beings] are sinners," he writes, "that justice can be achieved only by a certain degree of coercion on the one hand, and by resistance to coercion and tyranny on the other hand."[57] The justice achieved in following this course will be, Niebuhr admits, a "precarious justice,"[58] leaving us in need still of God's mercy. But his recommendation is subject nevertheless to the very critique he offers against pacifism, namely that it involves the heretical supposition that human beings themselves have the capacity to defeat evil and bring about justice in the world.

Niebuhr's claim that justice can be achieved among sinful human beings

---

[57]Niebuhr, *Why the Christian Church Is Not Pacifist*, p. 23.
[58]Ibid., p. 11.

"only by a certain degree of coercion" makes light of the fact that those claiming the prerogative to employ coercive means are themselves sinners whose judgments about how much coercion is "acceptable," in the case of war especially, can rarely be relied upon. Those fighting the "just war" against Hitler, for example, ended it through a campaign of carpet-bombing across the cities of Germany and by dropping nuclear bombs on Hiroshima and Nagasaki. Defending the campaign of obliteration in Germany, Niebuhr commented, "It is not possible to defeat a foe without causing innocent people to suffer with the guilty. . . . It is not possible to engage in any act of collective evil without involving the innocent with the guilty. It is not possible to move in history without becoming tainted with guilt."[59] True though this final claim may be, the pragmatist approach comes too close here to absolving the war-makers of moral responsibility. Niebuhr's conclusions thus reflect his problematic assertion to begin with of the normativity of human sin. Christianly understood, we do better, I suggest, to resist the complacent acceptance of sin as normative. This is not at all to deny the universality of sin but to recognize, rather, that God's purpose revealed in Jesus establishes a radically different starting point for Christian ethics, namely the new creation inaugurated in and through Christ.

Oliver O'Donovan offers a more promising point of departure in the affirmation that "the will of God for humankind is peace." God's peace is "the original ontological truth of creation," "the goal of history," and "a practical demand laid upon us."[60] From there O'Donovan develops his argument that governments are charged with the responsibility of seeking and upholding peace including, where necessary, through the armed and forceful suppression of criminal acts that constitute a threat to peace.

Karl Barth offers a similar argument. The basic fact of our human situation is not the normativity of sin but the new order of righteousness and fullness of life established in the resurrection of Jesus from the dead. That is

---

[59]Niebuhr, "The Bombing of Germany," in *Love and Justice: Selections from the Shorter Writings of Reinhold Niebuhr*, ed. D. B. Robertson (New York: Meridian Books, 1967), p. 222. Cited in Keith Pavlischek, "Reinhold Niebuhr, Christian Realism, and Just War Theory: A Critique," in *Christianity and Power Politics Today: Christian Realism and Contemporary Political Dilemmas*, ed. Eric Patterson (New York: Palgrave Macmillan, 2008), pp. 53-71. Pavlischek offers further critique of Niebuhr's position.

[60]O'Donovan, *The Just War Revisited*, pp. 1-2.

the primary reality to be reckoned with in Christian ethics. Christians are called upon to act in accordance with that reality and to serve only that end. All threats to that reality, which are thereby evil and demonic, must be opposed. O'Donovan and Barth both contend, furthermore, that in some cases evil must be opposed by military action. In such *very rare* cases, Barth does not demur from calling the conflict a righteous war, a war fought on behalf of and under the command of God. O'Donovan refuses to describe a war in its totality as just or righteous, for any major historical event is "a concatenation and agglomeration of many separate actions and many varied results. . . . [W]ars as such . . . present only a great question mark, a continual invitation to reflect further on which decisions were, and which were not, justified at the time and in the circumstances." Yet war, he argues, "can be brought within the scope of the *authority* on which governments may normally call, and . . . it can be undertaken in such a manner as to *establish* justice."[61]

Barth and O'Donovan both come to the view that evil must be opposed in the name of God, if necessary, through war. Christians could not sit idly by, for instance, as Hitler undertook his program to exterminate Jews and those others he regarded as a threat to the development of a master race. Neither can Christians turn a blind eye to the genocide, torture, oppression and so on that are common realities of human history. These must be opposed. The question, however, is whether we must accept O'Donovan's contention that "judgement has only the same material means available to it as crime." Must we agree that "armed conflict is the means it requires, because armed conflict is the means by which the crime of war is practiced"?[62]

There is much in the New Testament that conflicts with O'Donovan's view. Paul's instruction, "if your enemies are hungry, feed them; if they are thirsty, give them something to drink," and his further counsel to "overcome evil with good" (Rom 12: 20, 21) sets out a clear requirement not to engage enemies on their own terms. Jesus' own instructions superseding the *lex talionis* and his repeated injunctions to forgive and to love one's enemies likewise encourage a praxis that is quite different from the conventions of a

---

[61]Ibid., pp. 13, 14.
[62]Ibid., p. 7. A claim like this suggests that an armed response should always be the first resort rather than the last in the face of armed aggression.

sinful world. The consistent theme of the New Testament's ethical advice is that a different means *is* available to and required of those who seek to live in conformity with the purposes of God.

The case in support of an alternative praxis does not rely, however, only or primarily upon bits and pieces of ethical teaching, be they dominical or apostolic, for that teaching has its basis and justification in the path that Jesus himself took in opposing human evil and sin. Christian faith holds that Jesus, the one true judge of the world's sinfulness, opposed sin and evil by taking its consequences upon himself. His opposition to sin took the form of suffering and self-sacrifice, precisely so that the lives of his enemies would be spared. "Father forgive them," he prayed, "for they know not what they do." He went his way among us, flesh of our flesh, bone of our bone, full participant in the conditions of this sinful world. In the midst of our history Jesus opposed sin and evil not by coercion as Niebuhr commends, nor, as O'Donovan says is our only option, by adopting the same material means as crime, but rather through suffering love. It is important to note that the outcome was by no means assured. Jesus did not take this path of suffering because of a naïve belief that "love is guaranteed an easy victory in the world."[63] According to the calculations of worldly success, the path Jesus chose had nothing to commend it. Jesus was bound, rather, to be just another of history's victims, overpowered and defeated by human brutality and sin. But God sided with *him*. In the raising of Jesus to new life, human brutality and evil was unmasked. They were shown to have no ultimate power. The purposes of God cannot be defeated by the worst that we do. We come again to the generative affirmation of Christian ethics: in the resurrection of Jesus from the dead a new order is established in which God's intention that the creature should have life triumphs over death and over our death dealing ways.[64]

Christians, as Barth and O'Donovan rightly point out, are called upon to live within, uphold and testify to this new ordering of things. The death and resurrection of Christ is, for Christians, the paradigm within which they are

---

[63]We here recall Niebuhr's allegation against the "naiveté" of the pacifist position.

[64]This is a point made powerfully by O'Donovan in his *Resurrection and Moral Order*. It is not clear to me how the point may be sustained while also defending the prerogative of the state to engage in warfare and killing as O'Donovan does in *The Just War Revisited*.

to think through and enact their opposition to sin and evil. One of the metaphors of atonement present in Scripture and developed by the tradition is that Jesus on the cross does battle against the forces of evil in this world. It is here that the "holy war" is waged, not with arms, but with suffering love. God's "holy war" against evil is waged through cross and resurrection by which symbols the violent are shown to have no final power. Those who *acknowledge* the crucifixion as an act of divine judgment, who testify to its saving power, and who proclaim the promise of resurrection life, are also *commissioned* to participate in this divine form of opposition to evil and sin. They are bound to be far more thoughtful than they have typically been about what love of one's enemies really entails and about the dominical command to forgive the wrong that is done.

It might be objected, and commonly is, that God in Old Testament times did sanction and even commanded the use of war to punish evil and to advance his own purposes. The texts bearing witness to God's sanctioning of war must be taken seriously, as is done elsewhere in this volume; but Christians must take more seriously still the characteristic propensity of Jesus to heighten the ethical demand, to introduce a new commandment more stringent than the old: "You have heard that it was said . . . but I say to you." And the new commandment Jesus offers, modifying the summary command of the law to love your neighbor as yourself, is to "love one another as I have loved you." Christ's love finds its fullest expression at Calvary. The battle against evil waged there sets the pattern for those who seek to love others as Christ has loved us.

Christ puts himself in the way of evil, intervenes on behalf of the oppressed and the weak and the downtrodden, not with swords and spears but by bearing the blows and not striking back. Christ confronts the cycle of violence and declares through the costly gestures of love that the violence stops with me. He suffers in his own person the wrong that is done and trusts the outcome to God. That is the pattern of obedient life that Christians are called to follow. Forgiveness, compassion and sacrifice are the tools taken up by Christ to wage war against evil and sin.[65] When instead the

---

[65]I am puzzled by O'Donovan's claim that "the cross is not the sum of how Jesus 'went about doing good'" (*The Just War Revisited*, p. 11). He offers no indication of what other features of Christ's life or teaching might justify an alternative paradigm.

followers of Christ take up arms to wage war and argue that such action is necessary, unavoidable and a last resort, they are resorting to a logic other than that of the Logos incarnate.[66] It must be confessed therefore that they (we!) have failed in the call to inhabit God's new ordering of things. By the standard of Christ's engagement with evil, war waged with the implements of violence and destruction is always a failure in Christian discipleship. Such war can never be holy.

---

[66]This is the heart of the criticism leveled against Barth by John Howard Yoder. See Yoder, *Karl Barth and the Problem of War*, pp. 111-18.

14

"HOLY WAR" AND THE
NEW ATHEISM

A Theological Response

Stephen N. Williams

———————— ✝ ————————

BEHIND HOLY WAR

"In addition to demanding that we fulfill every 'jot' and 'tittle' of Old Testament law, Jesus seems to have suggested, in John 15:6, further refinements to the practice of killing heretics and unbelievers."[1] Presumably, some readers of this essay have just anxiously suspended their reading for a minute in order to look up their Bibles, as troubled by the fact that they had never noticed this before as they are by its putative content. Picking up the New International Version (1984) and turning to the designated spot, we read that Jesus said to his disciples: "If anyone does not remain in me, he is like a branch that is thrown away and withers; such branches are picked up, thrown into the fire and burned." Of course, there are different translations. But this makes no relevant difference. It would have been one thing if Sam Harris, the New Atheist whose words I have quoted, had contented himself with wrestling over the meaning of Matthew 5:18, the verse which features the "jot and tittle" (though it does not speak of *our* fulfilling the law). Christians have themselves long pondered its meaning. But the allusion to John

---

[1]Sam Harris, *The End of Faith: Religion, Terror and the Future of Reason* (London: Simon & Schuster, 2005), p. 82.

15:6 is an unmistakable sign that we are in the realm of the bizarre and not party to a rational discussion of the Christian Scriptures. True, Harris concedes, Jesus' words could be interpreted metaphorically, but he finds little consolation in that, for the chaos of Scripture still permits a literal reading of the Johannine text which "can be used to justify atrocities in defense of the faith."[2] Actually, only something even worse than hermeneutical chaos accounts for this remark. Even if John 15:6 were interpreted literally, it would have nothing to do with killing heretics and unbelievers.

Herein lies our problem in treating "holy war" and the New Atheism. If Harris is representative of New Atheism on this point, argument is obviously futile, because those who are intellectually serious need first to be intellectually informed. Doubtless the ancient proverb that one swallow makes not a Spring is irreproachable; but biblically informed readers of the New Atheist commentators on biblical texts will scarcely doubt that Harris' comments are indeed pretty typical.[3] This feeds into the more broadly based judgment that New Atheism is a secular fundamentalism and therefore impervious to the requirements of rational exchange.[4] Should we then not apply to New Atheism the principle announced by Christopher Hitchens: "What can be asserted without evidence can also be dismissed without evidence"?[5] After all, we seem fated to trade in assertions that are not only ungrounded in evidence but also palpably false. The answer is no, we should not dismiss consideration of New Atheism on "holy war," for at least three reasons.

First, even though New Atheists themselves characteristically state their views without seriously arguing a case, they manifestly touch on issues that can and should be taken with utmost intellectual seriousness and which thoughtful atheists are entitled to bring before Christians.[6] Second, New

---

[2]Ibid., p. 83. See also Sam Harris, *Letter to a Christian Nation* (London: Bantam, 2007), p. 13.

[3]See, e.g., Christopher Hitchens, *God Is Not Great: How Religion Poisons Everything* (London: Atlantic, 2007), pp. 97-122. Picking up a remark that he makes in this book, Tina Beattie quite rightly says that "[o]ne cannot possibly have an intelligent debate with this kind of polemic, for Hitchens is so defiantly obtuse in his representation of Scripture and its role in the Christian life that there is no point of entry into a sensible and informed discussion," *The New Atheists: The Twilight of Reason and the War on Religion* (London: Darton, Longman & Todd, 2007), p. 53.

[4]In the paperback edition of *The God Delusion* (London: Bantam, 2007), pp. 18-19, Richard Dawkins saw fit to rebut this allegation.

[5]Hitchens, *God Is Not Great*, p. 150.

[6]In this essay, I confine myself to the Christian religion, although New Atheism attacks religion

Atheism is a sufficient cultural force for us to attend to it, if not on its intellectual surface, certainly on account of the psychological, moral and sociological forces which it partly represents. Third, the question of the religious
terror of "holy war" and its rooting in the biblical text has long occupied the
perplexed attention of Christians independently of atheist criticism. Even if
the intractability of the second consideration in a brief compass means that
we leave it out of account and attend only to the first and third, the simple
arithmetical mind will conclude that we have a doubly difficult theological
journey before us, and this calculation will not be far off the mark. We could
spend the whole space afforded to this essay in a reconnaissance of our
stockpile of intellectual provisions and in meticulously mapping our theological campaign (if we may deploy metaphors which risk confirming
critics convinced of Christianity's incorrigible crusading mentality).
However, we must get on with the job. My aim is not to try to persuade New
Atheists of anything, for reasons that are already clear, but to attempt to
think about "holy war" from a Christian point of view against the background of their criticisms.[7]

New Atheists make a number of points in connection with "holy war"
and, as we should expect, prominent amongst them is reference to the great
number of religious or religiously inspired conflicts in the historical fore-
ground and to the warfare celebrated in the Christian Scriptures in the
theological background.[8] But the principal objection pivots on the point
that dogmatic religious conviction, irrationally maintained, breeds violence.
Here New Atheists take up, as a matter of urgency, concerns that were
dawning upon conscientious European thinkers in the aftermath of the

---

more broadly. Unfortunately, the fact that professional philosophers such as A. C. Grayling and
Daniel Dennett could seriously commend Hitchens's *God Is Not Great* for being "razor-sharp"
or "trenchant" (see the blurb on the back jacket) demonstrates that the atheistic philosopher is
not necessarily the thoughtful atheist. See the comments by Michael Ruse quoted in Alister
McGrath with Joanna C. McGrath, *The Dawkins Delusion: Atheist Fundamentalism and the
Denial of the Divine* (London: SPCK, 2007), p. 26. An observation by Ruse appears on the front
cover of this book.

[7]See too the poignant record of Tina Beattie's conversation with Keith Ward, *The New Atheists*, p.
16. For why persuasion is impossible here, see Terry Eagleton's conclusion to his devastating
study of *Reason, Faith and Revolution: Reflections on the God Debate* (New Haven, CT: Yale
University Press, 2009), p. 168.

[8]The works cited above, by Harris, Dawkins and Hitchens all address these questions. I am unable to discuss in this essay the specific question of anti-Semitism, which features in New Atheist polemics.

centuries of the Reformation and the Thirty Years' War. Contemporary theologians are amongst those who are persuaded that the rise of European secularism is largely accounted for by the strife of this period.[9] At the time when religious bitterness and bloodshed were staining the European scene, texts of ancient Skeptics from the pre-Christian Classical world were being republished.[10] Skeptics who proposed that nothing could be known were trumped by other skeptics who responded that this proposal was dogmatic, for it advances the dogmatic and non-skeptical claim that nothing can be known. The consistent skeptic will say that we cannot know whether or not anything can be known. At first glance, all this might appear to be no more than standard fare in the philosophy classroom, but it was productive of a culturally momentous contribution. For if, at a time when feuding religious dogmatisms litter the European stage, you publish the reasoned philosophical enquiries of those who ask whether we can know anything, a diagnosis of the contemporary social malaise seems now to be ready at hand: the problem is that everyone thinks that he (literally "he") knows more than he does. The cure follows: a little less religious dogmatism will surely mean a little more social peace. New Atheists take up this line of thought with ostentatious moral fervor and plenty of verve.

The underlying problem, as they present it, lies with the bare form of religious conviction, whatever its substantive content.[11] To adhere to religious convictions dogmatically and baselessly spells trouble, whatever those convictions may be. Now Christians will be predictably surprised to learn that those who follow the way of Jesus Christ should be viewed as little cauldrons of violence. We thought that the way of Jesus was the way of suffering and the cross, and that we were supposed to be poor in spirit, mourning, meek, hungering and thirsting for righteousness, merciful, pure in heart, peacemaking, ready to endure persecution and bless those who persecute us. We know that, all too often, we are not like this; lament that we are not more like this; agree that, when we are unlike this, we may well be agents of violence and not of peace and thus deserve the opprobrium that this brings

---

[9]For a short statement, see, e.g., Wolfhart Pannenberg, *Christianity in a Secularized World* (London: SCM, 1988), chapter 1, pp. 3-19.

[10]R. H. Popkin, *The History of Scepticism from Erasmus to Spinoza* (Berkeley: University of California Press, 1979).

[11]But see Sam Harris's positive remarks on Jainism, *The End of Faith*, p. 108, for example.

upon us. But it does not help the New Atheist case if we admit that we frequently behave differently in practice from what our principles require. For its problem lies not with an inconsistent Christianity, but with consistent Christianity. *Qua* baseless and groundless creed, even a substantively pacific Christianity is dangerous.[12] The irrational foundation and dogmatic form of Christianity are the twin generators of the evil of religious war.

More than one response is possible to the charge of epistemological irresponsibility, and Christian thinkers have repeated them time and time again. Whatever line we take, the fact is that faith is simply (and, it seems, willfully) misunderstood in New Atheist writing. The production of the Gospels embraced the express design of showing that the Christian movement was grounded in the testimony of eyes, ears and touch (see 1 Jn 1:1), and it is unsurprising that the father of modern philosophical empiricism, John Locke, put Christianity to the empirical test and was persuaded by it.[13] Whatever should be challenged either in the foundations or the adumbration of his philosophy, he certainly understood the store which Christianity set by the historical-empirical domain from its very inception. In the light of the allegation that Christianity makes a virtue of blind faith, it is scarcely stretching matters to say that, in the prologue to his Gospel, Luke informs his reader that he wrote precisely because it was better not to believe something just because you had been taught to believe it and that, instead, the grounds of faith must be investigated (Lk 1:1-4). Obviously this does not of itself mean that Luke's account is reliable or that he was not weaving fables under the cover of empirical pretence, but the foundational documents of Christianity (for here Luke is representative) inform us about the kind of faith which it aspires to promote and to instill.[14] Of course, the

---

[12]By "pacific" is not meant "pacifist," even though many Christians are pacifists as a matter of theological principle. What is undeniable is that the teaching of Jesus conduces to a pacific disposition.

[13]See Locke's *The Reasonableness of Christianity as Delivered in the Scriptures*, ed. J. Higgins-Biddle (New York: Oxford University Press, 1999) against the background of his *Essay on Human Understanding*, ed. P. Nidditch (Oxford: Clarendon, 1975), especially IV.14 onward.

[14]For an example of how Dawkins's argument on the biblical texts cannot be taken seriously, see his contrast between Doubting Thomas and the other disciples in a passage where he chastises biblically-based Christianity for the ideal of blind faith: *The Selfish Gene* (Oxford: Oxford University Press, 2006), p. 198. According to Dawkins, Thomas needed evidence, whereas the apostles did not. According to John's account, Thomas is chastised because the apostles advanced their testimony precisely because they had evidence and Thomas refused testimony based on evidence!

Gospels' testimony is undergirded by belief in the existence of God, but rational arguments for that too have long been advanced, even where those who advance them find no reason to doubt the basic validity of Israel's religious experience. New Atheists may dismiss the arguments and Christians themselves differ on their validity or force, but what Christianity certainly does not do is to commend the virtue of blind faith.

Discussion of the grounds of Christian belief lies outside the boundaries of this essay, but it is important to touch on this issue because it takes us to the foundations of New Atheist interpretations of the roots of Christian violence. There is no reason whatsoever to accept the New Atheist claim that the epistemological form of Christian religious conviction is warped in the alleged manner, its blind irrationality breeding a violence that overrides the pacific content on its luminous surface. Of course, dogmatism and irrationality are not the same thing; a belief may be irrational without being dogmatic and dogmatic without being irrational. Supposing, then, we affirm that Christian faith does not celebrate the virtue of groundlessness, can Christianity nevertheless be successfully indicted by New Atheism on the charge of harboring a dogmatism which is a menace to world peace? In moving from the question of the foundation to the question of the form of belief, we are bound also to slide into the question of content, for the allegation is that Christians are exclusivists and that its narrow dogmatism is expressed at the very substantive core of its belief: "The central tenet of every religious tradition is that all others are mere repositories of error or, at best, dangerously incomplete."[15] If this is so, we may parade the vestiges of rationality in the Christian tradition and trumpet its principles of peace, but our attitude toward "the other" will remain a source of strife. Currently in theological circles there is much debate on nonviolent atonement and although the concept of "the other" can function rather technically in this context, it can also be interpreted generally: traditional views of the atonement, portraying a wrathful God doing violence to his Son are allegedly pregnant with undesirable social consequences toward "the other," with their valorizing glorification of suffering.[16] The issues that arise here

---

[15]Harris, *The End of Faith*, p. 13.
[16]See the discussion, e.g., in Brad Jersak and Michael Hardin, eds., *Stricken by God? Nonviolent Identification and the Victory of Christ* (Grand Rapids: Eerdmans, 2007).

are not at all distinct from those which exercise New Atheism, but we cannot pursue them at present.[17] Atonement aside, how do things stand with Christianity as regards exclusion of the other? Are we in the realm of hostile dogmatism?

Here again, New Atheists fail to understand Christianity. What Christians have traditionally believed is that there is a God who made the world in such a way that he could enter into it in his own person, a feat which presents no problem for its Creator. Further, they hold that the human plight is such that the supreme expression of the Creator's love and will to put things right is entry into that world in the form of incarnation. To identify with the human condition to the uttermost, which is the work of love, entails being human and being human means, by definition, inhabiting one earthly space and time. So to become human is to become, by necessity, subject to the constraints of a particular space and time. To be human is to belong of necessity to a lineage, people or culture one way or another. So God's way into the world requires the preparation of a people to whom the Son will belong; the election of Israel is the expression of a maximally inclusivist intention.[18] God's inclusivist agenda is signified by two things: a Bible which is translatable so that there is no sacred and esoteric language of revelation, and a missionary task which is universal so that none should be deprived of the knowledge of God's way of salvation. The question of whether eschatological salvation is the privilege only of those who have heard the news of Jesus Christ has long been debated and a variety of views on it reside within the Christian church. Despite its importance, it is a question that joins the list of questions acknowledged but set aside in this essay. Let us, however, be sure to grasp the inner logic of so-called exclusivism. Christian belief in incarnation, atonement and resurrection does not for one moment entail that there is no truth outside Christianity, and wherever such truth is found it will be celebrated. It entails only that God with and for us in incarnation, atonement and resurrection could

---

[17]Richard Dawkins describes "atonement, the central doctrine of Christianity, as vicious, sadomasochistic and repellent," not to mention "barking mad," *The God Delusion*, p. 287.

[18]The word *inclusivist* here is not used in the particular sense that it bears in the context of debate on Christianity and other religious traditions but in the wider sense of God's aspiration to include humanity in his redeeming action.

have been embodied only in one space and time.[19] To derive from this outlook a principle of excluding hostility toward those who are not Christian is to get things as completely the wrong way round as is possible.[20]

GOD OF "HOLY WAR"

Attention is often drawn to the fact that 9/11 has generated or fueled much New Atheist writing, even if publications such as those by Richard Dawkins were earlier than that. Islam is not taken into account in the present essay; but the Christian New Testament is bound with the Hebrew Scriptures into the one Christian Bible and therein, it appears, lies the problem. Not all warfare is of the same kind in the Old Testament, but the designation "holy war" will be understood in the context of New Atheist critiques to embrace all that goes on in the killing fields in the name of Yahweh. It seems that the New Testament cannot innocently distance itself from what we read there: witness the book of Revelation and other passages, which indicate divine eschatological judgment. As other essays in this collection focus on these materials, the following remarks are general in relation to the biblical text. "Holy war" is a horizontal horror within history, but New Atheists naturally indicate that immediately behind and accounting for it lies the vertical terror which instigates it: God. The first sustained biblical quotation by Sam Harris in *The End of Faith* picks out some violent injunctions in Deuteronomy that constitute Moses' felicitous legacy to the people of Israel, commanding and not just commending intolerance and mercilessness.[21] Christians worship *this* God? Christians *worship* this God?[22]

At the time that this essay goes to press, I have lived in Northern Ireland for over eighteen years and gazed at chilling Protestant murals applying to the Republican, Nationalist or Catholic enemy the solemn Mosaic words

---

[19]Christians do not believe in reincarnation, so a self-identical human being cannot be the subject of multiple incarnations on this earth. Even if the hypothesis were floated, in the desire to show that a nonexclusive God could have appeared in history several times, an individual corporeal being could only occupy one space at any one time, so almost all of the world almost all of the time would lack the proximate presence of God incarnate.

[20]It is most regrettable that in his most recent work Jürgen Moltmann succumbs to a cognate misrepresentation of Christian attitudes, *Sun of Righteousness, Arise! God's Future for Humanity and the Earth* (Minneapolis: Fortress, 2010), pp. 142-48.

[21]Harris, *The End of Faith*, p. 18; cf. Harris, *Letter to a Christian Nation*, p. 82.

[22]However, it is unclear to what extent Richard Dawkins believes that Jesus is the opposite of Yahweh in *The God Delusion*, pp. 51-52.

which enjoin extermination of the Canaanite. No one who has seen them can pass glibly over New Atheist criticism. Yet as far as biblical readers are concerned, puzzlement should precede the excoriation of Yahweh. For the God depicted on the pages that begin the Judeo-Christian Scriptures is one who grieves over the incidence of violence. Correspondingly, what delights him and what he purposes to establish is the prospect of *shalom*, proclaimed particularly by the prophets. Jesus is regarded in the New Testament as the fulfillment of prophetic hope. The biblical narrative recounts God's instigation of a counter-violence in the form of the flood and the occupation of Canaan. Israel fights wars and the dénouement of world history is apocalyptically imagined in the book of Revelation. Summarily stated: the flood is a judicial execution portrayed as exceptional; following it, and by way of divine response to the actuality of human violence, the judicial taking of life for life in post-Noahic human community is sanctioned. The extermination of Canaanites is also a judicial matter, exceptionally inserted into world history, evil being so rife in that land that it will vomit out its inhabitants (Lev 18:25). The wars of the Israelite monarchy are canonically presented in terms of an accommodation to the people's desire for a king who will behave according to the pattern of other kings (1 Sam 8:1-23). The apocalyptic imagery of the book of Revelation must be interpreted not only by grasping the genre of apocalypse but also from a hermeneutical center in the revelation of God in Jesus Christ seen, heard and handled.[23] Whatever accounts for the canonical shaping of Scripture, I am simply delineating here, with the exception of the comment on Revelation, the shape in which it has been received in the church.

What are we to make of this? Divine action in history is properly the theme of theological description, dissection and discussion point by point, but all thought of God is distasteful to New Atheists, never mind any attempt

---

[23]Friedrich Nietzsche has not been alone in regarding the book of Revelation as "the wildest of all outbursts ever written which revenge has on its conscience," *On the Genealogy of Morality*, trans. C. Diethe (Cambridge: Cambridge University Press, 1994), I.16. I am particularly indebted to the work of Richard Bauckham in this area, including his general study of *The Theology of the Book of Revelation* (Cambridge: Cambridge University Press, 1993). Colossal ignorance of the nature of this book accompanies the confident castigation of its violence in such works as Charles B. Strozier, David M. Terman and James W. Jones, eds., *The Fundamentalist Mindset: Psychological Perspectives on Religion, Violence, and History* (Oxford: Oxford University Press, 2010), including chapter 10.

to account for his supposed actions. "Distasteful" is an apt word. Nietzsche, fiercest of nineteenth-century critics of Christianity and massively influential on both the succeeding and the present century hitherto, made a peculiarly transparent and illuminating remark in his book *The Gay Science.*[24] "What decides against Christianity now is our taste, not our reasons."[25] One strategy for handling this is to try to make the notion of God attractive. Before Nietzsche, Schleiermacher, for example, had attempted this.[26] Whether or not it was an enterprise well-advised in his own day or is well-advised in ours, it will obviously make little headway in the circles most affected by and reflected in New Atheism. Even so, we should approach "holy war" not by scrutinizing "holy war," but by asking about the God who was behind it. Suppose I detest George Bush and oppose his action in Iraq. If you are in favor of his action—whether or not you dislike the man—you might try to persuade me that military intervention was justified. But as long as I hate the man, I will not easily be swayed. If you are an intellectually effective advocate and I am not entirely immune to rational exchange, I might grudgingly concede that it is remotely and marginally conceivable, perhaps, that a sane person could just about see it your way; but it will take only the slightest tip of the balance of the argument, a barely perceptible chink in your reasoning, to send me scurrying back to unqualified opposition. For I do not like Bush and am not disposed to give him the benefit of the doubt in respect of any of his actions. It would all look very different if I liked Bush. I might like him but disagree with his action in Iraq; still, in that case, I should be disposed in spirit to give a sympathetic hearing to the case on his behalf. As New Atheists detest the God in whose existence they do not believe, they will not be disposed to listen to explanations of "holy war." Yet it is with God that everything in theology, as in life, starts and ends. If we fix our eyes on the wars, they may perplex us and perhaps lead us to conclude that we should dissociate the New Testament from the Hebrew Scriptures at this point, judging the witness of the latter a product of human misperception of God corrected

---

[24] I refer to it by this title in deference to a widespread convention, but "gay" no longer bears the meaning that it does in the title of Nietzsche's book, where "merry" or "joyous" is meant.

[25] Friedrich Nietzsche, *The Gay Science*, ed. Bernard Williams (Cambridge: Cambridge University Press, 2001), III.132.

[26] Friedrich Schleiermacher, *On Religion: Speeches to Its Cultured Despisers*, ed. R. Crouter (Cambridge: Cambridge University Press, 1996).

in the New Testament. Perhaps we shall recall in this context Jesus' rebuke to his disciples when they entertained the prospect of a fire from heaven breaking forth in judgment on Samaritan unbelief.[27] But, irrespective of whether we eventually subscribe to this familiar outlook and whatever we conclude on the question of the relations between Old and New Testaments, we surely approach the question of "holy war" most helpfully by reflecting on the nature of God himself as portrayed within their pages. To repeat: in the context of New Atheism and of the Hebrew Scriptures, by "holy war" we mean those wars of Israel fought in the name of Yahweh.

What attributes of God, in connection with "holy war," most revolt New Atheists? Two are obvious: power and vengefulness. What is problematic about God is not sheer power, although that is bad enough; it is power exercised in conjunction with his self-appointed role as judge of human life.[28] Presumably, Christian and atheist will agree that we self-regarding human beings disposed to describe ourselves as "enlightened" typically want to be free to think and do as we wish. So we find the thought of being judged anathema. When power is further conjoined with vengefulness, we have an intolerable situation. This is what we are up against when Israel's martial actions are not only sanctioned but commanded. This all-powerful judge, who, just by virtue of this very description, sounds portentously like a character bordering on the vindictive, is demonstrably vindictive when he breaks out in an orgy of violence toward those who do not worship him.

What are we to make of the notions of divine power and of vindictiveness expressed in this response and informing our horrified judgments about "holy war"? One of the most famous axioms in twentieth-century theology is that of Dietrich Bonhoeffer: "Only the suffering God can help."[29]

---

[27] According to Oliver O'Donovan, "[t]here is, in Jesus' own references to Elijah, more than a hint of criticism of the holy war conceptions that the prophet attempted to restore (*e.g.*, Lk 9.52-26)," *Resurrection and Moral Order: An Outline for Evangelical Ethics* (Leicester, UK: Inter-Varsity Press, 1986), pp. 158-59.

[28] See the "New Atheist" discussion offered by Daniel C. Dennett, *Breaking the Spell: Religion as a Natural Phenomenon* (New York: Allen Lane, 2006), especially chap. 8. Would Dennett be so upset by God's knowledge if he simply thought about God knowing about and seeing all the good things that we think that we have done? For the importance of omniscience in this connection, see Stephen N. Williams, *The Shadow of the Antichrist: Nietzsche's Critique of Christianity* (Grand Rapids: Baker, 2006), pp. 173-74.

[29] This and the following references are from the letter of 16 July 1944 in *Letters and Papers from Prison* (London: SCM, 1971), pp. 357-63.

This God "lets himself be pushed out of the world on to the cross." Bon-hoeffer's portrayal is one-sided, neglecting the connection of the Matthean text which he quotes (Mt 8:17) with the story of powerful signs and wonders in the ministry of Jesus and of the early apostles. However, his remark has a significant purchase on theological truth. "Anyone who has seen me has seen the Father" (Jn 14:9 NIV). We see in Jesus Christ an unfathomable ex-tremity of suffering. The suffering is not only the suffering of the cross in its uniquely atoning nature; the Matthean text which occasioned Bonhoef-fer's observation highlights, in connection with Jesus' healing ministry, the prophetic anticipation that "He took up our infirmities and carried our diseases." The suffering of Jesus Christ is exemplary for the disciple's suf-fering (1 Pet 2:21). In reading these passages, we are acutely aware of the distinction between the former (old) and the latter (new) dispensation; to this kind of suffering and weakness the "heroes" of the Old Testament were not summoned.[30]

This might strike us as affording an adequate platform from which to confess our beliefs: we can respond to the New Atheist revulsion toward "holy war" by sharing its moral reaction, by proceeding to pronounce it a thing of the past, which can pose no threat in the third millennium. For whatever else we say about it, we can be sure that it belongs generically to a pre-Christian dispensation. Is this an adequate response? There is certainly some truth in it, as far as the theological claim is concerned, that mandates to go to war in the name of God belong to a bygone era.[31] This is a case which surely can be made compellingly enough.[32] But supposing we wanted to go a step further and embrace this response wholeheartedly, including the terms of its moral reaction, would that response be adequate? A re-

---

[30]This is obviously not to gainsay the experience of figures such as Jeremiah and Hosea.

[31]By "going to war in the name of God" I do not have in mind here cases where religious reasons might be given for supporting a war which has absolutely nothing to do with religion. David Martin, in his fine book, *Does Christianity Cause War?* (Oxford: Oxford University Press, 1997) rightly raises the question of New Atheist attitudes to religion and just war today (p. 97). As the reader will have guessed, we encounter here yet another subject which lies outside the scope of our discussion. Yet important questions arise here about precisely how we conceptualize the range of "religious" or "holy" wars described in the Old Testament.

[32]See J. Gordon McConville and Stephen N. Williams, *Joshua* (Grand Rapids: Eerdmans, 2010), pp. 108-24. The argument offered in these pages has been adapted in "Could God Have Commanded the Slaughter of the Canaanites?" *Tyndale Bulletin* 63, no. 2 (November 2012): 161-78.

joinder that it remains inadequate could be offered along the following lines. We must make not only the dispensation and the morality a thing of the past, but the God of Old Testament power a God of the past, if he is truly to pose no threat in the third millennium. While the God of the Old Testament lingers, we cannot sleep safely at night. Someone will come up with the exceptional case: granted that the days of the Old Testament are generally over; nevertheless, there is the odd occasion when a little holy hacking is in religious order. And so the Old Testament terror is upon us again because the Supreme Terrorist is still abroad, like Communist politicians from before the 1990s who have morphed into democratic appearances in the new order, but whose character remains unchanged. On this reasoning, even if New Atheism is mistaken in judging followers of Jesus a constitutional threat to world safety, we cannot allay fears that as long as they refuse to disown the Old Testament God, they might (with theological consistency) launch the odd attempt at the extermination of Muslims, atheists or assorted unbelievers. Is this right? Do we need a radical break not only with the Old Testament dispensation and not even just with Old Testament morality but also with the Old Testament God?

The theological question of the relation between Old and New Testament haunts us here, just as it has exercised the church since its beginning, and it will not go away just because we must banish it from discussion, along with so much else, on the grounds that it is too big to handle. However our first port of call, I believe, is to seek to understand the ways of God in the Old Testament; he cannot well be banished (more than supported) until we have done this. This is the Creator God, who saw that creation was good and that the sum of its good constituent parts or principle of its formation was "very good" (Gen 1:31). The devastation wrought upon its summation, humanity, by the fratricidal outbreak of inter-human violence causes grief to God. It is under that sign that we are obligated to read everything that follows. God takes no joy in the flood, nor in the revision of the creation provision in relation to animals and the institution of a penal code (Gen 9:1-7). We are now in the world of divine concession, of an accommodation in its way distasteful to God as are those human ways which have called it forth. Behind the violence of Cain lies the unfathomable mystery of evil— the inexplicable presence of theophobic malice in Eden in the form of the

snake, and the success, not much less mysterious, of the serpent in per-
suading Eve, who persuades Adam, to take the serpentine rather than divine
route through life. The story practically announces the inextricability of the
metaphysical knot which is the problem of evil. It is not a problem foisted
on Judeo-Christianity from outside itself but a problem paraded early from
within the pages of its Scriptures. The very fact of creation entails the theoretical possibility of the creature's turning away from the Creator, for creation is other than the Creator and can be regarded by the supremely con-
scious form of that creation—humanity—independently of the Creator.
Given human freedom, the possibility is not just purely theoretical. We
know that it has been actualized. None of this illuminates the fact or force
of evil, a phenomenon dark to the point of impenetrability.

In accordance with terms on which he has set up the created order, God
takes neither of two paths. On the one hand, creation and creature are not
utterly destroyed. On the other, the creature is not given untrammeled
liberty to act *etsi deus non daretur*, as though God were now in permanent
deistic retirement.[33] If the *causes* of evil action in the world lie not in God
but in humanity, the Old Testament speaks of a God who may nonetheless
direct its *courses* so that they serve some purpose. This does not warrant the
conclusion that every evil has its purpose. It does not constitute a simple
and felicitous theological resolution. It entails only that God may use what
is already there to accomplish intentions which he continues to entertain in
relation to the world. It entails that where God is supposed to have commanded slaughter, if it was indeed commanded, it can only have been commanded with the heaviest of hearts, disposing of the human (or should we
say "male"?) propensity to violence and determining to cut its channel
rather than permitting its entirely autonomous flow and allowing violence
its own eternally autonomous integrity (if any form of *nomos* can be conceptually attributed to violence). This is the underlying theology of the Old
Testament, although it is not suggested that all the characters in its drama

---

[33]This Latin phrase about living as if there were no God was popularized by Bonhoeffer in the 16
July letter. Earlier in the letter, he remarked that the universal development towards autonomy
which was expressed in the sphere of theology went back to Herbert of Cherbury, who has often
(rightly or wrongly) been regarded as "the father of Deism." Even Deists, however, did not take
the retirement of God to mean that he did not reward the good and punish the evil; in this,
Herbert himself, in *De Veritate*, trans. M. H. Carré (Bristol: Arrowsmith, 1937) was typical.

are depicted as having seen things in this light.

The description offered here in the service of an attempt to protect us against the possibility of Christians bringing the Old Testament days back again is an alternative to driving a radical wedge between the powerful God of the Old Testament and the suffering God of the New. It involves ascribing possibility to God. This has long been a familiar position taken in modern theology. Of course it has been challenged and divine impassibility defended.[34] Obviously, it is a point that merits discussion on its own terms, as does the whole question of how God-language (including "grieving" and "commanding") applies to God. Yet even if we acquiesce in belief in divine passibility, it could be argued that the line that I have taken does not afford sufficient protection against the possibility of "holy war" today. What God once did, albeit with a heavy heart, can he not do again? Does not the very imagery of Revelation disclose that this is not an emotionally alien way of viewing God's action? The testimony of Revelation has been studiously omitted from consideration in the present discussion, but the gain of ascribing passibility to God along the lines set out above is that of conditioning from the very outset our view of his power, that vengeful power which was allegedly demonstrated in the command to kill enemies and take land. We actually have no idea of the depths of divine sorrow. We are not talking about a slight passing regret on God's part about the way things are. While the exercise of divine power in the Old Testament and the God of its wars are misunderstood, the Christian claim that those days have gone but that the God of those days remains will doubtless remain vulnerable to New Atheist criticism.[35] The crucial point about the distinction of dispensations is only held firm by a sober, uncomprehending, yet obedient acknowledgement of what the terrors of war must have meant for a God of love and peace.[36] It is really crucial to grasp

---

[34]See Thomas Weinandy, *Does God Suffer?* (Edinburgh: T&T Clark, 2000). H. P. Owen rather unusually moved back toward belief in impassibility, having previously adhered to classical theism in all but this respect. See *Christian Theism: A Study in Its Basic Principles* (Edinburgh: T&T Clark, 1984), p. 111n17.

[35]Not only to New Atheist criticism: I obviously take a position here on God, Scripture and revelation which is at odds with much modern theology.

[36]I agree that Paul's "*God of peace* appellation has not received the attention in Pauline theology that it merits"; Willard M. Swartley, *Covenant of Peace: The Missing Peace in New Testament Ethics* (Grand Rapids: Eerdmans, 2006), p. 210.

this as it was literally crucial that God suffer for the world.

Our discussion of divine power has shaded over into—or, at least, has clear implications with regard to—the question of divine vengeance. *Vengeance* is interpreted by critics of Christianity as *vengefulness* and the English word *vengeance* aids that interpretation. But talk of divine *vengeance* in Scripture, where that is the word used in translation, is talk of divine justice. There is a radical asymmetry between God's love and God's judicial activity as expressed in vengeance or wrath. Love is of the essence of God; the Trinitarian interpretation of God in the Christian church ascribes to Father, Son and Spirit unity in relations of mutual love. There is no wrath immanent in the eternal being of God. Wrath is God's reaction to human sin; it is the response of holiness to unholiness, necessary but unwelcome. Grace is the outflow of immanent love, not necessary, as though humanity were entitled to it as a matter of justice, but infinitely welcome to the one who exercises it with the welcome that greets the returning sinner. Without understanding its relation to God's immanent being, we shall never understand divine wrath. New Atheism does not even attempt to understand how Christians understand it.[37]

THE NEW ATHEIST PROMOTION OF "HOLY WAR"

By way of riposte to the New Atheist association of religion with violence, theologians have voiced in protest that (a) religion is frequently an excuse for political conflict; (b) the problem lies in human nature, not in religion; (c) religion can be a force for well-being; and (d) atheistic regimes have perpetrated worse horrors than anything else that we have seen in modern history. These lines of argument are all important and deserve the closest consideration.[38] I should wish to endorse them substantially. Rather than adumbrate these responses afresh, it may be worth blandly mentioning two things that Christians must be prepared to do in the contemporary world, not particularly under the pressure of New Atheist criticism but inevitably

---

[37]Emil Brunner, following Luther, offers an effective and succinct account here in *The Christian Doctrine of God* (London: Lutterworth, 1949), pp. 168-74.

[38]In addition to much that is well said on this question in above-mentioned studies by Tina Beattie, Terry Eagleton, David Martin and Alister McGrath, see two solid and germane discussions by David Fergusson, *Faith and Its Critics: A Conversation* (Oxford: Oxford University Press, 2009), pp. 120-50, and Keith Ward, *Is Religion Dangerous?* (Oxford: Lion, 2006), pp. 23-82.

with the consciousness that it features on the scene.

First, we need to be prepared to be chastened in our use of and tacit or overt celebration of political power. There is a whole critical world to be explored here in connection with feminist, postcolonialist and postmodernist thought. Here I simply note the tendency of Christians to leap to make the distinction between the interpersonal realm of humility, suffering, self-sacrifice or forgiveness and the public, political realm which demands a different ethic. This is not the place to take sides on the issues that arise here. However, it must be remembered that those principles of conduct that putatively characterize the realm of interpersonal dealings are not merely principles of conduct; they reflect the character to which the Christian aspires in his or her person. There is no realm of Christian activity that requires that these be set aside; on the contrary, it is impossible that they should be, for they characterize not a sphere of operations but the person who is the agent. It is a truism that power tends to have a corrupting and addictive effect on us, a fact which we conceal from ourselves by maintaining the separation of spheres. We have no idea of the power of power; we are its dupes. As a matter of fact, I do not hold that actions appropriate to interpersonal relationships can simply be transplanted into the public-political sphere; in fact, I am not even assuming that the issue before us is rightly described in the terms familiarly employed. Nonetheless, the requirements of Christian discipleship as set out in the New Testament must not be compromised or surrendered.

Second, we need to be highly discriminating in our rhetoric of good and evil. Imperative as it is to conform to the teaching of Jesus on the nature of discipleship, it is equally imperative to name good and evil; indeed, the imperative of such naming is entailed in the imperative of discipleship. There is no question of that. However, we should name it with proper discrimination. The forms of public political rhetoric make that difficult. Arguments go on about whether the United States got involved in Middle Eastern conflict because of the desirability of regime change or out of genuine fear of threatening nuclear weaponry or in order to access oil reserves, but the fact of it is that some supporters of military action wanted to go in for one reason, others for another. Yet we continue to talk simplistically of why "the United States" got involved. The caution that this example bids should be applied to the language of good and evil. On this point, at least, Reinhold Niebuhr was right: we are too prone to forget the relativities of history and to absolutize.[39] To say as much is not for one second to diminish the aforesaid need to name good and evil boldly, clearly and unambiguously, but only to insist on a dialectical pairing of moral requirements (which is also according to the spirit and, indeed, the letter of Niebuhr's work).

The contrast between New Atheism and intellectually serious forms of atheism makes us liable to forget both the fact and the significance of the fact that New Atheism is a species of atheism. Four of its representatives— Richard Dawkins, Sam Harris, Christopher Hitchens and Daniel Dennett— have been described as the four horsemen of the apocalypse (although I am not sure where this phrase actually originated).[40] This is the language and imagery of "holy war" launched against religion. It is salutary to observe historical connections. "The selection of religion as the source of evil needs itself to be analysed as a cultural trope residually derived from the massive conflict in European culture, especially Latin European culture, over the role of religion during the past two centuries."[41] I want to go a couple of centuries further back to one of the great makers of the modern world: Francis Bacon (1561–1626). Bacon, who set so much modern science on the experimental road, is credited with being the figure who has done most in the modern world to create a new set of values and to attempt the recon-figuration of the task of the philosopher by turning philosophers into scien-tists.[42] He aimed to see to it that empirically acquired knowledge grounds social life where theological or philosophical principles had, in the past, ob-scured its reality and our whole worldly reality. Bacon may not have said that knowledge in all the spheres of life was generically of the experimen-tally scientific kind, but he shaped culture in such a way that, "to a large

---

[39]See Niebuhr's remarks on the peculiar difficulties Protestantism has in this regard in the first volume of *The Nature and Destiny of Man*, titled *Human Nature* (London: Nisbet, 1941), p. 64.

[40]Actually, it is arguable that Philip Pullman in his three-volume *Dark Materials* trilogy conducts a more effective war campaign than the horsemen. See *Northern Lights* (London: Scholastic Press, 1995); *The Subtle Knife* (London: Scholastic Press, 1997); *The Amber Spyglass* (London: Scholastic Press, 2000).

[41]David Martin, *Does Christianity Cause War?* p. 20.

[42]See Stephen Gaukroger, *Francis Bacon and the Transformation of Early-Modern Philosophy* (Cambridge: Cambridge University Press, 2001).

extent, cognitive values came to be shaped around scientific values."[43] His words stand proudly at the head of both Kant's *Critique of Pure Reason* and Darwin's *Origin of Species*.[44] A figure like Richard Dawkins seems to fit this culture like a glove.

But there is another interpretation of Bacon in part compatible with the first. It has been promoted with force by Laurence Lampert.[45] In 1622, Bacon wrote a fragment entitled *An Advertisement Touching on Holy War*, apparently a minor work in the Bacon canon geared toward the Catholic-Protestant conflicts of its time, when Europe was in the grip of what became a Thirty Years' War (1618–1648). On Lampert's interpretation, what Bacon was really up to in this work was something that he could not do openly and something which has lain concealed for a long time: he was declaring the necessity of "holy war" against Christianity.[46] If this interpretation is correct, New Atheism assumes the mantle of Francis Bacon. Even if it is questionable, New Atheism is the expression of an impetus in atheism that is much deeper than itself, and Bacon still repays attention in this connection. Even if Bacon's proposals about experimental science had much to commend them, inattention to the wider religious, intellectual and cultural context of their commendation may have tended to conceal their implications. Pondering the thrust of Bacon's enterprise against the background of what he rejected in philosophical theology helps us to get a perspective on New Atheism. Modern science has a background not only in the Christian doctrine of creation or the ambition of Christian scientists to read the book of nature alongside the book of Scripture, but also in the work of the enigmatic and influential Francis Bacon, ambitious to found a New Atlantis. The new Atlantis is something very different from Christendom—and something much better.[47]

---

[43]Ibid., p. 226.

[44]Admittedly, the words heading up Darwin's *On the origin of species by means of natural selection or the preservation of favoured races in the struggle for life* (London: Penguin, 2009) do not portend anything very radical, nor do those heading up Kant's *Critique of Pure Reason*, ed., Norman Kemp Smith (London and Basingstoke: Macmillan, 1933), unless we begin to ponder the allusion to "sects" in the latter case and recall their impact on the European mind.

[45]Laurence Lampert, *Nietzsche and Modern Times: A Study of Bacon, Descartes and Nietzsche* (New Haven: Yale University Press, 1993).

[46]I have unfortunately been unable to access Lampert's own edition of Bacon's *An Advertisement Touching a Holy War* (Chicago: Waveland, 2000).

[47]See in B. Vickers, ed., *Francis Bacon: the Major Works* (Oxford: Oxford University Press, 2002).

At the beginning of the essay, allusion was made to the psychological, moral and sociological forces that New Atheism manifests. It is arguable that, behind the epistemological challenge to Christianity which, it was thought, was posed by scientific reason, lay an opposition to a scheme of sin and reconciliation that offended the "moral" sensibility of the post–Renaissance European.[48] Whatever we make of Bacon on this (or any other) score, of this we can be sure: humanity is involved in the most unholy war against its Creator. Eve and Adam's refusal of God's commandment was implicit deicide in the making, whose climactic outcome took place on a hill outside Jerusalem a long time later.[49] New Atheism's antagonism toward holy, religious war is part of an explicit attempt to eradicate religious belief. What weapons will it not be prepared to use?[50]

The actual "construction of the model of warfare between science and religion as a guiding theme of Western history" is, of course, considerably later than Bacon: Stephen J. Gould, *Rock of Ages: Science and Religion in the Fulness of Life* (London: Vintage, 2002), p. 117.

[48]See Stephen N. Williams, *Revelation and Reconciliation: A Window on Modernity* (Cambridge: Cambridge University Press, 1995). Supplementing the study to which I refer there (p. xiii) see now Charles Taylor's *A Secular Age* (Cambridge, MA: Belknap, 2007), especially the argument in part 2 about the relationship of scientific to moral considerations in the turn against Christianity in Latin Christendom. In the later part of the book, Taylor also treats the question of violence, beginning in chapter 17, pp. 618-75.

[49]In order to say this in this context, no decision needs to be taken on the literary genre of the relevant account in Genesis or the historical possibilities of Adam and Eve.

[50]Tina Beattie is particularly sensitive to the sinister possibilities here. See, e.g., her remarks on Hitchens's comparison of religious believers with rats, *The New Atheists*, p. 15. She justifiably invokes the work of John Gray, *Black Mass: Apocalyptic Religion and the Death of Utopia* (London: Allen Lane, 2007). In connection with the New Atheist scapegoating of religion, further exploration is needed of the theology, psychology and sociology of making scapegoats. Terry Eagleton, whose prominent work on New Atheism was cited above (n. 7) has given this some attention in *Holy Terror* (Oxford: Oxford University Press, 2005), chapter 6, pp. 128-40.

Afterword

OLD TESTAMENT "HOLY WAR" AND CHRISTIAN MORALITY

Where Do We Go from Here?

Jeremy Evans and Heath Thomas

———————— ✝ ————————

IT IS TRIVIALLY TRUE THAT THIS VOLUME will not provide the final word on the problems of war and violence in the Bible. In fact, this volume does not even provide a consensus view on the matter. The discussion that has emerged remains complex and, indeed, it is this very complexity that must be acknowledged in the future. It is appropriate at this point to identify some areas that have been overlooked in this volume and some avenues for future investigation. So the question that must be asked is, Where do we go from here? That is, what is a positive paradigm that will help us think as we move forward, both about the nature of ethics and the precepts for handling difficult passages of Scripture when confronted by them in our reading the Bible? We will offer philosophical/ethical considerations first followed by theological/biblical issues second.

PHILOSOPHICAL AND ETHICAL CONSIDERATIONS

It is important to make a difference between a *descriptive* claim and a *prescriptive* claim. A descriptive claim, obviously, only intends to provide the reader with an account of the facts. For example, Genesis 19:5-11 records the story of Lot and his daughters. Infamously, when a mob of men approached Lot's house and requested that Lot send out his guests so that they could have sex with them, Lot offers up his two virgin daughters so that they could do whatever they wanted with them. The text never *affirms* Lot's offering up his daughters to be raped; it tells us *that* Lot offered up his daughters to be raped.

Since we are discussing Lot, consider a second example embedded in the same chapter that is equally troubling. Genesis 19:30-38 records the story of Lot's incestuous relationship with his two daughters. Both of Lot's daughters made him drunk with wine, after which they seduced him and became impregnated with his children (Moab and Ben Ammi respectively). The text never indicates that Lot should have allowed himself to get drunk, nor does it indicate that incest is a proper form of sexual activity; it *reports* that these events occurred.

So the moral concerning descriptive narratives: when the text records an event, we are not then entitled to infer that the text is affirming what is recorded in the event—only that the event happened.

In contrast to descriptive claims are prescriptive claims. A prescriptive claim is one in which an action or actions are not just allowed but required— it tells us what ought to be done. A divine command serves as a case and point. God's commands generate obligations on the one to whom the command is addressed. Once the command is given, the person or persons *ought* to do what is commanded. The difference between descriptive and prescriptive content is very important, for as the old ethical adage goes, we cannot derive an "ought" from an "is."

The challenging part of this book centers on passages in which God commands actions that seem to be immoral. Commanding actions that are typically deemed immoral likens God to Charles Manson. Manson, it must be remembered, did not personally murder anyone in 1969 but sent several members of his cult to do his bidding. Manson was the mastermind of the horrors and, as such, is deemed responsible for the infamous Tate/Labianca murders. Analogously, if God commands the sacrifice of a child, or for his people to war against other people groups thereby bringing harm to women and children, is not God morally responsible for the carnage that ensues by virtue of his obligating agents to such actions? For example, Genesis 22:2 (NIV) reads, "Then God said, 'Take your son, your only son, whom you love—Isaac—and go to the region of Moriah. Sacrifice him there as a burnt offering on a mountain I will show you.'" The same type of reasoning applies to other narratives, as when the army of God drove out the Canaanites, except on a much larger scale.

What are some principles of ethics that help us understand these commands? First, we must make a distinction between those obligations/values that are objective and those that are absolute. When we use the word objective, it refers to a value or obligation that exists independently of human minds and human constructions. In other words, humans do not make these things up either conventionally (as a society) or subjectively (a man is the measure of all things). When we use the word absolute, we are referring to a value/obligation that is binding in all times, in all places and for all people. So to make the point clear: all absolute values/obligations are objective, but that does not mean that all objective values/obligations are absolute. Sometimes a moral authority issues a specific command to a specific person (or people) for a specific purpose.

To make an application, consider again the case of Abraham and Isaac. We can agree that God has generated an obligation on Abraham to sacrifice Isaac by commanding him to do so. However, this does not mean that God wants all people at all times and places to sacrifice their child. It is an objective obligation (derived independently of Abraham's mind and construction), but it is not an absolute obligation. God's *purposes* in obligating Abraham may be (1) to test Abraham's faith in God's provision or (2) to demonstrate that God, unlike the pagan cultures surrounding Abraham that require child sacrifice to placate the gods, does *not* require child sacrifice. In other words, the binding of Isaac demonstrated to Abraham that God is both faithful to his promises and morally superior to the gods found in the surrounding context.

The objective/absolute distinction is helpful for other matters of inquiry, including certain Old Testament food and clothing laws or even rituals for cleansing before worship.[1] Yet one wonders about how we distinguish objective obligations from those that are absolute? This is a good question, and one that deserves its own thorough treatment—but we'll provide one insight here. If the obligation is found to be without exception in the text,

---

[1]For a detailed treatment see Paul Copan, *Is God a Moral Monster: Making Sense of the Old Testament God* (Grand Rapids: Baker Books, 2011).

then you have good reason to think the obligation is absolute. For example, there are no exceptions to the prohibition against homosexuality (Lev 18:22; 20:13; Rom 1:25-27; 1 Cor 6:9-11); yet another example concerns the divine command to love God and others (Lev 19:18; Deut 6:5; Jn 13:34; 1 Jn 3:11, 23). It is reasonable to hold that many of the objective (but not absolute) commands in the Old Testament were given in lieu of the fact that the descendants of Abraham were separating themselves out from other people groups, providing distinctive marks of demarcation between the worship of false gods and their arbitrary requirements, and the obligations derived from the God who commands according to his perfect nature and creative purposes.

Though there is more that can be said, these two points are helpful when dealing with the moral implications of a text: (1) make sure not to confuse an "is" with an "ought"; and (2) study to determine if the command should be read as an absolute command binding on all people at all times for a specific purpose, or if it is an objective command given to a specific person/ people for a specific time and divine purpose.

Related to the precision needed to distinguish "is" from "ought," another major discovery that has emerged from this volume is the need for well-considered philosophical positions that inform arguments. Proper account of foundational theological and philosophical assumptions remains essential for clarity and precision in dialogue, as indicated in the essays by Stewart, Copan and Flannagan, and Williams with the New Atheists. Christian engagement with the concept of "holy war" needs such precision as well, as it too can move along without sustained reflection on philosophical and theological frameworks that give support to arguments. This practice, in our view, is essential to future engagement on the difficult question of "holy war" so as to safeguard against infelicitous interaction.

Future engagement must move beyond simple proof texting in order to identify difficult issues as "solved." That God indeed commanded "holy war" in the Bible (although note the arguments by Copan and Flannagan and Earl, respectively, in this volume), does not lead to the correlate that the command is real, normative and repeatable in modern society. Such a suggestion would ignore its own underlying assumptions. Basic philosophical underpinnings must be interrogated and then addressed in a careful argument. Drawing out the philosophical and theological points will help elucidate the rationale behind future arguments regarding divine war.

Further, future work should carefully address the conception of "justice" that gives ground to arguments concerning the morality of divine warfare. Proper thinking here remains crucial, because appropriate criteria will help to define and clarify virtues like *justice* in critical discourse and in everyday practice. Current discussions of justice in today's world are often contested because the meaning of the term remains underdetermined in scholarly and popular discourse. As a result, it is not surprising that different conceptions of justice abound. If little agreement exists concerning the appropriate rules for establishing what justice actually is, then it is not surprising that there are disagreements regarding the justice of God's commands/actions in divine war.[2] Is one simply left to choose which conception of justice is useful, workable or virtuous in the marketplace of ideas?[3] A Christian account of justice will take account of God's disclosure of himself and his ways with his world, which is deposited in Scripture.

THEOLOGICAL AND BIBLICAL CONSIDERATIONS

This brings us to a third point that arises from this volume. For future *Christian* engagement, it will be necessary to take note of the vital role of Scripture. The point seems rather redundant, but it remains (deceptively) relevant. Christianity has been since its inception a rather "bookish" faith.[4] Scripture provides the rule for faith and practice as Scripture is unified, comprehensive and true. It faithfully testifies to the primacy of Christ in both creation, salvation and eschatological new creation.

This means, in part, that the church has understood from its beginning that the Bible has a storied shape that gives history meaning and shape with its climax in Christ. Saint Ireneaus is often credited with elucidating this

---

[2]E. Clinton Gardner, *Justice and Christian Ethics*, NSCE (Cambridge: Cambridge University Press, 1995), p. 13; Alasdair MacIntyre, *Whose Justice? Which Rationality?* (Notre Dame, IN: University of Notre Dame Press, 1988), pp. 1-11, 349-403.

[3]These represent three major philosophical strands in the construction of a concept of justice. Compare Michael Sandel, *Justice: What's the Right Thing to Do?* (New York: Farrar, Straus and Giroux, 2009). See also Nicholas Wolterstorff, *Justice: Rights and Wrongs* (Princeton: Princeton University Press, 2008).

[4]See Denis Farkasfalvy, *Inspiration and Interpretation: A Theological Introduction to Sacred Scripture* (Washington, DC: Catholic University of America Press, 2010).

biblical insight in his teaching on preaching.[5] If this is the case, then anything within the world fits within the context of the biblical story, and conceptions of justice, including related implications of the nature, aims, expressions and *telos* of justice, should be contextualized within that story.
This is where, for instance, one notes in the section on biblical theology in
this volume both Lamb and Earl treat Old Testament and New Testament
visions of divine war to gain access to a fuller biblical theology of it.

Fourth, the unified and unfolding biblical narrative will be more productive in Christian engagement than a listing of dichotomies between Old
and New Testament. A simple listing of differences and similarities of
divine warfare in the Old and New Testaments only gets one so far in the
discussion. There will be differences between biblical presentations to be
sure, but a temptation in the "listing" approach is to omit the Old Testament
from Christian relevance. This temptation goes at least as far back as
Marcion, whose rejection of the Old Testament God was matched by his
embrace of the New Testament Jesus. It is the Old Testament God, however,
that gives purchase to the very identity of Jesus. The narratival shape of the
whole Bible, as indicated above, offers a profound and distinctive testimony
to the meaning of history itself.

Divine warfare is set within this testimony. Such an insight reveals that
divine war is neither the first nor last word in the biblical witness. Nor is the
divine warrior the first or last metaphor for God in the Bible. In this, there
is a unified story in which the question of divine warfare plays a part. From
this narratival basis, questions of divine warfare may be subsumed into
bigger questions concerning the meaning of history itself, by no means a
neutral question.[6] Again, this is one of the underlying assumptions that
must be surfaced to gain headway on the discussion, especially amongst
opposing views.

Fifth, a focus upon the full testimony of Scripture should in no way di-

---

[5]Saint Irenaeus, *On the Demonstration of the Apostolic Preaching*, trans. and intro. J. Armitage
Robinson (London: SPCK, 1920).

[6]See R. C. Dentan, ed., *The Idea of History in the Ancient Near East* (New Haven, CT: Yale University Press, 1967); John Burrow, *A History of Histories* (New York: Vintage, 2009). For a helpful discussion on the relationship between Scripture and developing a theology of history, see
David Bebbington, *Patterns in History: A Christian Perspective on Historical Thought* (Vancouver, BC: Regent College Publishing, 2000).

minish engagement of specific questions related to "holy war" with specific texts. It is precisely this point that draws Thomas to notice the distinctive testimony of Lamentations 2 as it speaks to divine warfare. There is ample evidence in the biblical testimony (especially but not exclusively in the Writings) that refuses to accept theodicy as a sufficient explanation of divine war. Prayer is, in this biblical testimony, a fertile way of engaging divine warfare. This point on spirituality and prayer opens up a fertile area that relates to the modern existential challenges that arise with divine warfare.

Finally, future research ought to pay attention to the specific texts that characterize God's own experience associated with divine warfare as testified in the biblical witness. Fretheim's *The Suffering of God* assesses these texts and may prove to be a valuable resource in future study. It is well known in Old Testament studies that in the midst of divine judgment one finds "divine laments," especially in the prophetic corpus.[7] The pathos of God here is unrivaled, as the violence of his people against their Lord leaves him mourning their rebellion and anguishing in their impending judgment (Jer 9:9; 12:7-12; 15:5-9; 48:29-33; Ezek 27:3-11, 26-36). God suffers pain on account of human sin against him, which then leads him to enforce judgment. Micah 1:8-9 (NRSV) is a potent text that reveals God's pain: "For this I will lament and wail; I will go barefoot and naked; I will make lamentation like the jackals, and mourning like the ostriches. For her wound is incurable. It has come to Judah; it has reached to the gate of my people, to Jerusalem." Further, the prophetic corpus reveals that God suffers *with* those who are suffering even divine judgment! In these texts that certainly relate to divine warfare, if they are not explicitly identified with them (Is 15:5; 16:9-11; Jer 9:10, 17-18; 12:7; 31:20; 48:30-36), God mourns with the mourning, hurts with the hurting, and thereby identifies with suffering from the "inside." Heschel in particular highlights the vision of God's suffering *with* peoples in his magisterial work on the prophets.[8] The prophets also present God as suffering *for* humanity (Is 43:23-24; 48:9; 57:11; Jer 15:6; Ezek 20:21-22; 24:12; Mal 2:17). These texts reveal that even in

---

[7]B. O. Long, "The Divine Funeral Lament," *JBL* 85 (1966): 85-86; M. S. Smith, "Jeremiah IX 9: A Divine Lament," *VT* 37 (1987): 97-99; see also T. Fretheim, *The Suffering of God: An Old Testament Perspective*, OBT (Minneapolis: Augsburg Fortress, 1984).

[8]A. J. Heschel, *The Prophets: An Introduction*, vol. 1 (New York: Harper & Row, 1969).

the face of sin against him, God becomes "weary" of restraining his judgment against the rebellious. God suffers *on account of* the peoples' sins, bears that sin and delays judgment against it. In so doing, he suffers for the sins of humanity (but unlike the vicarious suffering presented in Isaiah 53). Still, like a dam that finally breaks loose, God gives way to judgment and punishes a rebellious people.[9] The point is, however, that God is not presented as overly quick in his judgment: his mercy is long and his anguish in bearing sin is sure.

---

[9]So Fretheim, *The Suffering of God*, pp. 138-48.

SELECTED BIBLIOGRAPHY

Bainton, Roland. *Christian Attitudes Toward War and Peace*. Nashville: Abingdon, 1960.

Barth, Karl. *A Letter to Great Britain from Switzerland*. London: The Sheldon Press, 1941.

Bergmann, Michael, Michael J. Murray and Michael C. Rea, eds. *Divine Evil? The Moral Character of the God of Abraham*. New York: Oxford University Press, 2010.

Bonhoeffer, Dietrich. *Letters and Papers from Prison*. London: SCM, 1971.

Brueggemann, Walter. *Divine Presence and Violence: Contextualizing the Book of Joshua*. Eugene, OR: Cascade Books, 2009.

Bull, Marcus, and Norman Housley, eds. *The Experience of Crusading*. Vol. 1, *Western Approaches*. Cambridge: Cambridge University Press, 2003.

Cole, P. J. *The Preaching of the Crusades to the Holy Land, 1095–1270*. Cambridge, MA: The Medieval Academy of America, 1991.

Copan, Paul. *Is God a Moral Monster? Making Sense of the Old Testament*. Grand Rapids: Baker Books, 2011.

Copan, Paul, and William Lane Craig, eds. *Come Let Us Reason: New Essays in Christian Apologetics*. Nashville: B&H Academic, 2012.

Craigie, Peter C. *The Problem of War in the Old Testament*. Grand Rapids: Eerdmans, 1978.

Crouch, C. L. *War and Ethics in the Ancient Near East: Military Violence in Light of Cosmology and History*. Beihefte zur Zeitschrift für die alttetestamentliche Wissenschaft 407. Berlin: de Gruyter, 2009.

Dawkins, Richard. *The God Delusion*. New York: Houghton Mifflin, 2006.

"Did God Mandate Genocide?" Symposium in *Philosophia Christi* 11, no. 1 (2009): 3–92.

Eagleton, Terry. *Reason, Faith and Revolution: Reflections on the God Debate*. New Haven, CT: Yale University Press, 2009.

Earl, D. S. *Reading Joshua as Christian Scripture*. Journal for Theological Interpretation Supplements 2. Winona Lake, IN: Eisenbrauns, 2010.

Ellens, J. Harold, ed. *The Destructive Power of Religion: Violence in Judaism, Christianity, and Islam.* 4 vols. Westport, CT: Praeger, 2004.

Elssner, T. R. *Josua und seine Kriege in jüdischer und christlicher Rezeptionsgeschichte.* Theologie und Frieden 37. Stuttgart: W. Kohlhammer, 2008.

Frederiksson, Henning. *Jahwe als Krieger: Studien zum alttestamentlichen Gottesbild.* Lund: Gleerup, 1945.

Garcia, Robert K., and Nathan L. King, eds. *Is Goodness Without God Good Enough? A Debate on Faith, Secularism and Ethics.* Lanham, MD: Rowman & Littlefield, 2008.

Gardner, E. Clinton. *Justice and Christian Ethics.* New Studies in Christian Ethics. Cambridge: Cambridge University Press, 1995.

Gombis, Timothy G. *The Drama of Ephesians: Participating in the Triumph of God.* Downers Grove, IL: IVP Academic, 2010.

Gottwald, Norman K. *All the Kingdoms of the Earth: Israelite Prophecy and International Relations in the Ancient Near East.* New York: Harper & Row, 1964.

Gundry, Stanley N., ed. *Show them no Mercy: 4 Views on God and Canaanite Genocide.* Counterpoints. Grand Rapids: Zondervan, 2003.

Harris, Sam. *Letter to a Christian Nation.* London: Bantam, 2007.

———. *The End of Faith: Religion, Terror and the Future of Reason.* London: Simon & Schuster, 2005.

Hays, Richard B. *The Moral Vision of the New Testament: Community, Cross, New Creation.* San Francisco: Harper, 1996.

Hess, Richard S., and Elmer A. Martens, eds. *War in the Bible and Terrorism in the Twenty-First Century.* Bulletin for Biblical Research Supplements. Winona Lake, IN: Eisenbrauns, 2008.

Hitchens, Christopher. *God Is Not Great: How Religion Poisons Everything.* London: Atlantic, 2007.

———. *The New Atheists: The Twilight of Reason and the War on Religion.* London: Darton, Longman & Todd, 2007.

Hobbs, T. R. *A Time for War: A Study of Warfare in the Old Testament.* Old Testament Studies 3. Wilmington, DE: Michael Glazier, 1989.

Jersak, Brad, and Michael Hardin. *Stricken by God? Nonviolent Identification and the Victory of Christ.* Grand Rapids: Eerdmans, 2007.

Kang, Sa-Moon. *Divine War in the Old Testament and in the Ancient Near East.* Beihefte zur Zeitschrift für die alttetestamentliche Wissenschaft 177. Berlin: de Gruyter, 1989.

Klingbeil, Martin. *Yahweh Fighting from Heaven: God as Warrior and as God of Heaven in the Hebrew Psalter and Ancient Near Eastern Iconography.* Orbis Biblicus et Orientalis 169. Göttingen: Vandenhoeck and Ruprecht, 1999.

Lamb, David T. *God Behaving Badly: Is the God of the Old Testament Angry, Sexist and Racist?* Downers Grove, IL: InterVarsity Press, 2011.

Lind, Millard C. *Yahweh Is a Warrior: The Theology of Warfare in Ancient Israel.* Scottdale, PA: Herald Press, 1980.

Lock, Peter. *The Routledge Companion to the Crusades.* Routledge Companions to History. London: Routledge, 2006.

Longman, Tremper, III, and Daniel G. Reid. *God Is a Warrior.* Studies in Old Testament Biblical Theology. Grand Rapids: Zondervan, 1995.

MacIntyre, Alasdair. *Whose Justice? Which Rationality?* Notre Dame, IN: University of Notre Dame Press, 1988.

Maier, Cristoph T. *Crusade Propaganda and Ideology: Model Sermons for Preaching the Cross.* Cambridge: Cambridge University Press, 2000.

Martin, David. *Does Christianity Cause War?* New York: Oxford University Press, 1997.

McConville, J. Gordon, and Stephen N. Williams. *Joshua.* Two Horizons Old Testament Commentary. Grand Rapids: Eerdmans, 2010.

McGrath, Alister, with Joanna C. McGrath. *The Dawkins Delusion: Atheist Fundamentalism and the Denial of the Divine.* London: SPCK, 2007.

Miller, Patrick D., Jr. *The Divine Warrior in Early Israel.* Harvard Semitic Monographs 5. Cambridge, MA: Harvard University Press, 1973.

Niditch, Susan. *War in the Hebrew Bible: A Study in the Ethics of Violence.* New York: Oxford University Press, 1993.

Niebuhr, Reinhold. *Why the Christian Church Is not Pacifist.* London: SCM Press, 1940.

O'Donovan, Oliver. *The Just War Revisited.* Cambridge: Cambridge University Press, 2003.

———. *Resurrection and Moral Order: An Outline for Evangelical Ethics.* Grand Rapids: Eerdmans, 1986.

———. *The Ways of Judgment.* Grand Rapids: Eerdmans, 2005.

O'Donovan, Oliver, and Joan Lockwood O'Donovan. *Bonds of Imperfection: Christian Politics, Past and Present.* Grand Rapids: Eerdmans, 2004.

Reichberg, Gregory M., Henrik Syse and Endre Begby, eds. *The Ethics of War: Classic and Contemporary Readings.* Malden, MA: Blackwell, 2006.

Rowlett, Lori L. *Joshua and the Rhetoric of Violence: A New Historicist Analysis.* New York: Continuum, 1996.

Sandel, Michael. *Justice: What's the Right Thing to Do?* New York: Farrar, Straus and Giroux, 2009.

Schmitt, Rüdiger. *Der "Heilige Krieg" im Pentateuch und im deuteronomistischen*

Geschichtswerk: Studien zur Forschungs-, Rezeptions- und Religionsgeschichte von Krieg und Bann im Alten Testament. Ater Orient und Alten Testament 381. Munster: Ugarit-Verlag, 2011.

Schreiner, Klaus, with Elisabeth Müller-Luckner, eds. *Heilige Kriege: Religiöse Begründungen militärischer Gewaltanwendung: Judentum, Christentum und Islam im Vergleich.* Schriften des Historischen Kollegs 78. Munich: Oldenbourg, 2008.

Schwager, Raymund. *Must There Be Scapegoats? Violence and Redemption in the Bible.* San Francisco: Harper & Row, 1987.

Schwally, Friedrich. *Der heilige Krieg im alten Israel.* Leipzig: Deiterich, 1901.

Siebert, Eric A. *Disturbing Divine Behavior: Troubling Old Testament Images of God.* Minneapolis: Fortress, 2009.

Smend, Rudolf. *Yahweh War and Tribal Confederation: Reflections upon Israel's Earliest History.* Nashville: Abingdon, 1970.

Stassen. Glen. *Just Peacemaking: Transforming Initiatives for Justice and Peace.* Louisville, KY: Westminster John Knox, 1992.

———. *Just Peacemaking: The New Paradigm for the Ethics of Peace and War.* Cleveland, OH: Pilgrim Press, 2008.

Syse, Henrik, and Gregory M. Reichberg, eds. *Ethics, Nationalism, and Just War: Medieval and Contemporary Perspectives.* Washington, DC: Catholic University of America Press, 2007.

Thistlethwaite, Susan, ed. *Interfaith Just Peacemaking.* New York: Palgrave Macmillan, 2012.

Ward, Keith. *Is Religion Dangerous?* Oxford: Lion, 2006.

Williams, Stephen N. *The Shadow of the Antichrist: Nietzsche's Critique of Christianity.* Grand Rapids: Baker, 2006.

Wright, Christopher. *The God I Don't Understand: Reflections on Tough Questions of Faith.* Grand Rapids: Zondervan, 2008.

Yoder, John Howard. *Karl Barth and the Problem of War.* Nashville: Abingdon, 1970.

———. *The Original Revolution: Essays on Christian Pacifism.* Scottdale, PA: Herald Press, 1977.

Yoder Neufeld, Thomas R. *"Put on the Armour of God": The Divine Warrior from Isaiah to Ephesians.* Journal for the Study of the New Testament Supplement Series 40. Sheffield, UK: Sheffield Academic Press, 1997.

Younger, K. Lawson, Jr. *Ancient Conquest Accounts: A Study in Ancient Near Eastern and Biblical History Writing.* Journal for the Study of the Old Testament Supplement Series 98. Sheffield, UK: JSOT Press, 1990.

CONTRIBUTORS

Geth Allison (M.Div., Southeastern Baptist Theological Seminary) is adjunct faculty at Hampton University.

Alan S. Bandy (Ph.D., Southeastern Baptist Theological Seminary) is the Rowena R. Strickland Assistant Professor of New Testament and Greek at Oklahoma Baptist University.

Stephen B. Chapman (Ph.D., Yale) is associate professor of Old Testament at Duke Divinity School. He is the author of *The Law and the Prophets* (Mohr Siebeck).

Paul Copan (Ph.D., philosophy, Marquette) is the Pledger Family Chair of Philosophy and Ethics at Palm Beach Atlantic University. He is author and editor of over twenty books, including *Is God a Moral Monster?* (Baker) and *Creation Out of Nothing* (Baker Academic).

Douglas Earl (Ph.D., University of Durham) is the author of *The Joshua Delusion?* (Cascade Books) and *Reading Joshua as Christian Scripture* (Eisenbrauns).

Jeremy Evans (Ph.D., Texas A&M University) is associate professor of Philosophy at Southeastern Seminary in Wake Forest, North Carolina. He is the editor of *Taking Christian Moral Thought Seriously* (B&H Academic) and a forthcoming volume, *The Problem of Evil*, for the B&H Studies in Christian Apologetics series.

Matthew Flannagan is a theologian with proficiency in contemporary analytic philosophy. He holds a Ph.D. in Theology from the University of Otago in Dunedin, New Zealand.

Timothy G. Gombis (Ph.D., University of St. Andrews) is associate professor of New Testament at Grand Rapids Theological Seminary, Grand Rapids, Michigan. He is the author of *The Drama of Ephesians* (IVP Academic).

Daniel R. Heimbach is senior professor of Christian ethics at Southeastern Baptist Theological Seminary, research fellow with the SBC Ethics and Religious Liberty Commission and general editor of the B&H Christian Ethics series. He has written or contributed to fifteen books, written more than sixty articles and reviews, and helped write and produce thirteen articles on ethical issues appearing in the *English Standard Version Study Bible*.

David T. Lamb (D.Phil., Oxford) is associate professor of Old Testament at Biblical Theological Seminary in Hatfield, Pennsylvania. He is the author of *Righteous Jehu and His Evil Heirs* (Oxford) and *God Behaving Badly* (IVP Books).

Reid Powell (M. Div., Southeastern Baptist Theological Seminary) is a graduate student in Philosophy at the University of Houston.

Murray Rae (Ph.D., King's College, London) is head of the Department of Theology and Religion at the University of Otago in Dunedin, New Zealand. He is the author of *Kierkegaard and Theology* (T & T Clark), *History and Hermeneutics* (T & T Clark), and *Kierkegaard's Vision of the Incarnation* (Clarendon Press).

Glen H. Stassen is Lewis B. Smedes Professor of Christian Ethics at Fuller Theological Seminary in Pasadena, California, author of *A Thicker Jesus: Incarnational Discipleship in a Secular Age* (WJK) and coauthor of *Kingdom Ethics* (IVP Academic)

Robert B. Stewart (Ph.D., Southwestern Baptist Theological Seminary) is professor of philosophy and theology and holds the Greer-Heard Chair of Faith and Culture at New Orleans Baptist Theological Seminary.

Heath A. Thomas (Ph.D., University of Gloucestershire) is associate professor of Old Testament and Hebrew and director of Ph.D. Studies at Southeastern Seminary in Wake Forest, North Carolina. He also serves as Fellow in Old Testament at the Paideia Centre for Public Theology in Ontario, Canada. He is the author of *Poetry and Theology in the Book of Lamentations* (Sheffield Phoenix).

Stephen N. Williams (Ph.D., Yale) is professor of systematic theology at Union Theological College in Belfast, Northern Ireland. He is the author of *The Shadow of the AntiChrist: Nietzsche's Critique of Christianity* (Baker Academic) and coauthored a commentary, *Joshua*, with J. Gordon McConville (Eerdmans, 2010).

Names Index

Scripture Index